C. S. Lewis—Revelation,
Conversion, and Apologetics

C. S. Lewis—Revelation, Conversion, and Apologetics

P. H. Brazier

Foreword by Stephen R. Holmes

SERIES: C. S. LEWIS: REVELATION AND THE CHRIST
www.cslewisandthechrist.net

PICKWICK Publications · Eugene, Oregon

C. S. LEWIS—REVELATION, CONVERSION, AND APOLOGETICS

Series: C. S. Lewis: Revelation and the Christ 1

Copyright © 2012 Paul H. Brazier. All rights reserved. Except for brief quotations in critical publications or reviews, no part of this book may be reproduced in any manner without prior written permission from the publisher. Write: Permissions, Wipf and Stock Publishers, 199 W. 8th Ave., Suite 3, Eugene, OR 97401.

Pickwick Publications
An Imprint of Wipf and Stock Publishers
199 W. 8th Ave., Suite 3
Eugene, OR 97401

www.wipfandstock.com

ISBN 13: 978-1-61097-718-0

Cataloging-in-Publication data:

Brazier, Paul.

C. S. Lewis—revelation, conversion, and apologetics / P. H. Brazier.

Series: C. S. Lewis: Revelation and the Christ 1

xxii + 292 p. ; 23 cm. Includes bibliographical references and index.

ISBN 13: 978-1-61097-718-0

1. Lewis, C. S. (Clive Staples), 1898–1963—Religion. 2. Lewis, C. S. (Clive Staples), 1898–1963—Theology. 3. Apologetics. I. Title. II. Series.

BX5199.L53 B639 2012

Manufactured in the U.S.A.

All royalties from this series are donated to the University of Oxford C. S. Lewis Society

Typeset by P. H. Brazier, Ash Design,
Minion Pro 10.75pt on 14pt

SERIES PREFACE
C. S. LEWIS: REVELATION AND THE CHRIST

This is a series of books that have a common theme: the understanding of Christ, and therefore the revelation of God, in the work of C. S. Lewis. These books are a systematic study of Lewis's theology, Christology, and doctrine of revelation; as such they draw on his life and work. They are written for academics and students, but also, crucially, for those people, ordinary Christians, without a theology degree who enjoy and gain sustenance from reading Lewis's work.

Book One
Revelation, Conversion, and Apologetics

Book Two
The Work of Christ Revealed

Book Three
The Christ of a Religious Economy

A fourth volume, consisting of an in-depth bibliography, plus an introductory essay on Christology as the study of Christ, and a glossary, completes the series:

C. S. Lewis—An Annotated Bibliography and Resource

There is a website to accompany (www.cslewisandthechrist.net) that provides material and downloads to complement these books. Those who feel somewhat bemused by the concepts in Christology (the study of Christ) may gain understanding from browsing the site, which will give an introduction to the series. In addition a full detailed contents, including all sections can be downloaded and printed as an aide-memoire and guide to each book in the series.

This series has been many years in the making. The serious writing of it started in 2007; however, sketches relating to some of the topics go back much further. With writing the work grew. Lewis was not a systematic theologian, nor did he attempt to write a systematic theology (though the aim of *Mere Christianity* gets close to it). What this work attempts is to present a systematic study of what Lewis understood about Jesus Christ, and the revelation of God, who is at the heart of orthodox, traditional, theology.

For Hilary

Contents

List of Illustrations / xi

Foreword / xiii

Acknowledgements / xix

Introduction: C. S. Lewis—Revelation, Conversion, and Apologetics / 1

PART ONE
THE PERSONAL GOD OF SALVATION—CONVERSION AND ACCEPTANCE

1. Conversion: God is God / 19
2. Acceptance: God is God, in Christ / 39
3. Helen Joy Davidman: Intellect and Imagination / 51
4. C. S. Lewis and Karl Barth I: Religious Experience—Revelation and Modernity / 65
5. C. S. Lewis and Karl Barth II: A Doctrinal Realization—God is God, in Christ / 83

PART TWO
C. S. LEWIS—THEOLOGIAN AND "MERE" CHRISTIAN

6. C. S. Lewis the Classical Philosopher Theologian I: Witness and Method—"Mere" Christianity / 103
7. C. S. Lewis the Classical Philosopher Theologian II: praeparatio evangelica—A Catholic-Evangelical / 119
8. C. S. Lewis the Classical Philosopher Theologian III: Orthodoxy and Heresy—The Pittenger-Lewis Debate / 133

PART THREE
C. S. LEWIS—APOLOGIST, BROADCASTER, AND PUBLIC FIGURE

9. Apologist and Defender of the Faith I: Revelation and Christology, 1931–44—The Early Works / 149
10. Apologist and Defender of the Faith II: Revelation and Christology, 1941–47—The Middle Works / 177
11. Apologist and Defender of the Faith III: Revelation and Christology, 1948–63—The Later Works: Mere Christology / 205
12. Apologist and Defender of the Faith IV: Revelation and Christology, 1948–63—The Later Works: Christlikeness / 227

Conclusion. Apologist and Defender of the Faith / 261

Select Bibliography / 265

Indexes / 273

Sectional Contents / 287

List of Illustrations

Figure 1 (Chapter 4)
The Tensions that can affect all Christologies / 77

Figure 2 (Chapter 4)
The Tensions Inherent in the Doctrine of the Trinity / 77

Figure 3 (Chapter 5)
Karl Barth (1920) and C. S. Lewis (1925), pen and ink drawing, P. H. Brazier / 85

Figure 4 (Chapter 5)
Karl Barth and C. S. Lewis in the 1950s, charcoal and graphite drawing, P. H. Brazier / 97

Figure 5 (Chapter 6)
Page xvii from "What History is Credible, and What Not." The introductory essay, in Richard Baxter's *Church-History of the Government of Bishops and their Councils*, 1680 / 111

Figure 6 (Chapter 6)
Content-Driven Method in C. S. Lewis's Theology / 113

Figure 7 (Chapter 8)
Pittenger-Lewis—the fundamental distinction between a Liberal and a Creedal-orthodox position on the very nature of Jesus Christ / 141

Figure 8 (Chapter 8)
C. S. Lewis and W. Norman Pittenger, pen and ink drawing, P. H. Brazier / 143

Figure 9 (Chapter 9)
The Three Periods of Lewis's Apologetics and Theology / 150

Figure 10 (Chapter 9)
C. S. Lewis, the BBC Broadcast Talks 1941–44 (1) / 160

Figure 11 (Chapter 9)
C. S. Lewis, the BBC Broadcast Talks 1941–44 (2) / 161

Figure 12 (Chapter 9)
C. S. Lewis: the Key Theological and Philosophical Works—
The Early Period (1931–44) and the Middle Period (1931–47) / 175

Figure 13 (Chapter 10)
The Dialectical Tension in a Christian Doctrine of Death / 189

Figure 14 (Chapter 10)
The Relation between the Universal and the Particular / 195

Figure 15 (Chapter 11)
C. S. Lewis: the Key Theological and Philosophical Works—
The Mature Period (1948–63) / 209

Figure 16 (Chapter 11)
The Framework of a Doctrine of Salvation from *Mere Christianity* / 211

Figure 17 (Chapter 11)
The Apostles' Creed / 217

Foreword

The world of academic theology has not yet come to terms with Clive Staples Lewis. In his own lifetime he faced disdain and dismissal as a mere populist who had no real understanding of the crucial issues—but he was also awarded an honorary DD by my own university, St Andrews, fairly early on in his writing career (1946). In the years since his death, his books have mostly been ignored by academics, even as they were devoured by readers.

If considered as contributions to the academic debate, Lewis's various works show real weaknesses. He often proceeds, for instance, as if serenely unaware of the challenges of post-Kantian epistemology or higher biblical criticism. (The scholar need not accept the justness of every such challenge, of course, but cannot simply ignore them.) He appears to be what, in truth, he was: an amateur theologian. That title, however, conceals an important distinction: in Lewis's day, the amateur was distinguished from the professional not by lack of skill, but by performing for love of the game rather than payment; today, the word carries the strong implication of a weaker performer. Was Lewis an amateur in the sense of his own day, or of ours?

The Christian church has long had its amateurs in the first sense: writers who, despite (or perhaps because of) their lack of awareness of the current state of the academic questions, were able to make genuine contributions to the theological task of understanding and explicating the inner logic of the gospel story. Early in the fourth century, we find Lactantius offering idiosyncratic musings on the doctrine of the Trinity, which show clearly that he was unaware of the recent debates, but nonetheless he offers something of great worth to ongoing discussion; in the high Middle Ages the contribution of the likes of Catherine of Sienna or Teresa of Avila, both teachers outside the universities, was significant enough for them to be recognized (later) as "doctors of the church." Lewis fits into this noble tradition of truly talented amateurs; he is not paid to be a theologian, but he succeeds brilliantly in being one nonetheless.

Lewis has, it should be said, not been completely neglected by scholarship. In particular, in recent years analytic philosophers of religion have given extensive and respectful attention to a number of his arguments, particularly some of his accounts of how Christ's death on the cross might bring salvation to humanity. These engagements have, however, generally been piecemeal: this or that argument is discovered in Lewis and tested. Paul Brazier has given us something new in the series that this volume begins: a full account of Lewis's theology, set out in systematic order, with attention paid to the developments in his thought and to his biography. For this, we are greatly in Paul's debt.

The Lewis who we discover in these pages is not the occasional thinker we have grown used to who wrote often idiosyncratic, if sometimes brilliant, essays on this or that question, but never pulled his ideas together into a whole. Here we discover a deep commitment to central truths, which worked out in those various essays in different ways, but which was well formed and coherent. Paul Brazier shows us Lewis the systematic theologian with a clarity that has never been approached before.

We should not be surprised, of course, to find such coherence in Lewis. He was an academic of some distinction, albeit with his primary expertise in literature. He was also fascinated by the big systems of Platonic philosophy, accounts of the nature of things that are astonishingly ambitious in their attempts to encompass the whole of reality in one closed system. Lewis's major academic contributions focused on the medieval allegorical poets and on sixteenth-century English writers (he wrote on English literature in the sixteenth century for the *Oxford History of English Literature*; published a *Preface to Paradise Lost*; and traced the development of the medieval traditions into Spencer's *Faerie Queene* in arguably his greatest work, *The Allegory of Love*); in these writers we find, fundamentally, a colossal endeavor to *make sense* of the world. Allegory is an exercise in linking together endless partial meanings into an encompassing whole.

Allegory, of course, became a part of Lewis's theological arsenal. Although perhaps only *The Pilgrim's Regress* is pure allegory in his corpus of work, the author of *The Allegory of Love* knew well how traditions of allegorical writing could morph and develop into unexpected and new forms—this was close to the heart of his argument for the importance of *The Faerie Queene*, even. Just so, books as diverse as *The Great Divorce*, *The Screwtape Letters*, the Narnia series, the Ransom trilogy, and *Till We Have Faces* all draw on different facets of medieval allegorical traditions to communicate their points in imaginative ways. In several of these works, spiritual truth is conveyed by physical condition—the hardness of heavenly grass in *The Great Divorce*, or the sad condition of Narnia under the Queen ("always winter, but it never gets to Christmas"), for example. This sort of linkage has deep roots in Platonic and medieval allegorical traditions: all things are interconnected, and this has real consequences that can be perceived by the one who has eyes to see. Given that his professional interests concerned such grand and ambitious systematizing, and that this demonstrably spills over into his fiction, could it really be credible that Lewis's theological contributions were merely occasional and piecemeal?

Here, again, however, we come up against Lewis's separation from the mainstream of academic theological and philosophical thought in his day. We might reflect on two Swiss-German contemporaries to make the point forcibly: Karl Barth and Hermann Hesse. Barth was the leading Protestant theologian of the day, indeed of the twentieth century. When one thinks of the visceral anger of Barth's response to his long-time friend Emil Brunner's hesitant allowance that perhaps there were traces of an inherent rationality in creation (Barth's published response was memorably entitled *"Nein!"*), it is difficult to imagine how he might have responded to an apparently-dilettante theologian in England who was recovering medieval traditions in which the very weather patterns are true indicators of the spiritual state of a place! The energy of Barth's repudiation of Brunner came from the context of the need to oppose appeals to natural theology that were being deployed to justify church support for the National Socialist regime; its intellectual roots, however, go much deeper, to Barth's encounter with, and rejection of, the Roman Catholic theology of his day, and its reliance on the *analogia entis*, the "analogy of being." Barth could not accept an argument that truth about how God must be could be derived from an examination of the ways in which God had chosen to order creation.

Lewis's faith, however, tended to the catholic—resolutely Anglo-Catholic, rather than Roman, but nonetheless, the explanatory schemes he reached for were those which saw and rejoiced in close connections between creation and redemption; if it was a school of theology that was passing from fashion in the academy when he wrote, that was hardly his fault. Indeed, in his day, it still had formidable champions: its greatest exponent, Reginald Garrigou-Lagrange, might now be almost forgotten, but he towered over Roman Catholic theological education for two generations, formed the greatest minds of the Church (among many others, he supervised the doctorate of Karol Wojtyla, who later became Pope John Paul II), and only retired from the Angelicum in 1960. I suppose that Lewis never in fact read Garrigou-Lagrange's careful syllogisms—I certainly know of no evidence that he did—and I also suppose that he would have found the logic cold and unappealing had he read it. I suppose further that Garrigou-Lagrange would have found Lewis's imaginative flourishes even more uncongenial, had he encountered them; the impulse driving their systems, however, was fundamentally the same. If it was also everything Barth set his face against, Garrigou-Lagrange's presence in Rome is ample demonstration that Lewis's theological orientation, however unfashionable, was not simply at odds with all that was going on in the academy.

Dr Brazier here runs an extended comparison with Barth. The focus is on the sense that both Lewis and Barth had a profound experience of conversion that led each man to accept that all that he had believed and held to before needed to be revised in the light of the gospel. This comparison is apposite, and well carried through here; Barth worked in a context where the later distinctions loomed very large; for Lewis, they could be subsumed under the category of "mere Christianity" and so set aside. If Lewis had been in Munich or Heidelberg and not Oxford, would he have thought similarly? Almost certainly not, but God's providence led him to Oxford, and there is little question that the thoughts he forged there were of service to the kingdom of God, as were the thoughts Barth forged in opposition to "German Christianity" in his own context.

Hesse might seem a more surprising comparison: a great writer, certainly, who rejected his pietistic upbringing to become fascinated by the spiritual traditions of the Indian subcontinent (see his 1922 novel, *Siddhartha*) and particularly by some of the briefly-popular syncretistic amalgams of Christian and Indian themes, notably theosophy. He understood, however, the desire to find a systematic view of life, and understood the literary impulse to find it through allegory and the connections between seemingly-unrelated areas of human existence—which is to say he understood what drove Lewis.

All of this is explored in the eponymous system of endless meaning-transfer in Hesse's Nobel-cited novel *Das Glassperlenspeil* (1942). The novel is set in an unspecified future; the Game of the title is the perfection of allegory: every system of meaning making can be translated into positions in the game, and moves are made by invoking musical logic or economics or choreography or theology indifferently (or perhaps simultaneously) to move the beads around. It is taught and played in a separated province devoted entirely to intellectual concerns. Hesse can see, in a way that Barth could not, the possibility and attraction of the grand system of allegory that Lewis found in his medieval poets.

Hesse's hero, Knecht, masters the game—but then walks away. The game is merely an imitation of life, a substitute for worthwhile involvement in the world. He leaves, intending to offer his insights and gifts in service to the world, and then dies in a tragic accident a few days later. The novel was written in neutral Switzerland, whence Hesse was watching the rise of National Socialism in Germany with increasing concern; indeed, he was active in aiding at least a few German intellectuals and writers to escape to Swiss safety. The imagination of an intellectual ivory tower, a whole province devoted to thought, thought that had been elevated in its purest form to a game, perhaps serves as an implicit criticism of the neutral society in which Hesse had made his home.

Hesse, I am sure, never thought of the 1940s English universities in this connection, but the connections are not hard to draw. An isolated oasis of intellectual play, removed from any responsibility for the problems of the world—could the finger not point at the broad streets of Oxford, as much as the mountains of Switzerland? Hesse's novel reflects a cultural mood: the urgencies of contemporary life are too pressing to allow for leisured speculation about deep systematic connections. The theologian, perhaps particularly the lay theologian, who seeks a hearing in culture should focus on direct solutions to felt problems, not on constructing grand systems.

Lewis sought a hearing; his writing and speaking was almost all occasional, addressing this question or that problem, some of which had been posed to him, some of which he felt himself. He knew—before he read *Das Glassperlenspiel*, if he ever did—that intellectual games of drawing surprising connections played at the highest levels of abstraction, with or without glass beads, would not just be perceived as irrelevant, but would alienate a public impatient for direct answers to pressing issues. So if it is not surprising, given his intellectual interests, that he had a system, it is no more surprising, given his sense of vocation, that he kept it largely hidden. It would gain nothing for him with either academic or popular audiences.

Paul Brazier has uncovered what was hidden for us. In this volume, he skillfully weaves an account of Lewis's biography into an account of his religious epistemology, showing us how Lewis's own crises of faith led to a developing awareness of the claims

Foreword

of God in Christ by the Spirit. Lewis lived in an age fascinated by autobiographical analysis—a fact he himself mocks in *The Screwtape Letters*, when Screwtape advises Wormwood to encourage his patient to dismiss his Christian conversion as "a phase," commenting that modern people are endlessly going through "phases." Despite his mockery, Lewis was not immune from his generation's fascination: he wrote two book-length works of autobiography, *Surprised by Joy* and *A Grief Observed* and ran autobiographical allusions through many of his other works.

This is not just a bowing to contemporary fashion, however: published spiritual autobiography has a long history in the Christian tradition, reaching back at least as far as Augustine's *Confessions*. The attempt to narrate the workings of the Spirit of God in the human heart by offering as exact an account as possible of one's own experiences of grace seems a natural one for Christian pastors and apologists. Lewis narrates his own conversion to Christianity in a series of stages ("phases"?!), the two main ones being the development of a belief in God, or general theism, and then a conviction that God is revealed in Jesus Christ. Paul Brazier traces all this with care, and—taking the genre of spiritual autobiography with appropriate seriousness—mines Lewis's various accounts of his journey of conversion to understand further his core convictions about how God becomes real to the particular human heart.

The third chapter here turns to a comparison between Lewis and his wife Joy, exploring their different conversion narratives to open up the question of the imagination in theological knowing. Dr Brazier suggests to us that "the baptism of the imagination" comes first in Lewis's account of the processes of conversion: for Lewis himself, the call of the North and the glimpses of "joy" were—explicitly, in his own narratives—a *praeparatio evangelica*, a divinely-ordained preparation for the gospel to be received and believed. When the imagination is shaped in certain, godly, directions, then it will be easy to receive the truth of the gospel intellectually.

This claim is interesting and worthy of reflection. On the one hand, it explains the shape of significant portions of Lewis's corpus. Many of his most celebrated works—notably Narnia—are novels and narratives, not carefully-argued apologetic treatises. He could write the latter, of course—quite brilliantly; *Mere Christianity* is arguably still unsurpassed—but he saw that until the imagination was rightly directed, the arguments of a book such as *Mere Christianity* would inevitably fall on deaf ears. The heart had to be changed, before the mind could be.

I have noted already the comparison with Barth; Lewis's distinctive position is the postulation of "mere Christianity." Dr Brazier explores this in chapters 6–8 of the present volume. Mere Christianity is, almost, a Platonic ideal; there is an eternal truth, but our appropriations of it are always partial and distorted. This, on Brazier's analysis, is the reason for the development of differing—and competing—traditions of Christianity; Lewis is concerned to find the core around which all lively traditions of Christianity revolve. At the heart of this, for Lewis, is a commitment to certain points of doctrinal orthodoxy. This is demonstrated well in the (entertaining) story of Pittenger's attack on Lewis, covered here in chapter 8: Pittenger thought he could silence—perhaps bully—Lewis by invoking academic theological categories; Lewis responded with an acute awareness of the fundamental contours of historic orthodoxy. Perhaps some of his phraseology had been unfortunate—he was a non-specialist, after all—but fundamentally he stood in an orthodox tradition that Pittenger, for all his academic sophistication, had abandoned.

Dr Brazier finally here turns to a series of chapters analyzing Lewis's development as an apologist, offering a close reading of each work in chronological order. There is little point in summarizing this story here: it is told elegantly and convincingly in the relevant chapters. Here we find Lewis growing and maturing into his chosen vocation of making the faith comprehensible and credible to the people of his generation. He heard, felt, and responded to challenges; refined and developed earlier positions; and gradually developed into a formidable defender of the faith. The systematic connections with the epistemological positions developed before are made clear, and we begin to see the richness of the development of Lewis's theological thought.

Two further volumes are promised, which will fill out and develop the portrait of Lewis's theological system. For anyone interested in Lewis's thought, they should be eagerly awaited; in the meantime, what we have in this volume is already a convincing demonstration of the coherence of the system Lewis developed. Like Catherine of Sienna or Teresa of Avila, his location outside the contemporary academic debates should not blind us to the distinctiveness and value of his contribution; Dr Brazier gives us reason to believe that, like them, he is genuinely worthy of the honorific title "doctor [= teacher] of the church."

Stephen R. Holmes
Senior Lecturer in Systematic Theology
University of St Andrews, Scotland

Acknowledgements

My initial interest in C. S. Lewis started with a Sunday afternoon TV serialization of *The Lion, the Witch and the Wardrobe* in, I think, 1967. Crude by today's CGI standards, and in black-and-white, I only saw the first episode amidst a chaotic time of my life, yet a seed was sown, thoughts which I could not get out of my mind. Credit should also be given to a fellow student, Debbie Gould, when I was at art college, who commented pointedly to me that I should read Lewis's works. Something I started to do seriously when I became a Christian in 1980. Acknowledgement must be accorded to Dr. Murray Rae and Dr. Brian Horne (both formerly of King's College London) for engendering in me a serious study of Lewis from 1999, which culminated in this work. Thanks must also be given to Dr. Pat Madigan S. J., (Editor of *The Heythrop Journal*, for encouragement—and for publishing articles generated by this research), Judith and Brendan Wolfe (The University of Oxford C. S. Lewis Society), and also to John Field, a well-read Christian, for advice in reading early drafts. My thanks go to N. T. (Tom) Wright, for discussions (conducted by e-mailed message) on the nature of *the Christ* as presented in this work. My deepest thanks must go to Robin Parry (editor, Wipf and Stock) for countless ideas and advice, and his unrivaled expertise as a biblical scholar, particularly in his editing of this series. But ultimately acknowledgement and thanks must go to Hilary, my wife, without whom I would not be the person I am, and this work would never have existed.

Acknowledgement and thanks is given to the C. S. Lewis Co. Pte., for permission to quote from the following works.

Correspondence
C. S. Lewis, *Collected Letters, Vol. I: Family Letters 1905–1931* (2004). Extracts by C. S. Lewis, copyright © C. S. Lewis Co. Pte. Reprinted by permission.

C. S. Lewis, *Collected Letters, Vol. II: Books, Broadcasts and War 1931–1949* (2004). Extracts by C. S. Lewis, copyright © C. S. Lewis Co. Pte. Reprinted by permission.

C. S. Lewis, *Collected Letters, Vol. III: Narnia, Cambridge and Joy 1950–1963* (2007). Extracts by C. S. Lewis, copyright © C. S. Lewis Co. Pte. Reprinted by permission.

Single Volumes
C. S. Lewis, *Beyond Personality: the Christian Idea of God* (1944). Extracts by C. S. Lewis, copyright © C. S. Lewis Co. Pte. Reprinted by permission.

C. S. Lewis, *Broadcast Talks*. Reprinted with some alterations from two series of Broadcast Talks "Right and Wrong: A Clue to the Meaning of the Universe" and "What Christians Believe" given in 1941 and 1942 (1942). Extracts by C. S. Lewis, copyright © C. S. Lewis Co. Pte. Reprinted by permission.

C. S. Lewis, *Christian Behaviour* (1943). Extracts by C. S. Lewis, copyright © C. S. Lewis Co. Pte. Reprinted by permission.

C. S. Lewis, *Mere Christianity* (1952). Extracts by C. S. Lewis, copyright © C. S. Lewis Co. Pte. Reprinted by permission.

C. S. Lewis, *Miracles* (1st Edition, 1947). Extracts by C. S. Lewis, copyright © C. S. Lewis Co. Pte. Reprinted by permission.

C. S. Lewis, *Reflections on the Psalms* (1958). Extracts by C. S. Lewis, copyright © C. S. Lewis Co. Pte. Reprinted by permission.

C. S. Lewis, *Surprised by Joy: The Shape of my Early Life* (1955). Extracts by C. S. Lewis, copyright © C. S. Lewis Co. Pte. Reprinted by permission.

C. S. Lewis, *The Great Divorce* (1945). Extracts by C. S. Lewis, copyright © C. S. Lewis Co. Pte. Reprinted by permission.

C. S. Lewis, *The Pilgrim's Regress: An Allegorical Apology for Christianity, Reason and Romanticism* (3rd edition, 1944). Extracts by C. S. Lewis, copyright © C. S. Lewis Co. Pte. Reprinted by permission.

C. S. Lewis, *The Problem of Pain* (1940). Extracts by C. S. Lewis, copyright © C. S. Lewis Co. Pte. Reprinted by permission.

C. S. Lewis, *The Screwtape Letters* (1942). Extracts by C. S. Lewis, copyright © C. S. Lewis Co. Pte. Reprinted by permission.

The Chronicles of Narnia

C. S. Lewis, *The Chronicles of Narnia. The Silver Chair* (1953). Extracts by C. S. Lewis, copyright © C. S. Lewis Co. Pte. Reprinted by permission.

C. S. Lewis, *The Chronicles of Narnia. The Voyage of the Dawn Treader* (1952). Extracts by C. S. Lewis, copyright © C. S. Lewis Co. Pte. Reprinted by permission.

Volumes of Essays

C. S. Lewis, *Christian Reflections* (1967). Extracts by C. S. Lewis, copyright © C. S. Lewis Co. Pte. Reprinted by permission.

C. S. Lewis, *Essay Collection and Other Short Pieces* (2000). Extracts by C. S. Lewis, copyright © C. S. Lewis Co. Pte. Reprinted by permission.

C. S. Lewis, *Letters to Malcolm: Chiefly on Prayer* (1964). Extracts by C. S. Lewis, copyright © C. S. Lewis Co. Pte. Reprinted by permission.

C. S. Lewis, *Of Other Worlds* (1966). Extracts by C. S. Lewis, copyright © C. S. Lewis Co. Pte. Reprinted by permission.

C. S. Lewis, *The World's Last Night and Other Essays* (1960). Extracts by C. S. Lewis, copyright © C. S. Lewis Co. Pte. Reprinted by permission.

C. S. Lewis, *They Asked for a Paper* (1962). Extracts by C. S. Lewis, copyright © C. S. Lewis Co. Pte. Reprinted by permission.

C. S. Lewis, *Transposition and Other Addresses* (1949). Extracts by C. S. Lewis, copyright © C. S. Lewis Co. Pte. Reprinted by permission.

C. S. Lewis, *Undeceptions: Essays on Theology and Ethics* (1971). Extracts by C. S. Lewis, copyright © C. S. Lewis Co. Pte. Reprinted by permission.

Single Papers in Journals or as Guest Writer
C. S. Lewis, "Avant-Propos a l'édition Française," in, *Le Problème de la Souffrance* (trans. Marguerite Faguer, 1950). Extracts by C. S. Lewis, copyright © C. S. Lewis Co. Pte. Reprinted by permission.

C. S. Lewis, "Introduction," in, *English Literature in the Sixteenth Century* (1954). Extracts by C. S. Lewis, copyright © C. S. Lewis Co. Pte. Reprinted by permission.

C. S. Lewis, "Introduction," in, *St. Athanasius, The Incarnation of the Word. Being the Treatise of St Athanasius, De incarnatione Verbi Dei* (trans. Sr. Penelope CSMV, 1944). Extracts by C. S. Lewis, copyright © C. S. Lewis Co. Pte. Reprinted by permission.

C. S. Lewis, "It All Began with a Picture...", in, *The Radio Times, Junior Section* (15 July 1960). Extracts by C. S. Lewis, copyright © C. S. Lewis Co. Pte. Reprinted by permission.

C. S. Lewis, "Must Our Image of God Go?," in, David L. Edwards, ed., *The Honest to God Debate: Some Reactions to the Book 'Honest to God' with a New Chapter by its Author, J. A. T. Robinson, Bishop of Woolwich* (1963). Extracts by C. S. Lewis, copyright © C. S. Lewis Co. Pte. Reprinted by permission.

Acknowledgement and thanks is given to Houghton Mifflin Harcourt for the U.S. right for permission to quote from the following works:

Excerpts from REFLECTIONS ON THE PSALMS, copyright © 1958 by C. S. Lewis, renewed 1986 by Arthur Owen Barfield, reprinted by permission of Harcourt, Inc.

Excerpts from SURPRISED BY JOY: THE SHAPE OF MY EARLY LIFE, by C. S. Lewis, copyright © 1956 by C. S. Lewis and renewed 1984 by Arthur Owen Barfield, reprinted by permission of Harcourt, Inc.

Extracts from the Bible used with permission:

Revised Standard Version of the Bible, copyright 1952 [2nd edition, 1971] by the Division of Christian Education of the National Council of the Churches of Christ in the United States of America. Used by permission. All rights reserved.

New Revised Standard Version Bible, copyright 1989, Division of Christian Education of the National Council of the Churches of Christ in the United States of America. Used by permission. All rights reserved.

New Revised Standard Version Bible: Anglicized Edition, copyright 1989, 1995, Division of Christian Education of the National Council of the Churches of Christ in the United States of America. Used by permission. All rights reserved.

THE HOLY BIBLE, NEW INTERNATIONAL VERSION®, NIV® Copyright © 1973, 1978, 1984, 2011 by Biblica, Inc.™ Used by permission. All rights reserved worldwide.

Nestle-Aland, Novum Testamentum Graece, 27th Revised Edition, edited by Barbara Aland, Kurt Aland, Johannes Karavidopoulos, Carlo M. Martini, and Bruce M. Metzger in cooperation with the Institute for New Testament Textual Research, Münster/Westphalia, © 1993 by Deutsche Bibelgesellschaft, Stuttgart. Used by permission.

Introduction
C. S. Lewis—Revelation, Conversion, and Apologetics

This is a book about Jesus Christ.

Jesus of Nazareth, the Christ, is of central importance to humanity.

Jesus Christ is considered by orthodox Christians to be the unique revelation of God, the God above all gods, the God beyond all gods.

These are strong, dynamic, and assertive claims. There are various ideas and interpretations of who or what this Jesus of Nazareth, the Christ, was and is; these theories vary across the churches. However, down the centuries there has been a constant and steady seam of knowledge and understanding as to who Jesus Christ is, how he is God, and how this affects all of humanity.

To talk about Jesus Christ is to speak of revelation—God's self-revelation, God's revealedness to humanity. Therefore, God is the one who initiates both in our knowledge and understanding about these most important of matters, but also, crucially, in our salvation.

1. WHO OR WHAT IS *THE* CHRIST

This is one of a series of books entitled *C. S. Lewis: Revelation and the Christ*. Like many ancient names that had cultural or religious meanings, the name Jesus—in Hebrew, *Yeshua*, given to Mary by Gabriel, the angel at the annunciation—was known to those who heard it as signifying "God is savior," or "Jehovah is savior"; Christ means "anointed one," messiah. The word Messiah was commonly used in the era between the two testaments, Old and New (i.e., the intertestamental period), the concept of messiahship having developed in later Judaism (from the early Hebrew *Mashiach*, the anointed one, derived from the ancient Hebrew tradition of anointing the king with oil). Messiah was not necessarily a name, but a label, an attribution, an office, a role, essentially a title. By the time of Jesus of Nazareth the title "Messiah" was often attributed to someone the people liked, whom they believed could fulfill, they hoped, a role for them. However, *the* Messiah was to be the one anointed at the end of days. Jesus is therefore taken by those around him to be *the* Messiah; hence the early attribution that he is the Christ. The word Christ is simply a translation from the Greek (χριστός, *Christos*) and the Latin (*Christus*) for messiah. Therefore Jesus Christ, in name and title, was God's salvation, the anointed one. This did not necessarily imply that he was the second person of the Trinity. The trinitarian perception is part of the dawning realization in the early church, with ample pointers and examples of Jesus's trinitarian nature in the books that became the New Testament (texts produced by the earliest church in the years after the resurrection and ascension).

Around the time of Jesus's birth messiahship carried expectations. Some saw the coming messiah as a political leader who would expel the Romans; others expected a messiah who would be a partisan revolutionary whose aims were unclear; to yet more the messiah would return the Temple religion back to a happier time, he would oversee the restoration of Israel. To an extent these can be seen as purely human offices. During the intertestamental period there were many false messiahs, men raised up to realize a revolutionary, political, or religious role supported by a group or sect to save Israel in some way or other. However, false messiahs lapsed, disappeared, or were killed by the Romans or the Jewish religious authorities. The Jews were left still hoping.

The idea of redemption, salvation, was part of these multitudinous expectations of a messiah figure during the intertestamental period—but saved *from what*, redeemed *to what*? The answers to those questions were as varied as the messianic expectations of these false messiahs. As a redeemer figure, expected and foretold, Jesus does not necessarily live up to the expectations of his fellow Jews. However, on reflection, the clues were there all along in Jesus's life and ministry, and crucially in the Old Testament. The ancient Hebrew priests and kings were anointed, they were messiahs (Exod 30:22–25); later, this messiahship entitled one anointed by God as a leader, a king from the line of David. Therefore, Jesus of Nazareth was perceived by many who saw and heard him to be *the* long awaited Messiah, with different and often subjective expectations as to his role. What is important is that *a posteriori*, after the event, the proto early church interpreted this messiahship in the context of Jesus's role as God descended to earth to judge and forgive humanity, hence the use of the Greek word χριστός (*Christos*), Christ, by the writers of the New Testament. Jesus is then the final Messiah of messiahs.

Messiah, Christ, is then revealed to be trinitarian: God anoints God to descend to save his chosen people, in potential, along with all humanity, reascending with them into the divine life. Only in the fullness of the incarnation-cross-resurrection and the ascension is messiahship finally defined by Jesus. Then his life and ministry, his sayings and actions, take on new meaning, a significance and understanding veiled to many during his lifetime. Whatever the expectations of messiahship, Jesus of Nazareth is *the* Messiah (therefore, *the* Christ), not *a* messiah, political or otherwise. It is fair to say that some of the Hebrew expectations were blown away by God's revelation; whatever people expected, it fell short of what was given by God in this Jesus. People couldn't see or fully understand what Messiah was to be, even though the evidence was there in the Old Testament.

The witness of the apostles, disciples, and the early church is then a form of revelation equal to Scripture. The early church tradition replaces the old Hebrew categories of messiahship; the expectations of Jesus's contemporaries were fulfilled by God's revelation, but not necessarily in accordance with what they desired or expected. This divergence also extended to the interpretation of messiahship that the Jewish religious authorities held to in Jerusalem. For many years the Western church concentrated only on the early church tradition and the conclusions of the church councils in the fourth and fifth centuries, often, in effect, ignoring the Hebrew tradition that Jesus of Nazareth was born into. In recent years many theologians and Bible scholars, for example the orthodox Christian N. T. Wright, derive most of their conclusions about Jesus of Nazareth from an understanding of the New Testament's Jewish background, a setting in the life of the times in some ways. Perhaps the answer is to hold in balance the Hebrew tradition and categories, the perceptions of the earliest church, and also the conclusions of the later church councils, about the person and nature of Jesus. This is how to see and understand the term Messiah, *the Christ*.

This is a work, in many ways, of Christology; that is, the work and person of Christ, Jesus of Nazareth. Christology is thinking about Christ; explaining using the faculty of reason, mostly in written form, so as to explicate who and what Jesus Christ was and is. Lewis's work was very much in the context of the developed understanding of who and what Christ was; an understanding that took shape in the first seven centuries of the Christian era. As with the Bible, this understanding became something of a compass as to what counts as sound doctrine about Christ and what does not. This body of understanding of what is a traditional and orthodox understanding of Jesus Christ developed gradually during the early church, and then through the following centuries, and was complete by around the year 750 AD. Christology is therefore seen to be the study of the person and work of Christ, fully human and fully divine, historical and universal, and his significance for humanity: this systematic study is therefore the doctrine of Christ, but it must always understand the Hebrew roots into which Jesus of Nazareth was born and lived.

2. WHY C. S. LEWIS

This is a book about one man's understanding of, and his encounter with, Jesus Christ. That man is Clive Staples Lewis—C. S. Lewis, Jack, at his insistence, to all he knew—who wrote many, many books to defend Christianity and the witness of the churches. Lewis's aim was to defend Christianity itself, not Anglican or Roman Catholic, not Methodist or Baptist, not Presbyterian or Evangelical. Why? He sought to defend what he famously called "Mere Christianity," which was not his own personal religion, or his own personal selection from Christian theology and church history, but the faith set out in the creeds and explained by the church fathers living more than fifteen hundred years ago, the faith that originated with the apostles who knew this Jesus of Nazareth. Lewis sought to defend the faith that the martyrs died for. Being a "Mere Christian" for him represented the distilled basics of the faith rooted in the God-man Jesus Christ. This was to be distinguished, for Lewis, from watered-down Christianity, from human-centered religion.

Lewis's "Mere Christianity" was, therefore, polemical in its assertiveness. This "Mere Christianity" was there to a greater or lesser degree in all the churches of Lewis's day, but had been compromised by disputes between the churches; indeed the very fragmentation of the church into so many denominations or groupings weakened the basic core of the faith. Games of one-upmanship and power politics between bishops from competing denominations, or arguments over the finer points of worship, or in some instances a wholesale rejection of the beliefs set out in the creed, this all weakened the gospel: that God became incarnate as a human being in Jesus of Nazareth and died for our sins to open up a way for us into heaven. This was at the heart of the Christian faith. This Jesus of Nazareth, the Christ, did not simply live two thousand years ago leaving us alone in the world: the Holy Spirit of this Christ is active, alive, presses on us, seeks to convert us, to save us.

Lewis believed strongly in a basic core to the faith, a "mere" Christian core. All else could be considered to be an embellishment, details that are to a greater or lesser degree important to individual denominations, and are valid to a greater or lesser extent before God, but nonetheless these details and differences are culturally relative, they are in many ways subjective religion. Lewis therefore distinguished what he called "Mere Christianity" from this subjective religion. Lewis was an Anglican; he saw this "Mere Christianity" in the Church of England of his day, that it was at its strongest in the Catholic and Evangelical wings, as distinct from the liberal, modernist, central ground, which he believed marginalized this core of "Mere Christianity": Lewis could therefore be fairly described as a Catholic-Evangelical, indeed he described himself as such.

This book then is written for students and theologians, but also general readers familiar with Lewis's works. Because Lewis was an Anglican this is a work written to be appreciated by Anglicans; however, it can also be appreciated by Roman Catholics who in recent years have developed an interest more and more in the writings of C. S. Lewis; it is also aimed at Evangelicals who have long had a love of Lewis's work, but have been selective about what they agree with and disagree with in Lewis's presentation of the basic core of the Christian faith. Evangelicals may not like the way Lewis subscribed to what can be considered a traditional Catholic position on the sacraments and on purgatory, but he held these beliefs for good reason. And Evangelical readers would do well to think why he did. Likewise Roman Catholic readers would do well to see how Lewis could get beyond the external structure of religion to appreciate the immediacy of relationship any believer can have with the Lord Jesus, which in some ways by-passes the structures and authority of the church(es).

3. AIMS AND OBJECTIVES

This series, *C. S. Lewis: Revelation and the Christ*, is a study of C. S. Lewis's Christology, and his doctrine as such of revelation: that is, his understanding of the person and the work of Jesus Christ, and how this is God's self-revelation. This study includes Lewis's conversion, his acceptance of what Jesus Christ had done for him, but also his understanding of the church, which is to be seen as the body of Christ. Therefore this book is about how he put that understanding into words, but it is also about his encounter with Jesus Christ, how Christ revealed of Christ's person, Christ's self, to Lewis, and therefore brought him to the one true trinitarian God. This is, in effect, what this book is about: who and what Jesus Christ is, and what *he* does.

The aim of this book is to show what C. S. Lewis understood about Jesus Christ. The objective is to examine what he then wrote, but also how he came to know and to believe in the God behind and in the Christ. This book is–

- A systematic study of the person and work of Christ Jesus in the writings of C. S. Lewis, and the place this understanding has in the wider church, contemporary and historical.

- A systematic study of Lewis's understanding of revelation—God's self-revelation to humanity—and with it humanity's salvation.

- This is therefore a work about Lewis's doctrine of Christ (including his understanding of the church—the body of Christ), his doctrine of salvation, and his doctrine of revelation (including the respectful criticism he had for "religion").

- A presentation of the personal God in Christ, which is central to understanding C. S. Lewis himself, both child and adult, public and private, and how this relates to his work as a philosopher and theologian, and his personal salvation.

- A work that presents an understanding for thinking Christians and professional academics, which ranks Lewis amongst the more important theologians and philosophers of the twentieth century.

- An analysis of Lewis's method and technique (both theological and philosophical) in the way he re-presented the basic non-negotiable core of the faith in his apologetic, his analogical stories, and in his theological narrative.

- A study of Lewis's Christology that acknowledges the Catholic (for example, a high sacramental theology, a belief in purgatory) and the Evangelical (his acknowledgement of the need for personal conversion in the form of a direct relationship with the Lord) within his faith as a Catholic-Evangelical.

Many books relating to C. S. Lewis's theology assume that he was an amateur theologian who simply summarized Christian doctrine and ethics for his audience, that he was not an original thinker or a systematician on the scale of more noted professionals. This series of books, *C. S. Lewis: Revelation and the Christ*, demonstrates that this is *not* so, that such conclusions are spurious. Lewis may not have been employed as a religious professional but the same can be said for many theologians and apologists in church history. Lewis's work is original, underlyingly systematic, and orthodox (i.e., traditional).

Lewis excelled at a cohesive expounding of the essentials at the heart of the Christian belief, nonetheless he held to an understanding of the wider logical sweep of the faith, without becoming embroiled in the more controversial details that have bedevilled the churches, individual denominations, for centuries. Lewis's understanding of Christ was grounded in his conversion. This was a conversion that paralleled, in many ways, that of Augustine in his acceptance of what God had done for him in the incarnation and in his invocation of Christ as the light of the world, and was given its systematic edge by his daily reading of key works of theology and related philosophy from before the modern era (that is, works written prior to the Age of Reason and the Enlightenment in the eighteenth and nineteenth centuries, and the modernism-postmodernism of the twentieth century).

Revelation and salvation are all intertwined with what we know of and understand about Jesus Christ. Therefore we are dealing with three doctrines (that is, doctrine as a set of beliefs or principles held and taught by a group, whether the church, a political party, or academics, from the Latin *doctrina* "teaching, learning"). These three doctrines are closely related: a doctrine of *revelation*, a doctrine of *Christ*, and a doctrine of *salvation*. We cannot separate who and what Jesus is from what he came to achieve, and what this person reveals to us about God. This work is a systematic study of Lewis's presentation and understanding of Jesus Christ that, following his conversion, underpinned his work. It assesses the implications of what he wrote and how Lewis the philosopher/theologian—when writing on Christ—is to be seen in relation to the church. This is in regard to his reputation as a Christian theologian, but also how the person and work of Christ Jesus is central to the human that he was.

4. EXPLANATIONS, QUALIFICATIONS

Despite often being classified as an amateur, Lewis was a highly educated man. Although he had no formal training in theology, his intellect was confirmed in that he received, within four years of study, two BA Hons degrees from the University of Oxford, having passed all three required public examinations with first class honors. These degrees were in Greats (Greek and Roman Literature and Classical Philosophy) and in English. Despite the astute sharpness and strength of his intellect, Lewis tried to avoid specialized theological language (jargon). However, a few terms do need to explained before we proceed. Some readers familiar with Lewis's books may not appreciate the full meaning and use of the terms used here. Professionals familiar with these terms may still gain some understanding of the context in which they are used in this book. Many Catholics and Evangelicals are familiar with these terms derived from New Testament Greek, and from *ecclesial* (i.e., church) Latin—ironically it is often Lewis's Anglicans who are ignorant of them.

i. Revelation and Reason

Revelation is personal, as in the realization of perception and understanding many people will have—a eureka moment when one finds something, or when something is revealed to one. But it is also more than that, more than the personal and subjective. Revelation is about God's *self-disclosure* to humanity. Lewis understood and accepted how God had revealed of God's self to humanity in multifarious and diverse ways down the millennia and across vast geographical and cultural eons, but as an orthodox Christian he knew, both as fact and from personal encounter, that Christ was the unique, the highest, form of self-revelation of the one true living God. So to talk about Christ is to talk about God; to speak of Christ is to speak of revelation. Over recent centuries revelation has often been pitted against reason. Because of the confidence emanating from the Age of Reason and the Enlightenment, a confidence issuing from the belief that the human capacity to reason things out for ourselves was all that was needed, revelation became, in certain quarters, obsolete.[1] Lewis seeks to try to hold both revelation and reason in balance; as a trained philosopher he knew and understood the background against which he was writing.

ii. Patristic

The patristic era is from the time of Christ's resurrection through to the mid-eighth century. The church leaders and theologians of this period of over 700 years are called "patristic"—from the Greek for Fathers, πατήρ, *patēr*, *patros*—hence the theology of these centuries is patristic, formed by the early church fathers. The immediate years after Christ's resurrection is called the apostolic era—the era or period of the apostles, essentially the people who knew Jesus of Nazareth or were of his generation, all of whom had died by around the year 100 AD. We then have the sub-apostolic era, which is essentially the second century, then fully the patristic era.

iii. Platonism

Platonism is the name given to the philosophy of Plato (c.424/423BC–348/347BC), and his writings. The term also applies to systems of philosophy derived from Plato's work and ideas, for example, Neo-Platonism or Platonic Realism. Central to Platonism is the theory of forms. The forms are transcendent archetypes; what we take for reality is in some way a pale imitation of the forms—reality relates to the forms as an imperfect copy does to an original. The forms tell us that what we take for reality is *perceivable* but not *intelligible*, but that there is another higher reality that is *intelligible* but not *perceivable*. Lewis was a trained philosopher; indeed early in his career he taught philosophy. Platonism is a type of philosophy that he not only subscribed to but which characterized his work throughout his life. Most patristic theologians were Platonists, to varying degrees; Neo-Platonism was in many ways part of patristic theology. Many Protestant, Reformed, or Evangelical supporters of Lewis's work today object strongly to his Platonism, not realizing that it is fundamental to Lewis's interpretation of the gospel and is at the heart of his understanding of revelation. The precise nature of Lewis's Platonism will be fully explained at the appropriate point in this work.

---

1   For an understanding of the relationship between revelation and reason in terms of the disciplines of theology and philosophy, see: Gunton, *Revelation and Reason*.

iv. Apologist/Apologetics

C. S. Lewis is an apologist. Apologetics are defined by the Oxford English Dictionary as, *reasoned arguments in justification of a theory or doctrine*. An apologist is one who argues, who confronts the disagreements and divergences that are evident between different belief systems. The term comes from the Greek word, ἀπολογία, *apologia*, meaning *to speak in defense*. Christian apologetics are written to defend the truth of the gospel against attack from atheists, scientists, philosophers, exponents of non-Christian religions, indeed anyone that denies the heart of the Christian faith. Christian apologetics are considered different to theology *per se*, because in apologetics the truth of the gospel is represented in such a way as possibly to change the content in reaction to a perceived threat, indeed the apologetic content may be defined by the threat. Academic theology is considered by some to be impartial, disinterested, and neutral—in theory—and therefore in some ways superior. Yet if the gospel is true we cannot hold to an impartial multi-faith position that regards all religions and philosophies as equal, more pertinently that regards the content of all world religions as equally valid. Lewis did not: he understood that the gospel stands in contrast to the world, was *against* the world in many ways. Most of the theological writings in the early church are considered to be apologetics because they were written against the background of pagan Roman religion and politics, and were therefore written under persecution.

v. Creation, Fall, Incarnation, Resurrection, Second Coming, and the Four Last Things

The heart of the Christian faith, the basics, are in some ways summarized by the creation and the fall into original sin set out in the Book of Genesis; by the incarnation, crucifixion, resurrection, and second coming of God in Christ, in the New Testament; but also the four "last things" from the Book of Revelation as well as the Gospels. This is Lewis's basic summary of the faith. Lewis believed in the traditional faith, set out by the apostles, the early church, and the early church fathers, which was biblical. At the centre of the Bible story, in some ways summarized by the creeds, is, as Lewis asserted "the Creation, the Fall, the Incarnation, the Resurrection, the Second Coming, and the Four Last Things."[2] Some of this may be obvious but it separates Lewis from many modern theologians and churchmen who have watered down the faith. First, whatever we may learn about evolution and the origin of the world and the universe, God created everything out of nothing and sustains it. Second, that humanity, through its own fault, disobeyed God and was infected by original sin; furthermore we brought this on ourselves, and the predicament we find ourselves in is perilous. Third, God became incarnated as a human being, Jesus Christ, who was crucified for our sins and was resurrected, all to atone for our fall into original sin and restore us to a right relationship with God. Fourth, that this same Jesus Christ will return to judge all at the end of the world, which will be, as Lewis terms it, the four last things: death, judgment, heaven, and hell. This is the *eschaton* (from the Greek, ἔσχατον, for last or final things).

---

2   Lewis writing to *The Church Times*, Feb. 8, 1952. Lewis, *Collected Letters Vol. III*, 164.

vi. Liberal/liberal, Modernism

C. S. Lewis's writings are set against the background of liberal culture and society in Britain specifically, and the United States and Europe generally. "Liberalism" is often seen as a contentious and problematic word—often it appears to generate an emotional response, may be considered pejorative, and may also be invoked in an equally subjective manner. In this work the words "Liberal" and "Liberalism" with an initial capital letter are used strictly in the context of theological Liberalism in the church: this is a position that more often than not denies the incarnation and resurrection, seeking to promote Jesus of Nazareth as an ordinary human being, furthermore, a Liberal theological position may not believe in God (with a capital "G") but happily allow people to believe in "gods" of their own making, their own invention. Lewis often referred to this as a modernist tendency. Theological Liberalism since the eighteenth-century has claimed freedom not only from traditional dogmas and creeds but also in the analysis of and value accorded to Scripture. Such theology was to a large degree formulated in the light of what were considered advances in the natural sciences and philosophy—the spirit of the Age of Reason and the Enlightenment. In this work, when cited with a lower case initial letter ("liberal"), the term refers to liberalism in society and culture generally, in ethics and morality in the twentieth-century. This has often been to do with sexual behavior, but is also seen in culture, the media, entertainment, etc. Therefore a distinction needs to be drawn between Liberalism as a *theological* movement or belief system and what is often euphemistically called a liberal perspective in Western society generally. Today those who subscribe to ethical liberalism (particularly in the area of sexuality and marriage) may or may not to a greater or lesser degree subscribe to theological Liberalism. For example, there are East Coast American Episcopalians today who support the legitimization of homosexual behavior within Christian ethics yet who are strongly orthodox and creedal in their doctrinal beliefs; but then there are also those who subscribe to this ethical liberalism whilst simultaneously denying Christ's divinity and regarding him as just another ordinary man, therefore these two liberals (differentiated by an upper or lower case initial letter) cannot be seen as identical, or as completely separate from each other. Lewis uses the term "Modernism"/"Modernist" very much in the same context as Liberalism—he was often scathing about Modernist tendencies in the Church of England, tendencies that essentially were theological Liberalism, which argued that all our ideas about God were wrong, that there was no supernatural God beyond the ideas in our minds, our deepest desires, and wishes.

vii. Pagan

Lewis's theological writings, as indeed with his conversion, are played out against the backdrop of what is termed pagan religion or paganism. A pagan is essentially someone holding beliefs from outside of the world's main religions. "Pagan" therefore refers to this form of religion and religious myths from outside of, in our instance, the Jewish and Christian traditions. It is important to remember that the term "pagan" was used by Lewis, and is likewise used here, with no derogatory intent, nor as a term of abuse. Lewis used the term simply to refer to those peoples and cultures outside of the Jewish and Christian traditions: that is, Oriental, Middle Eastern, Indian, and European tribes and nations, but particularly in the ancient world (Greek and Roman philosophy and literature, religion, and mythology) and especially the religion and mythology of the North European tribes (Celtic, Norse, etc.), with whom the name pagan is most often associated. In comparison to the post-Christian world in the West today (Lewis was amongst the first to coin the term "post-Christian" at a time when Britain still perceived its civic pageantry and public religion, and its people as Christian, first using the term "post-Christian" publically in an address on November 29, 1954[3]), where it was often being asserted that Britain is "slipping," "descending," "regressing" into paganism, Lewis was quite adamant:

> When grave persons express their fear that England is relapsing into Paganism, I am tempted to reply, "Would that she were." For I do not think it at all likely that we shall ever see Parliament opened by the slaughtering of a garlanded white bull in the House of Lords or Cabinet Ministers leaving sandwiches in Hyde Park as an offering for the Dryads. If such a state of affairs came about, then the Christian apologist would have something to work on. For a Pagan, as history shows, is a man eminently convertible to Christianity. He is essentially, the pre-Christian, or sub-Christian, religious man. The Post-Christian man of our own day differs from him as much as a divorcée differs from a virgin. The Christian and the Pagan have much more in common with one another than either has with the writers of the *New Statesman*; and those writers would of course agree with me.[4]

When Lewis is talking about Paganism he is therefore speaking of the pre-Christian world of peoples and cultures diverse from the Christian but moving towards the fulfillment of some sort of understanding of the revelation of Jesus Christ. Essentially the difference between a pre-Christian pagan and the contemporary post-Christian pagan is one of movement: the pre was moving *towards* in his/her theistic beliefs, the post is moving *away* in his/her atheistic beliefs.

viii. Romantic

The term Romantic, with an initial capital letter, has nothing to do with cheap romantic novels or magazines, or romance! The term Romantic represents a movement in art and culture—poets such as Longfellow, Wordsworth, and Keats were considered Romantics, as were painters such as Constable and Turner, and composers such as Beethoven and, to a degree, Wagner. As an artistic and cultural term Romantic is to do with feeling, with expressing oneself, with responding to the innate beauty in landscape and the natural world. Romanticism was in some ways a reaction against the scientific rationalism of the Age of Reason. The Romantic Movement was often

---

3   Lewis's inaugural lecture at Cambridge, Nov. 29, 1954. C. S. Lewis, "De Descriptione Temporum," 9–25.
4   Lewis, "Is Theism Important?," 138.

associated with the cult of the individual—of emaciated, troubled artists starving in garrets and producing works of genius entirely by themselves without any input and involvement from anyone else.

5. "... AND THE COLLECTED WORKS OF C. S. LEWIS"

Many people over the last one hundred and fifty years have tried to encapsulate the intellectual rigor, the cogency, and veracity of the gospel, while communicating it to an audience of ordinary people, often interested skeptics. The Bible scholar and bishop N. T. Wright, commenting on Lewis's writings, notes how "millions around the world have been introduced to, and nurtured within, the Christian faith through his work where their own preachers and teachers were not giving them what they needed."[5] Wright was a case in point; he notes how his tutors, when an undergraduate at the University of Oxford, "looked down their noses if you so much as mentioned him [Lewis] in a tutorial. This was, we may suppose, mere jealousy: He sold and they didn't. It may also have been the frustration of the professional who, busy about his footnotes, sees the amateur effortlessly sailing past to the winning post." But Wright, like other academics, raises questions about just how universal Lewis's work was—it was about the gospel, was a defense of the gospel, but it was not *the* gospel: "the Christianity offered by Lewis both was and wasn't the 'mere' thing he made it out to be... But above all it worked; a lot of people have become Christians through reading Lewis." There is, therefore, a universal appeal to Lewis's work that is lacking in many other apologists and academic theologians, whose work is often soon forgotten, being relative to and emerging from particular cultural, human, subjective positions. This has not been the case with Lewis's defense of the gospel. For example, the writer Joseph Pearce has noted how Joseph Fessio S. J. cited this universal appeal in comments at a theological conference in the mid-1990s. Quoting from an address given by the philosopher Peter Kreeft, Pearce notes Fessio's comments, initially given somewhat tongue-in-cheek, which were roundly endorsed across all denominational divisions:

> Father Fessio made these remarks during a theological conference in the mid-1990s, which Peter Kreeft recalled in 1998 as "the most memorable moment of the most memorable conference I ever attended." Attending the meeting, says Kreeft, were "dozens of high-octane Roman Catholics, Anglicans, Eastern Orthodox and Protestant Evangelicals," who, despite their noted theological differences, converged near the end of the conference in a crescendo of agreement. Kreeft continues: "In the concluding session Father Fessio got up and proposed that we issue a joint statement of theological agreement among all the historic, orthodox branches of Christendom saying that what united us was 'Scripture, the Apostles' Creed, the first six ecumenical councils and the collected works of C. S. Lewis.' The proposal was universally cheered."[6]

---

5   This and the following quotations are from, Wright, "Simply Lewis," 39–40. Online: http://www.touchstonemag.com/archives/article.php?id=20-02-028-f.

6   Pearce, *C. S. Lewis and the Catholic Church*, xiii–xiv. Joseph Pearce quotes from, Peter Kreeft, "The Achievement of C. S. Lewis: A Millennial Assessment," unpublished address given at Boston College, 1998.

Pearce notes how Protestants, Catholics, and Eastern Orthodox have managed to find areas of substantial agreement in Lewis's works. For example, Pearce notes, the centrality to salvation history of Christ's atoning death on the cross, the historical event of the resurrection, the authority of Scripture, and the unchanging reality of moral law. So despite flaws, despite Lewis's humanity, there is categorically, objectively, something to Lewis's work that transcends the relative, the fashionable and transient, the subjective, the slanted, prejudiced, and blatantly one-sided (i.e., denominational), in ways that other apologists and theologians have failed in.

6. LEWIS ON THE CHRIST: GOD AND REDEEMER

As the first book in the series, *C. S. Lewis—Revelation, Conversion, and Apologetics*, consists of three parts, twelve chapters in all. Some chapters are quite long, but nonetheless are a coherent thematic whole despite their length. All chapters are divided into multiple sections and sub-sections to allow for ease of access to the material contained in these long chapters. (A full, detailed, sectional contents can be found at the end of this volume.)

i. Part One, The Personal God of Salvation—Conversion and Acceptance

Part One (chapters 1–5) is about Lewis's relationship with and acceptance of Christ; therefore we examine Lewis's protracted conversion. Lewis became a Christian as a boy, but fell away from an active faith to become an apostate self-confessed atheist as a young man. As a young Oxford don he started to become religious—first a Hegelian, then a deist; but then Christ revealed to him the reality of life, and he became a Christian. The question we address is this: "What was Lewis's conversion *from* and *to*?"

Lewis learned from George MacDonald, the Scottish author, poet, and Christian minister, the critical value of a baptized imagination, which was crucial in his conversion and his vocation as a Christian apologist. We can compare Lewis's conversion to the conversion of Joy Davidman, who later in life was to marry Lewis: how similar/dissimilar are they? Lewis can be compared with other people who underwent a similar conversion. Lewis's conversion can be elucidated by comparison with the conversion of the Swiss Reformed theologian Karl Barth: both arrive at a point where they must own that God is God (Barth 1915; Lewis 1929), which leads both of them to point to the unique self-revelation of God in Jesus, the Christ (Lewis is more the Romantic whereas Barth believes he must still measure all against Kant). In their mature work both are muscular, intellectual Christians who despite their denominational differences are orthodox-traditional, biblical-creedal Christians who argue against the zeitgeist of an Enlightenment-spawned modernism. However, there are significant differences—particularly related to religious experience. Therefore how do the two conversions compare? And what does this tell us about Lewis's relationship with Jesus Christ?

ii. Part Two, C. S. Lewis—Theologian and "Mere" Christian

Part Two (chapters 6–8) examines what was the basis or ground of Lewis's work as a theologian, and apologist—what was his method, and what did he mean by "Mere Christianity?" The sources for this method came from a fifth-century Catholic monk by the name of Vincentius of Lérins ("What has been held Always, Everywhere, by Everybody"), and a seventeenth-century Puritan called Richard Baxter ("I am a Christian, a Mere Christian"). Therefore Lewis sought to promote a basic core, a sheer, undiluted, essence that was at the heart of the faith endorsed by Scripture, and by this developed patristic church tradition. Lewis distrusted anything modern as compared to the patristic foundations of theology. We can consider what it meant for Lewis to declare that he was a Catholic Evangelical, but also why so many professional churchmen and theologians claim he is not one of them; that he was an amateur.

What picture of Christ do we read from Lewis's numerous theological writings as *praeparatio evangelica* (his phrase—for he saw himself as preparing his readers for the gospel, not necessarily converting them)? How did Lewis see his role—public and private—in bearing witness to Christ? How did he react against the modern world, for Christ's sake? In 1958 the theologian, apologist, and process theologian, W. Norman Pittenger publicly accused Lewis of christological heresy. Lewis, however, refutes the accusation and then proceeded to demolish Pittenger's Christology as dangerously liberal. Their differences come down to ontology and status: is Jesus Christ defined by the very nature of his being in and before God, or is he who he is because of humanely conferred status?

iii. Part Three, C. S. Lewis—Apologist, Broadcaster, and Public Figure

Part Three (chapters 9–12) considers what picture of Christ we can read from Lewis's numerous theological writings. What is the nature of the Christology, along with the understanding of revelation and salvation, in Lewis's apologetics published after his conversion? We can give particular attention to his role as a public figure and apologist, and his attempt to present an interdenominational basic core of the content of the faith relating to the Christ (in particular his work at the BBC).

Lewis's understanding of revelation relates closely to his doctrine of God, and is both orthodox and original in identifying areas of study which return the faith to orthodoxy while opening up human religiosity to the Christ event. Lewis considers theodicy and human pain, how we approach God's justification in relation to affliction (*The Problem of Pain*). This is seen to be rooted in the person and the office of Jesus Christ. Although written to be broadcast to the general public *The Broadcast Talks* provide the strongest insight into Lewis's technique as an apologist grounded in *reductio ad absurdum* (reduce to the absurd), and into his Christology and doctrine of revelation. How does the incarnation, "The Grand Miracle" relate to God's supra-natural action within this world? In the *infinitum capax finiti* (the infinite capable of the finite) revelation defines what our understanding of God's infinity should be—the truly infinite capacity of God is also to be finite, specific, incarnated. This contradicts our religious expectations for a distant singular "god," an unknowable and unattainable "god," whereas transposition reveals the incarnation.

We can then consider what picture of Christ we can read from Lewis's numerous mature theological writings, and how they are considered different to his popular apologetics from the 1940s, when he was at the height of his skill as an apologist and defender of the faith. Is Lewis's *Mere Christianity* broadly creedal, orthodox? The answer is yes, but there are shortcomings. Some criticize it for a lack of emphasis on the cross; however, it can be demonstrated that Lewis's understanding of the cross appears to be focused on the nature of atonement that issues from the death of Jesus of Nazareth, the Christ, and how this repays the debt generated by humanity through sin. Does this marginalize the place of punishment? Or is punishment subservient to the debt repaid through the Christ's lifeblood spilt? It is the blood of the lamb, Jesus the Messiah, slain for our salvation, that is the key to Lewis's understanding of the cross, not necessarily the means (crucifixion) of his death; this is confirmed by the Hebrew categories defining the relationship between blood and atonement. This is clear from Lewis's writings—particularly in *The Chronicles of Narnia*.

Towards the end of his life Lewis became more and more preoccupied in his writings with what may be termed "Christlikeness": how Christ is translated into ordinary mortal humans. These people are not Christ, but exhibit some of the characteristics, such as the ability to sustain altruistic love, self-sacrifice, a graceful acceptance of a God-given reality, and so forth (for example, *Till We Have Faces*, *Reflections on the Psalms*, and both positively and negatively in *The Chronicles of Narnia*), where this is more than simply a comparison but is *caused* by the indwelling of the Holy Spirit. In his mature work Lewis points to the primacy of the Christ event, consistently.

7. LEWIS'S CHRIST

We can ask what do we make of Lewis's understanding of Jesus Christ, the incarnation of the one true living God? How do we assess the rare accusations by some professional theologians/writers that there are elements of christological heresy in some of Lewis's writings? How do we define/categorize Lewis's objective understanding of Christ, and likewise his subjective appropriation? What christological model does Lewis draw? Lewis's Christ, that is the picture he gives us in his Christology, is essentially a picture in words, a Christ from below, not primarily from above because it starts with Immanuel, God with us. This is balanced, initiated, by a shift (a Platonic shift for Lewis) from eternity into our reality: the Christ descends to raise us up; in doing so we are drawn into the divine life. However, humanity is not overwhelmed by Christ: Christ is the loving servant, but authoritative in *his* divine claim on all creation, a creation that, for Lewis, Christ sang into being, into existence, *ex nihilo* (out of nothing). Lewis's Christology is therefore high—this is God incarnate, not a wandering preacher/healer who was super-religious, or a Palestinian carpenter who was a good moral teacher.

Introduction

The key to Lewis's Christology is in the authority of Christ in majesty, in the Last Judgment. This was represented in Patristic art by the Pantocrator, the risen and ascended Christ enthroned in majesty, surveying, sustaining and judging creation: Christ as the ruler of the universe. This was seen especially in Byzantine art (for example, The Christ Pantocrator, a mosaic in the apse of Monreale Cathedral in Sicily, see: www.cslewisandthechrist.net). Christ, the second person of the Trinity was always shown in paintings and mosaics of the Pantocrator in the form of a Jewish man, God descended to be the humble servant, though reigning in the future, on high. Lewis's understanding of Christ is grounded in many ways in the future, the pure transcendent action of the loving God, the God of love, manifested in and with humanity that comes to us: Immanuel (this is essentially, the timeless breaking into space-time rather than an anticipation). We will see this in Lewis's own personal relationship with God in Christ. For Lewis, the conscious start of this relationship is in his conversion, which was both emotional and reasoned. The reasoning was very much pressed on him by J. R. R. Tolkien, the Roman Catholic Oxford Professor of Anglo-Saxon, in bringing Lewis to accept the truth of what is stated in the creed: that Jesus Christ is God incarnate and that this Christ died because of our sins and for our redemption. Though he could then reason this out, for Lewis acceptance was very much through the Holy Spirit, which pressed upon him, possessed and converted him. We must also consider as part of this relationship his deeper conversion after the death of his wife, Joy Davidman, in 1960.

Therefore Lewis reads his Christology initially from below in the light of the evidence of the self-revelation of the one true living God in Jesus of Nazareth: this is the ground, the reality behind his conversion experience and his assertive apologetics. This points repeatedly to Christ from above, the Universal Christ of the Trinity, uncreated, eternally begotten with the Father, the universal light of the world that comes down to redeem in, as Lewis termed our world, "the shadowlands." Reasoning comes after this has happened, after the event, but is revealed to a degree in our minds because God has put this knowledge, this understanding, in our hearts and minds: it is, in effect, retained as a fragment of the *imago Dei* (the image of God) despite our Fallen state, our willfulness to deny God and God's claims on our lives. Christ is within as well as without. Lewis's understanding/knowledge is after the event, after the incarnation, cross, and resurrection reveals the absolute—God—drawing us all towards eternity from above. This is Immanuel's descent to raise us up, to draw us into God, to bring us home; therefore it is the potential salvation of all, subject to our appropriation of Christ's atonement. Holiness/sanctification, for Lewis, is the key here: we are to be perfect—whatever it takes (even a purifying after death, if needed). We will see how this is often presented by Lewis using nature metaphors and therefore is in many ways an organic Christology. Because there is a dialectical balance between the humanity and humility of Jesus Christ as compared to the authority and freedom of the Father from above we are not overwhelmed—despite the direction of God's actions. This is shown in Lewis's writings and his Christian symbolic narratives (for example, *The Chronicles of Narnia*). In Lewis's writings Christ is characterized often by beauty, a beauty that comes to us from the future. This is a beauty that simultaneously judges and forgives, that is, if the human accepts in repentance this judgment and forgiveness. Despite the religious upbringing and education, even religious prejudices, of many of the characters in these Christian symbolic narratives (for example, Narnia) each and every individual must at some point meet with the Christ-Aslan, the embodiment of the love and salvation of the Father; these meetings represent a crisis in each individual's life: they must choose one way or the other. Subject to the vagaries and vicissitudes of the Narnian reality (i.e., he can be killed by the White Witch on the stone table), the Christ-Aslan changes not as we do, our perception changes as we grow spiritually in Christ.

Lewis's picture of Christ in his writings is not simply a restatement of orthodox, classic or high Christology in the form of apologetic writings and symbolic narratives; Lewis's Christology is important in its vibrant balance between the humanity of Immanuel and the power and authority of the shift from the above, the timeless, to here below, into to the world of shadows. Lewis's Christ is significant and important and has often been overlooked in the history of twentieth-century theology.

Part One

The Personal God of Salvation—Conversion and Acceptance

"I was the object rather than the subject in this affair. I was decided upon."

C. S. Lewis talking about his conversion, in,
"Cross Examinations" (1963)

1

Conversion: God is God

SYNOPSIS:
Christ did not come primarily to give humanity knowledge; knowledge is in some ways a by-product: salvation is the work and purpose of the incarnation, and therefore of the cross and resurrection. Christology is more than reasoning about Jesus Christ, the Spirit of the Christ indwells the church: therefore the Holy Spirit that proceeds from the Father and the Son works in and through the people of God. All people, including children, can be religious. Children can respond implicitly to the love of God in Christ in an unselfconscious way. Where was this relationship in C. S. Lewis's childhood? What was the boy Lewis's relationship with Christ, implicit and hidden though it may have been for most of the time? Were there moments of grace? What was Lewis's religious background? What role does the death of his mother play when he was ten-years of age, likewise the Edwardian public school system? As an adult C. S. Lewis is to be seen as an explicitly *Christian* religious person, not just theistic or deistic or generally religious, but from the final point of his protracted conversion he expounds an explicit belief in the God revealed in Jesus Christ. But why was Lewis's conversion so long and drawn-out, so delayed and prolonged? It was a conversion that happened in several distinct stages. What was Lewis's conversion *from* and *to*? Initially, as we shall see in this chapter, it is to theism. Lewis knew intense moments of longing (*Sehnsucht*), a piercing disabling longing, a desire that disappeared as swiftly as it had crept up on him, which he called "Joy." These intense moments are of immense importance and are in effect to be seen as the work of the Holy Spirit. With hindsight Lewis could see how this sense of *Sehnsucht*/"Joy" had pointed him to the truth of the Christian revelation. Lewis's autobiographical works—*The Pilgrim's Regress* (1933) and *Surprised by Joy* (1955)—illuminate much that we can understand about his conversion through which God laid claim to his life, and in response Lewis wrote for God's glory.

1. INTRODUCTION

The purpose of the incarnation, crucifixion, and resurrection is the salvation of humanity. Knowledge is in some ways accidental, or a by-product, even though there is this hunger in humanity to know about God, to be reassured that God exists. This reassurance is often in human terms: people want to believe in the "god" they would feel most comfortable with. If they truly come across God, if God announces himself to them, seeks to enter their lives, they are often shocked and want to retreat into the picture of the ideal god of their fantasies, the "god" they can control, that doesn't pressurize them, that doesn't threaten their religious ideas. If the whole purpose of the incarnation, crucifixion, and resurrection is the potential salvation of all of humanity then any resulting knowledge will relate very closely to God's desire to redeem us, to know us in our redemption.

In many ways it is impossible for us to know God because to do so means we must turn God into an object—an object to study, to observe, maybe even interrogate, an object to dissect like a scientist. We will want God to justify God's self, give good reason for, prove, that God exists, give an explanation for how he has treated us, and so on. C. S. Lewis called this putting "God in the dock": we put God on trial and expect him to prove his innocence![1] This makes us the subject and God the object (this is to explicitly use the language of grammar and sentence structure). The correct relationship is where God is the subject, the eternal subject, and we are the object, the created object of his love. This means we know God in the way a baby or an infant knows its parents. This is why in one way we know God as Father. But, in becoming incarnate as a human being, in Jesus of Nazareth, God essentially makes himself an object—the self-objectification of God. As Christ, as an object, we can know God; we can study God in a way that before was impossible, or at best limited. But, this knowledge comes about because of what God does for our salvation. In these first two chapters we will look at C. S. Lewis's conversion, how God cut through all the false "gods" that Lewis believed in as an atheist. We will see how this relationship of subject and object relates very closely to how Lewis the intellectual, the academic, began to perceive and realize how God is, and how God expected Lewis to be in relation to God's love.[2]

2. C. S. LEWIS'S PILGRIMAGE: CHILDHOOD

Lewis was excellent at writing about the faith, about Jesus Christ. However, this is only part of what Christology is, or should be, about. Christ is not only an object for study; the church has proclaimed from the time of Peter and the disciples—who were gathered, huddled and frightened, in upstairs rooms—that the Spirit of the Christ was alive and indwelt them. So, what was Lewis's relationship with Jesus Christ?—and how does it affect our study?

i. Lewis's Background

Lewis was a pilgrim. In effect Lewis's pilgrimage is from a child with a sincere faith, to a self-confessed atheist, to an Hegelian idealist as a young don, to a theist, then to a Christian—a trinitarian theologian rooted in the Anglican tradition. Lewis's teenage atheism is confirmed by his experiences in the trenches of the First World War (he

---

1 See, Lewis, "God in the Dock", 88–94.
2 Much of the material in these next two chapters was initially presented to the Research Institute in Systematic Theology, King's College London, on July 27, 2004 in a paper entitled, *C. S. Lewis' Conversion and Karl Barth's Retraktation—"God is God,"* a Realisation. I extend my thanks to those in the Institute who offered advice on the paper, in particular, Revd. Dr. Alan Spence.

was wounded and invalided out before he was slaughtered like the millions who died). Nothing he came across as a student at Oxford after the war threatened his atheism. However, it is when he is teaching at Oxford that he begins to find difficulties with his atheistic belief system. At the centre of Lewis's pilgrimage is what he termed "Joy." Indeed Lewis regards this mystical experience as central to his conversion, his faith, and his work as a Christian apologist.

Born in Belfast, Ireland, on the November 29, 1898, Clive Staples Lewis was baptized into the Church of Ireland, as a baby. Albert James Lewis (1863–1929), his father, was a solicitor whose family roots were in Welsh Methodism, Evangelicalism, and the Church of England. Flora Augusta Hamilton (1862–1908), Lewis's mother, was the daughter of a Church of Ireland minister, the Revd. Thomas R. Hamilton. Flora's family was steeped in an ecclesiastical tradition, the family having settled in Ulster in the early seventeenth century, with a number of establishment chaplains, a bishop, and a First in theology amongst her forbears.[3] C. S. Lewis had an older brother named Warren Hamilton Lewis (1895–1973). From the age of four years C. S. Lewis insisted he was "Jacksie," or Jack, and that his brother was Warnie. At the age of six years the family moved into a large, substantial, detached house named Little Lea. Jack was therefore raised in a solidly Victorian middle-class professional home in Ireland; his father was called to the bar, his mother was a graduate in mathematics—a First from Queen's University, Belfast. Lewis was raised in his early years to read whatever he could find amongst his parents' library. However, the settled secure and secluded life at home with his brother for companion was shattered and irretrievably lost when his mother died of cancer in 1908. Thereafter, from the age of ten years, Lewis is educated at several public schools. It is through these rigid Edwardian institutions that Lewis's religious, social, and personal development takes place.

ii. Childhood Religion

All children will have religious experiences. All children of whatever age can be religious. The spiritual life in and with Christ is not necessarily something cultural that is learnt from other people. The outward form of our religion will be cultural and will depend on where we are born, the family we are born into, the culture or society we grow up in. However, the ability of the human being to respond to God is innate: we were made to love and worship God, in this is our greatest happiness. Whatever love we have is a reflection in us of the love of God. Children can love God as profoundly as the most mature saints or martyrs, priests, religious, or bishops. However, most children are not *self-consciously* religious; such religious self-consciousness is learnt, absorbed. However, what is important is not how religious we are in our childhood but that God in Christ loves children:

> People were bringing little children to him in order that he might touch them; and the disciples spoke sternly to them. But when Jesus saw this, he was

---

3 For full biographical details of Lewis, his parents, and his background, see: Green and Hooper, *C. S. Lewis: A Biography*.

> indignant and said to them, "Let the little children come to me; do not stop them; for it is to such as these that the kingdom of God belongs. Truly I tell you, whoever does not receive the kingdom of God as a little child will never enter it." And he took them up in his arms, laid his hands on them, and blessed them.
> Mark 10:13–16

To receive the kingdom of God we must receive it like a little child. Jesus is not saying that all children are innately innocent and can do no wrong. There is an openness in children which is, to a degree, lost by adults. Children are dependent in a way that adults are not. This relates to original sin: children are as affected by original sin as adults, but adults are much more decisive and in control of their lives and often the lives of others. Children can bully and exercise power over others, it is true, but to much, much, less of a degree than adults because of their dependence. Children can exhibit flexibility in their views and opinions; they can also appear to be more forgiving than adults. This is probably what Jesus was talking about. However, being dependent, relying upon adults and the adult world, can disrupt a child's religious world when the adult world is threatened. But in that threat there may be the potential for spiritual growth even if this growth is delayed until adulthood. This is what happened to C. S. Lewis. The security and dependability of the world he lived in as a child was shattered. And the growth in Christ which issued from it was delayed until his adult years.

So where was Christ in Lewis's childhood, his upbringing and schooling? Where was the love of God in the security and dependability of the world he lived in? And what happened to that world? To answer these questions we need to look at what Lewis tells us in his spiritual autobiography and other writings.

iii. Moments of Grace

Written over forty years after the childhood events it recalls, Lewis the intellectual, in his spiritual autobiography, *Surprised by Joy* (subtitled, *The Shape of My Early Life*), does a good job of trying to account for what was important in his childhood. Lewis is in many ways a Romantic in the sense of being open to and valuing beauty and magnificence, feeling and emotion; also he holds imagination in great esteem. Lewis writes of a moment of intense beauty which must been seen as a moment of grace: the Holy Spirit of Christ touching Lewis's mind and soul in a way that does not normally happen in everyday discourse and actions. Lewis was probably about four or five years of age (the incident occurs prior to the move to Little Lea). Lewis classifies this as the earliest of his aesthetic experiences, though it is probably more spiritual, even religious, than aesthetic, not because it evokes pantheism but because it perhaps was authored by the Holy Spirit. He describes how his brother presented him with a lid from a biscuit tin decked with twig, moss, flowers, in effect a model garden: "That was the first beauty I ever knew . . . As long as I live my imagination of Paradise will retain something of my brother's toy garden."[4] Along with the childhood glimpses of the far distant hills—the Castlereagh Hills—this generated a wistful yearning, a desire always

---

4   Lewis, *Surprised by Joy*, 5.

1. Conversion: God is God

unfulfilled: "They taught me longing—*Sehnsucht*; made me for good or ill, and before I was six years old, a votary of the Blue Flower"[5] More than half a century later, in *The Chronicles of Narnia*, Lewis would often present the Aslan-Christ as characterized by, above all, beauty; often a terrible beauty that judges by its very presence but also a beauty that children fall in love with, a beauty whose innate attractiveness will draw in all, a beauty that cannot be controlled or predicted. What we have here is the first hint of something which is of profound importance to Lewis, particularly the apostate atheistic young Lewis: *Sehnsucht*, which we will define and deal with later, but for now we will simply call it a longing, a yearning. Several years afterwards, Lewis noted what he termed the memory of a memory, how these moments from his childhood returned to possess him momentarily:

> It is difficult to find words strong enough for the sensation which came over me; Milton's "enormous bliss" of Eden (giving the full, ancient meaning to "enormous") comes somewhere near it. It was a sensation, of course, of desire; but desire for what? not, certainly, for a biscuit tin filled with moss . . . before I knew what I desired, the desire itself was gone, the whole glimpse withdrawn, the world turned commonplace again, or only stirred by a longing for the longing that had just ceased. It had taken only a moment of time; and in a certain sense everything else that had ever happened to me was insignificant in comparison.[6]

Lewis actually writes in *Surprised by Joy* that religious experiences were non-existent in his childhood;[7] so what did he regard the above experience as? He defines it as an *aesthetic* experience, simply an encounter with beauty. But is this an encounter with Christ? Religion for the young Lewis was something external, cultural, imposed by his parents, by school, and by society, and as such was part of an incomprehensible adult world. He also asserts that his parents did not fit in with the stereotypical idea of puritanical Presbyterian Ulster religion, they were far more Anglican than most around him (for example, Annie Harper, the Presbyterian governess). Within the context of implicit religious experience it is important to note how when the Lewis family moved to the new, large, detached house, Little Lea, Jack now saw himself as the product of "long corridors, empty sunlit rooms, upstairs indoor silences."[8] Lewis developed a degree of isolated quietude, which set him apart, which contributed to him developing as a writer. In these early years the close friendship developed between him and Warnie that would last a lifetime.

Lewis's glimpses of this spiritual world, the longing and yearning, seem at times more important than people to him. However, this sense of isolation, if that is what it is, also helped develop him as a poet, as hints in his later work suggest. He noted how when reading he could be caught by something unexpected that triggered this sense of longing and yearning:

---

5   Ibid., 5.
6   Ibid., 14.
7   Ibid., 5.
8   Ibid., 8.

> There came a moment when I idly turned the pages of the book and found the unrhymed translation of Tegner's "Drapa" and read
>
>> I heard a voice that cried,
>> Balder the beautiful
>> Is dead, is dead—
>
> I knew nothing about Balder; but instantly I was uplifted into huge regions of northern sky, I desired with almost sickening intensity something never to be . . . and then, as in the other examples, found myself at the very same moment already falling out of that desire and wishing I were back in it.[9]

Lewis regards these early spiritual experiences—though he does not necessarily see them in a religious context—as important, even key to anyone who seeks to understand his life and work.

iv. Death

The most profound religious experience the child that was Clive Staples Lewis went through has to be the death of his mother in 1908 from cancer. Lewis was but ten years of age. Lewis writes poignantly of the illness and loss, very much from a child's perspective: the innocence and yet apparent self-centred view of a child. Flora was treated at home, leading to an apparent recovery but then a relapse and death. The Lewis boys were not told of the cancer, not till after she had died, and were lost in puzzlement at what was happening. Jack wrote about how his father in his inconsolable grief ignored the boys, resulting in Jack and Warnie seeking solace in their own company.[10]

It is at this point that Lewis owns up to what he considered some sort of religious experience: his mother's death. "When her case was pronounced hopeless I remembered what I had been taught; that prayers offered in faith would be granted. I accordingly set myself to produce by will power a firm belief that my prayers for her recovery would be successful; and, as I thought, I achieved it."[11] Lewis was not gripped by a crisis of faith when his prayers were apparently unanswered, he comments that he thought no more about it. Lewis prayed for healing; then with his mother's death presumably he prayed for resuscitation-resurrection, which if it had happened would have been reminiscent of Lazarus in John's Gospel. However, Lewis does see something of this:

> I think the truth is that the belief into which I had hypnotized myself was itself too irreligious for its failure to cause any religious revolution. I had approached God, or my idea of God, without love, without awe, even without fear. He was, in my mental picture of this miracle, to appear neither as Saviour nor as Judge,

---

9   Ibid., 15. Lewis is referring to Esaias Tegnér's poem, "Drapa," in Longfellow, *The Seaside and the Fireside*. Esaias Tegnér (1782–1846), Professor of Greek, Swedish writer, and folklorist composed poems derived from the Norse myths, for instance, *Frithjof's Saga*.
10   Lewis, *Surprised by Joy*, 16–17.
11   Ibid., 18.

but merely as a magician; and when He had done what was required of him I supposed he would simply—well, go away.[12]

Perhaps it may be asserted that the will of the Father through the incarnate and crucified Son was in Flora's suffering precisely because of what would happen to her son, the man he would become, the witness he would be to God's glory. This is the cross—but it is so rarely recognized—the Lord of heaven and earth used Flora's cancer and death to create the man that Lewis was to become. For the child Jack this was a profound encounter from which he reacted. The death of his mother, the intensity of his prayer, the result which may have appeared as no answer but was still an answer from the Lord of heaven and earth, all of this was intensely religious. Looking at Lewis's life and career and writings after the event, which had been formed to a large degree by the event of his mother death, then Christ was walking with him, sustaining him, but he knew not. Then nineteen years later—Lewis's conversion—Christ revealed himself to the strident young Oxford don. Clive Staples Lewis's life was fractured and disrupted, a dislocation from which he never really recovered. Would the mature adult Lewis have written the vast and critically important volume of books, of Christian apologetics, a crucial contribution to the witness of the church in the twentieth century if his mother had recovered? He certainly would not have been the man he became: "With my mother's death all settled happiness, all that was tranquil and reliable, disappeared from my life." [13]

3. C. S. LEWIS'S PILGRIMAGE: YOUTH

Within weeks of his mother's death C. S. Lewis was sent away by his father, with Warnie, to boarding school. Lewis records with poignancy the journey, the reliance on his brother (for whom this was not the first time away at school), and the lack of reconciliation in him regarding his mother's death. He was still grieving; indeed the repression of grief and feeling amongst the Victorian-Edwardian middle class was considered essential, mandatory—Lewis was forced to develop what so often is characteristically called a "stiff upper lip." He was not allowed to grieve or to miss his mother. This was the social norm.

i. Schooling, Anglo-Catholicism, and Northernness

Both Jack and Warnie were boarded at the Wynyard School in Watford, Hertfordshire. According to Jack the school was characterized by mathematics lessons, Latin grammar (but never any Roman literature), and an unusual and excessive brutality: when the school closed within a couple of years of Jack's arrival the Headmaster was certified and locked away in an insane asylum. Lewis returned to Northern Ireland and went to school at Campbell College in Belfast. Because of ill-health he was sent to the health-resort town of Malvern in England, to a preparatory public school named Cherbourg House. At the age of fifteen years in 1913 he was sent to Malvern

12   Ibid., 18–19.
13   Ibid., 19.

College for a year. Malvern was considered a good English public school without the sadism and paucity of curriculum that had characterized Wynyard. However, Lewis hated the traditional Edwardian public school ethos dominated by class and social status, pecking order, fagging and sports; nothing but sports, gymnastics, rugby, and ambition, or so it seemed to Jack. Warnie saw no problem with Malvern; however, their father acquiesced and withdrew Jack, sending him to be privately tutored by William T. Kirkpatrick, a retired headmaster living in Surrey. Kirkpatrick—who had tutored Lewis's father, Albert—was a formidable intellect, very much a logician who could expose the weaknesses in an opponent's argument without mercy. Kirkpatrick was also a passionately committed philosophical atheist. It is to Kirkpatrick—"The Great Knock" as Lewis called him—that we must attribute a sound base to Jack's education, but also the incisive skill in logic that so often characterizes Lewis's mature Christian writings. Lewis's use of logic was grounded in the unforgiving teaching technique that Kirkpatrick used: he would accept absolutely no sloppy thinking or undefended argument or position.

Where was religion and spirituality in Lewis's youth and schooling? What was it that was of value to him? Whilst at Wynyard School Lewis began to attend an Anglo-Catholic church, the parish church of St. John the Apostle and Evangelist in Watford.[14] Lewis regards it as the most important thing that befell him at Wynyard: "There first I became an effective believer."[15] Lewis notes how as an Ulster Protestant he reacted against much that was high Anglo-Catholic in the church, in later life he claimed to be filled with disgust at the excessively Anglo-Catholic practices of St. John's. However, this was an important grounding and he was perceptive enough at the time to realize that it was in hearing Christian doctrine as distinct to what he terms religious uplift that was crucially important: "I began seriously to pray and to read my Bible and to attempt to obey my conscience."[16] This was a good beginning. Despite the nihilistic brutality of Wynyard School, St. John's gave Lewis a grounding, the value of which, coming soon after his mother's death, is to be seen as immeasurable. However much he would walk away from this start over the coming years, the grounding was there and his prayers were answered: he was hooked to invoke a fishing analogy common in the early church. St. John's church fished for men and women and children and through the vicar, the Revd. Canon R. H. L. James (incumbent from 1904–54, who must be seen as one of the most important people in Lewis's life, yet he rarely if ever gets a mention), God had hooked Lewis. However much Lewis wandered, the Lord God played him like a fish, giving him line, to wear himself out with all manner of philosophical, cultural, and pseudo-religious thought systems, before reeling him in nearly twenty years later.

---

14   The parish church of St. John the Apostle and Evangelist, Sutton Road, Watford, WD17 2QQ, was consecrated in 1873, a temporary building was replaced with the present church in 1893 with a rood screen by architect and designer Sir John Ninian Comper; for Lewis's reaction to St. John's, see, Green and Hooper, *C. S. Lewis: A Biography*.

15   Lewis, *Surprised by Joy*, 31.

16   Ibid., 32.

During his teen years Lewis developed a strong passionate interest in pagan Norse myth, Wagner, Icelandic sagas, Irish mythology, and Celtic mysticism. This was epitomized in a word: "Northernness." A Northernness that became like a religion to him, characterized by sheer wide open spaces, skies hung over vast forests and mountains, infinite seascapes with the fall of a winter sun behind the horizon. There was a coldness in this northernness, coupled with a love for nature, for landscape, for sunrises and sunsets, and autumn evenings. What characterized all of these phenomena for Lewis was "otherness"; an otherness where eternity, what was really real, could be glimpsed through the veil, the curtain, of our reality. Lewis was a Romantic in the artistic and cultural sense of the word. Although it is fair to say that Lewis was something of a loner he did develop a deep friendship at this time with another teenager by the name of Arthur Greeves—both realized their deep love for Wagner, illustrated by Arthur Rackham, and this sense of Northernness, mythology and saga. Both Lewis and Greeves shared a life-long correspondence.

ii. Atheism

Lewis's childhood faith, from the days attending St. John's church when he was ten to eleven years of age, was genuine; however, he lapsed into apostasy as he grew up and embraced atheism in his teens. What happened? While Warnie was at Malvern College, Jack was boarding at Cherbourg House, the preparatory feeder school for Malvern College: the Matron[17]—cited as Miss C, by Lewis—was the person who perhaps unwittingly triggered Lewis's crisis of faith and descent into atheism. Lewis notes how caring she was in her professional role but that also she was lost in a sea of belief systems with no ability to discern: Theosophy, Rosicrucianism, Spiritualism, and what Lewis terms "the whole Anglo-American Occultist tradition."[18] Lewis writes about how discussions with this Matron triggered his interest in and desire for the preternatural, the supernatural, which he describes as a spiritual disease, a lust.[19] Lewis notes how one reason why the devil, the Enemy, could so easily destroy his true understanding of God with false religion was because he was ripe for atheistic spirituality. He notes how his practice of the Christian religion had become burdensome, particularly as he had become more and more anxious and even neurotic in his prayer. When he first came to

---

17   The Matron of a boarding/residential public school was the person responsible for the care, welfare and well-being, and health of the residential pupils. This was not a teaching/academic role and in Edwardian England it was always a woman.

18   Lewis, *Surprised by Joy*, 56. Theosophy is a study of religion, philosophy, and metaphysics developed from the late nineteenth century (though is rooted in many ancient religions) as a spiritual philosophy by Helena Blavatsky (1831–91), who also co-founded of the Theosophical Society. As a belief system it holds that all religions are equal, or that there are elements in all religions that point to truth (truth being the highest form of religion). Religions are an effort by the so-called spiritual hierarchy to show people how to develop excellence. Theosophy is, as with all religions, characterized by diversity of belief. Some hold to reincarnation; often the human spiritual self is known as "the monad": this is the higher self. Originating in the seventeenth century, Rosicrucianism was a secretive order where inner realms or worlds aided people in their spiritual development. Both Theosophy and Rosicrucianism contain what appears to many to be an unhealthy element of Gnosticism.

19   Lewis, *Surprised by Joy*, 57.

"a serious belief" through St. John's church he was eager to pray, but as the years passed he became almost neurotic about the genuineness of his prayer, the efficacy of it, the level of concentration, and so on, so he would repeat the prayers, getting more and more anxious.[20] Lewis was in many ways alone. Being a boarder at a public school with no real friends, being in many ways an orphan (his father having withdrawn virtually all contact but polite conversation with his sons), so the interest/friendship of the Matron at Cherbourg House was in many ways the only human warmth, friendship, and sense of love he received. If he had attended a day school and had been part of a more normal family Lewis perhaps would not have become so anxious and neurotic in his prayers, and would not have seen his practice of orthodox Christian religion as so burdensome. But he did not.

Lewis the intellectual was also confused by the apparent truthfulness of the one religion that he was asked to subscribe to (Christianity), when he was exposed to the existence of thousands of other religions, philosophies, and thought systems. The only solution to Lewis as a fifteen-year-old was to dismiss them all as nonsense, but to dip into some of them, as seemed to satisfy his desires and pleasures. Although Lewis now moved away from Christianity (it is always important to remember that from the age of ten to around thirteen years—he is quite vague on dates, ages, and times—Lewis was a seriously believing Christian) and claimed to be an atheist, it is fair in reality to assert that he was a *religious* atheist. He dismissed the existence of the Christian God, called himself an atheist, but was actually very religious. However, his religion was a religion of feeling, of myth and story, of nature, of experience, all of which was orientated around self, around Lewis's ego. Lewis writes that he was something of a pessimist and had inherited a worrisome nature from his father. Despite this personal, experiential, mythological religion (which to Lewis was not religion); despite his avowed disbelief—or more pertinently lack of acknowledgement of God and the truth of the Christian gospel—Lewis still went forward for confirmation into the Church of England, again at public school, very much to please his father, and because it was a rite of passage for good middle-class Edwardian young gentlemen. What does Lewis have to say, in an attempt at self-analysis almost half-a-century later? "Asgard and the Valkyries seemed to me incomparably more important than anything else in my experience."[21] What is more, these pagan myths were more important than his Christian beliefs, plagued as the latter were by doubts. Lewis asserts that the phenomenon of Northernness was, or at least appeared to be to him, greater and more important than religion, yet he can see that part of this Northernness was religious, that it contained elements which his religion, or church practice, ought to have contained. Yet he asserts that it was not itself a new religion,[22] because, he argues, it contained no trace of belief in a god or gods and was not externally imposed. Here Lewis's understanding of religion is somewhat off the mark: religion does not necessarily require belief in a god, and is not always externally imposed. Indeed Buddhism, it can be argued, is in essence an atheistic

20   Ibid., 57–61.
21   Ibid., 72.
22   Ibid., 72–73.

religion for it has no "god," and leaves the question of God open. Lewis is prepared to admit something of this, "There was in it something very like adoration, some kind of quite disinterested self-abandonment to an object which securely claimed this by simply being the object it was . . . Sometimes I can almost think that I was sent back to the false gods there to acquire some capacity for worship against the day when the true God should recall me to *himself*."[23] Was the god (note lower case "g") that Lewis sought to deny behind a screen of atheistic religion, was this god really the God revealed by Jesus Christ? Considering the formal civic religion he had been forced to observe and take part in at public school it is pertinent to ask this question. Without much in the way of corroborating detail it would seem fair to assert that Lewis did meet the God of and in Christ Jesus at St. John's church when he was ten to eleven years of age; however, with the deeply shattering effect of his mother's death and being forced to live the life of an orphan amongst public school English aristocrats, it is of no surprise that he was, in some ways, clearing out his mind and soul of false gods. As we will see, the real God he had met at St. John's church near Wynyard School did not let go or leave-off Lewis despite the intellectual atheism he developed for himself, and God reminded Jack of what was required of him later when he was a young Oxford don.

iii. Sehnsucht

A literal translation of the German concept *Sehnsucht* (pronounced zein-zukt)—for it is more than simply a word—is "a yearning," "a longing." The problem is that there is no direct translation: it is a German concept that is only really covered by several related words in English. A yearning for, a longing for, implies an object, an object of desire, but there is so often with *Sehnsucht* no object, it is the sensation itself. Therefore *Sehnsucht* is often seen to have mystical overtones relating to something unattainable. It is then characterized by a fervent and passionate desire or longing, a yearning or craving, a hunger or even an addiction. In many ways this feeling, the concept of this desire, is destructive, negative, even seen by some as self-defeating because of the regret and, simultaneously, the deeply corrosive sense of unattainability and loss.

As a teenager and as a young man C. S. Lewis experienced *Sehnsucht*. He saw it as an inconsolable longing for an ill-defined or unknown object, a longing that struck with a sickening intensity: "That unnameable something, desire for which pierces us like a rapier at the smell of bonfire, the sound of wild ducks flying overhead, the title of *The Well at the World's End*, the opening lines of *Kubla Khan*, the morning cobwebs in late summer, or the noise of falling waves."[24] There is, then, sometimes a sense of nostalgia about the longing/yearning because if the object of desire is not known, or is ill-defined, there is then the association of "it" being from or in the past—often it is associated with childhood, or childhood memories, or simply, past times, better times. For many like Lewis the ache, the yearning or longing—Lewis often uses the term "pang," because it was so like a stabbing—was transient and short-lived but was

---

23   Ibid., 73.
24   Lewis, "Preface to Third Edition." Lewis, *The Pilgrim's Regress*, xiv.

so intense that the sense of *Sehnsucht* was in itself the object desired. Lewis considered the longing better than fulfillment. There is then an element of the secretive, the esoteric, about the longing because it is always different for each individual. Despite these individualistic characteristics Lewis considered that *Sehnsucht* was widespread, a common occurrence in humanity. Lewis occasionally uses the German word/concept, but defines this experience, this pang of *Sehnsucht* in himself, as "Joy" (which hereafter will be set with a capital J, and enclosed by inverted commas to distinguish Lewis's pang of *Sehnsucht* from ordinary joy).

Sehnsucht—Lewis's "Joy"—is a human concept, it is real, but the name, the concept, is to a degree a human imposition. As the person experiences this yearning, this longing, which pierces the soul, cuts to the core of the very being, strikes and disables with a sickening intensity, there is an external cause, a trigger. However, this is no psychological illusion or projection. So what triggers, what creates, these experiences? It must be seen as caused by the Holy Spirit. There have been secular atheistic writers who have written on this yearning, this un-nameable longing, but the intellectual construction they employ to name and explain falls short of what is happening. Lewis, like so many others who had focused on the experience of *Sehnsucht*, found after their conversion, after they had surrendered to God, that the pain and the disabling nature of this longing was satiated. However, if this sense of the Holy Spirit (which is essentially convicting the person of sin in not living a life orientated to God in Christ) is ignored, and if this sense of *Sehnsucht* is then cultivated for the experience in itself, then it becomes idolatrous and often amongst an educated and cultured elite it leads to suicide. This intimation of the Holy Spirit which is *Sehnsucht*/"Joy" therefore must be seen as an element of conscience—in these instances, an element of a *guilty* conscience. This experience as conscience relates to the beauty of God, which perhaps explains why the experience seems to come up on the individual unawares, afflict and retreat, before the individual has realized what has happened, and why the instances of *Sehnsucht*/"Joy" are so often associated with a sense of beauty (a landscape, a sunrise, a piece of music or poetry) because if we idolize an aesthetic experience, turn it into a "god," without realizing what we are doing then there will be a sense of guilt associated with the experience. If what is an intimation of the Holy Spirit, if what is the Spirit of the resurrected and ascended Christ acting on an individual in an attempt to convict them of sin and re-orientate them towards God, if this is turned into an idol to be sought, cultivated, experienced for itself then we are up against just how depraved and sinful humanity after the fall into original sin has become.

Such idolatry is a form of religion. Religion itself then can become an idol that works against the purposes of God in seeking the salvation of humanity. The danger with such idolatry, indeed with all idolatry and why it is explicitly outlawed in the Ten Commandments, is because in creating a substitute for God we not only lose sight of the real living God but we ruin any capacity in ourselves that God has placed in us whereby we can be responsive to God's Holy Spirit. Idolatry is not always in wooden statues or carved stone gods. The Bible can become an idol, likewise a church building. We can equally be idolatrous about a piece of music, about clothes, houses, a lifestyle; but worst of all are the idols that are mental models in our minds: *Sehnsucht* is so often an idolatrous mental model in the mind. Lewis writing of the experience commented: "It is that of an unsatisfied desire which is itself more desirable than any other satisfaction. I call it 'Joy,' which is here a technical term and must be sharply distinguished both from Happiness and from Pleasure. 'Joy' (in my sense) has indeed one characteristic, and one only, in common with them; the fact that anyone who has experienced it will want it again."[25] *Sehnsucht* is eschatological: if *Sehnsucht* is a glimpse of the judgment of God—not directed to any specific behavior but at the orientation of the individual person towards God, or not as the case may be—then for those who do turn it is a glimpse of heaven; for those who do not turn to God this is a glimpse of hell. *Sehnsucht* in Lewis's life is in many ways a systematic acting out of what Jesus says to Nicodemus in John's Gospel: that the individual must be born again, only the Spirit can bequeath life, flesh can only give birth to flesh. It is then essential for the individual to be drawn into the community we call church. So, if *Sehnsucht*/"Joy" is in many ways an intimation enacted by the Holy Spirit in laying claim to the person Lewis was, seeking to re-orientate him to God, then let us explore what actually happened to the young Lewis.

4. C. S. LEWIS'S PILGRIMAGE: CONVERSION

Lewis wrote of his conversion in two books. The first, *The Pilgrim's Regress* (1933), is disguised; it is somewhat allegorical; that is, the degree to which the story's hero is based on Lewis is open to speculation and conjecture. *Surprised by Joy* (1955) is much more honest and open: it is a spiritual autobiography. The chapters on Lewis's adult conversion, his return to faith, are a detailed and intensely existential attempt at charting his development from not just the childhood faith we have explored but also his atheism and then the struggle to break free of various belief systems (mostly philosophical) in his twenties to return to the gospel. *Surprised by Joy* is a seminal conversion story and rightly ranks with Augustine's *Confessions*. Essentially Lewis's struggle with God is charted in two chapters—XI *Check* and XIV *Checkmate*. The first of these two chapters is set in 1915 when Lewis is seventeen years of age and receiving private tuition from William T. Kirkpatrick; the second charts the development of his beliefs as a young don from 1922 through to 1929.

i. "Huge Waves of Wagnerian Music"

Lewis writes much about *Sehnsucht*/"Joy," which as we have seen evokes a sense of desire but often with no object and is characterized, certainly for Lewis, by regret and, simultaneously, unattainability and loss. For Lewis this sense of *Sehnsucht* came as quickly as it went, and filled him with a sense of pure beauty, pure joy, a beauty independent of the world of flesh and desire, ambition and lust, and so forth. Lewis wrote that this mystical experience was often generated by "huge waves of Wagnerian

---

25   Lewis, *Surprised by Joy*, 15–16.

music and Norse and Celtic mythology."[26] Lewis admits candidly that as a teenager he sought to cultivate this sense of "Joy," he longed for it, searched for it, but found that he could not replicate—even when reading the same passages or listening to the same piece of music. "Joy" was elusive; it was not in his command. Lewis writes that he came to see how he made the mistake of believing that this mystical experience was the object of his desire in itself. However, he was to realize it was merely a pointer—the *source* of this mystical pang was the true object of his desire. If what was happening for Lewis was the Holy Spirit attempting to point him, re-orientate him, towards God, Lewis did not realize this that the source was outside of this world, outside of this reality, and therefore the true enjoyment that lasts was not to be attained in this world: you cannot grasp and keep the beauty of a sunrise enveloped in white mist, you cannot own or freeze in time the music that so captivates. If you try to attempt to control or to own these moments all you will have—certainly for Lewis—is the sense of inconsolable loss, the sickening intensity of longing for what cannot be grasped, when "it" does not really exist: only the source of the beauty exists—God. This is so because God is triune, and within the Godhead each of the three persons ever focuses on the other. This ever focusing on the other within the immanent Trinity is an essence of love that indwells humanity, flows through humanity; if humanity attempts to grasp it in its beauty it will cease, and all we are left with is the ashes of this longing. The beauty of the Spirit is not the object in itself but a pointer. Lewis wrestled with trying to understand this sense of "Joy" for several years from his late teens through into his twenties. Eventually he realizes that he is trying to capture the unattainable. But he has to overcome intellectual hurdles: therefore he initially thinks his way to faith and then justifies this conversion.

For Lewis the eventual realization that the mystical pang of "Joy" was not the object in itself but a pointer dawned on him very slowly. Reading and studying old Germanic literature, saga and myth, Verse Edda prose, Greek and Roman sagas, nineteenth-century German and English Romanticism, even some ancient Indian religious myths, did not help. He wrote: "Only very gradually did I realize that all this was something quite different from the original 'Joy.' And I went on adding detail to detail, progressing toward the moment when I should know most and should least enjoy. Finally I woke from building the temple to find that the god had flown. Of course I did not put it that way. I would have said simply that I didn't get the old thrill."[27] And so Lewis tried to recover the old thrill, to recall this desiring, by revisiting the place of a walk, or search for a morning of white mist; he would re-read, listen again, but the longing was gone. The stab of pain, this elation of "Joy" could not be conjured. What he did not realize until much later was that this pseudo-religious busyness was in itself something of a pilgrimage, but, "the very moment when I longed to be so stabbed again, was itself again such a stabbing. The Desirable which had once alighted on Valhalla was now alighting on a particular moment of my own past; and I would not recognize him there because, being an idolater and a formalist, I insisted that he ought

26   Ibid., 159.
27   Ibid., 160.

to appear in the temple I had built him; not knowing that he cares only for temples' building and not at all for temples built."[28] Reflecting further on this some forty years after the event, Lewis compared this with "that error which the angel at the Sepulchre rebuked when he said to the women, 'Why seek ye the living among the dead? He is not here, He is risen.'"[29] Ever the poet, Lewis continued, "The comparison is of course between something of infinite moment and something very small; like comparison between the Sun and the Sun's reflection in a dewdrop."[30]

Contrary to the liberalism that engulfed the West in much of the twentieth century, Lewis did not mistake the desiring of *Sehnsucht* as a license for sexual freedom. Neither, despite his passionate interest in Wagner, did it lead into right-wing politics; nor for that matter, despite his interest in the work and writings of William Morris, did it lead into left-wing politics. Neither did Lewis lapse into the occult; nor the narcissistic luxury of suicide, despite his comments that "no strictly infinite disaster could overtake" such was his atheistic belief system, for "Death ended all. And if ever finite disasters proved greater than one wished to bear, suicide would always be possible. The horror of the Christian universe was that it had no door marked exit."[31] At the centre of Christianity, so Lewis concluded at this time, was a transcendental interferer, which jarred with his desire for independence and insularity. Lewis realized even at the age of eighteen years that there was no possibility of a treaty with this Christian reality: "there was no region even in the innermost depth of one's soul which one could surround with a barbed wire fence and guard with a notice, 'No Admittance!'"[32] However, a matter of months before call-up to war service Lewis was visited by a profound mystical experience that effectively scattered and annihilated all these various pseudo religious belief systems—the discovery of a book by a Christian writer, George McDonald, entitled *Phantastes, a Faerie Romance* (something of a precursor to the work on Christina fantasy that both the mature Lewis and Tolkien were to produce—i.e., Narnia and Middle Earth). In addition he discovered the work on a station bookstall on a profoundly beautiful autumn evening, shrouded in mist in the heart of the Surrey countryside. Travelling by train through the Surrey countryside and arriving at Leatherhead station Lewis wrote lyrically about the moment of dusk, the violet hills, the sky tinged green, of the air frost, when the dusk light is on the cusp of turning to the night, when the steam train's fire box glowed in the mist, his senses were enlivened by the cold: "Turning to the bookstall, I picked out an Everyman in a dirty jacket, *Phantastes: A Faerie Romance*, George MacDonald. Then the train came in. I can still remember the voice of the porter calling out the village names, Saxon and sweet as a nut—'Bookham, Effingham, Horsley train.' That evening I began to read my new book."[33] So what sort of religious/spiritual experience was this for Lewis? Lewis actually begins to struggle for words to

28   Ibid., 161. See also 174–75 for Lewis's own analysis of what he believed was happening in these experiences and his reaction to them.
29   Ibid.
30   Ibid.
31   Ibid., 165.
32   Ibid., 166.
33   Ibid., 172–73.

describe what was happening as he read *Phantastes*: "It is as if I were carried sleeping across the frontier, or as if I had died in the old country and could never remember how I came alive in the new . . . It was Holiness. It was as though the voice which had called to me from the world's end were now speaking at my side."[34] Lewis, though he did not know it at the time, was encountering the Holy Spirit: God the Holy Spirit was using all that was in Lewis's life experience to try to change, to re-orientate him: "It was with me in the room, or in my own body, or behind me. If it had once eluded me by its distance, it now eluded me by proximity—something too near to see, too plain to be understood, on this side of knowledge."[35] The pang, the longing, of *Sehnsucht*/"Joy" returned just when he was most unprepared, unaware, with his defenses down, just when he believed he had intellectualized it, and thereby dismissed it. The pang then left him to try to understand with all his theories in tatters. After the war when he returned to Oxford as an undergraduate he dismissed all this as romantic longing, as nonsense. This new look, post-war Oxford excluded *Sehnsucht*/"Joy" in the sense that it was to be categorized as internal; all such experience was part of, contained within, a closed, single-level universe. Therefore *Sehnsucht*/"Joy" was now to be dismissed only as a psychological projection from his deepest unfulfilled desires. Realism had taken over.

ii. "The Fox had been Dislodged from the Hegelian Wood"

Having graduated in Greats, Lewis's father agreed to finance him to read English in the hope that he would, in the ensuing years, be awarded a fellowship. Lewis received, within four years of study, two BA Hons degrees from the University of Oxford, having passed all three required public examinations with first class honors. These degrees were in Greats (Greek and Roman Literature and Classical Philosophy) and in English. From his reading of philosophy Lewis had developed a belief system more akin to Hegelianism with more than an unhealthy dose of Gnosticism. Amongst his new friends in the English school were several whom Lewis believed had all the right ideas—but like Nevill Coghill they were Christian. How could they be so nearly right? Lewis reflected! As he read English he also found that all the books he rated highly turned against him: Milton, MacDonald, Chesterton, and Medieval literature. Lewis wrote that:

> Absurdly . . . I thought that "the Christian myth" conveyed to unphilosophic minds as much of the truth, that is of Absolute Idealism, as they were capable of grasping, and that even that much put them above the irreligious. Those who could not rise to the notion of the Absolute would come nearer to the truth by belief in a god than by disbelief . . . The implication—that something which I and most other undergraduates could master without extraordinary pains would have been too hard for Plato, Dante, Hooker, and Pascal—did not yet strike me as absurd.[36]

---

34   Ibid., 173.
35   Ibid., 173.
36   Ibid., 208.

1. Conversion: God is God

Realism had to be abandoned, the new look was damaged; also his belief in chronological snobbery (the idea that humanity today is innately more advanced and superior to people in previous ages) was shaken, particularly after he had read G. K. Chesterton's *The Everlasting Man*: "all over the board my pieces were in the most disadvantageous position."[37] Further, he wrote that "the great Angler played his fish but he never dreamed that the hook was in his tongue."[38] Furthermore, he was now in regular long discussions with people like Hugo Dyson and J. R. R. Tolkien. Lewis wrote that a crucial step came in reading Samuel Alexander's *Space, Time and Deity*,[39] where he came across the distinction between "enjoyment" and "contemplation"—it was this, in part, that enabled him to see how he had mistaken the mystical pang of *Sehnsucht*/"Joy" for an end in itself.[40] Alexander distinguishes between *enjoyment* and *contemplation*, between *enjoying* the act of seeing a table whilst *contemplating* the table: the two acts cannot be simultaneous. Therefore Lewis could understand that attention to the object was essential. If you love someone, they are the object of your love. To cease attending, to cease focusing on the other, is therefore—for Alexander and for Lewis—to cease to love. To attend to your own feeling of love and not to the object of your love is, therefore, to cease loving. If we fail to attend to the other and withdraw into our own narcissistic pseudo-love then we slip gradually into nothingness. In terms of this distinction between enjoyment and contemplation, Lewis comments, "The surest means of disarming an anger or lust was to turn your attention away from the girl or the insult and start examining the passion itself."[41] Alexander had analyzed and explicated this distinction between enjoyment and contemplation philosophically, and reading it was like a bombshell to Lewis. Lewis could then see how all his waiting and watching for *Sehnsucht*/"Joy" was vain and hopeless: the sensation of *Sehnsucht*/"Joy" had been not the wave, but, as Lewis asserts, the wave's imprint on the seashore. To mistake the wave's imprint on the sand for the wave itself led to the idolatry of worshipping the effect the Holy Spirit had on his mind rather than redirecting his attention to God at the invitation of the Holy Spirit. Conversion was near. Lewis admits that though he was teaching English and Philosophy, the only explanation he could offer to himself or his students was a form of diluted Hegelianism, which did not serve him when faced with tutorials. He therefore owns to be drawn into a form of Berkleyanism, but, "I distinguished this philosophical god very sharply from the god of popular religion. There was, I explained, no possibility of being in a personal relation with him."[42]

Lewis wrote that as God closed in he was given a choice. He recounts how whilst on a bus travelling up Headington Hill he was being presented with a choice—without words or images. Lewis was aware how he was holding something at bay, that he was not moved by desire: this was an existential moment, a decisive moment, when he

---

37 Ibid.
38 Ibid.
39 Alexander, *Space, Time and Deity*
40 Lewis, *Surprised by Joy*, 210.
41 Ibid., 211.
42 Ibid., 215.

appeared the nearest it is possible to be to a free agent: "The fox," wrote Lewis "had been dislodged from the Hegelian wood."[43]

iii. "A Young Atheist Cannot Guard his Faith too Carefully"

The Rubicon Lewis crosses is a realization of the separateness, *aseity*, and utter difference between God and humanity; yet this is a God who wills that we should know, contemplate, and become aware of God. This is not the result of philosophical speculation. Lewis realized that this God was what the experiences of *Sehnsucht*/"Joy" were pointing towards—the desiring that became close to what is in some ways religious experience at the height of his atheistic period. Lewis:

> [This] was no state of my own mind or body at all. In a way, I had proved this by elimination. I had tried everything in my own mind and body; as it were, asking myself, "Is it this you want? Is it this?" Last of all I had asked if "Joy" itself was what I wanted; and, labelling it "aesthetic experience," had pretended I could answer "Yes." But that answer too had broken down. Inexorably "Joy" proclaimed, "You want—I myself am your want of—something other, outside, not you nor any state of you." I did not yet ask, "Who is the desired?" only "What is it?"[44]

This realization brought Lewis into a region of awe, the intimation of a realization that there was a God who was beyond all that he could conjure, think, or construct that was utterly "other," purely perpendicular to our world (tangential even). Lewis wrote:

> For I thus understood that in deepest solitude there is a road right out of the self, a commerce with something which, by refusing to identify itself with any object of the senses, or anything whereof we have biological or social need, or anything imagined, or any state of our own minds, proclaims itself sheerly objective. Far more objective than bodies, for it is not, like them, clothed in our senses; the naked Other, imageless (though our imagination salutes it with a hundred images), unknown, undefined, desired.[45]

But this was only a realization of the existence beyond self of the absolute otherness of God. In effect this was a step between the Hegelian absolute spirit and the Platonic otherness of God—but this was not God as Lord of all, the origin and creator of all, the God revealed through the incarnation. But such a realization had fatally damaged Lewis's atheism: "Really," Lewis wrote, "a young atheist cannot guard his faith too carefully."[46] And so he was recourse to consider this absolute spirit, in effect the Hegelian "absolute" separated from humanity and human desire, yet he convinced himself that this contemplation was not prayer. But there was a problem—if this was so, that this absolute spirit was independent of humanity, then how could the initiative lie on Lewis's side? "It might, as I say, still be true that my 'spirit' differed in some way from 'the God of popular religion.' My adversary waved the point. It sank into utter

---

43 Ibid., 217.
44 Ibid., 213.
45 Ibid., 214.
46 Ibid., 219.

unimportance. He would not argue about it. He only said 'I am the Lord'; 'I am that I am'." [47] And so Lewis wrote of his moment of surrender:

> You must picture me alone in that room in Magdalen, night after night, feeling, whenever my mind lifted even for a second from my work, the steady unrelenting approach of him whom I so earnestly desired not to meet. That which I greatly feared had at last come upon me. In the Trinity Term of 1929 I gave in, and admitted that God was God, and knelt and prayed: perhaps that night, the most dejected and reluctant convert in all of England.[48]

This is crossing the Rubicon. Lewis wrote that at least the prodigal son walked home on his own feet, but he had surrendered to a Love that opened the gates to a kicking, struggling, resentful prodigal. Lewis crossed the Rubicon and acknowledged that "*God was God.*" But what was this a conversion *to*? This was not necessarily, in Lewis's mind, the *Christian* God; it was not the God revealed in and through the incarnation. Or was it? It was in the sense that Lewis had said yes to God, the God above all gods, and now the Holy Spirit would re-orientate him to the full revelation displayed in the incarnation. Therefore initially this was only a conversion to theism; the second conversion to the gospel followed after a lengthy debate with J. R. R. Tolkien and Hugo Dyson that lasted all of one night, and a motorbike journey with his brother, after which Lewis simply knew that Jesus was the Christ, the incarnate, crucified, and resurrected Son of God. Upon this foundation stands Lewis's faith, and his work as theologian of orthodoxy.

---

47   Ibid., 220.
48   Ibid., 221.

2

Acceptance:
God is God, in Christ

SYNOPSIS:
C. S. Lewis's conversion is an encounter with the risen and ascended Christ, in the Spirit. Mary Magdalene, the mother, perhaps, of all theologians, met the crucified and risen Christ, and bore witness to the disciples; likewise Lewis bore witness in his work. If we are to understand Lewis's relationship with Jesus Christ and why it took him so long to be converted then we need to consider something of the belief systems that prevented his conversion: Popular Realism, Idealism and Pantheism, Deism, and so forth. A consistent factor in his thinking in the 1920s at Oxford was philosophical idealism; this is something of the intellectual background to his conversion. Lewis's conversion outlined so far is simply to *theism*, the belief in a personal God that had a claim on him, but where was Christ? Acceptance and conversion to Christ came two years later, initially through a conversation and debate with J. R. R. Tolkien and Hugo Dyson, much of it in Magdalen water meadows, along the tree-lined Addison Walk, which lasted into the early hours. However, the final realization came eight days later, during a journey in the sidecar of his brother's motorcycle. To what extent does the correspondence with his friend from childhood, Arthur Greeves, give us some indication of the depth of meaning and change of heart that Lewis underwent? Lewis's conversion was no Damascus Road experience; it was not a single event. Lewis's conversion was in four distinct encounters-events—the bus journey, the capitulating don, the critical conversation, and the motorcycle journey—and each needs to be assessed in its own right. Where is the church in Lewis's conversion? and what value can we place on Lewis's autobiographical accounts of his protracted conversion (*The Pilgrim's Regress* and *Surprised by Joy*), the progress and regress of the pilgrim? This chapter is essentially about how Lewis had to come to terms with the revelation of God in Jesus Christ: he simply had to accept what God had done in the incarnation, irrespective of whatever Lewis's intellectual ego expected of God.

1. ENCOUNTERS

In the early hours of the morning on the first day of the week Mary Magdalene went to the tomb. It was still dark, and as she arrived she knew things were not as they should have been: the stone had been moved. She did not investigate, she ran to inform the disciples. She ran to Peter and John, breathless she told them that they had taken the Lord from the tomb. Peter and John run through the half-light of the dawn to investigate; John outran Peter and reached the tomb first. He looked in, apprehensive and puzzled. Simon Peter caught up with him and went in. "Then the other disciple, who reached the tomb first, also went in, and he saw and believed, for as yet they did not understand the scripture, that he must rise from the dead" (John 20:8). John, the beloved disciple, looked, saw, perceived, and realized; he knew what had happened, he *accepted*, though he would probably have struggled to put this realization into words. In the early morning light Peter in his puzzlement, John in the quietude of his realization of the truth of the resurrection, returned to home; but not Mary. Mary loved Jesus too much to leave. Mary remained; she stayed as the light of the dawn gently lit the dew-laden ground; she could not leave; she stayed weeping outside the tomb. As the tears flowed, as she wrapped herself from the chill of the cool morning light, she bent again to look into the tomb, her clothes damp with the dew, and she saw two angels in white. They inquired of her why she was weeping. She answered:

> They have taken away my Lord, and I do not know where they have laid him. When she had said this, she turned around and saw Jesus standing there, but she did not know that it was Jesus. Jesus said to her, "Woman, why are you weeping? Whom are you looking for?" Supposing him to be the gardener, she said to him, "Sir, if you have carried him away, tell me where you have laid him, and I will take him away." Jesus said to her, "Mary!" She turned and said to him in Hebrew, "Rabboni!" (which means Teacher). (John 20:13–16)

Mary then went again to the disciples and told them, announced to them, that she had seen Jesus alive, that he had spoken to her and she to him. That he was real: "I have seen the Lord; and she told them that he had said these things to her" (John 20:18). They had a choice: simply to accept what had happened or not.

Mary was a reformed sinner who knew her need for the Lord of heaven and earth. Lewis was an un-reformed sinner, an atheist, an intellectual atheist, because he had developed elaborate philosophies and ideas that excluded God. The Russian writer Fyodor Mikhailovich Dostoevsky asserted that the worst of all sinners were those who had ideas: intellectual atheism which allowed the believer (and yes, atheists are believers) to do whatever he or she saw fit to do: by comparison, ruffians who sinned with their fists, shouted and bawled, or lapsed into sexual sins and then repented, posed, for Dostoevsky, no real threat to the gospel, and were often open to God in ways that intellectual atheists were not. However, this does not stop God the Holy Spirit working on people, preparing them for conversion. Both Mary Magdalene and C. S. Lewis had an encounter with the crucified and risen Christ. The encounter led Mary to witness to the disciples as to what had happened. Lewis's encounter led him to witness to his readership as a writer, as a theologian, and as a Christian apologist: in books, in radio broadcasts, and in argument with intellectuals in the common rooms of the colleges of the University of Oxford. Mary Magdalene was probably not an intellectual or a teacher. Lewis was. Lewis's conversion has much of the hallmark of intellectuals who are converted. So, what exactly was Lewis's conversion *from* and *to*.

2. A PROTRACTED CONVERSION

i. Popular Realism and Pantheism

If we are to understand Lewis's relationship with Jesus Christ and why it took him so long to be converted—he was over thirty years of age when he eventually gave in fully to creedal Christian belief—then we need to consider something of the belief systems that prevented his conversion. Lewis had a strong intellect, he was a double First from Oxford, and therefore it is inevitable that we must try to understand something of these philosophical beliefs that held him back. In his writing of his eventual return to Christ Lewis commented that his journey had been from popular realism to philosophical idealism, from this philosophical idealism to a pantheism of sorts, from pantheism to theism, then finally from theism to Christianity.[1] This final step was in many ways the most difficult, and the one that his intellectual ego, his intellectual prejudices, would not allow: if God existed then this god had to be on Lewis's terms only, God could only *be* if God fitted in with his intellectual worldview!

After the experience of the First World Was, and grounded in Kirkpatrick's atheistic logic, Lewis returned to Oxford subscribing to what he calls "popular realism," which was a polite way of describing atheism—Lewis simply was an atheist without any theories as to why; he looked at the world and claimed by design that there cannot be a God because the world was too flawed, too random, too dangerous and unfair; one only had to look at nature to see how the world had evolved by accident: if there was a God then the world would not be as it was. Gradually he moved to pantheism, which is where Lewis's God-given innate religious capacity still tried to convince him that there was more to reality that met the eye, more than his sense perception could tell him. If this is seen in the context of his Romantic-aesthetic love for nature, for long walks, for Northernness then you have pantheism, a religious worshipping of nature, perhaps even the proto-idea of some sort of innate spiritual force underpinning nature and world, but a god or the God?—No!

ii. Idealism and Theism

As an undergraduate at Oxford Lewis studied and was influenced by many writers and philosophers, many thought systems both ancient and modern. By the time he is teaching at Oxford he claims to believe in philosophical idealism. Idealism teaches that ideas are the whole or a key part of reality as distinct, to a degree, from a material world. Therefore, to some philosophers the idea that God would break into our world, be incarnated as a human being and die a horrible squalid painful death to save us is unacceptable: if God exists at all he will be known universally through ideas not through a particular event within the world. Philosophical idealism is really a development on from Lewis's pantheistic beliefs. There is for many an intimate connection between idealism and pantheism. But idealists are not consistent. Though some conceive of g/God as a distinct "idea," separate from this reality, for others the "g/God idea" is

---

1 Lewis, "Preface to 3rd Edition." *The Pilgrim's Regress*, ix.

reduced to a divine force within reality, often within each human, in many ways tied to reality, not an external personal God and not distinct, separate, from reality.

It is important to remember that Lewis was still not a Christian even after he had given in, moved from idealism, and admitted that God was God, for the question still remained of *which* g/God it was that Lewis had decided to acknowledge the existence of, and what he could know of this g/God. Lewis the reluctant *theist* had, in effect, simply acknowledged in the summer of 1929 (May-July?—Lewis gives no definite date), that there was a personal God, who was a definite person that sought him, had hunted him down, that waited for him to turn, to respond, this god was *the* God, the God that *was*, that *is*, behind all creation, all that we take for reality: objectively, God existed, God *was*. And this God sought him, laid claim to him and was thus a personal God. This understanding and encounter takes him way beyond Hegelian idealism. So this was the acknowledgement of the personal God; as such it was at least a step further than intellectual speculation, or the "maybe," that Lewis's idealism had pointed to (the god of the subjunctive!), but which had left him free to define this divinity in ways that suited his intellectual ego. Indeed there was an element of pride in Lewis at this time. Lewis's mind and his soul still inhabited a world of philosophical speculation. This was not necessarily the God of the Gospels or the creeds, even though it was surely the Holy Spirit of the risen Christ that had sought him, hunted him, and brought him to his knees! Lewis wrote that, "It must be understood that the conversion recorded . . . was only to Theism, pure and simple, not to Christianity. I knew nothing yet about the incarnation. The God to whom I surrendered was sheerly nonhuman. It may be asked whether my terror was at all relieved by the thought that I was now approaching the source from which those arrows of 'Joy' had been shot at me ever since childhood. Not in the least."[2] In many ways this would be how people who live outside of the possibility of knowledge about Jesus Christ would encounter the God that is in Christ, then after death it would be like the judgement described by Jesus in Matthew 25—the parable of the sheep and the goats. These people would be acceptable (or not, as the case may be) and then know the God that is in Christ in a way that they could not him while alive on earth because they did not come into contact with the church—either because of geographical isolation or time (i.e., they lived before the incarnation). This is important for it underpins much of Lewis's Christology. But Lewis lived in Western Europe in the early twentieth century and *did* know about the incarnation, crucifixion, and resurrection of God for his salvation. And this God was going to make sure he acknowledged and realized what had been done for him. And then this God in Christ was going to use Lewis, the philosophical apostate, as his missionary to and before the intellectual Oxford gentiles!—and beyond, to millions who have read his books and have been prepared for conversion by Lewis's writings.

So, how did Lewis get from being a theist to being a Christian? "My conversion involved as yet no belief in a future life," Lewis wrote.[3] There was therefore no element of fear and bribery involved—Lewis notes how this was rather like the ancient Jews who

2 Lewis, *Surprised by Joy*, 222.
3 Ibid., 223.

had to obey God simply because God was: "I was afraid that threats or promises would demoralize me; no threats or promises were made. The commands were inexorable, but they were backed by no 'sanctions'. God was to be obeyed simply because he was God."[4] Therefore to know God is to know that our obedience is owed to his sovereignty. Lewis started attending chapel services in Magdalen during the week—as a theist—and his parish church on Sundays, even though the idea of churchmanship was unattractive to him: "I was deeply antiecclesiastical."[5] However, Lewis does note that at this time he was more open to other people's beliefs and influence.

3. LEWIS, DYSON, TOLKIEN . . . AND REALIZATION

i. Debate

Lewis's final conversion to the God witnessed to by the Gospel writers and affirmed by the creeds was in many ways foisted onto Lewis the young don by the Roman Catholic Professor of Anglo Saxon at Oxford—John Ronald Reuel Tolkien. Two years after this conversion to theism a conversation took place on the evening of Saturday September 19, 1931, between J. R. R. Tolkien and Hugo Dyson, on the one hand, and Lewis, on the other. This debate was about myth and Christianity (part of the debate took place in Magdalen water meadows, along the tree-lined Addison Walk). It was, by all accounts, a heated conversation that lasted through the night till the early hours of the morning of Sunday September 20, and it finally convinced Lewis of the veracity of the claims of the Gospel writers and the creeds: that Jesus was the Christ, the incarnate Son of God, eternally begotten of the Father, God from God. Writing to Arthur Greeves two days later on Tuesday September 22, 1931,[6] Lewis outlines the meeting, how Dyson came to stay in his rooms at Magdalen, how Tolkien joined them to talk with them late into the night, then leaving at 3.00am, Lewis and Dyson seeing him out by the postern on Magdalen Bridge. Lewis and Dyson then retraced the walk through the water meadows and Addison walk talking further and recapitulating on their conversation, till 4.00am. Writing again to Greeves on the October 18, he explains how Tolkien and Dyson showed him how redemption was achieved, for it was this in many ways that proved the obstacle to Lewis. What had been holding him back from full belief was puzzlement over how the event of the cross and resurrection should achieve salvation for mankind:

> My puzzle was the whole doctrine of Redemption: in what sense the life and death of Christ "saved" or "opened salvation to" the world . . . What I couldn't see was how the life and death of Someone Else (whoever he was) two thousand years ago could help us here and now—except in so far as his example helped us. And the example business, tho' true and important, is not Christianity: right in the

---

4   Ibid.
5   Ibid., 226.
6   Lewis writing to Arthur Greeves, Sept. 22, 1931. Lewis, *Collected Letters Vol. I.*, 969–72.

> centre of Christianity, in the Gospels and St Paul, you keep on getting something quite different . . . "propitiation"—"sacrifice"—"the blood of the Lamb."[7]

It was this which Lewis found shocking, it led to an immediacy: the implications of the sacrifice of Christ were in the *here and now*, not isolated in the event two thousand years ago. Also, Lewis could not see how, when the world was full of stories of dying and resuscitated gods in pagan myths and Far Eastern religions, this one story could be unique and true. This was, in part, because Lewis had immersed himself so much during his atheistic "apostate" youth in Northernness and the pagan myths. However, now he could see that the doctrines we get out of the "true myth," to use Lewis's own words, are separate, a dilution in some ways, they are "translations into our concepts and ideas of that what God has already expressed in a language more adequate, namely the actual incarnation, crucifixion, and resurrection."[8]

ii. Awareness and Comprehension

This conversation with Tolkien and Dyson was still not the final giving in by Lewis to full Christian belief. Intellectually he could not see how God had acted unilaterally, uniquely, and there was still the problem of what Lewis saw as the language of atonement: propitiation, the sacrament of communion, the emphasis on the blood of Christ. It is fair to assert that much of this was cultural prejudice on Lewis's part, but there was also a deep ingrained resistance to finally giving in to this God. It was required that Lewis lay down his intellectual ego, his intellectual crown (cf. Rev 4:10[9]), but somehow this required more than belief, it was not simply a suspension of the intellect, it was something different. This moment came eight days later on Monday September 28, 1931; this realization of who and what Christ was suddenly became real to Lewis, this was while he was riding in the sidecar of his brother's motorcycle to Whipsnade Zoo!

> I was driven to Whipsnade one sunny morning. When we set out I did not believe that Jesus Christ is the Son of God, and when we reached the zoo I did. Yet I had not exactly spent the journey in thought. Nor in great emotion. "Emotional" is perhaps the last word we can apply to some of the most important events. It was more like when a man, after long sleep, still lying motionless in bed, becomes aware that he is now awake. And it was, like that moment on top of the bus, ambiguous.[10]

This realization was, in many ways, the gift of the Holy Spirit; an example of grace: the spiritual action of God affecting the human mind. But, Lewis had to prepare himself by slowly, painfully slowly, exorcising his false gods and the philosophical barriers which

---

7   Lewis writing to Arthur Greeves, Oct. 18, 1931. Lewis, *Collected Letters Vol. I.*, 975–77. Quote p. 974.

8   Ibid., 977.

9   "[T]he twenty-four elders fall before the one who is seated on the throne and worship the one who lives forever and ever; they cast their crowns before the throne." Rev 4:10.

10   Lewis, *Surprised by Joy*, 229.

prevented him seeing God. Warnie, incidentally, had returned to belief in Christianity eight months earlier on the May 9, 1931.

4. ENCOUNTERS ... AND THE CHURCH

Lewis's conversion was not a once and for all Damascus Road experience and encounter, a single event. Lewis's conversion was in four distinct encounters/events, probably because he had spent so many years building up his atheistic belief system: the bus journey; the capitulating don; the critical conversation; and the motorcycle journey

i. The Bus Journey

First, at some point in the first half of 1929 Lewis recalls how before God closed in on him he was offered what appeared to him to be a moment of free choice, a perfectly balanced free will choice: either-or. "I was going up Headington Hill on the top of a bus. Without words and (I think) almost without images, a fact about myself was somehow presented to me. I became aware that I was holding something at bay, or shutting something out . . . I felt myself being, there and then, given a free choice." [11] There was, for Lewis, no threat or promise attached to either, though he realized that to say yes meant the incalculable; it was a momentous choice, an unemotional choice. This was a meeting with Christ comparable with Nicodemus's encounter recorded in John's Gospel (John 3). For Lewis this was the closest he believed he ever came to a being a free agent. There were no motives involved, nothing to taint or act as bias, he was simply a free created will that could choose, could fall one way or the other. Lewis writes that he chose, he said yes, he effectively opened up to the Lord. A Lord he knew not in the realm of cognitive knowledge or thought but this was in effect the beginning of the end of his atheistic rebellion. This encounter for Lewis is reminiscent of the assertion in The Book of Revelation of how Christ will be pressing on the conscience of each and every individual, not continuously but at the most opportune moment/time in each life (Rev 3:20[12]). This moment for Lewis came whilst he was travelling on a bus going up Headington Hill at some point early in 1929.

ii. The Capitulating Don

Second, shortly after this encounter, came what we looked at in the previous chapter, Lewis's final giving in to God. This is where Lewis recounts how he gave in, capitulated, in his mind, to acknowledge the existence of the real personal God—kneeling in his room in Magdalen, the most dejected of converts. But this is more than merely a mental shift of emphasis, a changing of his mind. Intellectual sins are very, very real and, as we noted at the beginning of this chapter, are in many ways the worst of sins. What we believe, what we decide, affects profoundly the state of us and the eventual

---

11   Ibid., 216–17.
12   "Listen! I am standing at the door, knocking; if you hear my voice and open the door, I will come in to you and eat with you, and you with me." Rev 3:20.

destination of our soul and our resurrected body—will this being reside in eternal bliss before the divine beatific vision? Or will it reside in painful regret, agonizing over its life decisions in hell, a hell where it will not be alone, where it will crave a degree of solitude from that which it will fear above all else. Faith or no faith?—that is the question! Lewis was made to love and worship God, by God; all he does in his rooms in the Trinity term of 1929 is turn and acknowledge, yes, the existence of God, *the* God above all other gods sheerly divine and above all that is human, but this is also a letting in of the Holy Spirit. This was a profound realization, acknowledgement, and encounter for Lewis precisely because of his atheistic individualistic rebellion. For many other people, this moment of realization, acknowledgement, and encounter will be quieter, less isolated and in the context of a life of faith, in church, within the body of Christ.

iii. *The Critical Conversation*

Third, is the intense debate/conversation with Tolkien and Dyson mentioned above. Lewis's pilgrimage is a solitary pilgrimage. Reading *Surprised by Joy*, also the authoritative biographies, one is struck by how isolated, solitary, and individualistic Lewis was in his youth and in his twenties. His encounters with Christ are also individualistic, in the sense that they are when Lewis is at his most solitary, his most, we may say, vulnerable. That is with the exception of the third encounter—the debate with Tolkien and Dyson. Jesus Christ commented that when two or three are gathered he would be amongst them (Matt 18:20). This is precisely what happened in this encounter and we may say that it was the most fruitful encounter because it pushed Lewis out of himself, locked as he had been in himself since his mother's death, reinforced by the appalling sadism he had encountered at the Wynyard School. Tolkien and Dyson were in this encounter an example, we may assert, of the priesthood of all the baptized: Christians are part of the mystical body of the church, Christ's body, and their lives are—or should be—a witness to the truth of the gospel. We need not be ordained to witness to the gospel. Tolkien and Dyson were not ordained and had not the sacramental authority of the priesthood of Christ yet they affected Lewis in two ways: first, the Holy Spirit worked through them in breaking in to Lewis's intellectual defenses; second, because of their beliefs and their lives as Christians, they could impress on Lewis that he really did need to believe; he really did need to join them. Lewis, since he had become a theist two years earlier, had been attending church services, but probably did not involve himself with the congregation. He kept the people of God at arm's length; perhaps he feared they would break his intellectual defenses. Once the encounter with Tolkien and Dyson bore fruit eight days later on the journey to Whipsnade, Lewis in effect is open to the church, he is prepared to be involved explicitly as a Christian with the congregation of his local parish church in Headington; he is prepared to be known as, to be confronted as, a Christian in the common rooms, chapels, and halls of Oxford University; he is taking his first tentative steps as one of the people of God, a member of the church. He is prepared to stand up and be counted—for Christ's sake.

iv. The Motorcycle Journey

Fourth, is the final acceptance—while travelling in the sidecar of Warnie's motorcycle—that the truth lay beyond Lewis's intellectual ego. The truth that God is revealed uniquely in Jesus Christ who died for our sins on the cross is a reality that is beyond our intellectual and philosophical ideas, it is even beyond our religious prejudices. Lewis simply had to accept this: God had acted unilaterally. As his mind approached this final step he recalled how he felt a resistance almost as strong as the resistance he had felt to theism: "Every step I had taken, from the Absolute to 'Spirit,' to 'God,' had been a step towards the more concrete, the more imminent, the more compulsive." [13] Lewis knew when this final encounter happened but not how. The how it happened, the initiative, lay with the Lord Christ.

These four events, these four stages took over two years; in the case of Paul, they were rolled up in the one single cataclysmic event on the Damascus Road. But in both instances—Lewis and Paul—they constitute a form of revelation: revealed encounters with the risen and ascended Christ.

5. THE PROGRESS AND REGRESS OF THE PILGRIM

Lewis published two volumes of poetry in the years after the First World War.[14] The first book to be published after he became a Christian was *The Pilgrim's Regress*, published two years after the final stage of his conversion.[15] This is an allegorical novel illustrating the development of a character named John, who is an allegorical portrait of C. S. Lewis, as he meanders through a landscape reminiscent of the philosophical background of the nineteenth and early twentieth centuries: that is, the thought systems Lewis wandered through in his atheistic years. The character starts within orthodox/traditional Christianity and progresses through a wealth of philosophical thought systems and religions to end up where he started—traditional, orthodox, creedal Christianity. As such it is Lewis's personal version, a latter day edition, of *The Pilgrim's Progress* by the English dissenter and Puritan, John Bunyan (1628–88).

There have been plenty of studies of the complex, multi-layered allegory used by Lewis in *The Pilgrim's Regress*: who each mythological person represents, which philosophy, religion, or thought system was tempting John on his journey, his odyssey, his progress away from the truth, then his return to traditional/orthodox creedal Christianity.[16] These studies are excellent but we do not need to analyze Lewis's complex and multi-layered allegory here: suffice to say that what he presents is a scathing portrait of Enlightenment and post-Enlightenment thinking and the attempt by some churches to water down the gospel to accommodate atheism; what Lewis never ceased scathingly to call, "Modernist" and "Liberal" tendencies. *The Pilgrim's Regress* is not

---

13   Lewis, *Surprised by Joy* (1955), 229.
14   Hamilton, *Spirits in Bondage* and Hamilton, *Dymer*. Clive Hamilton was a pseudonym C. S. Lewis used, which was derived from his Christian name and his mother's maiden name.
15   Lewis, *The Pilgrim's Regress* (1st ed.).
16   A guide to the allegory, mythology and allusion used by Lewis in *The Pilgrim's Regress* can be found at: http://www.lewisiana.nl/regressquotes/index.htm.

autobiographical—leastwise it is autobiographical only by allegory. The path John takes is not identical to Jack's! However, the philosophies and religions that tempt John and ensnare him for a while are accurate to what ensnared the young Lewis. So what was *The Pilgrim's Regress* about? The character John is driven in many ways by this intense longing we have considered already—*Sehnsucht*, to Lewis, "Joy." For John this longing issues from an enchanted island, which is his goal, though he often appears to lose the sight of the goal he is working towards because he is waylaid by all these characters, allegorical characters, who attempt to seduce him with their belief systems, all of which are sincerely held but are simply false religions, false philosophies.

John is born and raised in Puritania, he lives in fear of the unseen landlord (institutionalized Protestant Christianity?), and is troubled by the sense of longing he experiences, by the visions he has of the enchanted island. Initially mistaking *Sehnsucht*/"Joy" for lust he sets off on his journey, escaping the snares and traps of Mr. Enlightenment (nineteenth-century rationalism), Freudian psychoanalysis, the modern literary movement, Mr. Mammon, Mr. Humanist, Mr. Sensible, and so on. The places traversed include a city by the name of Eschropolis and landscapes including the Valley of Humiliation and, importantly, the Grand Canyon (Books 5 to 7), which he must traverse, or fail. Along the way John is captured by the Spirit of the Age (Book 3, "Through Darkest Zeitgeistism"). It is often the allegorical personification of Reason that saves John, that influences him, and returns him to his quest.

Where is Christ in this? The body of Christ, the church—personified allegorically as "Mother Kirk" (Book 5, chapter 2)—explains to him that "The Grand Canyon" is the sin of Adam, and explains that she, the church alone, can guide him across, but importantly carry him. Does John accept?—no, he goes the long way round, leastwise he tries, and fails. He encounters cultured, sensible, worldliness, he meets Mr. Neo-Angular, and, of course, Liberal Humanism. He is accosted by Mr. Broad (modern religion—watered-down Liberal Christianity), who is deeply at one with the world and does not believe in the need for John's quest, his pilgrimage. Because he cannot cross the gulf John eventually ends up at Wisdom's house. It is only when he is within *Wisdom*, inside the allegorical house of Wisdom, that he can see that all these thought systems and pseudo religions, which had at one time seemed so attractive to him, were false; in particular, what we have encountered briefly already: pantheism, philosophical idealism/Hegelianism, and realism/materialism. When he leaves Wisdom's house John is assisted by a man who is the Christ, from whom he understands that he must accept grace—or his quest will fail and he will die. John still will not submit to the Lord's grace and continues to wander. Eventually he does accept grace; this is recounted by Lewis in a crucial chapter (Book 9 "Across the Canyon," chapter 4, "*Securus Te Projice*"—literally, "Throw yourself away with care"). John eventually finds the enchanted island, but realizes he knew it all along; he knew it while he walked the knife-edge between heaven and hell in his pilgrimage.

The Pilgrim's Regress was written while on holiday in Ireland in September 1932 with Arthur Greeves. This is then a year after the Tolkien/Dyson/Lewis debate and the trip to Whipsnade, which saw his final capitulation and submission to Christ: the terror of the Lord! The chapter entitled "Caught" (subtitled, "The Terror of the Lord— Where Now Is Sweet Desire," book 8 chapter 7), which comes about three-quarters of the way through the book, contains the kernel of what Lewis understands about his struggle against becoming a Christian. This chapter also contains material that he had sketched out in 1930 shortly after he became a theist, where Lewis wrestles with (the hidden?) Christ and passionately wants to hold on to his independence. This material written shortly after his conversion to theism was entitled, "Early Prose Joy," and was integrated by Lewis into chapter 7 of *The Pilgrim's Regress*.[17] In this material John/Lewis realizes that if he is to give in then his soul, his life, all that he is will never be his own ever again. The landlord (God in Christ) would be all:

> [W]ith his first waking thought the full-grown horror leaped upon him. The blue sky above the cliffs was watching him: the cliffs themselves were imprisoning him: the rocks behind were cutting off his retreat: the path ahead was ordering him on. In one night the Landlord—call him by what name you would—had come back to the world, and filled the world, quite full without a cranny. His eyes stared and his hand pointed and his voice commanded in everything that could be heard or seen, even from this place where John sat, to the end of the world: and if you passed the end of the world He would be there too. All things were indeed one—more truly than Mr. Wisdom dreamed—and all things said one word: CAUGHT—Caught into slavery again, to walk warily and on sufferance all his days, never to be alone; never the master of his own soul, to have no privacy, no corner whereof you could say to the whole universe: this is my own, here I can do as I please. Under that universal and inspecting gaze, John cowered like some small animal caught up in a giant's hands and held beneath a magnifying-glass.[18] [Lewis' emphasis.]

Although there is much valuable material in these early attempts to analyze what had happened to him ("Early Prose Joy" and *The Pilgrim's Regress*), their value is strictly limited because of their proximity to his protracted conversion. They lack the maturity that *Surprised by Joy* has, which was written nearly a quarter of a century after Lewis's conversion. In the preface to the third edition of *The Pilgrim's Regress*, published in 1944, Lewis does admit to something of this immaturity. He commented, "On rereading this book ten years after I wrote it, I find its chief faults to be those two which I least easily forgive in the books of other men: needless obscurity, and an uncharitable temper."[19] Lewis's first attempt at Christian autobiography in *The Pilgrim's Regress* reads in many ways like a theoretical account of thought systems with a Christian thought system being the adopted model at the end. In *Surprised by Joy* there is a much stronger sense of a single human being whose will is pitted against an objectively real God—the *Holy Ghost* to invoke the language of early modern English—who seeks the lost, the fallen, who actively hunts for the lost sheep that has gone astray. *Surprised by Joy* is intensely existential—that is to say, it is about human existence and the dilemma all

---

17   Lewis, *The Pilgrim's Regress* (3rd ed.), 183–85. The material, "Early Prose Joy," is an unpublished fragment of 58 pages held in the Bodleian Library, University of Oxford, dated 1930.
18   Ibid., 183–84.
19   Ibid., ix.

human individuals face. *Surprised by Joy* is, in fact, theological existentialism. Why?—because theological existentialism is the exposition of the character and nature of the relationship between God and humanity: human existence before God. This is often seen from an individual perspective—the crisis of faith of an individual characterized by decision-making. This decision-making, as Lewis shows so deftly, is between the fallen human will and the God who descended to earth to die and be resurrected to redeem us from our sins, and whose Holy Spirit seeks the lost to bring them back home.

3

Helen Joy Davidman: Intellect and Imagination

SYNOPSIS:
Lewis learned from the Scottish author, poet, and minister George MacDonald the critical value of a baptized imagination; indeed it was in part through MacDonald's work that Lewis the teenage atheist had his imagination baptized by the Holy Spirit, the intimation of God's beauty on a frost-bitten autumn evening on Leatherhead Station. What value is there to a baptized imagination when married to the sharp logicality of Lewis's intellect? Lewis was an intellectual atheist at the point of his encounters/conversion. What other such encounters help us to understand what was happening to him? Joy Davidman (his wife to be) was raised a Jewish atheist against a strict moral background of cultural Judaism in New York. She was a bright scholar, with a powerful intellect, who became a teacher, a Communist, a Hollywood screenwriter, and a novelist/poet. Joy could sense the beauty and transparency of God's creation as much as Lewis did, but for other reasons. To what extent did the cultural divergence account for a different "taste" of the supernatural? As an adult Joy underwent a profound conversion reminiscent of Lewis's, but her experience/encounter was characteristically different—she writes, "and God came in." What was Joy's conversion to and from? She writes of the sacrament at the heart of all beauty—what is her understanding and appreciation of the Holy Spirit? To what extent did Christ, in her words, haunt her during the rebellious years of her youth; a period characterized by poetry and imagination, communism, and intellect? Joy evokes Francis Thompson's *Hound of Heaven*, although she comments that God crept up on her stealthy like a cat. Teleologically the difference post conversion between Joy and her then husband William Gresham epitomizes the parable of the seed and the sower.

1. A BAPTIZED IMAGINATION

In many ways the crucial moment or point of conversion came when the teenage Lewis stood on Leatherhead station and was touched by the Holy Spirit as he looked out on a frost-bitten autumn evening, and then "found" George MacDonald's *Phantastes* on the station bookstall:[1] the smoke, the red glow on the underside of the engine, the eerie blue hills beyond the Dorking Valley, the sky green with frost, Lewis so alive as the world froze, as he heard the poetry of the Saxon village names called out; this was a moment of the glory of God as the Holy Spirit touched his mind and

---

1   Originally published 1858.

used his imagination so that sense perception was enlivened and the picture of the scene before him became pregnant with otherness; the intimation of a world beyond the shadowlands; the intimation of a truer reality glimpsed through the veil of our world; a reality to which we are all called. Lewis's imagination was, at this moment on Leatherhead station, baptized. Lewis had been baptized into the church by his maternal grandfather, the Revd. Thomas R. Hamilton, the rector, at St Mark's Church, Dundela, Belfast, on the January 29, 1899; he was then baptized by the Holy Spirit on this magical autumn evening when he was about seventeen years of age: he was born again of water, but then of the Spirit. It was then only a matter of time—all hope was lost, it was inevitable that he would become, as he put it, amongst the most dejected and reluctant of convert in all of England !² He went off to war, returned, graduated from Oxford with a double first, became a fellow but eventually "gave in," as he put it, in 1929, then "accepting" in 1931. The key to Lewis's conversion and the key to his work is this baptized imagination. It was through encountering the work—both theological and literary—of George MacDonald, the Scottish author, poet, and Christian minister (1824–1905) that C. S. Lewis's imagination, which had been baptized in a moment on Leatherhead station, was then confirmed by reading MacDonald that same evening. Thereafter, many years later, he could begin to reflect and understand with his intellect the importance of a baptized imagination, and what had happened.³

Lewis and MacDonald's understanding of the imagination, also their appreciation of the workings of the mind, were very similar, likewise their image-rich approach to theology: Lewis would often acknowledge MacDonald as his master and teacher.⁴ MacDonald understood how God used people's imagination to get through to them: "MacDonald was a person dedicated to the pursuit of Truth that he might serve the Truth with his entire being . . . Because MacDonald yearned above all to attend to God's Spirit, the truth he communicated expresses enduring wisdom."⁵ MacDonald viewed the intellect, imagination, and faith as gifted by the Holy Spirit, but there is still the freedom for people to accept or reject God on a conscious level, even if *he* is working on them in their subconscious minds. However, God will re-orientate to *his* will, to God's will. This is what happened to Lewis (in his rooms at Magdalen) many years after his imagination had been baptized, in and by the Holy Spirit, in that moment on Leatherhead station. For MacDonald a baptized imagination relates closely to and emerges from the incarnation: the creative-re-creative act of the incarnation validates the created forms of the imagination, because God took our flesh, shared our matter and a human mind, therefore the power of the Holy Spirit over a baptized imagination ensures the imagination's fruits are not subjective.⁶ "It is not surprising that for MacDonald the closer one is to Christ the Creator, the more faithful and vibrant the imagination will be . . . to see beyond and behind visible reality

---

2 Lewis, *Surprised by Joy*, 221.
3 Dearborn, *Baptized Imagination*.
4 Lewis, *The Great Divorce*, 66–67. See also, Lewis, "Introduction," in McDonald, *Phantastes*, v–xii.
5 Dearborn, *Baptized Imagination*, 65 & 66.
6 Ibid., 77–80.

with imaginative perceptiveness and depth requires humility, renewal and love."[7] This requires childlike humility. But we must always be aware that the imagination may be distorted and disordered: baptism in the Spirit should avoid this. It did for Lewis. Some of his most profound understanding of Christ comes across in his stories, so that MacDonald is in many ways behind Narnia. The baptizing of Lewis's imagination far from weakening, limiting, or restricting his intellect actually sharpened it and allowed it to blossom fully so that, coupled with the logical sharpness trained into his intellect by his teachers, Lewis's stories rose to be creative theology—a highly original re-telling of the gospel.

So what is a baptized imagination and why is it important? First, we must acknowledge that the imagination is part of the human mind, and that each and every human has—to a greater or lesser degree—an imagination, the ability to imagine. Although we observe and categorize the mind, and although this categorization might seem to be imposed on what we observe, there is an element in which the imagination is distinct from our other mental processes. What is the imagination? It is the capacity, the gift in many ways, to create mental images; the ability to generate, spontaneously, illustrations, pictures, or images in the mind, which give meaning to our experience of reality. The imagination helps us to make sense of the world and it is fundamental if we are going to learn; therefore it is very important to children but is often neglected by adults. Storytelling is the key to both imaginative creating and also to listening and learning. The imagination does not seem to work the way our cognitive mental processes work. With the imagination thoughts just seem to happen, ideas will appear to come out of nowhere. What is imagined is not the result of what we observe or think sequentially. The imagination is therefore creative, it invents. The imagination should therefore be governed by the Holy Spirit or there is no knowing what it might come up with. Therefore the imagination needs to be baptized by the Holy Spirit, and then God can use it. Lewis realized the importance of a baptized imagination, tied in with the sharpness of a developed intellect: it is developing the intellect, training it, developing the strategies of thinking (which he did under William T. Kirkpatrick in Surrey and as an Oxford undergraduate) that were so important. Lewis knew on reflection that his imagination had been baptized and that it was the key to his writings: his theology and his stories (*The Chronicles of Narnia*, *The Space Trilogy*, etc.), but also works such as *The Great Divorce* (1945), which use story and parable to explain the relationship between fallen humanity and the judgment of Christ, and therefore the reality of heaven and hell. Lewis had read and studied not just Jesus' use of parable and story but had also read and studied, as part of "Greats" at Oxford, Greek and Roman literature,[8] and had developed the capacity to write Christian story, allegory, and parable. But, without a baptized imagination the creative content of the story, allegory, and parable would either not have existed or have been so poor in quality and meaning as to be of no use in advancing the kingdom of God, in Christ.

7   Ibid., 81.
8   For an introduction to the christological value of the pagan classics, see, Markos, *From Achilles to Christ*.

2. HELEN JOY DAVIDMAN

Was the final stage of Lewis's protracted conversion (essentially from the summer of 1929 to the autumn of 1931), based as it was on an understanding of the God behind *Sehnsucht*/"Joy" and focused really on the event we have recalled, unique? Many other people go through conversion experiences. Many are similar to Lewis's.

i. Cultural Judaism: New York

Helen Joy Davidman's parents were, she asserts, self-confessed Jewish-atheists. Immigrants from Poland and the Ukraine, Joy's grandparents were orthodox Jews; her grandfather is reputed to have died through contracting pneumonia whilst preaching to the gentiles of Manhattan's Lower East Side.[9] Joy's parents, Joseph Davidman and Jeanette Spivack, subscribed to a form of humanism that acknowledged Judaism as a cultural religion that offered morality and a way to live, but they firmly subscribed to materialism and atheism. Joy wrote how her parents came to America as children from–

> [S]mall villages in Eastern Europe where for a thousand years the Jews had held desperately to their faith against fire and terror and murder. Cut off, hemmed in, embittered, the Judaism of such villages resembled the taboo systems of savages more than it resembled the prophetic Judaism of the Old Testament or the philosophic and scholarly Judaism of medieval Western Europe. Six hundred and more ritual taboos governed daily conduct; striking a match or stacking the dishes carelessly could be an offence against a very jealous God.[10]

In New York many of these immigrant Jews abandoned this form of Judaism as a religion, but retained belief in a vague ill-defined god of human progress, which Joy refers to as a form of Unitarianism, however, her parents rejected this cultural "god": "My father declared proudly that he had retained the ethics of Judaism, the only 'real' part of it, and got rid of the theology—rather as if he had kept the top floor of our house but torn down first floor and foundation. When I came along, I noticed that there was nothing supporting the ethics; down it crashed. It's not true that an atheist cannot have any morality; what he cannot have is a *rational* morality" [Joy's emphasis].[11] Therefore, for Joy, her parents' rigid morality, derived to a greater or lesser degree from the survival Judaism of Poland and the Ukraine, became habit and sentiment. Joy noted how her parents believed in temperance and justice, fortitude and prudence; however, she writes that her father never saw how these virtues were meaningless in an atheistic universe:

> Moral ideas could only be something men had put together for their own convenience, like the horse and buggy; something you could scrap as soon as an automobile morality came along. And he tried his level best to pass his virtues on

---

9 Davidman, "The Longest Way Round," 13–26. See also, Dorsett, *And God Came In*. See also, Sibley, *Shadowlands*, 64–77 and 79–94.
10 Davidman, "The Longest Way Round," 14.
11 Ibid., 14–15.

to me. Atheist virtues, however, don't keep very well. My parents had never been taught that faith and hope and charity were virtues at all. With no revealed law, no conviction of sin, no weekly reminder of shortcomings, no humility before God, no wonder at mystery, no hope of heaven, no help of grace—what can the best atheist do but turn Pharisee?[12]

Joy's razor sharp intellect could see that if there was no God then there was also no morality, nothing was inherently wrong—people would invent morals and ethics to suit a given situation, and such morality was movable, it was redefined according to the needs of the moment, according to whichever group in society shouted the loudest. She could also see that her parents' belief in justice and temperance, fortitude and prudence, was really only self-interest, thinly disguised—such morality had suited them, given them social and cultural advancement and wealth to go with it.

ii. Cultural Judaism: Childhood

Helen Joy Davidman was born on the 18th April 1915 in the Jewish ghetto in Manhattan. Joy had a comfortable childhood, a good education, private music lessons, and holidays to New England and the West Coast. The Davidmans moved to the Bronx, and then to Grand Concourse, which was characterized by bourgeois respectability, as their wealth and standing increased. Joy's father was a very strict disciplinarian who regularly subjected Joy and her brother, Howard, to corporal punishment. She had a very high IQ of over 150 and after graduation from Hunter College (BA, 1934, aged nineteen years) and Columbia University (MA, in English, 1935, aged twenty years), she taught English in high schools in New York from 1936 to 1938, but then took to writing. She became a radical card-carrying Communist, a famous American poet, novelist, and writer, and a scriptwriter for Hollywood. Then in 1946, in her thirties, she underwent a profound conversion to Christianity. At the time she was married to the writer William Lindsay Gresham and had two children—David (b.1944) and Douglas (b.1945). William Gresham, however, had become an alcoholic; he was unfaithful and violent and the marriage was collapsing. This is the background to her conversion. She came to England and met C. S. Lewis. The story is well-known and has been the topic of a TV docu-drama, a Hollywood film, and a stage play: they married after her divorce, initially as a formality to naturalize her as a British citizen, however when Joy was diagnosed with terminal cancer they were married before God in a Christian ceremony. She recovered, remission lasted a few years, then she died. Her death devastated Lewis and formed the trigger of another stage of conversion for him, perhaps the most profound of his conversions. So what was Joy's spiritual pilgrimage and how does it compare to Lewis's? What was her hidden, implicit, relationship with the Christ who sought her, courted her, approached and even hunted her as he had done with Lewis? What was Joy's conversion?—what was it *to* and *from*? What was it characterized by?

---

12   Ibid., 15.

C. S. LEWIS—REVELATION, CONVERSION, AND APOLOGETICS

3. CHRIST HAUNTED ME

i. *"The Sacrament at the Heart of all Beauty"*

Joy had declared her atheism to her parents when she was eight years old; by her teenage years she had rejected all morality as a human construct, setting her own standards according to pleasure. She recalls that when she was fourteen years old she experienced a profound aesthetic sense, which relates to *Sehnsucht* (though she does not use the German word or concept). This was an encounter in many ways, like Lewis's

> I went walking in the park on a Sunday afternoon, in clean, cold, luminous air. The trees tinkled with sleet; the city noises were muffled by the snow. Winter sunset, with a line of young maples sheathed in ice between me and the sun—as I looked up they burned unimaginably golden—burned and were not consumed. I heard the voice in the burning tree; the meaning of all things was revealed and the sacrament at the heart of all beauty lay bare; time and space fell away, and for a moment the world was only a door swinging ajar. Then the light faded, the cold stung my toes, and I went home, reflecting that I had had another aesthetic experience. I had them fairly often. That was what beautiful things did to you, I recognized, probably because of some visceral or glandular reaction that hadn't been fully explored by science just yet. For I was a well-brought-up, right-thinking child of materialism. Beauty, I knew, existed; but God, of course, did not.[13]

Joy initially categorized this as aesthetic—that is, it was concerned with or relating to beauty. But did she see this appreciation of beauty as within her mind only? Was the perception or awareness only inside her head? The Holy Spirit affected Joy's mind, triggered the perception. But is actual beauty something outside of her mind that exists in created reality? Joy realized, in retrospect, years later, that this was an encounter, but we may also assert that this was not just in her mind for she perceived *beauty*, and beauty is not just in the eye of the beholder. More than that, she perceived that beauty was a sacrament at the heart of all things. Why? God created and sustains and is at the heart of all things. Beauty was from God; beauty lay at the heart of all things because all created things are mysteriously imbued with God's sacramental grace. Grace was in a moment imparted to Joy *from* the sacramental beauty at the heart of all creation. The Holy Spirit simultaneously touched Joy's mind from within the sacramental beauty of sun, mist, ice, and trees, the created natural world. To worship this Spirit in the natural world *by itself* would be wrong, it would be pantheism. However, it is important to remember that God declared that creation was good (Genesis 1, specifically v. 31), and we will see, perceive, moments when we can almost grasp the goodness, the rightness, the wonder and the beauty at the heart of creation, particularly the natural world: Lewis on Leatherhead station (to name but one occasion) and Joy in Central Park New York. There are people whose brains are simply not wired (through nature or nurture)

---

13   Ibid., 13.

in such a way as to be receptive to such intimations from the Holy Spirit. There are others who are. Ironically, despite her, and her parents', atheism Joy was more open to God than Lewis, and had a sounder understanding of the theology behind these moments related to *Sehnsucht*; this was a theological understanding despite her lack of churching. She writes about how she sensed the voice in the burning tree as the bright winter sun burned through the bare frost-laden branches, how she had in a single moment an intimation of the meaning of all things—this was a revelation, it was not a human construct, this was revealed; but if so, by whom or by what? She writes in terms of sacramental theology, she perceived, as a fourteen year old atheistic cultural Jew, the sacramentality in all things, all creation! David and the prophets would have rejoiced at her perception, a perception we find in the Psalms, that creation actually sings praise joyously, beauteously, to the Lord.[14] She comments that she perceived that sacrament lay at the heart of all beauty, that this sacrament was laid bare, open for all to perceive, how this realization was a moment of temporal paradox when her mental cognitive awareness of time's relentless movement, of the physicality of space and distance (and hence separation and aloneness even) were gone: "time and space fell away, and for a moment the world was only a door swinging ajar."[15] Joy's perception is not conditioned by her religious or cultural heritage or background because she had been raised by moralistic atheists. The imagery, the mental categories she invokes to try to make sense, to try to explain, what had happened were, we may assert, more the result of revelation than her use of religious images and categories, for her upbringing had been devoid of religious images and categories. This was a vision. But a vision of what? That beauty is real; beauty is *actual*. It is not subjective; it is not a question of personal taste; it is not a human construct: beauty is *real*; it is sacramental; it issues from God and is, to one degree or another, in all created things. Therefore there is a God, who despite all our human confusion, wills to communicate to us in love often through the good creation that is imbued sacramentally with *his* beauty, *his* Spirit; a God who can touch our conscious minds and in that moment we will taste eternity and our lives thereafter will not be the same. Behind this encounter for Joy, as she came to realize, was Christ.

Joy's experience in Central Park New York was, yes, similar in many ways to Lewis's experiences, yet subtly different. Joy's experience certainly lacked the intense guilt-laden longing that Lewis recalled with such encounters with the Holy Spirit, probably because she had never known and therefore never rejected the living God behind and in creation. However, it is fair to assert that as with Lewis's experience of *Sehnsucht* on Leatherhead Station, this was the instant, the point where heaven and earth met in a moment, when Joy Davidman's imagination was baptized. In both cases this is perhaps also the point of commission for both of them of their vocation before the Lord. Both examples are of a conscious realization, regardless of what their

---

14   For example, "Let the floods clap their hands; let the hills sing together for joy" (Ps 98:8); see also Pss 65:12 and 114:4–6.
15   Davidman, "The Longest Way Round," 13.

personal religious egos would believe (or more pertinently not believe!), that God communicated to them through the innate beauty of the natural world, his creation.

ii. Poetry and Imagination

How did Joy respond to this encounter as an intellectual atheist? First, I think it is fair to say she was not a skeptic as Lewis was, for there was not the element of piercing guilt-ridden longing in her experience of the Spirit. She was an intellectual atheist and although she had decided that the only meaning in life was self-defined pleasure this did not mean sexual libertarianism, alcohol, drugs, etc., for her; the ultimate pleasure for Joy was in reading and writing poetry (!), therefore her school and college friends nicknamed her "forbidden joy," partly because of her parents repressiveness.[16] Joy therefore exhibited a caution and celibacy in her young life but was not afraid to love. Lewis was in many ways afraid to love and had created intellectual barriers against loving: he was quite a loner, much of which can be attributed to the trauma following his mother's death. So how did Joy respond? She comments that following this experience-encounter when she was fourteen years of age: "A young poet like myself could be seized and shaken by spiritual powers a dozen times a day, and still take it for granted that there was no such thing as spirit. What happened to me was easily explained away; it was 'only nerves' or 'only glands.' As soon as I discovered Freud, it became 'only sex.' And yet if ever a human life was haunted, Christ haunted me."[17]

Christ *haunted* me, she writes. She is writing a few years after her eventual conversion, but can clearly see how religious experience, if it is genuine, is only valid in the context of the Holy Spirit of the resurrected and ascended Christ of which, at the time, she had no knowledge. But this did not stop the Holy Ghost—to invoke more traditional language, particularly as Joy claims that she was *haunted* by Christ—acting on her, reassuring her in many ways, preparing her for the moment when *he* would fully reveal himself to her, give her the choice where she could turn and say yes, to follow *him*, or not. For Joy, anything resembling the religious impulse was channeled into her life, her education, and her parents growing prosperity. Therefore, by the time she was fifteen years of age she recalls that: "I believed in nothing but American prosperity; in 1930 I believed in nothing. Men, I said, are only apes. Virtue is only custom. Life is only an electrochemical reaction. Mind is only a set of conditioned reflexes, and anyway most people aren't rational like *ME*. Love, art, and altruism are only sex. The universe is only matter. Matter is only energy. I forget what I said energy was only. Portrait of the happy materialist" [Joy's emphasis].[18]

But, buried under all this brash assertive materialism was a girl who wrote poetry, who recognized and followed the creative impulse and lived a life contrary to these nihilistic materialistic beliefs. For Joy, her, "Inner personality was deeply interested

---

16   Sibley, *Shadowlands*, 69.
17   Davidman, "The Longest Way Round," 13–14.
18   Ibid., 15–16.

in Christ, and didn't know it."[19] Like her parents and many of her Jewish relatives and family friends she had been taught to feel what she describes as a cold chill at the mention of the name of Jesus Christ. This was her religio-cultural conditioning. But did this mean she was antagonistic to the genuine Christ? Probably not, for two reasons: first, her openness to Christ's Spirit as evidenced from what we have seen already; second, as she notes, for hundreds of years European Jews lived among people who interpreted Christ's will to mean Jews were flogged and burnt as heretics and were regarded as the anti-Christ, they were excluded by gentleman's agreements and closed universities. If, she writes, "nominal Christians so confuse their Master's teaching, surely a poor Jew may be pardoned a little confusion."[20] Despite her religio-cultural prejudices, triggered by and ingrained through centuries of persecution, racism, and disenfranchisement, she had nevertheless read the Bible. Why?—she argues she read the Bible for its literary beauty, simply as a work of literature. However, she found herself unconsciously quoting Jesus not only in her poetry and writings, but in conversations, particularly when she was fighting her parents' bourgeois moralistic hypocrisy: "My first published poem was called 'Resurrection'—a sort of private argument with Jesus, attempting to convince him (and myself) that he had never risen. I wrote it at Easter, of all possible seasons, and never guessed why. The Cross recurs through most of my early poems, and I seem to remember explaining that Jesus was 'a valuable literary convention.'"[21]

Despite her self-proclaimed atheism from the age of eight years, as a child and teenager she had loved reading fantasy works—in particular the work of George MacDonald, which we have encountered already through Lewis. So in many ways she had exposed herself to implicit Christian ideas. To paraphrase Lewis's comment we came across in the previous chapter, as a young atheist he could not guard his faith too carefully.[22] Joy did not believe in the supernatural, yet her cultural interests and reading generated a love of heaven, though she did not see it as such.

iii. Communism and Intellect

By the mid-nineteen-thirties, and in the American Depression, Joy espoused communism, further, she sought involvement with and membership of the Communist Party; paid her dues and became a card-carrying communist. She admits she would have killed for the Party had it asked her to. Ironically, she writes that "I think I was moved by the same unseen power that had directed my reading and my dreaming—I became a Communist because, later on, I was going to become a Christian."[23] With hardly any background—apart from having read Marx's *Communist Manifesto*, which she comments few of her colleagues in the party had—she was employed as journalist and critic for the Party's semi-official magazine, *New Masses*. She learned to lie for

19   Ibid., 16.
20   Ibid., 16.
21   Ibid.
22   Lewis, *Surprised by Joy* (1955), 219.
23   Davidman, "The Longest Way Round," 19.

the Party, that claiming love for the people, the proletariat, would justify any action: that the end justifies the means. This time working for the Party was interrupted by six months working as a scriptwriter in Hollywood. However, on return her interest in the Party was waning. She met and married a Spanish Civil War veteran, writer, and fellow poet, William Lindsay Gresham. The birth of her first son finally put paid to her involvement with the Party and with any communist activities. The false gods had fallen aside to be replaced by communism, which in turn was being exposed as an incoherent false "god" or "idol," which itself was falling by the wayside. Marriage and a young family now took her time and energies and focus, in addition she was a successful, published, poet, and novelist.

4. AND GOD CAME IN

In 1945 Joy's childlike interest in what she called fantasy had led her to read C. S. Lewis's *The Screwtape Letters* and *The Great Divorce* (interest in Lewis's Christian books was at that time sweeping America). She was still a card-carrying atheist—or so she believed—but, she writes, "I hadn't given quite enough attention to developing the proof of it." [24] Joy's involvement with the Party was waning; she notes how in the 1930s, during the Depression, a sincere rage at injustice and misery had led to many being involved in Party activities. America, or the American economic system, was seen to have failed. By the early- to mid-1940s, with the Second World War at its height, a renewed faith in America and dismay at the antics of the Soviet Union, had led to patriotism and a repudiation of Marxism amongst many who had been stalwart Party activists.[25] Joy saw those that remained as embittered failures more interested in revenge on the existing society than in building a better one. Joy's involvement grew less and less: "By 1946 I had two babies; I had no time for Party activity, and was glad of it; I hardly mentioned the Party except with impatience. And yet, out of sheer habit, I went on believing that Marxism was true . . . For I had no knowledge of divine help."[26]

Joy notes with poignancy that, as Francis Thompson symbolized God as the Hound of Heaven pursuing on relentless feet, with her God was acting more like a cat in that he had been stalking her for many years. Christ had been courting her patiently judging when to reveal *his* Lordship: "He crept nearer so silently that I never knew he was there. Then, all at once, he sprang."[27] In early spring 1946 there came a morning where Bill, her husband, phoned from she knew not where to announce he was having a nervous breakdown, his mind going. He did not return home. Bill had become an alcoholic and an adulterer, and his work as a novelist and poet was failing. Hours later Joy was desperate. She writes that she felt helpless for the first time in her life, that she was forced to acknowledge that she was no longer in charge of her fate, that she was certainly not, as she puts it, the captain of her soul.

---

24   Ibid., 22.
25   For example, see, Schama, *The American Future*. See, ch. 12.
26   Davidman, "The Longest Way Round," 22.
27   Ibid., 23.

> All my defences—the walls of arrogance and cocksureness and self-love behind which I had hid from God went down momentarily. And God came in. How can one describe the direct perception of God? It is infinite, unique; there are no words, there are no comparisons. Those who have known God will understand me; the others, I find, can neither listen nor understand. There was a Person with me in the room, directly present to my consciousness—a Person so real that all my previous life was by comparison mere shadow play. And I myself was more alive than I had ever been; it was like waking from sleep. My perception of God lasted perhaps half a minute. In that time, however, many things happened. I forgave some of my enemies. I understood that God had always been there and that since childhood I had been pouring half my energy into the task of keeping him out. When it was over I found myself on my knees, praying. I think I must have been the world's most astonished atheist.[28]

Was this awareness of God? Was it no more than a comforting illusion? asks Joy. She answers that in terms of her and Bill's life-crisis nothing had changed: afterwards she was just as worried and helpless as before. If it was an illusion, the awareness of God had not helped on a practical level. No, within this was the moment of choice for Joy, if anything was offered which could help her situation it was reassurance, an assurance of God's love. But this was not an assurance that was self-generated, sentimental, cosseting, like a cuddly soft toy; for Joy this was characterized by, "Terror and ecstasy, repentance and rebirth."[29] Christianity is true not because it meets a human need. Joy's experience was not simply a psychological projection produced as the mind's response to the desperate state she was in; on the contrary, the experience was sparked by a perception of that which came from outside of her mind. It met a human need precisely because it is true (the Word of God, the person of Christ Jesus resurrected and ascended, pressed on her at this the most desperate time in her life precisely because it was the most beneficial moment *from Christ's perspective*). What happened to her was eternal, external, true, and beautiful, and occurred at precisely the right moment. As with Lewis in his rooms in Magdalen in 1929, she had sensed the approach of God and had given in and admitted, realized, that God was indeed God. So is *all* religious experience valid? Are all conversion experiences from the Holy Spirit? No. We are the object, not the subject; we are not the author of valid conversion experiences, we are the object. Because of our fallen status we may delude ourselves to believe that it is God who has initiated the experience, who is courting us, seeking us, but, it might just well be a demonic or evil force acting, inviting, us. The measure of all religious experience has to be the self-revelation of God, which is in Christ Jesus. How does a religious experience measure-up against the gospel? The conversions of Lewis and Davidman are seen as valid in retrospect; first, because in each case the Spirit drew each of them to the knowledge of God's self-revelation in Christ; second, the way they lived their lives after the encounter is testimony to the truth of God's revelation. In the case of people who were born outside of the knowledge of the incarnation-cross-resurrection, the ultimate test of the validity of a conversion experience is *post mortem*,

---

28   Ibid., 23.
29   Ibid., 24.

after death, before the judgment seat of Christ where—as laid out in Matthew 25—the way they lived their lives after a conversion experience/encounter is testimony to the truth of God's revelation. There are a lot of issues here in the context of how God gave intimations to pagans (i.e., people outside of the Judaic-Christian revelation) and how Lewis valued such intimations christologically.

5. THE HOUND OF HEAVEN

When Bill eventually returned home Joy writes that he accepted what had happened to her, commenting that he was, "on the way to something of the kind himself."[30] Both knew that they needed to change, to reorder their life together. "If my knowledge of God was true, the thinking of my whole life had been false. I could not doubt the truth of my experience. It was so much the realest thing that had ever happened to me!"[31] In a gentle manner, in a less overwhelming manner, this encounter with the Holy Spirit continued as Joy reordered her mind, her ideas, her beliefs, her whole life: "I snatched at books I had despised before; re-read *The Hound of Heaven*, which I had ridiculed as a piece of phoney rhetoric—and, understanding it suddenly, burst into tears. (Also a new thing; I had seldom previously cried except with rage.) I went back to C. S. Lewis and learned from him, slowly, how I had gone wrong. Without his works, I wonder if I and many others might not still be infants 'crying in the night.'"[32]

Joy refers to Francis Thompson's (1859–1907) poem, *The Hound of Heaven*, first published in 1900, which charts the slow, gradual, at first imperceptible, progress of the God that courts, and awaits a response whilst the human seeks ever to escape. Who is this God?—it is not the self-righteous political "god" of communism, it is not the literary "god" of a successful writer and poet who basks in the limelight of publicity, it is the Christ, who had died for her on the cross and awaits her response. The initiative lay with Christ, but the response had to come from Joy. The Lion of Judah became for Francis Thompson the Hound of Heaven (though for Joy this had a more feline, stealth-like, quality):

> I fled Him, down the nights and down the days;
> I fled Him, down the arches of the years;
> I fled Him, down the labyrinthine ways
> Of my own mind; and in the mist of tears
> I hid from Him,[33]

Strangely, one of the first acts of faith, as Joy puts it, was a renewed interest in the Communist Party because she still considered that Marxist economic theory was relevant because she asserts that once she recognized God she also recognized the need for moral responsibility. Joy felt she had a duty to show the Party that it did not need atheism. Like Lewis following his crossing of the spiritual Rubicon in 1929, Joy was not

---

30 Ibid., 24.
31 Ibid.
32 Ibid.
33 Ibid.,

necessarily a Christian following her conversion encounter. Throughout all her atheist life she had regarded the apostate with traditional Jewish horror. So, initially what Joy desired was to develop into a good Jew, of the "comfortable Reformed type": "I had the usual delusion that all religions mean the same thing."[34] In studying religions she found them shot through with difference and contradiction. Some were characterized for her by wisdom, some by strong ethical intentions, some were characterized by insight:

> But only one of them had complete understanding of the grace and repentance and charity that had come to me from God. And the Redeemer who had made himself known, whose personality I would have recognized among ten thousand—well, when I read the New Testament, I recognized him. He was Jesus. The rest was fairly simple. I could not doubt the divinity of Jesus, and, step by step, orthodox Christian theology followed logically from it. My modernist objections to the miraculous proved to be mere superstition, unsupported by logic . . . I am a writer of fiction; I have made up stories myself, and I think I can tell a made-up story from a true one. The men who told of the resurrection told of something they had seen. Not Shakespeare himself could have invented the Synoptic Gospels. My beliefs took shape . . .[35]

There are two important points here: first, Joy recognized through a degree of comparative religious study that what had touched her was a person, not some inanimate abstract spiritual force, and that through simple comparative deduction that person was Jesus Christ; second, that she had no doubt about the divinity of this Jesus Christ—unlike C. S. Lewis who struggled to accept the fact of Christ's divinity, even after being preached at by Dyson and Tolkien.

Joy and Bill and the children were baptized in Pleasant Plains Presbyterian Church in 1948; and there she thought she would remain. Leastwise, that is how she finishes her spiritual autobiography written in 1949, and published two years later. Despite his apparent conversion William Gresham's alcoholism, his adultery, his abusive violence did not change. The marriage was on the rocks. He had an affair with Joy's cousin, Renee Rodriguez. Joy left him and took the children to England, eventually to divorce Bill, and to marry C. S. Lewis. She would contract cancer, recover, see the cancer to reassert itself, then die aged forty-five years on July 13, 1960—in the faith. Bill's conversion was most probably genuine but he still—like all Christians—had free will, a will he exercised. Joy and Bill are examples of the parable of the sower and the seed:[36] in the case of Joy the seed of conversion bore good fruit, an hundred fold, in the case of Bill, the seed of conversion fell on barren ground and was chocked by the weeds of this world. Joy knew that following her conversion encounter/experience she had to change. That change was analogous to the growth of the seeds in the parable of the sower and the seed.

---

34 Davidman, "The Longest Way Round," 25.
35 Ibid., 25.
36 Matt 13; Mark 4; Luke 8.

After years of substance abuse and transitory relationships William Gresham on the September 14, 1962, committed suicide in a run-down hotel room in New York by taking an overdose of sleeping pills.[37]

---

37 See Douglas Gresham in Wikipedia: http://en.wikipedia.org/wiki/William_Gresham.

4

C. S. Lewis and Karl Barth I: Religious Experience—Revelation and Modernity

SYNOPSIS:
What can we say about the conversion experiences we have looked at so far? Are they really no more than wish-fulfillment? Is the encounter no more than the projected desire of a troubled psyche? Or is a real encounter taking place with the God above all gods? Where is the *real* Christ in these experiences? Lewis had a strong intellect and a well-developed capacity for reasoning. Therefore we may ask, what is the relationship between intellectual sins and religious experience? If we filter these experiences then the measure of these encounters may tell us something about the individual, but pertinently about God. Was Lewis's capacity to reason as corrupt, as fallen, as his will? The encounter with Christ will affect the intellect in such as Lewis and Davidman. We can consider other encounters that will help us to understand what was happening to Lewis and Davidman? A brief look at the conversion of Augustine shows how reason and the will can block the desire of Christ to save. The individual experiences of the French philosopher Simone Weil, the German philosopher Edith Stein, and the Swiss theologian Karl Barth all illuminate in different ways what happened to Lewis. The theology of Lewis and Karl Barth can be considered as incompatible; however, they share a respect for an orthodox traditional creedal basis for Christian doctrine, grounded in the revelation of the triune God: the Word of God as person (Christ) and Scripture. What was the christological background to the conversions of C. S. Lewis and Karl Barth? Despite the importance of Scripture, the creeds, and the ecumenical church councils, the heritage of Lewis and Barth issuing from the Age of Reason and the Enlightenment, specifically from the de-Christianized Jesus of nineteenth-century Liberal Neo-Protestantism, is something that both have to work against. Both Barth and Lewis experience something of a watershed, a conversion. To Lewis this was like crossing the Rubicon; to Barth it was a *Wendung*, a profound change of heart expressed in belief, accompanied by a constant *Retraktation*, a constant reappraisal. Notwithstanding key differences it is possible to identify an element within their realization and perception of God that was diametric to the belief system each held prior to conversion/reconversion. This perception of the realism of God led in part to their mature work Similarities can therefore be observed because of a common source from which the encounter issues: God. However, the object of each encounter (the fallen human being) is characterized by diversity, by individual personality, by differences.

C. S. LEWIS—REVELATION, CONVERSION, AND APOLOGETICS

1. A CONVERTED INTELLECT?

i. Intellectual Sins and Religious Experience

Many other people go through conversion experiences. Many are similar to Lewis's. Many intellectuals undergo similar encounters with the risen and ascended Christ. But there are also important dissimilarities between each of them because each is an individual, therefore there are important components or elements to each conversion that are unique to an individual's character, their personality, and life development. Joy Davidman's conversion was similar to Lewis's, yet also different. The question has to be asked, "Just how genuine is a conversion?" The assumption is that there is an encounter with that which is without. Further that the conversion is initiated from outside of the individual's life and mind: that is, that it comes from God. It is important to remember, however, that some experiences/encounters may indeed be from outside the individual concerned but are from an altogether darker source: the principalities and powers, the spiritual darkness that Paul speaks of—demons or worse.[1] In addition, they may indeed not be from without, they may be no more than the heart-felt desires of the complex and manifold psyche of each individual projected onto the mind like a movie projected onto a screen. In other words, as the nineteenth-century German theologian Ludwig Feuerbach asserted, such experiences may simply be a projection: the mind may project the idea of a "god," then the experience may simply be from the deepest desires of a complex self, much of which is located in the sub-conscious.[2] As a theologian and self-confessed atheist Feuerbach, in effect, wrote-off all religion as mere wish fulfillment. He asserted that, "God is the realized wish of the heart, the wish exalted to the certainty of its fulfillment."[3] Furthermore, the secret, he writes, of theology is that it is nothing more than anthropology—religion and theology is no more than the study of humanity. Feuerbach—like so many theologians in the Age of Reason and the Enlightenment—had grounded Christianity on human religious experience. As a result it is not surprising that many of them lost sight of God, declaring themselves atheists. Alastair McGrath noted that Feuerbach's critique of religion loses much of its force when dealing with a divine encounter with humanity from outside, or, more pertinently, theologies that claim to deal with such an external encounter.[4] That is, when humanity realizes that there is a God outside of all human expectations; a God that can know them, seek them. Modern enlightened theology that secretly follows Feuerbach's psychological explanation of religion and appeals to atheism fails to follow through what it purports to believe. Robert Jenson the American Lutheran theologian commented:

---

1 "For our struggle is not against enemies of blood and flesh, but against the rulers, against the authorities, against the cosmic powers of this present darkness, against the spiritual forces of evil in the heavenly places." Eph 6:12.

2 See: Feuerbach, *The Essence of Christianity*.

3 Ibid., 121, 207.

4 McGrath, *Christian Theology*, 231. See also Gerrish, "Feuerbach's Religious Illusion," 362–65 and 367.

> But just if Feuerbach is right, if there is in fact no antecedent one God, there also can be no one antecedent community of humankind. Feuerbach dreamed of a universal humanity and so of a shared eternal vision of human value, but therein he remained parasitic on the faith he debunked. Thus Western unbelief has since had to abandon that dream and now knows only classes and genders and races and cultures. Insofar as religion interprets itself by the resultant neo-Feuerbachian theory, religion is revealed as a struggle for metaphysical power, for each such group necessarily projects its ideal or compensatory vision of itself to be the final good. It is just so that Scripture sees the gods of the peoples as idols and "nothings." Exactly as neo-Feuerbachian theory says, what each of the gods does is validate and enforce the particular human situation, with its structure of values, from which she/he/it is projected—in all the alienation and tyranny of every such situation.[5]

A Feuerbachian position is ultimately absurd—if there is no God then there is no truth, no morality and no meaning. If God is an illusion then so is certainty and meaning, which Feuerbachians and scientific atheists today rely upon, indeed their protestations of no g/God are grounded in a certainty that cannot exist according to their criteria. However, Feuerbach's observations are significant because they open up space between human religiousness and God. That is, space is opened up between the religious desire in humanity, the human capacity to invent gods and idols, on the one hand, and the one true living God who we can only truly know in Christ, on the other hand. God is therefore transcendent, beyond all that we can conceive of, even know. God is other—*wholly other*. From this transcendence and otherness God comes to us from beyond the world of Feuerbachian religion, an imaginary world peopled by projected gods or idols. God comes to us in the Word made flesh. While humanity invents all manner of religions and gods/idols, God comes to us in humility, divesting himself of much of his omnipotence and omniscience and omnipresence in the form of a vulnerable human baby. This is a concept or doctrine of God that humanity could never have dreamt up—God incarnate, utterly dependent on two ordinary people, Mary and Joseph, for his safety and growth, nurturing and education. This is the Christ.

ii. The Measure of Religious Experience

The measure of all religious experience and conversion is this Christ Jesus, crucified, resurrected, and ascended for our sins, and who comes to us now through the Holy Spirit, who will indwell in us. But we must not mistake this indwelling for our own projected ideas of what or who God should be. But it is not simply a case of either/or: there may be a degree, however small, in all conversion experiences that emanates from the human psyche, that colors the impact of the Holy Spirit. Personal development, cultural conditioning, our own religious ideas and prejudices will effect, more pertinently they will filter, how the Holy Spirit reveals God to us. And people may still worship their own desires, the projected "god" of their dreams, and take this

---

5   Jenson, *Systematic Theology* Vol. 1, 53.

projection for a real "god" to their own detriment, indeed to their own damnation: the parable of the sower and the seed again.[6]

iii. *The Human Filtering of Religious Experience*

The individual—Joy Davidman, C. S. Lewis, William Gresham—will filter the presence of the Holy Spirit and will color the resulting knowledge and understanding each individual has about God. Likewise the cultural situation, the family background, the beliefs, and prejudices will also affect the eventual understanding. Likewise childhood experiences will shape how we encounter God: how much, for example, is Lewis's understanding of his encounter with the risen Lord colored by the profound psychological disturbance the death of his mother had on him? Similarly, how much did God in Christ use this sublimated wound in the adult Lewis as a way to get across to the atheistic young don, whose intellectual ego would not allow God in? There will be those who say that if this wound from his mother's death had not been so deep and painful then Lewis would not have become religious in his adult years. There are those who may argue that Lewis's conversion and religious character was projected from his subconscious mind as a coping mechanism caused by the intolerable grief and pain from his relatively troubled childhood. Such a theory asserts that Lewis's religion was compensation for his troubled childhood. However, this is to invert what is happening. Those who have a "normal" untroubled life, who have nothing to challenge or break into the hermetic confident world of the self, are the ones who as a result are relatively immune to the action and effect of the Holy Spirit. By contrast, Lewis's childhood traumas may be seen as *initially* leading to atheism: his mother's death, the nihilistic world of Edwardian public schools—these are a blessing in disguise. Without them Lewis would not—eventually—have been open to God in the way he was to become. For example, Job comes to a sounder understanding and relationship with God through and after his troubles. The healthy, the sound, the confident and successful, these in their atheistic self-contained world are the ones subject to delusion. These are the ones to be pitied. The veracity of Lewis's conversion and his apologetic claims can, with hindsight, be seen as valid. Because we are fallen, and hence fallible, we will only truly know the genuineness of these and many more encounters with God eschatologically—that is, after death. Prior to the end of all things any claims we make for our religious experiences and encounters will be either deluded or genuine, to a million fine degrees. Only before the judgment seat of Christ will we know as we are known (1 Cor 13:12[7]) and thereby see what was authentic and indisputable.

---

6 Matthew 13; Mark 4; Luke 8.
7 "Now we see but a poor reflection as in a mirror; then we shall see face to face. Now I know in part; then I shall know fully, even as I am fully known." 1 Cor 13:12.

2. A SHARED ENCOUNTER?

i. Augustine and Religious Experience

Understanding does not come immediately with the moment of the encounter. Understanding comes afterwards: God touches us in a moment, in an instant, which seems not to exist in time, and we are left, so to speak, to pick up the pieces, try to make sense of what had happened. The patristic theologian Augustine is an example; consider the account of his conversion in his book, *Confessions*.[8] Despite his intellectual and philosophical ideas—even, we may say, prejudices—Augustine is brought to a point of crisis by the hidden Christ, a point where he must decide one way or the other. But this is more than a decision; it is most often characterized as a response. Elizabeth Fox-Genovese comments that:

> The conversion of St. Augustine differs markedly from that of St. Paul, yet ranks as no less exemplary and may well speak more directly to the condition of modern converts. St. Augustine came to intellectual certainty about the truth of Christianity before he embraced it in faith. "What I now longed for," he wrote in his *Confessions*, "was not greater certainty about you, but a more steadfast abiding in you." The obstacles lay not in his mind but in his heart, "which needed to be cleansed of the old leaven. I was attracted to the Way, which is our Savior himself, but the narrowness of the path daunted me and I still could not walk in it."[9]

Fox-Genovese continues by observing how Augustine saw himself as enslaved by obstacles that prevented his wholehearted conversion—he still focused on his fleshly sins. This, she rightly shows, is not necessarily so; his *intellectual* sins were far worse, and far more enslaving.

Augustine often focuses on the role of the *will* in conversion: a will divided against itself.[10] Such encounters as we have examined must not be seen from an egocentric perspective: it is not a case of the individual believing they are special, more precious before the Lord than all others, that the moment of grace is an endorsement of the life the person has lived. Such conversion experiences relate far more to sin than to selective endorsement. Although it is true to say that for some people the moment of conversion may be the result of a recognizable point in their life, for others being born again of the Spirit and of water may be a long, drawn out process lasting a lifetime. This may be so for many, but there are still those for whom there are instances where individuals do recognize that the past was wrong and that the future must be characterized by change—a change of heart, a change of lifestyle, and often a change of morality. Fundamentally this is a change in belief—as the person becomes a new person, a new creation. This moment is triggered by an encounter with the Holy Spirit:

---

8   Augustine, *Confessions*.
9   Fox-Genovese, "The Way of Conversion." *Crisis* 20.6 (June 2002). Online: http://www.catholicity.com/commentary/genovese/08018.html. Fox-Genovese is quoting from Book 8, ch. 12, §§. 28–30 of Augustine, *Confessions*.
10   Ibid.,

Paul on the road to Damascus must be seen as the classic example of such a conversion (Acts 9). Paul's conversion is a dramatic violent event precisely because of the level of sinfulness within him: his sinful ideas had serious implications for the growth of the church—the church being the locus of God's economy of salvation. So, perhaps we may suggest that the degree to which there is a noticeable and perceivable point of conversion is directly in relation to the degree of sinfulness in any given person. Lewis's conversion was much longer and more protracted than Joy Davidman's. Is this difference reflected in the degree of sinfulness in each? This is dangerous ground because no-one has a window into another person's soul, and the knowledge we would need to draw such a conclusion is private and in many people hidden, not only from observers but even from the individual's own knowledge. Only God truly knows every individual and their true state of sinfulness and grace.

Lewis and Augustine were both trained philosophers and teachers. Each fought in his mind against having to give in, to acknowledge what was happening to him. Lewis in his youth may not have been guilty of the fleshly lustful sins that Augustine acknowledges, but both had adopted non-Judaic-Christian religious beliefs (Augustine, Manichaeism; Lewis, Hegelian idealism), which ensnared the mind, and then the soul. By contrast, Joy Davidman's mind seemed less ensnared. Yes, she was an atheistic Jew, a communist, but what she writes of her conversion experience as a young married woman shows that she was more accepting: her conversion was less protracted and drawn-out, certainly by comparison with Lewis's (and for that matter, Augustine's)—was it simply that she was more open to love? Did Joy's Jewish heritage (her grandparents, relatives, etc.) make her more open to belief in Christ, when Christ decided to reveal himself to her?

ii. Simone Weil and Edith Stein and Religious Experience

Joy Davidman's conversion was therefore different, yet sharing common features with Lewis. Contemporary to Davidman in Europe were Simone Weil and Edith Stein, both of whom, like Joy, were converts from Judaism. Their conversions likewise share similarities yet are also unique, have unique characteristics that reflect each individual's journey, pilgrimage. Born and raised in Paris, Simone Weil (1909–43) describes her parents as agnostic cultural Jews; like Davidman she is a phenomenal intellect, only in this instance, a trained philosopher from the Sorbonne. As a student she flirted with communist-Bolshevik ideas, but saw from her youthful involvement in the Spanish Civil War what Marxism could lead to. Like Davidman, Weil also went into teaching but suffered ill-health and migraines. Despite this she subjected herself to intense physical/manual labor. In her late twenties she wrote of having been possessed by Christ as she recounts intense mystical experiences. It is important to remember that Weil's Christian beliefs developed gradually during the last six years of her life, from the initial mystical experiences at Solesmes in Portugal and Assisi in Italy (1937–38), through her regular discussions with a Dominican priest (Fr. Perrin) in the south of France during the early years of World War Two while trying to get her

4. C. S. Lewis and Karl Barth I: Religious Experience—Revelation and Modernity

parents to safety in New York away from the Nazis, through to her death at the age of thirty-four years in 1943 from tuberculosis. Somewhere in this human confusion of mixed emotions, a repressed upbringing, disillusionment with political activism, and the sharpness of a philosophical intellect Weil was genuinely touched by Christ and responded. From the agnostic crypto-communist philosophical brilliance of her youth, she realized the wholly otherness of the God who stoops in humility to redeem people, possessing them in love. Through the discussions with Fr. Perrin she became a believing Christian but refused to be baptized, questioning its necessity in the context of the Roman Catholic Church. Weil questioned the degree to which Rome perceived and acknowledged the way Christ's Holy Spirit was working amongst other people and cultures. She was also concerned as to whether Rome recognized when people were baptized by and in the Spirit, whether they were religious or not, or whether they were in the church(es) or not. However her writings exhibit a profound understanding of how we are converted (the metaphysics of conversion) and how our sufferings relate to Christ's cross. She is known as the patron saint of outsiders. Weil's conversion is unique and different to that of Lewis and Davidman, yet strangely familiar and reminiscent, as the individual struggles to make sense of what had happened in the experience of encountering Christ.[11]

Like Augustine, the form of the encounter may be triggered by reading—scriptural or otherwise. The path of Edith Stein (1891–1942) was probably the most serene and unperturbed of those whom we have looked at. That is, the path of her conversion was amongst the smoothest and untroubled, but the path of her pilgrimage in Christ was simultaneously the most troubled and the most Christian: it was the way of the cross. Born into an Orthodox Jewish family in Breslau, Silesia (Germany), she studied under the philosopher Edmund Husserl at the University of Göttingen, completing her doctorate under him, then working at the University of Freiburg. It was through reading the autobiography of the Catholic mystic Teresa of Avila whilst on holiday at the age of thirty years that she experienced her conversion. She was baptized into the Roman Catholic Church on the January 1, 1922, whereupon she

---

11   See, Weil, *Waiting on God*, 49. Key thoughts on Weil's understanding of her mystical encounters with God in Christ are to found in her notebooks; however, many of these ideas found a more coherent expression in the essays written in the South of France (June 1940–May 1942):

"Réflexions sur le bon usage des études scolaires en vue de l'amour de Dieu" ("Reflections on the Right Use of School Studies with a View to the Love of God"): spring 1941.

"L'Amour de Dieu et le malheur" ("On the Love of God and Affliction"): the first half sketched out in the spring of 1941 was published in Attente de Dieu, 1950; a second version, much extended and amended was discovered later in her papers from New York and London, the complete text was therefore published in, Weil, *The Simone Weil Reader*, (1977).

"Formes implicites de l'amour de Dieu" ("Forms of the Implicit Love of God") spring 1941.

"Réflexions/Pensées san ordre concernant l'amour de Dieu" ("Reflections Without Order on the Love of God") 1941.

There are two further essays both broadly titled "Réflexions/Pensées de l'amour de Dieu" written in this period.

All of these essays can be found in Weil Oeuvres Complètes (1988–97) or in earlier French editions; English translations of these essays are in: Weil, *Waiting on God*, Weil, *The Simone Weil Reader*, or Weil, *On Science, Necessity, and the Love of God*. See also, Weil, *First and Last Notebooks*.

gave up her university post to teach at a Dominican girls' school for ten years. She then taught at the Institute for Pedagogy in Münster, but the rise of Nazism forced her to leave teaching. She became a nun in 1934, entering the Discalced Carmelite monastery in Cologne. Because of Nazism Stein, now Teresa Benedicta of the Cross, was moved to Echt in the Netherlands (a Carmelite monastery). However, because she was racially a Jew she was arrested and along with her sister Rosa, also a convert, they were sent to their death in the gas chambers of the Auschwitz concentration camp. Stein was touched by the spirit of the resurrected and ascended Christ as she read about Teresa of Avila, and responded in a way that was much more unconditional than many other intellectual converts: she gave up her work, gave herself and all to Christ, and followed the path of martyrdom. She was canonized as Saint Teresa Benedicta of the Cross by Pope John Paul II in 1998.

3. C. S. LEWIS AND KARL BARTH

Writing to his brother in February 1940, C. S. Lewis noted how he was encountering students at Oxford who were enamored with the theology and teachings of a Swiss theologian by the name of Karl Barth. He wrote about how he feared for the way theology had been developing during the 1930s and now during the early years of the Second World War there was a degree of strident intolerance amongst Christian students that concerned him:

> [A] most distressing discovery I have been making these last two terms as I have been getting to know more and more of the Christian element in Oxford. Did you fondly believe—I did—that where you got among Christians, there, at least, you would escape (as behind a wall from a keen wind) from the horrible ferocity and grimness of modern thought? Not a bit of it. I blundered into it all, imagining that I was the upholder of the old, stern doctrines against modern quasi-Christian slush: only to find that my "sternness" was their "slush." They've all been reading a dreadful man called Karl Barth, who seems the right opposite number to Karl Marx. "Under judgment" is their great expression. They all talk like Covenanters or Old Testament prophets. They don't think human reason or human conscience of any value at all: they maintain, as stoutly as Calvin, that there's no reason why God's dealings should appear just (let alone, merciful) to us: and they maintain the doctrine that all our righteousness is filthy rags with a fierceness and sincerity which is like a blow in the face.[12]

Anyone who knows of Barth's theology will see here a caricature—a caricature not drawn by Lewis but by a group of zealous Barthian supporters, students barely out of the schoolroom or the dormitory of an English boarding school. Do we blame Calvin for Calvinism? Aquinas for Thomism? Do we blame Jesus for the sins of the church? Barth, I am sure, would have baulked at this caricature. Like Lewis, Barth enjoyed smoking and drinking; in addition Barth passionately defended Mozart and

---

12   Lewis writing to his brother, Feb. 18, 1940. Lewis, *Collected Letters, Vol. II*, 347–53, quotation, 351. See also, Lewis writing to his brother, Apr. 28, 1940. Lewis, *Collected Letters, Vol. II*, 404–6, specifically, 404.

4. C. S. Lewis and Karl Barth I: Religious Experience—Revelation and Modernity

his music as the revelation of God: they can say what they like about my theology, he was often reputed to say, as long as they leave Mozart alone. Barth was critical of post-war American evangelists who so destructively criticized and destroyed people so as to convert them. Speaking of Barth and the gospel, Colin E. Gunton commented that,

> It is important to remember that for Barth this does not encompass a pessimistic anthropology. It is not trying to grind the human nose in the dust. He has no sympathy at all with the kind of preacher who tries to frighten people into salvation. He once offended Evangelicals by saying what a dreadful man Billy Graham was, you see, because he heard him preaching—he heard Graham as he tried to hammer people into the ground with their sins, which he considered was dangerous, pastorally dangerous—because if the forgiveness doesn't follow, if you don't accept the forgiveness, you are just made to feel bad without being saved. Barth's view is that salvation is preached first and only in the light of it do you understand sin, nonetheless it is not a pessimistic anthropology.[13]

Barth also criticized people who tried to use The Sermon on the Mount as a legalistic code—"like telling us that it means we must never drink or smoke."[14]

C. S. Lewis and Karl Barth can be considered as very different theologians, indeed to many from a more extreme position, they could be seen as incompatible. Yet, as secularism has taken hold in the West since their respective deaths in the 1960s, Lewis and Barth have seemed closer in their thinking because of their respect for an orthodox, traditional, creedal basis for Christian doctrine, a basis grounded in the revelation of the triune God: the Word of God as person (Christ) and Scripture, and the church as a forgiving community. Both Barth and Lewis were operating from different positions when at the height of their powers in the 1940s and 1950s: Lewis the Anglican Oxford scholar, children's storywriter, and Christian apologist; Barth the Swiss Reformed Church minister and professor of dogmatics in Germany and Switzerland. However, for both there had been something of a watershed, a conversion: in Lewis's words crossing the Rubicon; to Barth, a *Wendung* (that is, a profound change of heart and belief) and *Retraktation* (a reassessment, a constant reappraisal). Furthermore, significant differences between Lewis and Barth notwithstanding, it is possible to identify an element within their realization and perception of God that was diametric to the belief system each held prior to conversion/reconversion. This perception of the realism of God led in part to their mature work.

4. KARL BARTH

i. The Castigation of Liberalism

Considered by many to be the scourge of liberal philosophy and theology when it denies the Christ—often by substituting the cross with religious feeling, human religiousness—the young Karl Barth (1868–1968) was praised by the Catholic

---

13   Gunton, *The Barth Lectures*, 78–79.
14   Ibid., 132–33.

theologian Karl Adam in 1926 because Barth's theological commentary on Paul's Epistle to the Romans (*Der Römerbrief*) was a wake-up call: "Barth's *Römerbrief* hit immediately in its first appearance—August 1919—like a bomb on the playground of the theologians, comparable in its effects with the encyclical on anti-modernisation of Pope Pius X."[15] A generation later Pope Pius XII,[16] commented in 1951 that the Swiss Reformed theologian Karl Barth was the greatest theologian since Thomas Aquinas.[17] Barth was Lewis's contemporary, he was a Reformed minister who cherished his Calvinistic heritage, but was also an ecumenical theologian in the sense that he wrote theology that transcended denominational boundaries. His mature work written over a thirty-five year period consists of fourteen volumes of *The Church Dogmatics*,[18] which—in an estimated six million words—re-established Christ at the centre of the church and at the heart of Christian theology, in the wake of modern skepticism.

There is a beauty, a poetic beauty and majesty, which is reminiscent of Lewis the poet, in the way Barth wrote about Christ in *The Church Dogmatics*. There is a measured cadence to his theology that has the authority one would normally associate with Scripture. He talks of "The Way of the Son into the Far Country," of "The Judge Judged in our Place."[19] Barth does not try to argue with you, he does not try to persuade you of the veracity of the gospel; he simply asserts its truth, its honesty and reliability, its cogency and that it is essentially beautiful, reflecting the beauty of God. *The Church Dogmatics* is heavily christological; it is strongly Christ-centered. Therefore, in the context of Lewis's Christology consider this: Barth writing on the incarnation and how it relates to our salvation:

> From §59 The Obedience of the Son of God
> The way of the Son of God into the far country is the way of obedience. This is, *in re* [in the matter (of)] the first and inner moment of the mystery of the deity of Christ . . . we are confronted with the revelation of what is and always will be to all other ways of looking and thinking a mystery, and indeed a mystery which offends. The mystery reveals to us that for God it is just as natural to be lowly as it is to be high, to be near as it is to be far, to be little as it is to be great, to be abroad as to be at home . . . by the sin of man he chooses to go into the far country, to conceal his form of lordship in the form of this world and therefore in the form of a servant, he is not untrue to himself but genuinely true to himself,

---

15 "Barths Römerbrief schlug gleich bei seinem ersten Erscheinen (August 1919) wie eine Bombe auf dem Spielplatz der Theologen ein, in seinen Wirkungen etwa vergleichbar der Antimodernistenenzyklika des Papstes Pius X." Adam, "Die Theologie der Krisis", 271–86. Adam referred to Pope Pius X (1835–1914; pontiff 1903-1914), his decree *Lamentabili sane exitu* (A Lamentable Departure Indeed), issued 3 July 1907, condemning sixty-five modernist or relativist propositions concerning the nature of the Church, revelation, biblical exegesis, the sacraments, and the divinity of Christ.

16 Pope Pius XII (1876–1958; pontiff 1939–1958).

17 Quoted in Barth, *Fragments Grave and Gay*, i. For a theological biography of Barth, see, Busch, *Karl Barths Lebenslauf*. For an introduction to Barth's theology see: Webster, *Barth*.

18 Barth, *The Church Dogmatics*.

19 Ibid., See, Vol. IV/1, Chapter XIV Jesus Christ, the Lord as Servant: §59.1: 'The Way of the Son of God into the Far Country', 157–210; §59.2: 'The Judge Judged in Our Place', 211–83; §59.3: 'The Verdict of the Father', 283–357.

to the freedom which is that of his love. He does not have to choose and do this. He is free in relation to it.

Even in the form of a servant, which is the form of his presence and action in Jesus Christ, we have to do with God himself in his true deity. The humility in which he dwells and acts in Jesus Christ is not alien to him, but proper to him. His humility is a *novum mysterium* [new mystery] for us in whose favour he executes it when he makes use of his freedom for it, when he shows his love even to his enemies and his life even in death, thus revealing them in a way which is quite contrary to all our false ideas of God. But for him this humility is no *novum mysterium*. It is his sovereign grace that he wills to be and is amongst us in humility, our God, God for us.

He gives himself to us in Jesus Christ, he exists and speaks and acts as the one he was from all eternity and will be to all eternity. The truth and actuality of our atonement depends on this being the case. The one who reconciles the world with God is necessarily the one God himself in his true Godhead. Otherwise the world would not be reconciled with God.[20]

Some twelve years older than Lewis, Barth served as parish pastor in a small town in neutral Switzerland while Lewis was in the trenches in World War One. Lewis's family had Anglican priests and a bishop in his mother's line; Barth's family likewise had boasted Reformed ministers in his father's line. Barth's religious heritage was solidly Swiss Reformed Church ministers and Bible scholars; his father Johann Friedrich (Fritz) was a pastor and patristic scholar, who taught at The College of Preachers in Basle (founded in opposition to liberal theology). Barth's grandfathers had been pastors; three of his uncles had read theology. Karl Barth may be considered as a cradle to grave Christian: he does not recount or own any period of disbelief or rejection of the faith he was born into. By contrast Lewis was raised in his early years to read freely whatever he could find amongst his parents hundreds of modern books, and exhibited an Anglican establishment freedom of sorts. Lewis, as we have seen, suffered at Edwardian public schools characterized by fagging and brutality, he had to carry the pain of his mother's death from cancer, though again as we have seen, Lewis's genuine childhood faith lapsed as he grew up and he embraced atheism in his teens despite being confirmed in the Church of England. Therefore he is conscious of his position and that he is converted from atheism. By contrast Barth never lost his faith but it was submerged when he was a student by his study of Liberal neo-Protestantism, which he then espoused as a young pastor in Geneva, a Liberal neo-Protestantism that in many ways reduced God to human desire and religion to human culture. Therefore we can identify a *re*-conversion for Barth in his late-twenties, from this human-centered cultural religion to an orthodox, traditional, creedal position. For Lewis we see a conversion from atheism to theism then to Christianity in the period of a couple of years. By comparison Barth's re-conversion from Liberal neo-Protestantism to orthodox, creedal Christianity took, in effect, ten years (from his arrival as pastor in Safenwil in 1911 through, generally, to the completion of the second edition of his

20 See, Vol. IV/1, chap. XIV, Jesus Christ, the Lord as Servant, §59 The Obedience of the Son of God, 157–357.

commentary on Romans in 1921). Both conversions are characterized by a realization of the realistic existence of God as axiomatic fact, God as *wholly other*, independent from all human affairs (for Barth 1915; Lewis 1929). This understanding then moves into the revelation of God in Christ: God speaking (i.e., the *Deus dixit*, God for us). Despite similarities and differences, both of them in their mature work wrote much to reassert and promote orthodox Christian doctrine in the face of many twentieth-century heresies: liberalism, political tyrannies, pseudo-Gnosticism, and the *Zeitgeist* of mid-twentieth-century European modernity. Importantly, both sought to deny mere religion and assert the revelation of God over what they termed "man's search for God"—that is, the human religious quest.

ii. Trinitarian Considerations

If we are to ask the question what was Lewis, and for that matter Barth, converted *from* and *to*, then this raises christological questions: talk of God is one thing; speaking of Jesus is another. But they are not detached and isolated (i.e., separate "gods"), but neither are they the same divine entity (first God, then Jesus . . .). We are here talking about the distinction between modalism and polytheism. This raises questions about orthodox Christology and heresy. The early church defined a sound, orthodox understanding of Jesus as *very God and very man*; as the second person of the Trinity incarnated in human flesh. Was this understanding dominant in the early twentieth century, the formative period in Lewis and Barth's development? What did those who influenced and taught Lewis and Barth believe about this Jesus of Nazareth? See figure 1 on the tensions that can affect all christologies, and figure 2 on the tensions inherent in the doctrine of the Trinity.

Nineteenth-Century Liberal Neo-Protestantism

Although he studied theology at the universities of Berne, Berlin, and Tübingen, it was at Marburg, much to his father's displeasure, that Barth felt at home—particularly under the tutelage of the liberal, Wilhelm Herrmann (1846–1922), Professor of Systematic Theology at Marburg from 1879. Hermann was a follower of Kant in philosophical terms and a follower of Albrecht Ritschl in his Christology. Herrmann insisted that what should be observed and taught about Jesus of Nazareth were those facts that would act upon humanity—for example, Jesus's moral teaching but not the story of the virginal conception or the resurrection. Furthermore Herrmann proposed that there might have been other aspects of the man Jesus of Nazareth that were considered relevant and of value by the apostles but these ideas/conclusions were not of importance to late nineteenth- and early twentieth-century humanity (essentially the German middle class or educated bourgeoisie). Herrmann held to a Ritschlian Christology. Albrecht Ritschl's (1822–89) understanding of Christ was that you start with this ordinary human, Jesus of Nazareth, and you develop a value judgment about him. Ritschl believed that you came to believe in the significance of Jesus as Christ by a value judgment. This was a Christology of value judgments: you subjectively valued

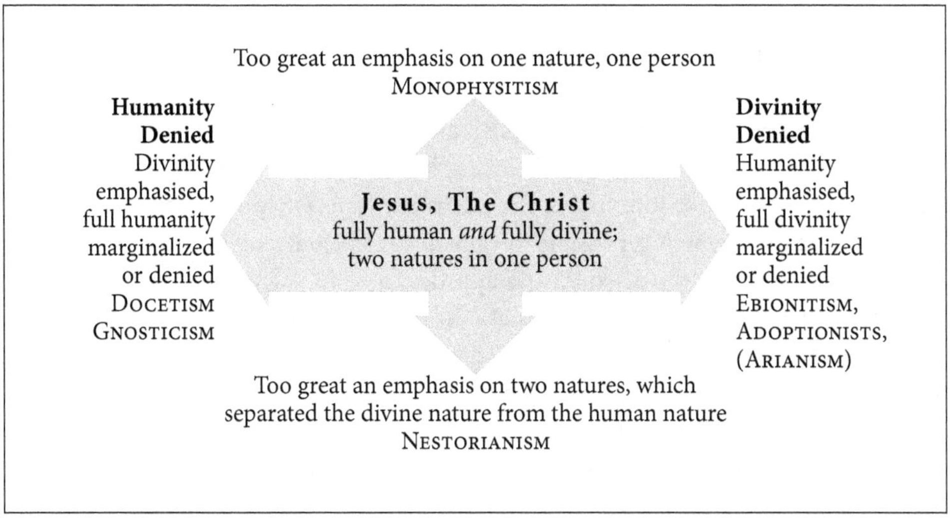

4. C. S. Lewis and Karl Barth I: Religious Experience—Revelation and Modernity

Too great an emphasis on one nature, one person
MONOPHYSITISM

Humanity Denied
Divinity emphasised, full humanity marginalized or denied
DOCETISM
GNOSTICISM

Jesus, The Christ
fully human *and* fully divine; two natures in one person

Divinity Denied
Humanity emphasised, full divinity marginalized or denied
EBIONITISM,
ADOPTIONISTS,
(ARIANISM)

Too great an emphasis on two natures, which separated the divine nature from the human nature
NESTORIANISM

Figure 1: The Tensions that can affect all Christologies

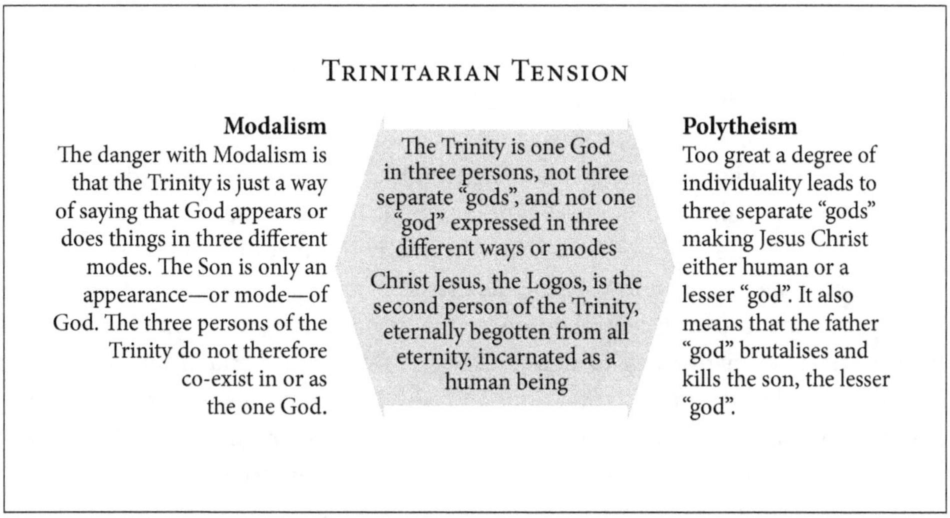

TRINITARIAN TENSION

Modalism
The danger with Modalism is that the Trinity is just a way of saying that God appears or does things in three different modes. The Son is only an appearance—or mode—of God. The three persons of the Trinity do not therefore co-exist in or as the one God.

The Trinity is one God in three persons, not three separate "gods", and not one "god" expressed in three different ways or modes

Christ Jesus, the Logos, is the second person of the Trinity, eternally begotten from all eternity, incarnated as a human being

Polytheism
Too great a degree of individuality leads to three separate "gods" making Jesus Christ either human or a lesser "god". It also means that the father "god" brutalises and kills the son, the lesser "god".

Figure 2: The Tensions Inherent in the Doctrine of the Trinity

this ordinary man *as if* he was God, or a "god." This is not the Christ of dogma; this is not the Christ of the creeds. Ritschl, as so many nineteenth-century theologians, reduced Jesus to a good moral teacher. For Ritschl, as for Herrmann and for Barth as a student (and, for that matter, Lewis as an Hegelian idealist, if he had thought about Jesus), Ritschl concentrated on the ethical teaching of Jesus, in particular his teaching of the kingdom of God. Ritschl did not teach that Jesus is God become man; he sets out ethical reasons why it is possible to value Jesus as God, *as if* he were God. Ritschl therefore claimed that the disciples and apostles came to value, they made a personal judgment, that said this man Jesus was *as if* he was God to them. However, Herrmann went further—he excluded both the mysticism of personal religious experience and the metaphysical speculation that underpinned any intellectual reasoning about ultimate reality. Any value to the historical Jesus was therefore in the man's moral teaching for humanity alone.[21] Original sin, atonement, the cross, did not really fit into this picture.

A De-Christianized Jesus

The consensus of agreement on the person and nature of the Christ that was laid out by the early church fathers in the centuries after the resurrection through the first six ecumenical councils (including Ephesus, Nicaea, Constantinople, and Chalcedon) established the faith of the church. None of this was really questioned in any detail, even during the fraught and fought over times of the Reformation: all sides in the sixteenth century (the Protestant Reformation churches and Rome's Counter Reformation, essentially the Council of Trent) accepted the canon of Scripture, the creeds, and the ecumenical councils. These creeds, councils, and Scriptures represented the givenness of the truth, as revealed truth. It was with the Age of Reason and the dawn of the period of the Enlightenment in the seventeenth and eighteenth centuries that this consensus was challenged. Many historians, philosophers, and theologians sought to reduce the divine status of Jesus Christ, in many instances to deny God in Christ completely.[22] Many sought to redefine the Christ as an ordinary human being. Much of this critique came from central European theologians, while the Church of England reduced itself, in many ways, to a cultural wing of the British establishment whereby senior clerics flirted with such questions and with Deism. In this context it was left to the Roman Catholic, the Eastern Orthodox and the Non-Conformist and Evangelical churches to witness to Christ's truth, along with lone nineteenth century prophets such as the Danish philosopher Søren Kierkegaard and the Russian writer Fyodor Mikhailovich Dostoevsky. The ground of this Enlightenment critique claimed to be rationalist but was essentially humanist: humanity was at the centre, humanity was the measure of all; God was allowed to exist if humanity patronisingly approved, allowing God to be. Within this a distinction is driven between the Jesus of history and the Christ of faith. There was then, particularly in nineteenth-century theology, a desire,

21   See, Herrmann, *The Communion of the Christian with God*.
22   For a survey of how Enlightenment and post Enlightenment thinkers in, essentially, Western Europe and North America have critiqued traditional Christology see: Macquarrie, *Jesus Christ in Modern Thought*.

4. C. S. Lewis and Karl Barth I: Religious Experience—Revelation and Modernity

a quest, to find out who this man Jesus of Nazareth was if the church's witness was to be rejected? Within this quest for the historic Jesus many even sought to deny that Jesus was a Jew: Jesus was recast as a bourgeois, cultured, enlightened white European. The writer George Tyrrell S. J. said about this so-called "historical" Jesus that he "is only the reflection of a Liberal Protestant face, seen at the bottom of a deep well." [23] The authority of the Bible was demolished; historians claimed that the Gospels were inaccurate and unreliable and sought to try paint what they saw to be a "true" portrait of Jesus: the historical Jesus, which the Christ of faith had smothered over. However, after two hundred years no one has managed to recapture/reconstruct this merely human Jesus of a Western liberal mind-set. During this time Bishops and theologians, priests and clergy, were effectively split into two broad, overlapping, camps: those who subscribed to the creeds, the Scriptures, and church authority, and those who did not. There have been good creedal orthodox/traditional bishops and priests, theologians, and ordinary Christians in this modern era, but their witness was so often drowned out by the skeptics, by the zeitgeist, the spirit of the age, in a world that sought more and more to define truth in its own fallen and willful image. This is the christological background to the conversions and the theological ministries of C. S. Lewis and Karl Barth. (Lewis explicitly criticized this de-Christianized Jesus in many of his works in the 1950s, in particular in the context of the reductionist doctrine of Scripture many high-ranking Anglican clerics subscribed to.[24])

iii. Barth: Wendung *and* Retraktation

Barth initially worked as assistant pastor to the German speaking church in Geneva; he then served for ten years in the small industrial town of Safenwil in the Aargau. Barth referred to the momentous and tumultuous changes that his beliefs went through during his time in Safenwil as his *Wendung*, that is, a profound turnabout, a diametric change of direction, and then later, his *Retraktation*, that is, a revision, a reassessment, a constant reappraisal to ensure the true path which had emerged from the *Wendung* was still being followed. Barth wrote of a *Wendung*—a 180° turn, an unexpected and decisive turn of events, a turn for the better.[25] This decisive, diametric change of heart and mind, a sea change, was so complete that there was no going back. Even in his mature work Barth continued to reappraise these changes—not to pull back, to change his mind, not to return to the liberalism of his theological training, but to ensure the cogency and permanence of this sea change. This *Retraktation* occurred throughout the period of his mature work, but especially in the late 1940s and the 1950s. However, the term *Retraktation* applies equally to the period of diametric change, the *Wendung*,

---

23   Tyrrell, *Christianity at the Cross-Roads*, 49, see also, generally, 46f.
24   See, Lewis, "Modern Theology and Biblical Criticism."
25   Barth spoke of, "Eine Wendung um 180°, eine unerwartete/entscheidende Wendung," "eine Wendung zum Besseren," also, "totale Veränderung" in a lecture delivered at the meeting of the Swiss Reformed Minister's Association in Aarau, Sept. 25, 1956: Barth, *Die Menschlichkeit Gottes*, 6.

during his time in Safenwil and centering on 1915–16. Barth is almost certainly using the term with Augustine's *Retractationes* in mind.[26]

Barth's *Wendung* is his development away from the nineteenth-century Liberal neo-Protestant heritage that had been at the heart of his theological formation. To reject this is more than a change of theological emphasis or a shift in theological allegiance; furthermore it covers a number of years in terms of development—it is a wholesale reorientation, a methodological shift so that once the change has been accomplished there is no going back. If so, why? Because Barth wanted to assert the irreversible permanence of his conversion/change of heart from the years 1915–16, with all the implications asserted for Christian doctrine. Writing in the 1950s Barth commented:

> Were we right or wrong? We were certainly right! Why? Let one read the doctrine of Tröltsch, and Stephan! Let one read also the dogmatics of Lüdemann, in its way so solid, or even that of Seeburg! If all that wasn't a blind alley! Beyond doubt what was then in order was not some kind of further shifting around within the complex of inherited questions, as this was finally attempted by Wobbermin, Schaeder, and Otto, but rather a *radikale Wendung*. The ship was threatening to run aground; the moment was at hand to turn the rudder an angle of exactly 180°. And in view of what is to be said later, let it immediately be stated: that which is gone does not return. Therefore there never could be a question of denying or reversing that change. It was however later on and it is today a question of "*Retraktation*."[27] (Barth's emphasis)

For Barth: "A genuine '*Retraktation*' in no way involves a subsequent retreat, but rather a new beginning and attack in which what previously has been said is to be said more than ever, but now even better." Barth continued, "If that which we then thought we had discovered and brought forth," commenting on the changes centered on the years 1915–16, "was no last word but one requiring '*Retraktation*' (revision, improvement, reassertion to a degree) it was nonetheless a true word."[28] If one looks closely at the multitudinous influences on Barth in the period 1911 to 1921—as evident from his sermons, addresses, and correspondence—then (like Lewis in the 1920s, searching through Theism, Hegelian idealism, etc.) there is a constant reappraisal (as with the influence and use of Fyodor Mikhailovich Dostoevsky and Søren Kierkegaard, or Franz Overbeck, or Platonic concepts), a constant reconsideration—a *Retraktation* even at this early stage in his work.[29] Barth discovers, absorbs, is influenced, critically assesses; however he soon reconsiders and reassesses; then he distances himself and his theology from the influence, to a degree, and moves on. Influences come thick and fast: this is *Wendung* and *Retraktation*, according to Barth's usage. Barth asserted that

---

26   See Augustine, *Sancti Aurelii Augustini Retractationum libri II*, and, Traupé, "Saint Augustine," 342, 360, in particular, 355.
27   Barth, *Die Menschlichkeit Gottes*, 6–7.
28   Ibid., 7.
29   For a full exposition of Barth's influences at the crucial time of 1915–16, see: Balthasar, *Karl Barth, Darstellung und Deutung seiner Theologie*; McCormack, *Karl Barth's Critically Realistic Dialectical Theology*; and, Brazier, *Barth and Dostoevsky*, 2008.

the decisive change of this period in Safenwil must stand, this true word must stand, cannot be bypassed, and that it constituted the presupposition of what must then in his mature work be considered the humanity of God—God's turn to us, God for us. The foundation, the decisive turn for Barth in 1915 was, as we shall see, the realization that "God is God," from which flows his mature work focusing on the turn of the hidden or absent God (the *Deus absconditus*) to and for humanity: the God that speaks, that communicates (the *Deus dixit*).

Safenwil (1911–21) was Barth's first full ministry. The conditions of the parish and congregation focused his concerns on the paucity of the nineteenth-century Liberal theological tradition. Safenwil was industrial, small scale, but had not experienced the reforming zeal of socialist/trade union activists who would have challenged the poverty and atrocious working conditions and the use of child labor. Workers and bosses/managers worshipped side-by-side on Sunday but were divided during the week—strikes, lock-outs, poor wages and working conditions, industrial strife. Colin E. Gunton comments that: "It was not so much the Socialism that influenced him but the incapacity of a liberal gospel, or a liberal form of preaching, actually to speak to this situation. You see, when you have got people fundamentally at loggerheads, preaching the religious life does not help much, at least that is what he came to feel. It is no good telling people to be religious when there are more serious problems dominating their lives."[30] There was a tension between his theological training and his social and political experience: "Even in my inner being I was a stranger to the bourgeois world of Ritschl and his pupils."[31] So, Barth became politicized and became known as the "Red Pastor" and "Comrade Barth." He was exposed to the influence of two leading radical Swiss Religious Socialists—Hermann Kutter and Leonard Ragaz. Through this involvement Barth fell under the influence of the Blumhardts. Christoph Blumhardt's father had found miracles happening amongst the people he was ministering to. These were not isolated incidents and he began to realize that there was a strong and dynamic element to Christianity, of the Holy Spirit breaking in to judge. In an era of liberal and scientific skepticism Blumhardt was witnessing healing and miracles. This impressed Barth and led him to regard the elder Blumhardt as a prophet.

The outbreak of the First World War was significant in Barth's changes. Many years afterwards he wrote, "Was it—this has played a decisive role for me personally—precisely the failure of the ethics of the modern theology . . . with the outbreak of the First World War, which caused us to grow puzzled . . . ?"[32] In August 1914 ninety-three intellectuals attempted to impress German public opinion by proclaiming support for the war policy of Kaiser Wilhelm II. Barth was horrified to discover many of his respected teachers amongst the signatories: he could no longer subscribe to their ethics, in particular their understanding of the Bible and history.[33] Questioning

---

30   Gunton, *The Barth Lectures*, 23.
31   Barth, "Concluding Unscientific Postscript on Schleiermacher."
32   "Die Menschlichkeit Gottes," 6.
33   Comments recounted by Barth from an address delivered at the meeting of the Goethegsellschaft in Hanover, 8 January 1957: Karl Barth, "Evangelische Theologie im 19. Jahrhundert," 14.

the validity of their teaching and doctrine he concluded that such support was grounded in religious liberalism: "He [Schleiermacher] was unmasked In a decisive way all the theology expressed in the manifesto and everything that followed it (even in *Die Christliche Welt*) proved to be founded and governed by him."[34] Barth is not alone: with the catastrophe of the First World War the stability, pride, and security of liberal neo-Protestant society and culture broke down. The Great War represented a fragmentation—a disappearance of all the certainties about the bourgeois social order in Germany (and for that matter the Victorian Middle Class "Christian" ethic in Britain and the strict Edwardian hierarchical social order Lewis had been raised in).

So, what was the significance of both Barth and Lewis's conversions? What exactly did they come to understand when each declared, prayerfully, that God is/was God? What value can we read from their doctrinal realization that God is God . . . in Christ? We can now turn to a systematic analysis of Lewis's (and Barth's) Christology and their doctrine of God as part of their respective conversion.

---

34   Barth, "Nachwort," 293.

5

C. S. Lewis and Karl Barth II:
A Doctrinal Realization—God is God, in Christ

SYNOPSIS:
C. S. Lewis and Karl Barth both arrive at a point where they must own that *God is God*, which leads them to point to the unique self-revelation of God in Jesus Christ. In their mature work both are muscular, intellectual Christians. Notwithstanding the individual denominational characteristics of each as a theologian, Lewis and Barth are orthodox-traditional, biblical-creedal Christians who argue against the *zeitgeist*, the spirit of an Enlightenment-spawned modernism. However, there are significant differences—particularly related to religious experience. Therefore how do the two conversions compare?—and how does this illuminate our understanding of Lewis's relationship with Christ? We can now turn to a systematic theological analysis of Lewis's and, by comparison, Barth's christologies and doctrines of God, which issues from their respective conversions. What understanding can we draw from their doctrinal realization that God was indeed God . . . in Christ? The profound realization for both Lewis and Barth is of a God that is wholly other, that is known in Lordship, but is a Lord that stoops to love humanity into redemption: this is seen in the proposition "God is God." However, the complement is shown to be qualified by Lordship: *personhood* is the nature of this Lordship—this *person* is revealed as the Christ, the second person of the holy and indivisible Trinity who acts in love toward humanity, who loves in freedom. Therefore how does this faith sit with an academic mind-set?—we are talking here of the difference between the notion of an abstract and negative deity, as distinct from, the living God. For both Barth and Lewis this is characterized by the difference between "man's search for God" (dabbling in religion) and "God's search for man" (God himself, the hunter, King and husband, approaching at an infinite speed). What problems does this expose in relation to Barth as a religious professional, as compared to Lewis who was officially an amateur with no theological or church status? A profound understanding of Lewis's relationship with, and his intellectual model of, the Christ related to his conversion can be read from an interview conducted in the last year of his life where he declared, "I did not Choose Christ: He Chose me," and that he was, in effect, "decided upon."

1. GOD IS GOD

Because of their churchmanship Lewis and Barth will appear different and, at times, at odds with each other. However, this is where secularism during the last thirty-five years of the twentieth century has helped Christianity: it has forced the churches to look at common ground rather than differences—Christians now huddle together, to a degree, as the sharp biting and critical wind of secularism blows. Lewis and Barth do exhibit a degree of commonality in their lives, education, and beliefs. At the heart of Barth's change is, like Lewis, an emergent, redefined understanding of God. Broadly speaking we see this doctrine developing away from the Schleiermachian immediacy and the Hegelian idealism (which had also ensnared the young Lewis), which tied God to religious experience and world history—the events of the First World War had exposed the fault lines in this doctrine. Here we have the genesis of Barth's concern for God's freedom, God's *aseity*—that is, God's right, so to speak, to be God, independent from all that humanity imposed in theological definitions and religious projections.

A year into the war Barth commented in a lecture given in Basle, "Kriegszeit und Gottesreich," "[that] world remains world . . . But God is God."[1] Herbert Anzinger wrote, encapsulating Barth's comments: "To recognize that God is God, 'To recognize God also, as well as he is in the life and words of Jesu,' that he is 'something other beyond reason, other as all' . . ."[2] What we find here is Barth's early use of negation in relation to speaking about God; further, we find the use of *ursprung* as well as the emphasis on the wholly otherness of God:

> What concern to us is the God who was introduced to us once as the highest idea of the ethics? That "Father in heaven," to whom Jesus points us is no Ideality, which lives from its opposition no formal, unreal magnitude, that finally belongs to this world, no idea of the justice or the precious in the rivalry of the ideas of ethics, but rather the reality, out of which our entire world has fallen. That God is our creator and origin in the other world is entirely new for us, this would be the only positive thing that we can say. All our other speaking of God is a stammering, or it must if it should count seriously, exist in pure negation.[3]

Furthermore Barth sees this distance, this separation between the world and God in terms of *diastasis*—a relationship whereby two entities stand over against each other with no possibility of a synthesis (certainly not into a higher form of being in the Hegelian sense). Barth is making a conscious effort to distance himself from this Hegelian idealism and religion. The moment Barth began to express doubts about the theology he had been schooled in, a criticism of religion was inevitable. Once Barth began doubting the way he had been prepared for ministry by his teachers, particularly to the congregation in industrial Safenwil, then he is starting to criticize religion. What is important is that this is a criticism of Protestant and Reformed religion generally and German Liberal neo-Protestantism specifically. In all cases it is in the service of the gospel: Barth is looking at the church he is part of, looking at the way it ministers, the doctrinal basis of that ministry, and criticizing in the light of his understanding of the Christian gospel. Barth's teacher, Wilhelm Herrmann,

---

1   "*Welt bleibt Welt, daß Gott Gott ist.*" Karl Barth, "Kriegszeit und Gottesreich," an unpublished lecture given in Basle, Switzerland, Nov. 15, 1915. All but the first 12 of 31 pages survive in the Karl Barth archive in Basle. Parts of the text are published in Anzinger, *Glaube und kommunikative Praxis*, 120–22.
2   Barth, "Kriegszeit und Gottesreich," 120-21.
3   Ibid., 121.

5. C. S. Lewis and Karl Barth II: A Doctrinal Realization—God is God, in Christ

Figure 3: Karl Barth (1920) and C. S. Lewis (1925), pen and ink drawing, P. H. Brazier

held no criticism of religion—the theologians, clergy and adherents of the Lutheran Church in the nineteenth century were, for Herrmann, an adequate representation for the liberalism of his doctrine. Herrmann's religion was primarily individualistic—the individual was encouraged to see how God was working in his/her life. Questions of sin and guilt did not play much of a role in this approach. Herrmann's attitude and approach to religion was wholly positive. Barth's attitude and approach to religion was becoming negative and critical, dismissive and destructive; his sermon for May 4, 1913, based on Amos 5:21–24, echoed the prophet's criticism of religion: justice and righteousness were the measure of good religion, and without a commitment to action on behalf of such a cause then religion is no more than dreadful lies: "Do you really think that your so called religion has any value at all?"[4]

By 1915 Barth was in a period of crisis: "The predicament in which Barth found himself when preaching was not primarily a technical and practical matter . . . but a problem which concerned the basic content of preaching (can I, may I, speak of God at all?). And the discovery that he now made was this, that to recognize the basic difficulty in speaking of God is in itself relevant knowledge of God."[5] There is no question here of doubting the existence of God but how ministers and theologians are to speak of God. Barth comments further on this predicament:

> [W]hat do sceptics know about "life and death" questions? They leave the question "Does God exist?" open . . . Don't things become critically dangerous only if and because God is? In that case does not the decisive question recoil on one . . . [I]n short the whole of human independence and self-assurance are weighed in the balance and finally found wanting? (This is notoriously not the case with the sceptics' question.) That is the question which I failed to recognize

---

4   Barth, *Predigten 1913*, 217.
5   Busch, *Karl Barths Lebenslauf*, 103.

> as a student or as a young pastor. It is the question, which then came down on me like a ton of bricks round about 1915.[6]

In the same year, in part through conversations with Hermann Kutter, Barth underwent something of a conversion—or a re-conversion?—in his understanding of God:

> From Kutter I simply learnt to speak the great word "God" seriously, responsibly and with a sense of its importance. When he preached, and indeed in private conversation, he could impress on one that this was a deadly serious matter, which could not be taken lightly. And it was this prophetic thinker and preacher ... [who] represented the insight that the sphere of God's power really is greater than the sphere of the Church and that from time to time it has pleased God, and still pleases him, to warn and to comfort his Church through the figures and the events of secular world history.[7]

Kutter inspired Barth to rediscover the separateness, the wholly otherness of God, over and against all human affairs. This is not necessarily a Christian conversion or re-conversion, for it is only a realization of the existence of the Hebrew God. Later Barth criticized Kutter, for the simplicity of this approach but he could not deny the foundational basis of this awesome realization of God's aseity and sovereignty.[8] But this is more than an understanding of God. There is something happening here which is at once deeply personal but also very, very real: Barth started to know God in a very real way, in an intimate way that transcends ordinary cognitive knowledge. Such knowledge is triggered by the Holy Spirit and has a, yes, supernatural element to it. Barth's intellect, we may speculate, was—like Lewis in his rooms in Magdalen at a similar age—baptized. This same year, for Barth, 1915, also saw the influence of the Russian writer Dostoevsky—in the form of a biblical/patristic understanding of sin, and the wrenching of conscience away from Liberal pietism. So Barth perceives finally that God is indeed God. Then he begins to realize how God is God, in Christ: Barth's christocentric development, the heavy Christ-centered nature of his mature work, starts more or less immediately with his return to the Bible as the basis or ground of his theology (rather than nineteenth-century philosophy—Kant and Hegel). This is built on what Colin Gunton terms the Schleiermachian problem:

> If God is immediately perceivable by all people of all religions then you do not need Christ. If you adopt the position of Schleiermacher, who would talk of the white heat of the soul communing with God, then the mediator is not needed. Either God is transcendent and redemption, revelation, comes through Christ, or Christ is redundant and all can know God immediately (fallenness does not enter the question). Wilhelm Herrmann wanted both; and Barth again always

---

6   Ibid., Barth writing to his brother Peter, Apr. 29, 1932.
7   Hermann Kutter (1863–1931), a Swiss Lutheran theologian who was pastor from 1898 of the Neumünster in Zürich. Pietistic in background, he founded Swiss Religious Socialism and saw Christian socialism as a necessary "tool" used by God for the advancement of the kingdom of God. For Kutter's comments see, Busch, Karl Barths *Lebenslauf*, 88. Busch is quoting from an interview between the Swiss Reformed theologian Karl Barth and H. Fischer-Barnicol from 1964; see also Barth, "Nachwort," 293.
8   See Barth writing to Eduard Thurneysen, May 30, 1929, Barth, *Karl Barth-Eduard Thurneysen Briefwechsel Band II*.

being the intellectual came to realize that you could not have your cake and eat it in that respect. Either you had religion, which was this immediate relation to God, or your relation to God was mediated by Jesus Christ.[9]

Barth became progressively disillusioned with his teachers, in part because the two positions appeared incompatible. Why?—because, "their teaching just didn't rise to the ethical challenges of the day, of the twentieth century . . . how do you teach people to value the pietistic religious life when the world is tearing itself to pieces in a world war."[10] The solution did not lie in politics, neither in his theological heritage: it lay with the Christ—*Christ mediates*. Working out, explicating, this solution became his life's work. Initially this is seen in his commentary on Romans, written from 1916 on. Therefore it is really in the two years of 1915 and 1916 that Barth undergoes this re-conversion: the new starting point of "World remains world—but God is God," essentially from Kutter; the eschatology of the Blumhardts; and the rediscovery of a biblical/patristic understanding of sin from Dostoevsky, all in 1915.[11] This is then built on in 1916 by accepting the Bible as the basis for a new theology, initially in the form of his study of Romans. Much of this is with and at the instigation of his friend and theological colleague Eduard Thurneysen. This two-year period is the Rubicon in Barth's personal pilgrimage in his ten-year profoundly dynamic about-turn in his belief system, his *Wendung*, and thereafter his constant reassessment, recommitment, re-examination of his belief system, his *Retraktation*.

2. LEWIS AND BARTH: A DOCTRINAL REALIZATION— GOD IS GOD, IN CHRIST

In the course of their conversion/re-conversion we find Barth and Lewis, and also pertinently Joy Davidman, responding to a realization in the mind. It is important to remember how the mind can be influenced by the Holy Spirit in terms of dreams, visions, and thoughts, pictures formed in the imagination. This realization in the mind is of the innate existence, the axiomatic transcendence of God, as God. Lewis, following the realization that Jesus was the Christ, in 1931, in the sidecar of his brother's motorcycle, could not explain in cognitive terms why he now realized this was so. This "idea" is of no human origin: it is the influence, the pressure of the Holy Spirit working on the human mind. It is important to remember that we do not, as so many scientists and philosophers would like to believe, live in a closed universe: we are open to the suggestions and influence of good as well as evil spirits (1 John 4:1). This brings us back to the principle of a baptized imagination: the effect, the pressure, that the Holy Spirit will bring to bear if the invitation is accepted: God does not force himself onto people in the way demons and evil spirits will try to.

So, God is God, and the Holy Spirit will draw all where possible into a recognition that God is God, in Christ: for as we have seen, either you have religion as an immediate

---

9   Gunton, *The Barth Lectures*, 20.
10   Ibid, 20.
11   Brazier, *Barth and Dostoevsky*, 31–45.

relation to God, or your relation to God is mediated by Jesus Christ (bearing in mind that actual knowledge of or about Jesus Christ is contingent—limited by when and where you were born and live). For Barth this realization is initially phrased as "God is God," in the present tense, then set of over and against the world, which remains itself; thus world remains world, but God is God.[12] For Lewis this realization is tied up with a personal conversion having been a self-confessed atheist for fifteen or so years. There is, therefore, a strong element of what could be considered noeticism in each case. It has often been asserted that Lewis thinks his way to faith. If this is so, then likewise Barth took several years to think his way to a sound doctrinal basis for ministry. But, this noetic progression is at the governance and will of the Holy Spirit: neither could have arrived at this point if they had been solely reliant on their own will and mental faculties, their intellect.

i. The Lord as "I Am."

For Lewis, that "God was God"[13] was more of an acknowledgement than a realization and he qualifies this by invoking the present tense: the realization that God stood over and against him simply, sheerly, and purely as Lord: "'I am the Lord'; 'I am that I am.'"[14] For both Barth and Lewis, this is a paradoxical statement as it tells little about God except for utter transcendence, and diametric being over and against the world. Both are coming from a position redolent with nineteenth-century German philosophy— the obvious influence of Hegelian metaphysics prior to conversion/re-conversion is clear. Perhaps this is why both stress the absolute transcendence and separation, aseity and independence of God from human reality so much. This realization is more than the acknowledgement of an abstract absolute spirit over and against the world: this is a personal Lord that knows us intimately and seeks a response. As we have seen, Lewis makes the link explicitly with Exod 3:14: "God said to Moses, 'I Am that I Am.' He said further, 'Thus you shall say to the Israelites, I Am has sent me to you.'" Eberhard Busch has noted how Barth's new starting point was in many ways an explication of Exod 3:14.[15] Busch describes how Barth began to use this phrase, how he sought to deny the "god" that parts of the church revered as a no-god; further, how the position "God is God" does not exclude a christocentric position. Neither does "God is God" mean "God is everything," for if God is everything then God is not God. What is more, explains Busch, this is not a mathematical equation: "The equation, therefore, is not self-evident because it implies the critical thesis that our speaking about God does not automatically speak about God."[16] To say that "God is God" invokes the realization that what we take for God is not God: therefore God is not acknowledged as God. Even in saying thus, all we can proclaim is that we fall short in our perceiving. Our speech

---

12 Barth, "Kriegszeit und Gottesreich," 120.
13 Lewis, *Surprised by Joy*, 220.
14 Ibid., 220.
15 Busch, "God is God: The Meaning of a Controversial Formula and the Fundamental Problem of Speaking about God," 101–13.
16 Ibid., 104.

is inevitably inadequate. As Busch notes, by placing our "god" "on the throne of the world we enthrone in him only ourselves."[17] Furthermore, to say, "God is God, is so unprotected that it seems to cry out for further explanatory definition."[18]

ii. The Paradoxical Difficulties of Defining the Complement in God is God

The proposition, "God is God" is subject-complement. This is to invoke, deliberately, the language of grammar. In calling God *subject*, this is as the *nominative* in a sentence; not the *object* (*accusative*), the object that we may study, investigate. In his mature work Barth asserted that God allows us to turn God into an object of study so as to gain some understanding, but this self-objectification does not deny the primacy of God as the *eternal* subject, the eternal origin from which all that is created flows. Grammatically the complement is not less than the subject.[19] Therefore, such a construct is in essence trinitarian, or points to the trinitarian—the relationship between the Father and the Son can be seen as subject-complement: the Son is not less than the Father; the Father does not exist before the Son; the Spirit is co-eternal, it proceeds from both the Son and the Father. They are, however, different persons. This question of personhood is important. However, what is predicated requires further elucidation. The complement in "God is God" implies unknowing; the complement opens up distance and hiddenness, aseity and sovereignty. This becomes a safeguard that prevents God being merged utterly into human affairs. Therefore, for Barth and Lewis, without this safeguard we have only a noetic idol: the no-"god" of human-centered churches/religion for Barth,[20] or C. S. Lewis's "absolute spirit" from his Hegelian phase. In his commentary on Romans, Barth faces the paradox that we *must* speak about God—it is a divine imperative—but we are human and therefore *cannot* speak about God. We must replace the complement "God" in Barth's and Lewis's declaration with a qualifier but herein lies danger for whenever we declare God is *love*, God is *glorious*, is *truth*, is *goodness*, God is *immeasurable, infinite, immutable*, there is compromise—we reduce God to a concept. And we so often draw these concepts from ancient Greek philosophy not from the ancient Hebrews, from the Old Testament, where God again and again stops the Hebrew patriarchs, the prophets, the kings and tribes from creating idols and little "gods" out of an idea or thought about God: they had to suffice again and again with this blank canvas—the, "I am that I am" that God is, but we must not fill in the detail with our own ideas about God, leastwise, not until God's full self-revelation in the incarnation. For hundreds and hundreds of years the Holy Spirit restrained and prepared the ancient Hebrews until qualification of the great "I am" happened as an event in human history. Therefore, we must always keep

---

17   Ibid., 105.
18   Ibid.
19   For example, in NT Greek Θεος εϲοτιν ὁ Λογος (*The Word is God*): the position of the article indicates the subject; the complement drops the article and is placed before the verb.
20   This is best expounded by Barth in a scathing attack on religion, an address delivered in the Town Church of Aarau on Jan. 16, 1916 published in *Neue Wege X* (1916). See, Barth, "Die Gerechtigkeit Gottes," 5–17.

before us the paradoxical revelation of this hidden God, the *deus abscondus*, rooted in the name given in Exodus: "I am that I am." Therefore the qualifier can only be "Lord." This then opens up space for the self-revealing of God in Christ Jesus: "God is God" is qualified by Lordship; personhood is thereby revealed as the nature of this Lordship—this person acts in love toward humanity. But this love, forgiveness, and mercy do not deny God's Lordship. This is rooted in the first commandment: "I am the Lord your God, and you shall have no other gods before me" (Exod 20:2). Therefore, to return to Busch, "The equation 'God is God' seeks initially to avoid the equating of God and our concepts of God."[21] Only if this is no definition at all can we avoid the pitfalls of qualifying and reducing God to a human idol. Busch rightly notes how the acknowledgement/declaration is a reflection of the revelation of God's name given to Moses. In Barthian terms this is simultaneously a revealing and a concealing, a veiling and unveiling, visible yet shrouded: "I am that I am." This name is both informative and given, yet obtuse and cryptic. Therefore, any conversion must be initiated by God and on God's terms: otherness and Lordship are essential to this, as both Barth and Lewis realized. It is this realization that separates Barth and Lewis's conversions from the Hegelian metaphysics they were both moving away from. There is perhaps a way in which the Holy Spirit rehearses and prepares individuals such as Lewis, Davidman, Weil, Stein, and Barth, as it did with the ancient Hebrews: a blank canvas is how to start a great painting. Lewis and Barth in particular had to clear out all false conceptions of God and start with this basic axiom—that God was indeed God.

iii. fides quaerens intellectum

There is another factor in this realization—namely the realization that faith precedes doctrine, or more pertinently, *faith is a necessary prerequisite for understanding*. The acceptance of God as God, of the Lord as "I am," is the correct prerequisite for any degree of understanding; it is also the basis of a sound Christology. What then follows is as Anselm of Canterbury (1033–1109), churchman, theologian, and philosopher, wrote, "I do not seek to understand so that I can believe, but I believe so that I may understand; and what is more, I believe that unless I do believe I shall not understand."[22] Anselm accepted that any degree of understanding of God initially involved accepting the Lordship of God. Therefore, *fides quaerens intellectum* (faith seeking understanding): faith may seek understanding but faith can only understand if such understanding is built upon faith. Lordship, however, is a constant: thus Anselm could write that he was not trying to make his way to the height, to penetrate the light inaccessible, he knew in humility that his understanding was not equal or capable. But out of love he desires to understand a little of the truth about God. For Lewis he had to take the step of faith; then he could seek to understand, but an important factor was humility—a trait that was lacking in the pseudo-Hegelian beliefs prior to his conversion. If he had remained with his own innate theological speculation he would have got no further than the

---

21   Busch, "God is God . . .," 107.
22   Anselm of Canterbury, *The Proslogion*, 82–104. Anselm is quoting from Isa 7:9.

idea he called "absolute spirit," which merely complemented all that he had become as a person. By comparison, Barth attempts to solve the crisis of faith manifested in his preaching and beliefs through left-wing politics. However, the year of the new starting point, 1915, for Barth is characterized by a realization of the distance and hiddenness, aseity, and sovereignty of God. This is a position that in Barth is redolent with humility. Both conversion/re-conversion for Barth and Lewis bear the hallmark of what Anselm asserted. It is of no mere coincidence that both Barth and Lewis developed a profound appreciation of Anselm of Canterbury in their mature work.

iv. *The Problem of Religious Professionals*

Whilst he was teaching philosophy and literature at Oxford in the 1920s Lewis's contemporaries knew him to be a self-confessed atheist; he may have exhibited a degree of embarrassment at declaring his faith after his conversion, but he soon rose to the challenge to be acknowledged as a Christian apologist and a theologian. By comparison with Barth's *Wendung* and *Retraktation*, Lewis's conversion was relatively swift. At the time of his re-conversion Barth is being paid as a religious professional— as a Reformed Church Minister—therefore it was expected of him that he believed and subscribed to Christian doctrine. However, Barth never ceased to acknowledge the paucity and inadequacy of his liberal beliefs. Both Lewis and Barth are in effect born again! Barth's re-conversion is more veiled because of his status as a religious professional; furthermore it is masked by his socialism/crypto-Marxism. Prior to conversion Lewis developed Hegelian beliefs, whereas Barth became politicized. (Within this Barth was the more communal; Lewis was effectively an individual loner.)

v. *The Problem of Religion*

Barth would readily, as we have seen, criticize religion; it was one of the ways in which he extracted himself from the tangle of nineteenth-century liberal neo-Protestantism. But Lewis also could see this distinction between religion as a human construct, on the one hand, and *the truth of God's revelation*, on the other. Writing on the period just before he finally knelt down and reluctantly admitted that God was God, Lewis wrote about his conversion: "But if a god—we are no longer polytheists—then not a god, but God. Here and here only in all time the myth must have become fact; the Word, flesh; God, man. This is not 'a religion,' nor 'a philosophy.' It is the summing up and actuality of them all."[23] So, for Lewis, the incarnation—God becoming man—is not a philosophy, it is not a religion or even part of a religion: it is the sum of all that is philosophy and religion and theology. The Christ is the centre of all and the Christ is beyond mere religion. This does not dismiss religion, the religious impulse in humanity is important, but it does put religion in its place.

We have alluded earlier to the criticism of religion in the service of the gospel in Barth's *Wendung* and *Retraktation*—this is something that continues into Barth's

---

23   Lewis, *Surprised by Joy*, 228.

mature work, the idea that all religion is, in some instances, a form of unbelief.[24] For both Barth and Lewis, religion is defined as humanity's search for God, a search that too often results in idol worship and destructive beliefs (for example, the pseudo-religious belief systems that beguile John in Lewis's quasi-autobiographical, *The Pilgrim's Regress*). By contrast—dialectically we may say—the gospel for both of them is about God's solution to the problem of humanity. These two aims or causes—the gospel, on the one hand, human religion, on the other—are often diametric. This does not denigrate any value religion, but religious speculation must be kept in its place.[25] Lewis, ever the poet, stated this succinctly by asserting that we do not start with the mystical love of the creature for the creator—but with the mystical love of the creator for the creature.[26] So, for Lewis, God's love for us precedes our religious impulse, even if, at its finest, we direct a loving impulse to God. Dietrich Bonhoeffer, influenced by reading Barth's work, and from meeting him, encapsulated something of this in the phrase, "religionless Christianity"; whereas Lewis sought to present the gospel in the Narnia myths for children, Christ as Aslan stripped of the suffocating formality of religion. Both Lewis and Barth therefore as mature Christians could simultaneously see value in religion while realizing how it was often a barrier between God and humanity. Barth in his mature work invokes the German word/concept, *Aufhebung*: religion is simultaneously put down, dismissed, yet raised up and valued.[27]

There is therefore something of a continuity between Barth's early work and his mature work in this independence of God from religion. We have noted already how at the height of his *Wendung* and *Retraktation* Barth commented, "Don't things become dangerous only if and because God is?"[28] Lewis commented in a similar vein how "even in this present life there is danger in the very concept of religion."[29] However, Lewis the poet communicated this at its best in one of his works of Christian apologetics:

> Men are reluctant to pass over from the notion of an abstract and negative deity to the living God. I do not wonder. Here lies the deepest tap-root of Pantheism and of the objection to traditional imagery. It was hated not, at bottom, because it pictured him as man but because it pictured him as king, or even as warrior. The Pantheist's God does nothing, demands nothing. He is there if you wish for him, like a book on a shelf. He will not pursue you. There is no danger that at any time heaven and earth should flee away at his glance . . . You have had a shock like that before, in connection with smaller matters—when the line pulls at your hand, when something breathes beside you in the darkness. So here; the shock comes at the precise moment when the thrill of life is communicated to us

---

24   Barth, *Church Dogmatics*. See, Vol. I/2, §17 The Revelation of God as the Abolition of Religion, 2. Religion as Unbelief.
25   For example, there is Barth's public debate about natural theology with Brunner in the early 1930s. See: Barth, *Natural Theology*.
26   Lewis, *The Four Loves*, 120–21.
27   *Aufhebung, die*: abolition, repeal; closure or lifting; rescindment or raising-up.
28   "Wird die Sache nicht erst dann lebensgefährlich, wenn und weil Gott ist." Barth, writing to his brother Peter, Apr. 29, 1932, quoted in Busch, *Karl Barths Lebenslauf*, 103.
29   Lewis, *Letters to Malcolm: Chiefly on Prayer*, 27–28.

along the clue we have been following. It is always shocking to meet life where we thought we were alone.[30]

Lewis decries the Hegelian gods, which he derogatively referred to as pantheistic. He recounted how people are unwilling, reticent, to pass over from the notion of an abstract and negative deity to the real living God because there is safety in the idols and little gods of our own making, our own personal religion, because they do nothing, demand nothing. Such gods/idols are tame projections (as Feuerbach asserted), which may be a panacea but they insidiously enslave, ensnare, for they protect us from the truth, God's truth, the God of truth. Such an idol or god will not chase or hunt, track or seduce you. As Lewis asserts, "There is no danger that at any time heaven and earth should flee away at his glance." But then, in conclusion, wrote Lewis, it is like the shock of realizing you are not alone. Here at his most poetic, Lewis encapsulates what his conversion had been all about, a word picture that applies equally to Barth's re-conversion and to Joy Davidman's conversion:

> And therefore this is the very point at which so many draw back—I would have done so myself if I could—and proceed no further with Christianity. An "impersonal God"—well and good. A subjective God of beauty, truth and goodness, inside our own heads—better still. A formless life-force surging through us, a vast power which we can tap—best of all. But God himself, alive, pulling at the other end of the cord, perhaps approaching at an infinite speed, the hunter, king, husband—that is quite another matter. There comes a moment when the children who have been playing at burglars hush suddenly: was that a real footstep in the hall? There comes a moment when people who have been dabbling in religion ("Man's search for God!") suddenly draw back. Supposing we really found him? We never meant it to come to that! Worse still, supposing he had found us? So it is a sort of Rubicon. One goes across; or not. But if one does, there is no manner of security against miracles. One may be in for anything.[31]

3. LEWIS AND BARTH: ACCEPTANCE

i. Prevenience

Karl Barth, from the point of his profound change of heart (his *Wendung*) and constant reassessment, recommitment to the true path (like Augustine, his *Retraktaion*) placed the emphasis and the initiative, the action, on God in Christ arguing that we can do nothing for ourselves, more pertinently, we can initiate nothing for ourselves. The initiative proceeds eternally from the Father; from the moment of creation this God seeks us. Works, good works, are important for Barth, for how else do we praise God, whether in prayer or worship, in charity or in art for that matter, but our works, as is our faith, are a response to God's initiative. Therefore, both Barth and Lewis are loath to claim a human decision at the point of a conversion because this immediately

---

30   Lewis, *Miracles* (1st ed. 1947), 113.
31   Ibid., 114.

places the initiative, the emphasis, and responsibility on the human, when (because of original sin) we fail to do the good we want to do even when we think we are doing good (Romans 7). So can we even make a decision to convert, to live for God?—or does the initiative always eternally proceed from God, who hunted and courted Lewis and Davidman down the years of their, we may say, miss-spent youth? In this context both Lewis and Barth talked of God's search for humanity, not of humanity's search for God.

This initiative by God is the action of grace. Such a graceful action by God to seek the conversion of an individual is reliant upon prevenience. The concept of prevenient grace is Augustinian and invokes a form of grace that precedes all human decisions, that necessarily exists prior to and without dependence upon anything that men and women and children have done either for or against God. Because of our fallen status, corrupted through original sin, prevenient grace permits people to respond, to accept or not, God's salvation proffered through Christ's sacrifice.

ii. "I did not choose Christ: He chose me"

How did Lewis see this prevenient grace working in him? How did he see his conversion—did he see himself as special, chosen? In was in his later years, after the publication of *Surprised by Joy* that he could see how this grace worked, that it was not so much the human decision that was important, indeed he could see that the human decision was perhaps not necessarily the result of apparent free will, but the effect of this prevenient grace working in him:

> What I *think* is this. Everyone looking back on *his own* conversion must feel—and I am sure the feeling is in some sense true—"It is not I who have done this. I did not choose Christ he chose me. It is all free grace, which I have done nothing to earn." That is the Pauline account: and I am sure it is the only true account of every conversion from the inside. Very well. It then seems to us logical and natural to turn this personal experience into a general rule, "All conversions depend on God's choice."[32]

Lewis further comments that whatever Paul implies in his emphasis on the faith response, we must not reject the parable of the sheep and the goats (Matthew 25), where the emphasis is on *works*. Lewis notes how reconciling these two approaches are beyond him, and that it even stumped the Apostle Peter.[33] Lewis, therefore, warns-off if people are trying to create a universal rule between works and faith and grace. Lewis had the wisdom to know when some things are beyond human comprehension:

> The real inter-relation between God's omnipotence and Man's freedom is something we can't find out. Looking at the Sheep and the Goats every man can

32   Lewis writing to Mrs Emily McLay, Aug. 3, 1953. Lewis, *Collected Letters Vol. III*, 354.

33   Ibid., 354f. Referring to 2 Pet 3:15–17: "So also our beloved brother Paul wrote to you according to the wisdom given him, speaking of this as he does in all his letters. There are some things in them hard to understand, which the ignorant and unstable twist to their own destruction, as they do the other scriptures. You therefore, beloved, since you are forewarned, beware that you are not carried away with the error of the lawless and lose your own stability."

5. C. S. Lewis and Karl Barth II: A Doctrinal Realization—God is God, in Christ

be quite sure that every kind act he does will be accepted by Christ. Yet, equally, we all do feel sure that all the good in us comes from Grace. We have to leave it at that. I find the best plan is to take the Calvinist view of my own virtues and other people's vices: and the other view of my own vices and other people's virtues.[34]

This raises questions about election. Do *we* decide, or does *Christ* decide?

iii. "I was decided upon"

On Tuesday, May 7, 1963, C. S. Lewis was interviewed by a representative of the Billy Graham Evangelistic Association, a man by the name of Sherwood E. Wirt. Only months before his death, Lewis spoke candidly about his conversion.[35] When pressed by Wirt as to the nature of his conversion, Lewis commented that it is not enough to want simply to be rid of one's sins, what is important is "to believe in the One who saves us from our sins. Not only do we need to recognize that we are sinners; we need to believe in a Saviour who takes away sin. Matthew Arnold once wrote, 'Nor does the being hungry prove that we have bread.' Because we know we are sinners, it does not follow that we are saved." [36] In the context of what Lewis had recounted in *Surprised by Joy*, Wirt asked whether he believed that he had made a decision at the time of his conversion:

> I would not put it that way. What I wrote in *Surprised by Joy* was that before God closed in on me, I was in fact offered what now appears a moment of wholly free choice. But I feel my decision was not so important. I was the object rather than the subject in this affair. I was decided upon. I was glad afterwards at the way it came out, but at the moment what I heard was God saying, "Put down your gun and we'll talk."[37]

Lewis the intellectual continued by asserting that what he did, his response to God, was a deeply *compelled* action, and yet paradoxically it was also in many ways the *freest* action because no part of him was beyond or outside the response. For Lewis it did not appear feasible to respond in any other way. Lewis understands that it is God who initiates, that God is the eternal subject. Does a servant really have a choice whether to obey or not the request of the master? It is in the nature of a servant to obey—if a servant disobeys then she or he ceases to be a servant—it is important to remember in our democratic age of self-fulfillment and self-aggrandizement that the New Testament books generally, the parables of Jesus specifically, are written in the language of servant and master, servants who merely do what is required of them. Lewis the rebellious servant merely, simply, had to put down his gun, the symbol of all his intellectual pride and egotism. Wirt, on behalf of the Billy Graham Evangelistic

---

34 Ibid., 355. Lewis is referring to Calvin, *Institutes, Vol. 1*, Bk. II, Ch. I, §.8, 250–52.
35 Conducted in Lewis's rooms in Magdalene College, Cambridge, on Tuesday, May 7, 1963, the interview was initially published in two parts, (Sherwood E. Wirt and C. S. Lewis, "Heaven, Earth and Outer Space" and "I was Decided Upon") in the American periodical *Decision*, later to be combined posthumously. See, Lewis, "Cross Examination", 215–21.
36 Ibid., 217.
37 Ibid.

Association is pressing Lewis to own that he controlled the situation of his conversion, yet Lewis quite rightly owns that the initiative lay with God and that though the point of assent was probably the freest moment in his life he could see on reflection that he could not have done anything else, he could not have responded in any other way. Lewis answered further that it was a case of everyone coming to terms with the claims of Jesus Christ upon his or her life, if not then they would be guilty of inattention or of evasion.

This is essentially about election, not necessarily the doctrine of election that we might find in the more traditional Roman Catholic approach or for that matter the more hardline Calvinistic doctrine, where there is to be identified a specific and particular elect. This is more to do with God's election of people raised up to bear witness to what God has done for our salvation, *in Christ*. Essentially what we have here is a doctrine of election that asserts that all are elected by, through, and in Christ's death on the cross; it is then a question of response, a question of turning to be for Christ, to put down one's gun of intellectual rebellion as Lewis terms it, or the crown of sin, religion, and pride (again, cf. Rev 4:10[38]). This implies the *potential* salvation of all. This does assert the place for human participation through free will in Lewis's understanding of salvation, which can be interpreted as coming from an Arminian perspective, or more pertinently, a position that is related in many ways with that of Jacobus Arminius (1560–1609): that Christ died for *all*, not merely for a limited number of "elect." Therefore, we can do no good for ourselves, any good in us comes from grace, but we can do ourselves an evil—we can refuse God; we can hold out against God. If this is so then the judgment of God in Christ is that we lock ourselves into hell from the inside. For example, Lewis has the nineteenth-century theologian and minister George MacDonald, in *The Great Divorce*, comment that in the end there will be only two groups: those who say to God, "Thy will be done," and those to whom God freely addresses the judgment, "Thy will be done."[39] Therefore though we can do nothing within ourselves for our salvation we can respond to God, we can respond to what Christ has done for us.

4. BARTH AND LEWIS: SIMILARITIES AND DISSIMILARITIES

So were Lewis's and Barth's conversion/reconversion the same? No, of course not, because each man was a unique creation, a distinctive and exceptional person. Although for both their conversion is characterized by a renewed awareness of a realistic God they were different men, from dissimilar backgrounds both religiously and culturally, and their mature work is likewise, characterized by difference, individuality; yet their mature work does, as we have noted, have more in common as the years pass because of the drift into postmodern liberalism in the churches in the West. Likewise, although both, at a point in their intellectual development, were influenced by

---

38 "[T]he twenty-four elders fall before the one who is seated on the throne and worship the one who lives forever and ever; they cast their crowns before the throne . . ." Rev 4:10.

39 Lewis, *The Great Divorce*, 58.

5. C. S. Lewis and Karl Barth II: A Doctrinal Realization—God is God, in Christ

Figure 4: Karl Barth and C. S. Lewis in the 1950s,
charcoal and graphite drawing, P. H. Brazier

Hegelian idealism, they handled the influence and reaction against it differently. In general terms Barth's reconversion was dogmatic, intellectual; Lewis's was likewise intellectual (he thought his way to faith) but it was also mystical. There was, I believe, a mystical element to Barth's conversion, but he was loathe to acknowledge this, he was reluctant to admit an encounter with the Holy Spirit. Barth, because of his youthful theological liberalism, was never comfortable with religious experience and would perhaps even have disowned referring to the changes in his late-twenties (the year of the new starting point) as a conversion or re-conversion. By contrast Lewis was comfortable with religious experience and mysticism: if it was focused on, governed by, asserted and did not deny the *Deus dixit*—God's self-revelation in Christ. Barth was strident in his denial of the value and relevance of natural theology (i.e., philosophy, or philosophical speculation about God) while Lewis was cautiously optimistic, and valued our capacity to reason things out. There are, therefore, significant differences that cannot be ignored. However, this notwithstanding what can be identified here is the similarity in their assertion of the *aseity* (the uncreated, underived freedom of God *to be*), sovereignty, yet personal governance of the realistic God at a crucial point in their lives, a turning point, a watershed, a conversion/reconversion—a point that could be referred to by Lewis as crossing the Rubicon, by Barth as *Wendung* and *Retraktation*.

So, Joy Davidman and C. S. Lewis, and to a different degree Karl Barth, were converted to and by the God of grace, the great "I am," who is simultaneously revealed

97

and hidden. There is clearly some common ground between the conversion of Lewis and that of Barth, particularly given their enormous importance as sound orthodox creedal twentieth-century theologians. But there are clearly differences, things that are unique to each, which, as also with the case of Joy Davidman, reflect the individual that each person had become. Do these differences outweigh any common ground? There are many theologians and Christian writers who would agree that "God is God, in Christ," that God is transcendent and beyond our understanding, that God is the eternal subject who stoops in his triune presence to redeem fallen humanity. Perhaps the differences between Barth and Lewis are not as important as this foundational similarity. In cultural terms Lewis was more of a Romantic (i.e., like the English Romantic poets Wordsworth, Keats, and Coleridge, etc.). Lewis valued the human capacity of reason, to reason things out. Both Lewis and Davidman were open to God revealing of himself in the natural world, the glory of the Lord shining through nature on a sunlit winter's day (Lewis as a strident seventeen year old on Leatherhead station; Joy as a confused fourteen-year-old in Central Park, New York)—that is, the analogy of being (*analogia entis*) in many ways. Barth would have none of this for he feared the Romantic. He categorically denied the analogy of being, that is, that God could be read from the natural world with the innate abilities in our minds. For Barth God was only and uniquely revealed in Jesus Christ; that the human capacity for reason was too corrupt from the fall, from original sin, and especially in the light of the Age of Reason and the Enlightenment.

In their mature work, in addition to what we noted from a handful of Barthian zealots, students, at Oxford in 1940, Lewis and Barth shared not only a skepticism as to the value of a human response to Christ, a human decision, when we must focus on God's initiative, but both of them also shared a belief that the gospel was essentially diametric to this world. This view is well known in Barth, but consider this from Lewis: "I believe that there are many accommodating preachers, and too many practitioners in the church who are not believers. Jesus Christ did not say 'Go into all the world and tell the world that it is quite right.' The Gospel is something completely different. In fact, it is directly opposed to the world."[40] In their mature work Lewis turned to stories and mythology, Barth turned to analogy/realistic narrative: there is some common ground. Lewis exhibited no uncertainty in writing about his conversion, initially in *The Pilgrim's Regress*, later in *Surprised by Joy* and in *A Grief Observed*. Barth never did, he did not regard the changes he went through around the year 1915–16 as a personal conversion forged by the Holy Spirit, leastwise he never publicly owned to this event/encounter being a conversion/reconversion. Why not? Barth had been raised a Calvinist but feared the descent into the personal and the subjective because of what he saw had happened to German and Swiss theology in the nineteenth century (Liberalism, Schleiermacher, Hegel, Feuerbach, etc.); Lewis was an Anglican and did not fear the Romantic, or what could be misinterpreted as the subjective: does this account for these differences over publicly acknowledging a conversion? But all these

---

40   Lewis, "Cross-Examination," 220.

5. C. S. Lewis and Karl Barth II: A Doctrinal Realization—God is God, in Christ

are differences that come after conversion. Joy Davidman's conversion is smoother; she is less rebellious in some ways, than Lewis. There are therefore similarities and dissimilarities. There is a greater similarity to all at the point of conversion precisely because God is the eternal subject (i.e., God is God) and all people have to change to arrive at the point of acknowledging God's transcendence and purity, hiddenness, then if possible within the limits of knowledge, to acknowledge, to accept, that God is God in Christ (remembering that such Christian knowledge is in some ways contingent—that is, dependent of an accident of birth, geographically and temporally). How Barth and Lewis understand their conversions was different. Genuine conversions will be relatively unique for different people. We could now look at what is the nature of an authentic conversion, but we have looked enough at Lewis's conversion for now to be able to proceed to examine what exactly he wrote about Jesus Christ. His mature work as a Christian apologist will reveal more about his relationship with Christ, as will the way he handled marriage to Joy Davidman and her death from cancer.

Part Two

C. S. Lewis—

Theologian and "Mere" Christian

"It is not enough to want to get rid of one's sins.
We also need to believe in the One who saves us from our sins."

Lewis speaking a few months before his death about his conversion,
and his relationship with the church.

6

C. S. Lewis the Classical Philosopher Theologian I: Witness and Method—"Mere" Christianity

SYNOPSIS:
Lewis was a trained philosopher, a *literatus*; he taught English literature and wrote theology, more specifically, Christian apologetics. Lewis was quite specific in his aims and objectives: to restate a basic or common core, a "Mere Christianity." This was achieved through a content-driven method: as the Christ event is a moment in history, method is defined by this event. The sources for this method came from a fifth-century Catholic monk by the name of Vincentius of Lérins (*"What has been held Always, Everywhere, by Everybody"*), and a seventeenth-century Puritan called Richard Baxter (*"I am a Christian, a Mere Christian"*). Therefore, Lewis sought to promote a basic core, an undiluted essence that was at the heart of the faith endorsed by Scripture, and by this developed patristic church tradition: essentially, what has been held by all without the drift into error, primarily endorsed by Scripture, secondarily endorsed by patristic church tradition, therefore a "Mere" (from the Medieval Middle English), a sheer, pure, simple, and undiluted core of "Mere Christianity." Such a method because it is content-driven involves a particular view of history. Therefore, we may ask what Lewis's understanding of history was. And what was his doctrine of history in relationship to "modernism" and "postmodernism"? In terms of a concept of history, Lewis defines a "single unifying universal principle," whereby he rejects "modern" interpretations where they depart from this orthodox tradition in favour of "the vast mass of doctrine which I find agreed on by Scripture, the Fathers, the Middle Ages ... mere 'modernism' I reject at once." For Lewis, this "Mere" core could best be identified in the Evangelical and Anglo-Catholic wings of the Church of England of his day (despite the often acrimonious differences between them), as distinct from the "Establishment," "Modernist," or "Liberal" groupings within the Anglican Church in England.

1. C. S. LEWIS: COMMISSION

All the Christian denominations, all the churches, have to a degree been compromised since the Reformation. This applies within the ever-fragmenting nature of Protestantism as much as in the established churches such as the Church of England. Roman Catholicism is not exempt from this—it is weighed down by centuries of religion, by externality, and by religious legalism; by decisions, particularly since the Reformation, that it cannot reject as wrong for fear of compromising the authority it claims. And Protestantism? In the average American town one can plot the splits, and counter-splits, of various Baptist and Presbyterian churches by driving around and observing the new church buildings with names indicating the secession of one part of a congregation from another: this is the fragmentation of Protestantism. Martin Luther may have been right in his assertions—on justification by faith, his criticism of indulgences and corruption in the Roman Catholic Church, that the true priesthood was the priesthood of all the baptized, that salvation is through faith in Christ alone; a faith which is often to be seen as unmediated by the "church"—but he was asserting *his* belief, *his* view, which opened, to a degree, the floodgates of *individualism* when the churches, like ancient Israel, should be characterized by *community*, therefore unity. The Reformation was a heightening of church, a return to biblical roots and the theology of the patristic era, but it was also the death-knell of universality and further enhanced what to many appears to be the elevation of human-centred religion over the revelation of God. No church or denomination can now claim the high ground, pure authenticity. All Christians can do is appeal to the Lord, the common heritage of faith. In effect, this is what C. S. Lewis's commission before the Lord was—to witness to what is at the *heart* of the faith.

So, Lewis became a Christian, all his barriers—in particular his intellectual ego—were down, and the Lord came in: the Holy Spirit reformed Lewis, gave him rebirth. On a more practical level he had to get used to being known as a Christian amongst the atheistic intellectuals of the common rooms of the University of Oxford: scientists, philosophers, etc. But also he discovered there were Church of England clerics—bishops, chaplains, vicars—who outwardly were pillars of the British establishment, men looked up to by ordinary people as examples to follow, who did not believe in essential Christianity. Lewis began to realize that the ordinary man in the streets of Oxford did not know that some of these Anglican clerics did not believe in what was represented by their clerical dress, by what they did in church, and by their words when they preached.

In Britain during the first half of the twentieth-century there were several so-called lay theologians who, to a degree, dominated the theological scene, particularly before, during, and after the Second World War. Some of these people were, unsurprisingly, Anglicans, but others were Roman Catholics. C. S. Lewis and J. R. R. Tolkien were among the best known of them but also included were the novelist and playwright Dorothy L. Sayers, the writer Charles Williams, the poet T. S. Eliot, and, to a lesser extent, G. K. Chesterton (who died in 1936). This is not the same as the Inklings, which we will come to later; these people were simply writers in Britain and American who witnessed to orthodoxy. As lay theologians their work was explicitly or implicitly theological, rooted in a creedal orthodoxy that many argue the official Church of England, in some quarters, either sought to abandon or was embarrassedly uncomfortable with. C. S. Lewis, in particular, had, and still does, provide a defense of the creedal tenets of orthodox Christian faith. In the context of what we noted about how Karl Barth was impressed by Hermann Kutter's assertion[1] with regards to the

---

1   Busch, *Karl Barths Lebenslauf*, 88. Busch is quoting from an interview between the Swiss Reformed theologian Karl Barth and H. Fischer-Barnicol from 1964; see also Barth, "Nachwort," 293.

Holy Spirit using people outside the churches to embarrass the official line, we may ask, "Did the Holy Spirit fill the perceived vacuum within English theology by raising up educated men and women outside the official ranks of the clergy to witness to the creed, the traditional beliefs of the faith?" Lewis and Tolkien's work never appears to be out-of-print and there has been a large volume of studies published on their work. Furthermore their work still reaches a missionary audience most priests/ministers can only dream of.

2. C. S. LEWIS: "MERE CHRISTIANITY"

i. "What has been held Always, Everywhere, by Everybody"

Primarily for Lewis the faith is creedal. In expounding what Christianity is about, it is simple: it is summarized in the creed. However, to go further, when questions arise, there has to be a method, a principle by which to address questions, doubts, queries, to expand and expound on the faith. If C. S. Lewis has a method in his theology it is two-fold: one element is broadly Catholic, the other broadly Evangelical (more pertinently, Puritan). First, was an appeal to the basic core of the faith established in the centuries after Christ's resurrection, a basic core that was essentially complete by the mid-fifth century, but with much of the detail worked out by the mid-eighth century, this common core to the faith was endorsed by Scripture and by the developing church tradition. Writing to the editor of one of the Church of England's weekly newspapers, *The Church Times*, in 1952, Lewis commented that, "To a layman, it seems obvious that what unites the Evangelical and the Anglo-Catholic against the 'Liberal' or 'Modernist' is something very clear and momentous, namely, the fact that both are thoroughgoing supernaturalists, who believe in the Creation, the Fall, the incarnation, the Resurrection, the Second Coming, and the Four Last Things. This unites them not only with one another, but with the Christian religion as understood '*ubique et ab omnibus*.'"[2] The phrase "*ubique et ab omnibus*" ("everywhere and by everyone") is important. It is from a fifth-century monk by the name of Vincentius of Lérins who was asserting that we should hold on to that which has been believed by all. Lewis is referring to Vincentius of Lérins key work, *The Commonitory* (written in 434AD), which was written to establish a general or common rule to identify truth from falsity. Vincentius's rule is in essence succinct and simple: it is the authority of the Bible, holy Scripture. All questions of doctrine and ethics must be measured against the canon of Scripture, answered from the Bible. But this, Vincentius acknowledges, is problematic because there are so many interpretations of Scripture. The rule of Scripture is then qualified by an appeal to that which has been endorsed universally since the earliest days of the church—from antiquity as he puts it, from the earliest times. The clergy and offices of the church imbue the Bible with this authority, thus: "*quod ubique, quod*

---

2 Lewis writing to *The Church Times*, Feb. 8, 1952. Lewis, *Collected Letters Vol. III*, 164.

semper, quod ab omnibus" ("what has been held always, everywhere, by everybody").³ So what did Vincentius of Lérins write?–

> But here someone perhaps will ask, since the canon of Scripture is complete, and sufficient of itself for everything, and more than sufficient, what need is there to join with it the authority of the Church's interpretation? For this reason—because, owing to the depth of holy Scripture, all do not accept it in one and the same sense.
>
> Moreover, in the Catholic Church itself, all possible care must be taken, that we hold that faith which has been believed everywhere, always, by all. For that is truly and in the strictest sense "Catholic," which, as the name itself and the reason of the thing declare, comprehends all universally. This rule we shall observe if we follow universality, antiquity, consent. We shall follow universality if we confess that one faith to be true, which the whole Church throughout the world confesses.⁴

In other words, there is a body of doctrine/belief, essentially about Jesus of Nazareth, the Christ, which is non-negotiable, authenticated by Scripture, held in faith by all, always, everywhere (hence, universally consented to from antiquity), which was established in the centuries after Christ, in the patristic era, that emerged from the apostles as the authority of the church: this body or knowledge was revealed, cumulatively, but it constitutes a form of revelation.

ii. "I am a Christian, a Mere Christian"

The second element to Lewis's content-driven method was, like Vincentius of Lérins, to identify a common ground or core, but in this instance to name it and in so doing identify some of its characteristics. The name?—"Mere Christianity." This common core, this "Mere Christianity," is then to be used as a measure of doctrine and ethics. Walter Hooper has shown how this element was there in comments Lewis made in correspondence from the early 1930s. Clearly one of Lewis's prime concerns from the earliest days of becoming a Christian was how non-Christians viewed the confusions and contradiction within the denominations and churches, and how there must be a common ground or core to the faith, which has to be seen as more important than the differences, the contradictions. In the immediate years after his conversion Lewis wrote to a former pupil, Dom Bede Griffiths, a convert to Roman Catholicism, in the context of refusing to discuss with him the differences between the Church of England and the Roman Catholic Church, "When all is said (and truly said) about the divisions of Christendom, there remains, by God's mercy, an enormous common ground."⁵ Because of the years he spent as an apostate in an atheistic wilderness Lewis was able

---

3 Vincent of Lérins, "The Commonitory of Vincent of Lérins," 207–60. For the statement, "q*uod ubique, quod semper, quod ab omnibus,*" alluded to by C. S. Lewis, see, ch. 2, §. 6 "A General Rule for Distinguishing the Truth of the Catholic Faith from the Falsehood of Heretical Pravity," 214, see also 219 and 223. An online text can be consulted at the Christian Classics Ethereal Library: www.ccel.org.

4 Ibid., 213–14.

5 Lewis writing to Dom Bede Griffiths, Apr. 4, 1934. Lewis, *Collected Letters, Vol. II*, 136. See also comments on this correspondence in, Hooper, *C. S. Lewis A Companion and Guide*, 295–96.

to perceive an aspect to the church that perhaps those on the inside, so to speak, did not recognize; namely that there was an essential unity that was evident to a greater or lesser degree in all denominations and churches whatever their differences; and this commonality was evident especially (for Lewis) in literature (Beowulf, Chaucer, Dante, Milton, Jane Austen, etc.). This common core is the basis and ground of the BBC radio talks given during the Second World War. It is then outlined again in 1944 in the introduction he wrote to a new edition of a key patristic work by Athanasius (296-373 AD)—*de incarnatione verbi Dei* (*The incarnation of the Word of God*). This was translated by an Anglican nun with whom Lewis exchanged correspondence over many years by the name of Sr. Penelope.[6] Here it is given a name for the first time—"Mere Christianity"—a name attributed to a seventeenth-century Puritan from the Evangelical tradition, Richard Baxter (1615–91). Lewis's research and thinking on this method was interrelated with his writing of the BBC radio broadcasts; he formulated this principle while writing the talks, which then was given its name from his reading of Richard Baxter's, *Church-History of the Government of Bishops and their Councils* (1680) sometime in 1943 or early 1944. The term "Mere Christian" or "Mere Christianity" is attributed by many to Lewis, though it is important to remember that he got the term from his reading of Richard Baxter's work. At the heart of Lewis's content-driven method was the principle—from Baxter and Vincentius of Lérins— that the revealed deposit of faith contained in Scripture and the patristic tradition was more reliable than much modern theology and philosophy. Therefore anything "new" must be tested against this revealed body of tradition, the deposit of faith, which was at its most intense for Lewis in the church fathers and the Scriptures. Lewis wrote in the introduction to Sr. Penelope's translation of Athanasius, in 1944:

> A new book is still on its trial and the amateur is not in a position to judge it. It has to be tested against the great body of Christian thought down the ages, and all its hidden implications (often unsuspected by the author himself) have to be brought to light. The only safety is to have a standard of plain, central Christianity ("Mere Christianity" as Baxter called it) which puts the controversies of the moment in their proper perspective. Such a standard can be acquired only from the old books. And that brings me to yet another reason for reading them. The divisions of Christendom are undeniable and are by some of these writers most fiercely expressed. But if any man is tempted to think—as one might be tempted who read only contemporaries—that "Christianity" is a word of so many meanings that it means nothing at all, he can learn beyond all doubt, by stepping out of his own century, that this is not so. Measured against the ages "Mere Christianity" turns out to be no insipid interdenominational transparency, but something positive, self-consistent, and inexhaustible.[7]

In effect, there is a falling away in the intensity of what we say and believe about the gospel as the centuries pass. Therefore, although this core will survive, we need, as the years pass, to measure the new cultural forms the gospel may take against this

---

6   Lewis, "Introduction." In Athanasius, The Incarnation of the Word, 5–12.
7   Ibid., 6–7.

common core: because, despite all the denominational differences, there is, for Lewis, an immensely formidable unity.[8]

There is an understanding here that he developed further, and, as ever, with Lewis, it is the visual imagery that helps expand and illuminate the concept. In the preface he wrote to the French edition of *The Problem of Pain* in 1950 where he employs the language of space and relationship.[9] Referring to different churches and denominations Lewis wrote that:

> If the unity of charity and intention between us were strong enough, perhaps our doctrinal differences would be resolved sooner; without that spiritual unity, a doctrinal agreement between our religious leaders would be sterile. In the meantime, it will be apparent that the man who is most faithful in living the Christian life in his own church is spiritually the closest to the faithful believers in other confessions: because the geography of the spiritual world is very different from that of the physical world. In the latter, countries touch each other at their borders, in the former, at their centre. It is the lukewarm and indifferent in each country who are furthest from all other countries.[10]

Therefore, the greater one's integrity to the revealed truth of the gospel within one's own denomination the greater one's unity with other denominations is displayed. The more Christians try to accommodate with the world, the more Christians try to water-down the centre of the faith; the more they reduce and deny the core in an attempt to get along with other denominations (or even other religions), the more they end up as, in Lewis's words, lukewarm and indifferent.

Lewis continued in the letter sent to *The Church Times* from 1952, quoted above, "Perhaps the trouble is that as supernaturalists, whether 'Low' or 'High' Church, thus taken together, they lack a name. May I suggest 'Deep Church'; or, if that fails, in humility, Baxter's 'mere Christians'?"[11] Baxter influences Lewis not only through this idea of being merely Christian but also in his understanding of the church. It is important to remember that Baxter lived at a time when religious civil war had razed England, Roman Catholicism was effectively illegal in the country (while it still persecuted its disobedient faithful in mainland Europe), the Church of England imprisoned people who would not attend its Sunday services and there were numerous Protestant groups who would not even look at each other, let alone talk to each other. Richard Baxter wrote that,

> You know not of what Party I am of; nor what to call me; I am sorrier for you in this than for myself; if you know not, I will tell you, I am a CHRISTIAN, a MEER

---

8 Ibid., 8.
9 Lewis, "Avant-Propos a l'édition Française," 11–12.
10 "Depuis ma conversion, il m'a semblé que c'était ma tâche particulière d'apprendre au monde extérieur ce que croient tous les chrétiens. Je laisse à d'autres les controverses; c'est une matière qui regarde les théologiens avertis. Je crois que vous et moi, le laïcat, les simples soldats de la foi, servirons mieux de manière habituelle la cause de la réconciliation, non en apportant notre contribution à de tels débats, mais par nos prières et par le partage en commun de tout ce qui peut être partagé de la vie chrétienne dès muintenant." Ibid., 12.
11 Lewis writing to *The Church Times*, Feb. 8, 1952. Lewis, *Collected Letters Vol. III*, 164

6. C. S. Lewis The Classical Philosopher Theologian I: Witness And Method—"Mere" Christianity

> CHRISTIAN, of no other Religion; and the Church that I am of is the Christian Church, and hath been visible where ever the Christian Religion and Church hath been visible: But must you know of what Sect or Party I am of? I am against all Sects and dividing Parties: But if any will call *Mere Christians* by the name of a *Party*, because they take up with *mere Christianity*, *Creed*, and *Scripture*, and will not be of any dividing or contentious Sect, I am of that Party which is so against Parties: If the name CHRISTIAN be not enough, call me a CATHOLIC CHRISTIAN; not as that word signifieth an hereticating majority of Bishops, but as it signifieth one that hath no Religion, but that which by Christ and the Apostles was left to the Catholic* Church, or the body of Jesus Christ on Earth.[12]
>
> [*: Note, for Baxter, the "catholic church" is simply the universal church, not specifically the Roman Catholic Church. Also, Baxter uses the Middle English spelling of "Meer"; italicization and capitalization is as from the 1680 first edition. See figure 5 overleaf.]

Richard Baxter is writing in the context of sectarian names and labels: he refutes that the claim that Luther was ever called a Lutheran, or Bishop Laud a Laudian. Therefore, he argues that if they insist on name-calling then he is a "Mere Christian." Baxter can see that despite all the acrimonious disputes and warring between denominations there was a common core that could be seen in most Christians to a greater or lesser degree. This he appealed to and labeled "mere." Lewis identifies with this. It is important to remember that although in modern English the adjective "mere" denotes that which is solely, no more, or no better, than what is specified (as in the phrase, "mere mortals"), and the word "merest," is used to indicate the smallest or slightest (as in the phrase "the merest hint"), Lewis and Baxter are using the word with its pre-modern meaning, its Medieval Middle English meaning in the sense of "pure," "sheer," or "downright" (*meer*, from the Latin, *merus*, meaning undiluted); a meaning that continued into the early modern English of Baxter's seventeenth century, but was lost with the modern English of the nineteenth and twentieth centuries. Against "all sects and sectarian names." Baxter continues: "I am sorry that you are not content with meer Christianity . . . I would say also that (nor as Protestants) did I not take the religion called Protestant (a name which I am not fond of) to be nothing but *simple Christian*."[13] It is this Medieval use of "mere," more than the modern English meaning, that characterizes Lewis's use of and invocation of "Mere Christianity." Therefore Lewis's appeal was to a basic Christian core, to be simply "Mere" or "Merely" Christian (i.e, pure, undiluted), and that this characterized his most popular book based on the BBC radio broadcasts from the Second World War, published in 1952, entitled *Mere Christianity*: "The reader should be warned that I offer no help to anyone who is hesitating between two Christian 'denominations.' You will not learn from me whether you ought to become

---

12 Baxter, "What History is Credible, and What Not." Introductory essay in, *Church-History of the Government of Bishops and their Councils*, xvii. Note, the forty-four pages of preliminaries—title, preface, introductory essay, and detailed contents—are not numbered; therefore counting from the title page, the reference quoted in the 1680 edition is on p. xvii. See figure 5 overleaf. All subsequent references are counted from the title page as p. i.

13 Ibid., xvii.

an Anglican, a Methodist, a Presbyterian, or a Roman Catholic. This omission is intentional (even in the list I have just given the order is alphabetical)."[14] Lewis's aim, as always, was to present, in his words, "an agreed, or common, or central, or 'mere' Christianity." [15] Lewis wrote to explain the simply basic, the merely, of the faith to unbelievers because the more you delved into the detail, the more denominationalism reared its ugly head: divisions, groupings, mine and thine. Church history had shown Lewis that disputations over obscure points would not help to convert the unbeliever. This in some ways was the aim of the writers of the three Synoptic Gospels (Matthew, Mark, and Luke), and Paul in his epistles: to convince people of the veracity of what had happened in Bethlehem, on Calvary, and in the tomb.

> I hope no reader will suppose that "mere" Christianity is here put forward as an alternative to the creeds of the existing communions—as if a man could adopt it in preference to Congregationalism or Greek Orthodoxy or anything else. It is more like a hall out of which doors open into several rooms. If I can bring anyone into that hall I shall have done what I attempted. But it is in the rooms, not in the hall, that there are fires and chairs and meals.[16]

So, Lewis's writing about Jesus Christ attempts to transcend the differences between denominations while simultaneously appealing back to the early church, the early tradition, and the emerging deposit of faith, endorsed by Scripture, before the fragmentation of the church into denominations and groupings, or the corruption of the Roman Catholic Church in the late Middle Ages which led in part to the Reformation, or the sectarianism of the Protestant and Reformed churches. This simple undiluted "mere," centered on the God-man Jesus Christ, this pure, sheer, core to the faith, *is not* the Church of England, it *is not* the Evangelical churches, it *is not* Rome, *neither is* it the Orthodox churches, the Presbyterian, and so on. This basic core, this "Mere Christianity," should lead individuals into the various churches and denominations, but however different the denominations are this creedal, biblical, patristic core should be present to a greater or lesser degree. If not, then questions have to be raised as to whether such a church/denomination is Christian. There is, therefore, a unity that transcends church boundaries amongst those whose lives and beliefs echo this mere core.

3. CONTENT METHOD IN C. S. LEWIS'S THEOLOGY

i. An Appeal

C. S. Lewis's writings were content-driven: as the Christ event is an occurrence, an incident in history, the method is primarily defined by this event. This event leads into church history, the content issuing from Jesus' request to his followers to remember

---

14 Lewis, *Mere Christianity*, vi.
15 Ibid., viii.
16 Ibid., xi.

would not you vouchsafe to name that Heresie which I have owned: I have given you large Field-room, in near 80 Books; and few men can so write, as that a willing man may not find some words which he is able to call Heresie: A little learning, wit, or honesty, will serve for such an hereticating presumption. 2. I never heard that *Arminius* was called an *Arminian*, nor *Luther* a *Lutheran*, nor Bishop *Laud* a *Laudian*; but if you be upon the knack of making Names, you best know your ends, and best know how to fit them to it. 3. But seriously, do you not know my Judgment? will not about 80 Books inform you? how then can I help it? 4. No, but you know not what Party I am of, nor what to call me; I am sorrier for you in this than for my self; if you know not, I will tell you, I am a CHRISTIAN, a MEER CHRISTIAN, of no other Religion; and the Church that I am of is the Christian Church, and hath been visible where ever the Christian Religion and Church hath been visible: But must you know what Sect or Party I am of? I am against all Sects and dividing Parties: But if any will call *Meer Christians* by the name of a *Party*, because they take up with *meer Christianity*, *Creed*, and *Scripture*, and will not be of any dividing or contentious Sect, I am of that Party which is so against Parties: If the Name CHRISTIAN be not enough, call me a CATHOLICK CHRISTIAN; not as that word signifieth an hereticating majority of Bishops, but as it signifieth one that hath no Religion, but that which by Christ and the Apostles was left to the Catholick Church, or the Body of Jesus Christ on Earth.

And now Sir, I am sorry that you are not content with meer Christianity, and to be a Member of the Catholick Church, and hold the Communion of Saints, but that you must needs also be of a Sect, and have some other Name: And how shall I know that your Sect is better than another? Were not the Papists Sectaries and Schismaticks, damning most of Christs Body on Earth, for not being subject to their Pope, I should not be so much against them. I find promises of Salvation in Scriptures to Believers, that is, Christians as such (if such sincerely,) but none of the salvation of men as *Papists, Diocesans, Grecians, Nestorians, Eutychians, &c.* I would say also [*nor as Protestants*] did I not take the Religion called *Protestant* (a Name which I am not fond of) to be nothing but *simple Christianity*, with opposition to Popery, and other such corruption. And now you know your own designs, your tongue is your own, and who can controul you, whatever you will call us; but I, and such others, call our selves MEER CHRISTIANS, or CATHOLICK CHRISTIANS, against all Sects and Sectarian names, and haters both of true *Heresie, Schisme*, and *proud, unrighteous, hereticating* and *Anathematizing*. Psal. 4. *O ye sons of men, how long will ye turn my glory into shame? how long will ye love vanity, and seek after lying? But know that the Lord hath set apart him that is godly for himself:* Psal. 12. 1, 2, 3, 4, 5. *Help Lord, for the godly man ceaseth; for the faithful fail from among the children of men: They speak vanity every one with his Neighbour, &c.* See the rest.

b

I will

Figure 5: Page xvii from "What History is Credible, and What Not." The introductory essay, in Richard Baxter's *Church-history of the Government of Bishops and their Councils*, 1680

him.[17] Therefore Lewis's method is to identify a body of knowledge and understanding that exists outside of human consciousness; this body of knowledge and understanding has not been invented by people, it is not the result of human culture, it does not vary within different societies, different ethical systems, and different religions, though there may be local and cultural variations in response to this body of knowledge and understanding (related to emphasis, or church practices, for example). This body of knowledge and understanding relates to what God has done for our salvation in Christ. The church, via its clergy and theologians in the centuries after Christ's resurrection, began to perceive and understand this. This led to the formulation of the creeds, which were essentially succinct summaries to be used by the faithful as a declaration of this core, as a profession of faith by those newly baptized, and in the context of worship. To go beyond this, to expand and expound on the creeds, is then to codify this understanding into a body of knowledge—propositions, doctrine. Primarily this body of knowledge and understanding is attested to by Scripture, it is endorsed by Scripture, it is about God's dealings with humanity culminating in the incarnation, crucifixion, and resurrection. Secondarily, when there are questions that cannot be directly answered by appeal to Scripture, this developing body of doctrine is secondarily endorsed by appeal to the developed patristic tradition—the early church. Therefore, there is identified a "Mere/*merus*," a sheer, pure, simple, undiluted core, a basic core of "Mere Christianity," that is at the heart of the Christian faith and provides the foundation for theological apologetics: Scripture, backed-up by the patristic tradition, identifies a "Mere" core, pure and undiluted. This underpins all of Lewis's work as a theologian.

ii. A Patristic Appeal

In some ways Lewis is not alone in his content-driven method, in his appeal to the roots of the church in the centuries after Christ's resurrection. This was in part what the Reformation was about: a return to the Bible and the church fathers. In the more extreme cases this led to a rallying cry of *sola scriptura* in many Protestant and Evangelical churches, ignoring the paradox that Scripture was the result of evolving church tradition (the books of the New Testament were composed in the decades after the resurrection, and the canon of Scripture was not fixed until the fourth century). Lewis knew that you could not exclude church tradition; even if it erred, it has an innate ability to right itself, to correct any drift into error. Lewis, like so many individuals in the nineteenth and twentieth centuries, was given by God a sort of prophetic role, characterized by a mistrust toward a Christendom that had become churches, become denominations. He sought to focus on the reminders, still preserved intact, as he believed, of the early history of Christendom, free from compromise, particularly when it declared the basic tenets of the creeds. Lewis could therefore identify a stream of truth centered on the God-man, Jesus Christ, that flowed from the early church. In reading theology the appeal is then to read from this patristic era

---

17   Matt 26.26–28; Mark 14.22–25; Luke 22.14–19; See also 1 Cor 11.24.

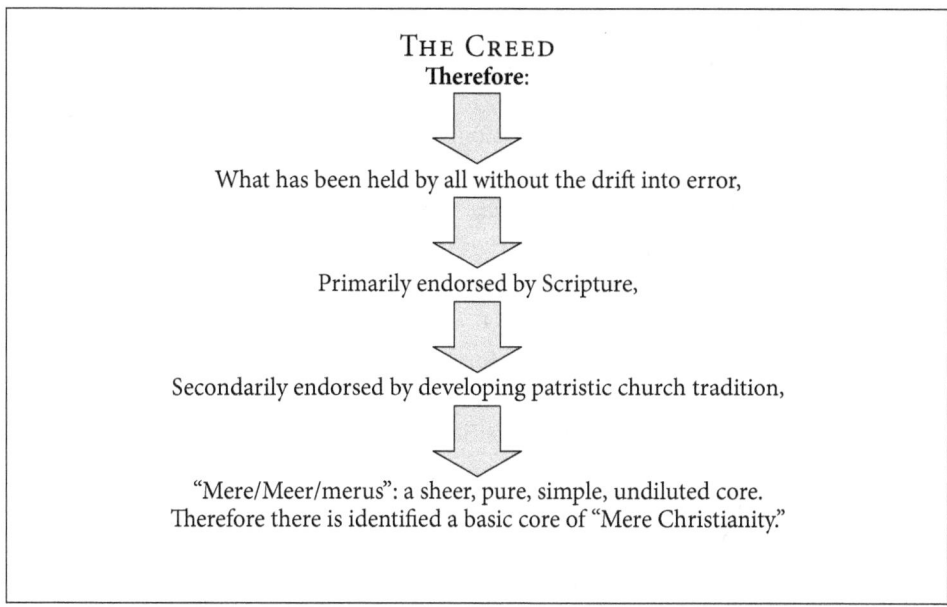

Figure 6: Content-Driven Method in C. S. Lewis's Theology

and into medieval scholasticism (for example, for Lewis, Thomas Aquinas). There is also value, for Lewis, in sixteenth- and seventeenth-century works, evidenced by his quoting the Puritan Richard Baxter, provided such works are rooted in and reflect the basic core of beliefs from the patristic era. Lewis did not really see much of value in the thinking of theologians and philosophers from the eighteenth and nineteenth centuries, that is, Age of Reason or the Enlightenment.

Lewis laid out his theological masters and the education he received from them, in a letter in response to an enquiry from a reader, in 1958.[18] When the reader, by the name of Corbin Scott Carnell, questions the complexity of the debts Lewis owes to modern theologians, he comments that his debt to the "moderns" is hardly anything at all, that he knows not the "moderns" and what they stand for, that Christianity reached him initially through the literature he taught in the 1920s (Dante, Spenser, Milton, George Herbert, and so forth). After his conversion he drank in Augustine, Richard Hooker, Traherne, and the work of many Medieval mystics; and the great patristic theologians. He admits his ignorance on many modern theologians and philosophers, with the exception of two orthodox and traditional Protestant-Reformed works: Anders Nygren's *Agape and Eros* (on the nature of Christian love) and Gustaf Aulén's seminal work on Christ's sacrifice, *Christus Victor*:[19] Both these works were not

---

18 Lewis writing to Corbin Scott Carnell, Oct. 13, 1958. Lewis, *Collected Letters, Vol. III*, 978–80
19 Ibid, 980. Lewis is referring to, Nygren, *Agape and Eros*, and, Aulén, *Christus Victor*.

"modern," but drew heavily on the patristic tradition and on the Reformation tradition from the sixteenth and seventeenth centuries.

Lewis was probably better read in many of the early church fathers, the patristic heritage of the church, than many theologians today. Much of this reading was in support of his professional work in Medieval and Renaissance literature, as well as his apologetics, though, as Mark Edwards has demonstrated, he did not spend as much time studying the fathers as many today would have expected of him: "[H]e appears to have devoted little time in his mature years to the perusal of the Fathers . . . [T]his is not to deny that he advanced the study of early Christian authors who are neglected in most histories of the 'development of doctrine'; it is not to deny that the contours of orthodoxy were more apparent to him than to many of the critics . . ."[20] In effect, Lewis pointed his readers to the early church fathers in the context of Vincentius of Lérins' comment that here you will find the measure of your faith; if you are puzzled and confused by contradictory doctrine and ethics, by "Modern" and "Liberal" tendencies, look to what was held always, by all. However, Lewis was no patristics scholar.

iii. History, Modernism and Postmodernism

Christianity—orthodox Christianity—is an historical religion because at the heart of the gospel is *an event*, an historical event: God breaking into this world in the form of the incarnation with all that flows from that event. Therefore any one writing theology must be working with some understanding of how history operates. Lewis was highly critical of "modernism," if it is to be seen as the culmination of the Age of Reason and the Enlightenment. As such it was essentially a series of intellectual and cultural movements that developed towards the end of the nineteenth century in Western Europe, rooted in the power of humanity to improve and reshape the world through science and technology, to question constantly every aspect of human existence. Religion, from this perspective, was often seen as preventing progress. Modernism asserted a rational view of history, which in effect, repudiated the idea of the incarnation, but then modernism also pushed God more and more into a corner, reducing and containing and eventually denying. Modernism was essentially built on the premise that things could only get better, that science and technology could solve all our problems. However, since the 1960s skepticism has replaced this optimism, to a large degree, though intellectually the roots of this disillusionment lay in the ruins of Europe at the end of the Second World War. Therefore, we now live in an age of so-called "postmodernism," in which belief systems and values are perceived to be self-contained and relative. Therefore, there are now no certainties, except for the certainty that there are no absolutes. There is now no grand narrative, no over-arching story that unites (Western) humanity and moves it in a particular direction

---

20 Edwards, "C. S. Lewis and Early Christian Literature." 23–24. Edwards detailed analysis focuses, in effect, on the lack of footnote referenced evidence in Lewis's mature Christian writings to patristic sources, though as we will see in chapter 12, Lewis was more concerned with Christlikeness and "Mere" Christology in his mature writings than an historical study and justification of the fathers. The fathers were a ground, a foundational ground, out of which sound doctrine could be written today.

(unless the fixation with a self-indulgent, consumerist, sex-driven lifestyle can be considered a worldview). Religion, of course, contradicts this, especially the gospel. However, this is now marginalized because, amongst other reasons, British society must accommodate several different religious narratives. In addition, there is not even consistent agreement over a definition of "postmodernism," only the relativity of individual belief systems that seek to insulate themselves against the contradictions evident when compared with other people, other groups, other belief systems. Postmodernism is then a cultural and intellectual (and inevitably religious) condition that lacks any clear and consistent principle or belief, and in itself is characterized by ambiguity and complex contradictions. If there is an organizing principle it is probably the contradictory certainly that diversity is absolute, that meaning is either elusive or non-existent: truth is then castigated as a social construct whereby humanity is the measure of all, and in the end that measure is meaningless. And amongst intellectuals the act of speaking and writing gets lost in semantic analysis and linguistic nihilism; critics end up not speaking or writing because the act of speaking and writing is considered to be culturally conditioned and oppressive, or any pronouncements are hedged around with ambiguity, relativity, and qualification so as to remove any sting from what is said or written.

Lewis repudiated modernism; however, he died before the full development of postmodernism as a (pseudo) worldview from the end of the 1960s. Lewis saw the incarnation as the central event of humanity: God became man. By Christianity he measured all things: "I believe in Christianity as I believe that the Sun has risen, not only because I see it, but because by it I see everything else."[21] Therefore Lewis saw Christianity as the worldview, a *Weltanschauung*. This "mere" core was the meta-narrative (an all-encompassing story, an overarching great narrative) above all competing meta-narratives, not because it was easy, fashionable, or a convenient and complimentary lifestyle, but because it was *true*. This *Weltbild* cohered with the situation humanity was in, and related to a greater or lesser degree to all other religions and philosophies, cultures, and peoples, throughout time, and, as such, contradicts humanity's discredited meta-narratives—the towers of Babel such as Marxism or the Enlightenment, or secular liberal humanism and postmodernism. Therefore, for Lewis a consistent thread could be traced through history: this was God's dealings with humanity, to save humanity from itself. This history, in many ways salvation history, is recounted in great detail in the Old Testament, culminating in the events of the Gospel narratives, then flowing forward through the events recounted in the book of the Acts of the Apostles, into the early church, and the patristic era. Postmodernism would want to see this history as subjective and relative to other religious histories. Not so, would have been Lewis's response. The Christ event does not necessarily deny other religions but it is pre-eminent, the culmination of God's dealings with humanity.

Richard Baxter's work, from which Lewis derived the concept of "Mere Christianity," was a work of church history, and he, like Lewis, realized the importance

---

21   Lewis, "Is Theology Poetry." 150–65. This concept was also used in *Mere Christianity*, and is derived essentially from the writings of Augustine and Anselm, but also G. K. Chesterton.

of identifying what was and what was not part of this salvation history. We must for the sake of Christ discriminate on questions of belief and ethics, but particularly on the question of what is, or is not, credible history, to use Baxter's term, in relation to the Christ event. Baxter wrote:

> But it is not all history that is needful or useful to us: there are many things done which we are not concerned to be acquainted with. But the history of the Church, of the propagation of the Christian faith, and what the doctrine was that was then received, and how it was practised, promoted and defended, and how it was corrupted, invaded and persecuted, is of so great use to posterity, that next to the Scripture and the illuminations of God's Spirit, I remember nothing more needful to be known.[22]

This is remarkably similar to Vincentius of Lérins balance between Scripture and the developing patristic church tradition. Baxter saw this as very important because, he argues, "Meer Christians" should know about the past, about church history, as they need to be "truly acquainted how things have gone in the Church from the beginning,"[23] thus the records and documents from the patristic period are of immense importance. This was also so for Lewis: history was not relative, our perception may to a degree be relative to our personal interests, but there was a thread—as Vincentius of Lérins had identified—of truth, of the emergence of sound beliefs about Christ, which was of importance.

iv. A Unifying Universal Principle

Lewis set out the principle underlying this two-fold content-driven method in a letter to an American Episcopalian, Hart Lyman Stebbins, who had written to him asking what would be "the arguments which throw the decision to the Anglican and against the Roman Catholic Church?"[24] Lewis's reply uses an image, a metaphor, almost a parable, inevitably Platonic. He writes that if he sought the fullest and truest interpretation of what Plato taught then he would be confident in accepting the interpretation which is common to all those who either claim to be Platonists or subscribe to his teaching, those who agree on what he took to be true Platonism: "Any purely modern views which claim to have discovered for the first time what Plato meant, and say that everyone from Aristotle down has misunderstood him, I reject out of hand."[25] Lewis then tackles the balance between the churches of his day, of the denominations in the twentieth century. He would also reject what purported to be an ancient Platonic Society that still existed in Athens and claimed to be the exclusive trustees of Plato's meaning (i.e., perhaps comparable to the Roman Catholic Church?):

> I should approach them with great respect. But if I found that their teaching in many ways was curiously unlike his actual text and unlike what ancient

---

22   Baxter, "Preface." In, *Church-History*, iv.
23   Ibid., vi–vii.
24   Lewis to H. Lyman Stebbins, May 8, 1945. Lewis, *Collected Letters Vol. II*, 645–47. The essential substance of Stebbins letter is presented on p. 645 at the beginning of the reply Lewis sent to him.
25   Ibid., 645–46.

6. C. S. Lewis The Classical Philosopher Theologian I: Witness And Method—"Mere" Christianity

interpreters said, and in some cases could not be traced back to within 1000 years of his time, I should reject these exclusive claims: while still ready, of course, to take any particular thing they taught on its merits. I do the same with Christianity. What is most certain is the vast mass of doctrine which I find agreed on by Scripture, the Fathers, the Middle Ages, modern RCs, modern Protestants. That is true "catholic" doctrine. Mere "modernism" I reject at once.[26]

Therefore, we have Lewis's content-driven method succinctly stated in one principle: continuity and agreement of a core of belief, agreed on by Scripture, the fathers, the Middle Ages, modern Roman Catholics, and Protestants, and tracing its heritage back to the apostles: this is true "catholic" for him. This is a universal principle, where universalism lies beyond any particularly denomination. Because Lewis's reply was in the context of Stebbins enquiry of the relationship between the Anglican and the Roman Catholic churches (Stebbins was to be received into the Roman Catholic church a year later) he did continue to explain how he rejected Roman Catholicism where it differed and dissented from this universal tradition and in particularly from apostolic Christianity, citing examples relating to Mary and Mariology, the papal principle, and the doctrine of transubstantiation, in relation to—importantly—the New Testament. It is important to remember that Lewis is writing in the context of pre-Vatican II Rome. For example, "In a word, the whole set-up of modern Romanism seems to me to be as much a provincial or local variation from the central, ancient tradition as any particular Protestant sect is. I must therefore reject their claim: though this does not mean rejecting particular things they say."[27] This is not simply an anti-Roman polemic; Lewis equally applied this universal principle to Protestantism—writing to his life-long friend Arthur Greeves there are detailed criticisms of the Puritan and more extreme Protestantism evident in their Ulster heritage, where such Puritanism departs from this universal principle and becomes provincial, parochial, and local, a variation from this central and mere, simple, and sheer core.[28] We may ask, importantly, what is the source of this unifying universal principle? Christ: the universal Christ from all eternity to all eternity, the second person of the Trinity, co-eternal with the Father and the Holy Spirit, the Word of God, who through and in the Spirit will lead us into all truth, who is the way the truth and the life: "When the Spirit of truth comes, he will guide you into all the truth; for he will not speak on his own, but will speak whatever he hears, and he will declare to you the things that are to come" (John 16:13; cf. John 8:32; 14:16).

---

26 Ibid., 646.
27 Ibid., 646–47.
28 See, Lewis to Arthur Greeves Dec. 6, 1931. Lewis, *Collected Letters*, Vol. II, 22–25.

7

C. S. Lewis the Classical Philosopher Theologian II: *praeparatio evangelica*—A Catholic-Evangelical

SYNOPSIS:
In identifying a "mere" core within the Catholic and Evangelical wings of the Church of England of his day Lewis effectively repudiated much that characterized the Anglican establishment, or "modern" and "liberal" centre. Lewis's adversaries were in effect theological Liberalism and religious atheism—terms which need to be very carefully defined as there are a myriad of subtle degrees of individual variation between "Liberal religious atheists" (such individuals can only be defined as such if they have claimed to be atheistic). Therefore, for Lewis, a priest who claims in print to disbelieve everything represented by his office and ministry is, *"a form of prostitution."* Lewis, drawing on his two-fold method, was, in effect, a Catholic Evangelical. What did Lewis mean by invoking such a description? He referred to his writings as *praeparatio evangelica* (preparation for evangelization) for he saw himself as preparing his readers for the gospel, not necessarily converting them. How did Lewis see his role—public and private—in bearing witness to Christ? How did he react against the modern world, for the sake of Christ? How did he come to construct the picture of Christ that we read from his numerous theological writings, a picture at the heart of his apologetics, which revealed the logicality of the faith in a basic transdenominational, pure but elusive, core at the heart of the faith? How do we assess C. S. Lewis—when writing on Christ—in relation to the history of the church? What is Lewis's place in the church as a Christian apologist? We can conclude that Lewis was a classical philosopher theologian in the mould of patristic theologians like Justin Martyr (c.100–165 AD) and Origen (c.185–c.254 AD). Lewis was specifically, a biblical patristic apologist. Is Lewis's "mere Christianity" no more than "Mere Lewisianity"? Some critics have asserted this; however, at the heart of Lewis's "mere" core is, *"the one who saves us from our sins."* Lewis's "mere," despite some personally favored minor details, can be seen as a defense of the truths of Christianity and not his own personal religion. How did Lewis achieve this? How did he avoid presenting "Mere Lewisianity"? His appeal is to the truth of the gospel as existing in eternity: we get glimpses, intimations, we can see shadows of the truth, but the real truth, the full revelation, is beyond us: it is *intelligible* but not completely *perceivable*. Lewis saw himself as an ordinary layman in the Church of England, but in relation to some of its clergy he commented that, "Missionary to the priests of one's own church is an embarrassing rôle." Therefore Lewis asserted Platonically that he walked *"in mirabilibus supra me"* (wonders too far beyond me, things too great for me), but this was in relation not just before the "professionals," but also before God.

C. S. LEWIS—REVELATION, CONVERSION, AND APOLOGETICS

1. INTRODUCTION: LEWIS'S ADVERSARY—RELIGIOUS ATHEISM

If, for Lewis, this "mere" core could best be identified in the Evangelical and Anglo-Catholic wings of the Church of England of his day, as distinct from the "Establishment," "Modernist" or "Liberal" groupings within the Anglican church; if these "fringe" groupings bore witness to this "mere" core, this sheer undiluted essence to the faith, as distinct from the centre ground that chose to water-down the faith, then in this context Lewis's adversaries can be identified as theological Liberals and religious atheists. C. S. Lewis was highly critical of theological Liberalism in the Church of England. Lewis uses the term "modernism"/"modernist" very much in the same context as his use of "Liberalism"; if such modernism argued that Jesus was an ordinary human being, that all our ideas about God were wrong, that since the eighteenth century traditional dogma, along with the creeds and Scripture, had, to a degree, been questioned and repudiated, then such progress in human understanding appeared to relegate God's revelation. The spirit of the Age of Reason and the Enlightenment was all-pervasive and had watered down Christianity, which for Lewis, had de-Christianized the church.

It is essentially religious atheism that is represented by the terms "Modern" or "Liberal" for Lewis. Religious atheism in the Church of England was Lewis's adversary, his opponent, which he did not cease to repudiate at every opportunity. What is religious atheism? Religious atheists are essentially people who are, often, closeted self-confessed atheists (though many are now openly anti-theistic), but who like to be religious. They may deny the divinity of Jesus Christ while conceiving of "god" as a monist singularity, but most often deny the supernatural, deny God, and repudiate the creed. There are a myriad of subtle degrees of individual variation between religious atheists, but what they have in common is that they *openly*, often *academically*, claim to be atheistic and yet continue to be religious. For Lewis these men were often priests and bishops in the Church of England.

Lewis therefore felt compelled to assert this common core in the Church of England of his day. Lewis was highly critical of what he termed the fashionable non-miraculous version of Christianity: a situation that has only worsened in the intervening years. For Lewis, theological Liberalism was worse than ethical liberalism—in other words, what we believe (or more pertinently do not believe) is worse than how we behave, even if that behavior is in a manner which does not strictly fit in with biblical ethics. Ethical liberalism is forgivable; doctrinal liberalism (beliefs) is not because it denies and repudiates the source of any forgiveness. Lewis wrote, "A great deal of what is being published by writers in the religious tradition is a scandal and is actually turning people away from the church. The liberal writers who are continually accommodating and whittling down the truth of the Gospel are responsible. I cannot understand how a man can appear in print claiming to disbelieve everything that he presupposes when he puts on the surplice. I feel it is a form of prostitution."[1] And today? Recently a senior cleric on retirement lamented that the Church of England was fast becoming a

---

1   Lewis, "Cross-Examination," 216.

religious society of amiable agnostics. Indeed the phrase "amiable agnostics" was used by Lewis in *Surprised by Joy* in his criticism of the broad religionists of his day![2]

2. C. S. LEWIS: A CATHOLIC EVANGELICAL?

i. *Theologian and Missionary*

This two-fold content-driven method characterized all of Lewis's theological and apologetic writings: Baxter's appeal to commonly held beliefs—this "mere Christianity"; and Vincentius of Lérins appeal to that which had been held by all—endorsed by Scripture and the developing church tradition in the patristic era. Lewis was traditional and orthodox, sacramental and biblical, in his theology. His writings expound a strong sacramental theology—he went to confession on a weekly basis, and he did have a relatively "high" view of the sacraments, especially the Eucharist: the sacraments were to be seen as the vehicle through which the new life of Christ is transmitted to us. This was from and in keeping with the Roman Catholic tradition. In addition, he believed strongly, logically, in the existence of purgatory after death—more pertinently purgation in the sense that people would still in a limited sense have the opportunity to change after death, move closer towards Christ and be sanctified. However, Lewis also had an understanding of the immediacy of relationship characterized by a personal encounter with Christ, a direct experience of conversion, an understanding more readily associated with the Evangelical and Free Church traditions; encounters that are in many ways independent of the churches, or church authority and control. It is important to remember that there was nothing Lewis believed as a Catholic-Evangelical in relation to Jesus Christ that departed from or contradicted the beliefs that were held by the early church and the theologians and churchmen of the patristic era. The one exception to this is his Mariology—his understanding of the Virgin Mary, the mother of Jesus—which is not as full as that accepted by many of the patristic theologians (however, Lewis did exclude much Roman Catholic Marian devotion, characteristic of recent centuries).

Ironically, as we shall see, Lewis's understanding of the church as the body of Christ reflected that of the great fifth-century Catholic theologian Augustine, who is attributed with first identifying and drawing the distinction between the visible church we see on earth and the invisible church of the redeemed and saved, the elected and chosen, who are truly at one with Christ and are at peace with one another. There is something of a dialectic here for one could not exist without the other, the invisible without the visible, yet such a view of the body of Christ, the church, does show that the true church lies outside of our perception and is not bedeviled by schism, sin, infighting, and evil. The broken and flawed churches we see will be absorbed, subsumed, into the invisible church—the community of the saved and elect in Christ—at the end of time. This distinction between the visible and the invisible church was also

---

2   "Amiable agnostics will talk cheerfully about 'man's search for God.' To me, as I then was, they might as well have talked about the mouse's search for the cat." Lewis, *Surprised by Joy*, 220.

understood by the Reformers in the sixteenth and seventeenth centuries. Indeed, it is there in C. S. Lewis's quotation from the Puritan Richard Baxter. For Baxter the true invisible church within the fragmented visible churches of his day was characterized by those who were "merely" Christian—those that "hath been visible where ever the Christian Religion and church hath been visible."[3] That Lewis could see this distinction between the visible and invisible church—shared by the Catholic Augustine and the Puritan Baxter—is to his credit and goes some way to explaining why he refused to get embroiled in the wranglings and squabbles between the churches of his day, always remembering that as an Ulsterman he had known first hand of the infighting between Catholics and Protestants.

Although it is easy to identify elements in Lewis's theology generally, his understanding of Jesus Christ specifically, that are in keeping with a Roman Catholic position and then also elements that are in keeping with an Evangelical (i.e., Protestant, Reformed, Puritan, etc.) position, Lewis was not really either. Lewis looked to see something of what was at the heart of the faith that transcended the party politics and entrenched dogma of various churches: hence his appeal to Catholics and Evangelicals that they should see themselves as merely Christian, subscribing to "mere Christianity," as exponents of "deep church" because of the seriousness of their faith, and their appeal to the deposit of faith and tradition that went back to the early church and the patristic era, a tradition validated and endorsed by holy Scripture. In an interview only months before his death, Lewis commented, "The great thing is to be found at one's post as a child of God, living each day as though it were our last, but planning as though our world might last a hundred years."[4]

ii. *"praeparatio evangelica"*

C. S. Lewis was therefore essentially a missionary: he wanted to bring people to the faith, to the point of conversion, irrespective of whether they claimed to be religious or not, went to church or not. Lewis's aim was also to enable people to find that their faith had become real (whether they were Roman Catholic or Anglican, Methodist or Presbyterian), that is, to see and to know God in and through Christ because what happened two thousand years ago was true. Lewis's aim was to bring about an encounter of the reader with Jesus Christ.[5] Therefore, when writing to Sr. Penelope on another occasion he described himself, his work, as a preparation for evangelism: "Mine are *praeparatio evangelica* rather than *evangelium*, an attempt to convince people that there is a moral law, that we disobey it, and that the existence of a Lawgiver is at least very probable and also (unless you add the Christian doctrine of the Atonement) that this imparts despair rather than comfort."[6] Therefore Lewis saw himself as preparing

---

3 Baxter, "What History is Credible, and What Not," xv.
4 Lewis, "Cross-Examination," 221.
5 Ibid., 218.
6 Lewis writing to Sister Penelope CSMV, May 15, 1941. Lewis, *Collected Letters Vol. II*, 484–85. See also, Lewis, "Preface to the Third Edition," in *The Pilgrim's Regress*, xvii. See also, Heck, "Praeparatio Evangelica," 235–57.

his readers for the gospel, not necessarily converting them. Lewis saw his role, public and private, in bearing witness to Christ. He was in effect a *pre*-evangelist: for Christ's sake. Lewis probably discovered the phrase *praeparatio evangelica* from the early church historian, Eusebius of Caesarea (c.263–c.339 AD), who used it for the title of his work, *Praeparatio Evangelica* (*Preparation for the Gospel*), written to demonstrate the veracity of the gospel over and against (Roman) pagan religion. It is an apologetic defense of Christianity in the face of Greek and Roman arguments that the Christian faith was irrational and impious. Eusebius uses clear, systematic, and sustained arguments.[7] Lewis did not just borrow, in all probability, the phrase from Eusebius; Lewis was working in the mould of the early church fathers, steeped in Greek and Roman philosophy (but working against it when necessary). Like Eusebius, Lewis was using clear, systematic, and sustained arguments, a technique borrowed in some ways from the Greek philosophers, and like Eusebius he was asserting the veracity of the gospel over and against the neo-pagan religions of his day.

Lewis was essentially a private man; he described himself as inherently anti-ecclesiastical[8] and can be considered something of a loner. This, in some ways, explains the self-perception that he was not necessarily a missionary but one who, like John the Baptist, prepared the way and pointed people to Christ. In the film *Shadowlands* (1993) about Lewis's relationship with Joy Davidman, there is a pertinent scene. Whether the actual words were spoken or not by them, the scene can be taken to be a reflection of Lewis's character. Joy Davidman embarrasses Lewis by calling out his name when she is trying to find him in a restaurant for a pre-arranged first meeting. When Joy questions his embarrassment he comments that he is not what she might call a public figure. Joy's response is brash and quick—if this is so why does be write all the books he has published, and why does he give public talks. As Lewis's brother suppresses a laugh, Lewis replies quietly that despite the fact that they have only just met Joy has seen right through him. It is important to remember that Lewis's vocation as someone who prepared others for conversion was very much a reflection of his character, a man who always chose the safe path, who had been something of a loner. Do Evangelical missionaries convert people?—or is it the Holy Spirit? All any missionary can do is prepare the ground and point the way—like Lewis did, *praeparatio evangelica*.

3. C. S. LEWIS: A CLASSICAL PHILOSOPHER THEOLOGIAN

So where is C. S. Lewis in the tradition of christological reasoning? Lewis is not a conventionally trained theologian, which in itself does not disqualify him. The radio broadcasts were criticized by many within the Church of England establishment as the work of an amateur, one who was unqualified to speak on the subject of faith

---

7   Eusebius of Caesarea's, Προπαρασκευη Ευαγγελικη (*Preparation for the Gospel*, written sometime between 313 and 324 AD), usually known by its Latin title, *Praeparatio evangelica*, was written to demonstrate the veracity of the gospel over and against pagan religion through clear and sustained argument, it is an apologetic defence of Christianity. See: Johnson, *Ethnicity and Argument in Eusebius' Praeparatio Evangelica*.

8   Lewis, *Surprised by Joy*, 226.

and theology. However, Lewis is comparable with the philosophically trained patristic theologians, rather than with his contemporaries steeped in modern philosophy and the skepticism of the Age of Reason and the Enlightenment. The work of the great patristic theologians was effectively grounded in their faith. They were essentially from two groups. In the first group were priests and bishops who wrote theology to meet a challenge, a demand, often from the Roman state, but also to counter heretical ideas. The second group were ordinary lay Christians who were most often trained philosophers; they had been through the Greek Academy. Lewis's education, his conversion, his faith, and his mission are similar in many ways to the second century apologist, Justin Martyr. Justin Martyr was a trained philosopher who became a Christian who then taught the faith and sought to show how the faith was rational and coherent. Justin Martyr (c.100–165 AD) was so named because he was martyred by the Romans for not believing in "god" (i.e., the Roman Emperor, to whom Justin was required to make sacrifice), and worshiping a man as God: Jesus Christ. Justin sought to show how Jesus was the Christ and was truly man and truly God. Raised as a pagan, he studied philosophy, taught philosophy (he wore the *pallium*, the philosopher's gown), then converted to Christianity, thereafter he dedicated his life to teaching Christianity as the true philosophy. He continued to wear the *pallium* to point out that he had reached the Truth in Christ. He sought to teach the rationality of the gospel, how Jesus was the Messiah, God's word, his Logos (John 1:14). The Logos was seen as the enveloping principle of rationality in the universe in Greek philosophy (essentially from the Stoics): Justin Martyr therefore claimed that Christ Jesus was not only human, but was the eternal and universal Word/Logos of God. Justin therefore founded in many ways what is called Logos Christology, which was a way of explicating how Jesus was the Christ and was both fully human and fully divine.[9] The one Logos of God is known, for Justin, by Greek pagan philosophers as *reason*, by the ancient Hebrews in the *law*, but by Christians as *Lord*. Christ was thus known implicitly amongst the ancient Hebrews and the ancient philosophers; however, Christians have the fullest and the most profound understanding because of their encounter with Christ both historical (the Jesus of history) and universal (the Spirit of the resurrected Christ that indwells his people, his followers, his church). For Justin, the Greek pagan philosophers had only an incomplete and fragmented understanding of Christ the Logos; however, for Justin, the Logos had sowed seeds (he used the term *Logos Spermatikos*, derived from Middle Platonism) throughout human history and therefore Christ was known in part, implicitly and in fragments of revelation, amongst different peoples at different times. Christianity is therefore the culmination and conclusion of all these philosophies and religions, many of which anticipated the Truth. So, Justin Martyr is presenting not reason or law alone, but a person—both fully human and fully divine—as the fullest

---

9   See, Justin Martyr's *First Apology*, specifically §. 1–12. Karen O'Dell Bullock, *Shepherd's Notes: Writings of Justin Martyr*. Justin is essentially drawing on Stoic philosophy and Middle Platonism in asserting Jesus as the Logos (Gk: Λογος—as used in the opening of John's Gospel), but Jesus was also not just the *Logos* but also the *nomos* (the law, in Gk: νομος) of the ancient Hebrews.

7. C. S. Lewis the Classical Philosopher Theologian II: praeparatio evangelica

revelation of God; a revelation that the ancient Hebrew law makers and the ancient pagan philosophers could point towards, could glimpse.[10]

Origen of Alexandria (c.185–c.254 AD) is another example. Born to a Christian family in Alexandria, he was educated and trained by his father. Origen became a scholar and theologian, one of the early church fathers. He revived the Catechetical School of Alexandria where Clement (c.150–211 AD) had taught. He was ordained in Caesarea at the age of forty-five years, where he remained. He was tortured for being a Christian in Caesarea in 252 AD, dying from injuries sustained two years later. Origen, like C. S. Lewis, was a Platonist and produced what is essentially the first attempt to describe Christianity intellectually. He is in many ways the first systematic theologian because he attempts to lay out systematically, as a system, the elements of the faith and its worldview. Unfortunately there were questionable elements in his theology, such as universalism (the idea that all souls will, after an immeasurably long period of "time" in hell, be reunited with God and be in heaven, though whether Origen was truly a universalist is open to debate). Origen further developed the Logos Christology that Justin had been working on two generations earlier. Origen was an intellectual, trained by his philosopher father, who, like Lewis, wrote theology (though Origen was ordained in middle-age and Lewis was not). Lewis was in many ways better off outside of the clerical ranks of the Church of England of his day.

Like Justin Martyr, and like many lay theologians, Lewis was a philosopher: from his student days he was a trained classical philosopher. This, of course, was the intellectual tradition that patristic theology grew out of, as we have seen already. Lewis was therefore a trained philosopher and logician, something he used with incisive sharpness when writing theology and when in debate with colleagues in Oxford. However, Lewis did not attempt what a systematic theologian would attempt today: to lay out, with the correct emphasis on all aspects, a full and true orthodox picture of Christ.

Was Lewis a theologian? Many who write on Lewis argue he is not a professional theologian, he was not trained as one, that he wrote no systematic theological treatise. Lewis often referred to himself as a layman and an amateur.[11] Lewis may not have graduated with a project-based module degree (with no written exams) in pick-and-mix theology and general religious studies, but it may be asserted that he was far more qualified than thousands of theology graduates today. Why? Although he had no formal training in theology, his intellect was confirmed in that he received, within four years of study, two BA Hons degrees from the University of Oxford, having passed all three required public examinations with first class honors. These degrees were in Greats (Greek and Roman Literature and Classical Philosophy) and in English, and he was a believing Christian, a Catholic and Evangelical who did not hide behind a supposed academically disinterested exposition of what other theologians might have

---

10 This was brought out at its clearest in Justin Martyr's *Second Apology*, which was a supplement to his first apology and was written specifically for a Roman Senator by Justin in an attempt to justify his beliefs as a Christian. It was written probably ten years before his martyrdom, around 154–57 AD.

11 Lewis, *Mere Christianity*, vi.

said. Lewis implicitly reflected Anselm of Canterbury's assertion that God has given us language so that we may use it to praise and worship God; if we fail to use language—speech—for praise and worship, focused on God, then language will become more and more meaningless—which is what has happened within much postmodern philosophical reflection and speculation about language. Lewis sought to return to theology's patristic and biblical roots. Like most patristic theologians, Lewis was a trained philosopher who believed; not a trained theologian, a religious professional, who did not believe. In addition, Lewis was better read, in terms of this patristic and medieval theological heritage than, it may be argued, most theology lecturers today (though not as comprehensively as a patristics expert). Indeed Lewis was in effect a classically trained philosopher theologian. To paraphrase an element of the ancient Greek and Roman literature and philosophy he was schooled in, what we do in the here-and-now echoes through eternity: this is what characterizes Lewis's work—the end game of life, the what-is-to-come. The philosophically educated, classically trained patristic theologians knew that all they wrote was about the business of heaven, and so did Lewis. This, of course, raises serious questions about what a theologian is, or, more pertinently, is not. Lewis was, yes, an amateur in the strict sense of the word; he was not *employed* as a cleric or a religious bureaucrat, but this is to his advantage—he did not write and publish books because the research rating of the university employing him required it every two years, he did so because he loved the truth of the gospel. Lewis wrote as a disciple of Christ. If Lewis was not a theologian then neither were the church fathers he read on a daily basis, and neither was the Apostle Paul. And Constable and Picasso were not painters because they did not have an art college degree. Did Mozart have paper qualifications from a music college?

4. "THE ONE WHO SAVES US FROM OUR SINS?"

i. Lewisianity?

Some critics have claimed that C. S. Lewis's "mere Christianity," his method, is a personal view—that Lewis selected those elements from the tradition that complemented his spirituality and religion and then claimed this position was universal. Are these criticisms justified? The Roman Catholic convert and writer Joseph Pearce echoes some of these criticisms in his book on C. S. Lewis in relation to the Roman Catholic Church.[12] He criticizes the churchmanship of the Puritan Richard Baxter from whom Lewis took the name "mere Christianity," looking at the partisan nature of the man's religion and political allegiances: "The fact that the first person to coin the phrase 'mere Christian' was a Puritan Protestant who called himself catholic highlights the difficulties involved in discussing and defining 'mere Christianity.'"[13] Pearce notes how the ability to pick and choose from the deposit of faith has resulted in a plethora of Protestant parties and sects today, but he fails to acknowledge that the Roman

---

12   Pearce, *C. S. Lewis and the Catholic Church*.
13   Ibid., 117. See also, Derrick, *C. S. Lewis and the Church of Rome*, 174–211.

7. C. S. Lewis the Classical Philosopher Theologian II: praeparatio evangelica

Catholic Church is, since the Reformation, also one such party or sect. Pearce argues that Lewis failed to identify the cause of this fragmentation in the personal schism triggered by Henry VIII, but neither does Pearce; he assumes it is the Protestant and Reformed churches that caused the fragmentation, but fails to attribute guilt to Rome in triggering the Reformation through its corruption and its violence towards the faithful (for example, the pertinent issue of the English Bible). Pearce criticizes Lewis's *Mere Christianity* for not including Roman Mariology. But this is precisely why Lewis did not see a place for most of Roman Mariology in the "mere" core: it was not there in the New Testament or in the early church, and was in effect an add-on to the Roman Catholic denomination: much Mariology was therefore optional.

Pearce compares Lewis's work with G. K. Chesterton's *Orthodoxy*, as a basic summary of the faith, which is predictable as Chesterton was an Anglican convert to Roman Catholicism. Perhaps the difference here lies in Lewis's comment a matter of months before his death, part of the interview with the representative of the Billy Graham Evangelistic Association:

> Mr Wirt: "I believe it was Chesterton who was asked why he became a member of the Church, and he replied, 'To get rid of my sins.'"
>
> Lewis: "It is not enough to want to get rid of one's sins. We also need to believe in the One who saves us from our sins. Not only do we need to recognize that we are sinners; we need to believe in a Saviour who takes away sin. Matthew Arnold once wrote, 'Nor does the being hungry prove that we have bread.' Because we know we are sinners, it does not follow that we are saved."[14]

In many ways this summarizes the differences between Lewis and the Roman Catholic Church and explains why he did not feel the need to become a Roman Catholic. Lewis knew the immediacy of relationship from his conversion with the crucified and resurrected Lord, and that the forgiveness that flowed from Christ's pierced body was not owned or controlled by the churches.

Is Lewis guilty of inventing his own religion—Lewisianity? Mark Brumley, another Roman Catholic, addresses this question succinctly and with wisdom:

> Another reason for Lewis' potency: he was no innovator. He presented Christ and Christianity, not Lewis and Lewisianity. The publisher of that paperback edition of *Mere Christianity* that I mentioned at the outset got it only half right when on the back cover Lewis was dubbed, "The most original Christian writer of our century." I say "half right" because insofar as Lewis was a superb stylist who incarnated the Christian vision in fiction as well as essay, not to mention a uniquely effective theological populariser, he was indeed "original." But he was not "original" in the sense of concocting his own theological synthesis or customizing his own creed. "We are to defend Christianity itself," he told the Welsh clergymen in his talk on Christian apologetics, "the faith preached by the Apostles, attested by the martyrs, embodied in the creeds, expounded by the

---

14   Lewis, "Cross-Examination," 216.

Fathers. This must be clearly distinguished from the whole of what any one of us may think about God and Man."[15]

Therefore Brumley can identify and demonstrate how Lewis attempted to defend Christianity not his own personal religion.

ii. The Confusion of Men and the Providence of God

We established in the previous chapter Lewis's unifying universal principle, which underlay his two-fold content-driven method, rooted as it was in the universal Christ; a principle that transcended all of the churches and denominations, yet could be seen to a greater or lesser degree in all of the churches and denominations. The question then is how successful Lewis was in steering a path away from denominational sectarianism and personal religion so as to identify and promote this "mere" core of the Christian faith; this sheer, simple, core about Christ. Lewis, because he is human, will have colored some of this "mere Christianity" with his personal preferences; this was inevitable and impossible to avoid because he was human and not the author of the "mere" truth. However, his academic credentials should have helped him to be as detached and disinterested as possible. And to invoke Lewis's Platonism, this "mere" core exists as truth, God's truth, in eternity. Lewis's (and Richard Baxter's) Middle English use of "mere" as pure and unadulterated means that whatever we see in this world of shadows will be tainted and will be a compromise, but we must strive to identify and remain steadfast to this undiluted core however much it may be elusive, however much it may seem to be outside of our grasp, however much it appears to be transcendent. Therefore it is important not to view all as subjective, personal, relative; it is important to realize that there is this pure undiluted core to the Christian faith that exists in eternity, outside of our control, but not completely beyond our grasp. This is where Lewis's Platonism comes to the fore: this mere core of Christian doctrine exists in eternity as *intelligible* but not completely *perceivable*; by comparison we may assert that Lewis regarded the Church of England establishment as *perceivable* but not *intelligible*.

How successful was Lewis in identifying this Platonic "mere" of the Christian faith? The answer to this question lies in the remainder of this book, but also perhaps in the manner in which the Holy Spirit ensures the place of Lewis's work in the popular consciousness of Christians today. However, whatever we say and do our perception of this truth of the gospel will be subject to "*hominum confusione et Dei providentia*" (the confusion of men and the Providence of God).[16] Karl Barth, speaking here in the context of the many in-depth discussions he held with Roman Catholic theologians and philosophers of religion in the late 1920s, readily asserted that the course of the Christian church had been determined by human confusion and short-sightedness, where we believed we saw the truth, the right path, but had been clearly mistaken; yet, within those human efforts at church, at defining doctrine, was the light of Christ, the

---

15   Brumley, "The Relevance and Challenge of C. S. Lewis," para. 13.
16   Barth, "Der römische Katholizismus als Frage an die protestantische Kirche," 363.

7. C. S. Lewis the Classical Philosopher Theologian II: praeparatio evangelica

providence of God. However, because of the confusion of men (*hominum confusione et Dei providentia*) Barth asserted, the Reformation was necessary.[17] Therefore *all* churches and denominations since the Reformation are relative to each other and, for Lewis, the "mere," in the pure, undiluted sense of the gospel in eternity, exists untainted by the confusion of men. Again, these are issues to do with the nature of church that we will deal with later. Roman Catholicism's question arises out of this confusion: the true substance of the church can no longer be found in one church/denomination alone: hence Lewis's appeal to the patristic era and Scripture, and the need for his detachment from the official ranks of clergy in the Church of England.

5. "MISSIONARY TO THE PRIESTS OF ONE'S OWN CHURCH"

i. A Prophetic Outsider?

It is perhaps in the context of Lewis's content-driven method, his mission, that we must therefore re-evaluate Lewis's own comments that he was an amateur. For example, in *The Problem of Pain*, Lewis states that, "the only purpose of the book is to solve the intellectual problem raised by suffering."[18] There are those who would consider this aim to be non-theological, unless the writer is a so-called qualified expert. It can be argued that perhaps the only people who are qualified to talk about pain and suffering in relation to God are those who are, or have, suffered, are in pain, or have been afflicted. So what qualifies someone like Lewis to write theology? Lewis has a foot in both camps, so to speak, for he suffered during his childhood and his academic ability also qualifies him. Lewis continued:

> If any real theologian reads these pages he will very easily see that they are the work of a layman and an amateur. Except in the last two chapters, parts of which are admittedly speculative, I have believed myself to be restating ancient and orthodox doctrines. If any parts of the book are "original," in the sense of being novel or unorthodox, they are so against my will and as a result of my ignorance. I write, of course, as a layman of the Church of England: but I have tried to assume nothing that is not professed by all baptised and communicating Christians.[19]

Lewis, writing here in the preface to *The Problem of Pain*, is qualified to write on the theology of pain because he is a baptized and communicating Christian with a highly developed intellect. His qualifications are beyond those conferred by a secular university or a professional body. Again, in *Mere Christianity* he wrote,

> There is no mystery about my own position. I am a very ordinary layman of the Church of England, not especially "high," nor especially "low," nor especially

---

17 Re., Karl Barth's massive *corpus* into these concepts, see: Brazier, "Barth and Rome: A Critical Engagement," 137–52; and, Brazier, "Barth and Rome—II: Socialism, the Church and a Theocratic Illusion," 61–78.
18 Lewis, *The Problem of Pain*, ix–x.
19 Ibid., x.

anything else. But in this book I am not trying to convert anyone to my own position. Ever since I became a Christian I have thought that the best, perhaps the only, service I could do for my unbelieving neighbours was to explain and defend the belief that has been common to nearly all Christians at all times.[20]

In one of his most stinging criticism of modernism in the Church of England (aimed at the use by Liberal clergy of reductionist Bible study), Lewis asserts that he is an educated laymen, not theologically educated, not a professional; he then proceeds to demolish the pretence of certain clergy in claiming to be experts.[21] He concludes by commenting that, "Once the layman was anxious to hide the fact that he believed so much less than the Vicar: he now tends to hide the fact that he believes so much more. Missionary to the priests of one's own church is an embarrassing rôle."[22] Lewis therefore considers himself to be a missionary to wayward-thinking Anglican clerics—perhaps his role is actual more of a prophet. He commented in an address to an assembly of Anglican priests and youth leaders that it really ought to be the priests teaching him—not the other way round—but concluded that we need one another's help—*oremus pro invicem* (Let us pray for each other—a Latin phrase common amongst Roman Catholics).[23] He may not have produced a complete systematic theology of the Christian faith, but his apologetics are perhaps more use than a systematic treatise in proclaiming orthodoxy. Despite what he said about himself and his work, Lewis was most definitely not an ordinary layman in the Church of England. If he was, then it is to the shame of a clerical elite, the establishment. Lewis's phenomenal intellect, his piercing capacity for philosophy and logic, his two first class honors degrees from Oxford, set him apart as not an ordinary member of the Church of England. Perhaps Lewis's self-deprecating remarks must be seen as tongue-in-cheek, a smoke screen, particularly given the level of theological illiteracy and biblical ignorance that could be attributed in some quarters to the modern church.

ii. Lewis: "in mirabilibus supra me"

In the context of his relationship with official theologians Lewis commented that, "I walk *in mirabilibus supra me* and submit all to the verdict of real theologians."[24] Lewis's use of *in mirabilibus supra me* is important for he is referring to *wonders far beyond me*, or even, in Lewis's context, *things too great for me*.[25] He apparently acknowledged the superiority of professional theologians. Or does he? He also uses this phrase on another occasion. Writing on God's relationship to law and truth, Lewis commented:

20   Lewis, *Mere Christianity*, vi.
21   "Let us pray for one another." Lewis, "Christian Apologetics," 64–65 and 76.
22   Lewis, "Modern Theology and Biblical Criticism," 166.
23   Ibid.
24   Lewis, "Transposition," 1st ed. 9–20. A reworked and extended edition of the sermon as an academic paper was published seventeen years later: Lewis, "Transposition," 2nd ed. *They Asked for a Paper*, 166–82, quote from 181.
25   *mirabilis, mirabilis, mirabile*: wonderful, marvellous, astonishing and extraordinary, remarkable or admirable; even strange, wonderful to say, to speak of.

supra: above, before, formerly, beyond, over, more than; also, in charge of, in authority over.

7. C. S. Lewis the Classical Philosopher Theologian II: praeparatio evangelica

"But it is probably just here that our categories betray us. It would be idle, with our merely mortal resources, to attempt a positive correction of our categories—*ambulavi in mirabilibus supra me.*"[26] Only in this instance he walks (*ambulavi*) not before the professional theologians who claim superiority but before God: therefore Lewis the "amateur" and his theologian critics, the "professionals," are all inferior to God in matters and wonders that are far beyond them, things too great for them. On the question of Christ's Second Coming Lewis commented that, "I have no claim to speak as an expert in any of the studies involved, and merely put forward the reflections which have arisen in my own mind and have seemed to me (perhaps wrongly) to be helpful. They are all submitted to the correction of wiser heads."[27] However, he continues that, "There are many reasons why the modern Christian and even the modern theologian may hesitate to give to the doctrine of Christ's second coming that emphasis which was usually laid on it by our ancestors." So neither the modern Christian (Lewis?) nor the modern theologian (the professionals?) are in a position to speak fully, completely, and in superior tones, on this question (particularly in the context of Jesus' comments: "But about that day and hour no one knows, neither the angels of heaven, nor the Son, but only the Father." Matt 24:36; and "But about that day or hour no one knows, neither the angels in heaven, nor the Son, but only the Father." Mark 13:32).

Lewis's categorization is therefore Platonic, and it is inspired by the Holy Spirit. Lewis's invocation of *in mirabilibus supra me* is Platonic because it claims that the truth is beyond us, in the other realm, eternity. We get glimpses, intimations, we can see shadows of the truth, but the real truth, the full revelation, is beyond us. Theological talk about these matters is important, it guides us and keeps us on the right track, but writing today about Jesus Christ *is not* Christ, in the same way that talking about being in love is not being *in* love, though it does relate closely and may be informative. Therefore neither so-called "amateurs" such as Lewis, nor the so-called "professionals" (such as the Church of England establishment that criticized Lewis's success with his radio broadcasts, whose pride was dented by Lewis's success), or for that matter a Roman Catholic *curia* (court, or senate, or inquisition), are in a position to claim superiority over another's understanding. Lewis's invocation of *in mirabilibus supra me* is prompted by the Holy Spirit because it is fair to say that he was inspired by the Holy Spirit, his mind was baptized and illumined by the Holy Spirit, which, to a degree, authenticated and authorized his work. It is important to remember that no one church or individual controls or owns the authority of the Holy Spirit: the Spirit moves where it will. Therefore the "mere" core is identified from the work of many: the writers of Scripture, the creeds, the church fathers, and the classically trained philosopher-apologists of the early church. Lewis was therefore, in effect, a classical philosopher theologian, specifically, a biblical patristic apologist.

---

26 Lewis, "The Poison of Subjectivism," 80–81.
27 Lewis, "The World's Last Night," 93.

8

C. S. Lewis the Classical Philosopher Theologian III: Orthodoxy and Heresy—The Pittenger-Lewis Debate

SYNOPSIS:
Detractors and supporters; orthodoxy and heresy: there were criticisms by some religious professionals (clergy and university lecturers—often within the closed common rooms of Oxford) that Lewis was, in the strictest sense of the word, an amateur who had strayed into theological matters reserved for clergy and professionals. However, there were many who valued his work in writing and broadcasting theology for ordinary people, a target audience other than an educated, oligarchic, "liberal" and "modern" elite. For example, in 1946 the University of St. Andrews awarded Lewis an honorary Doctor of Divinity degree. But why the detractors and what were there criticisms? In 1958 the theologian, apologist and Process Theologian, W. Norman Pittenger accused Lewis of christological heresy—criticisms published in the leading American weekly, *The Christian Century*. Lewis likewise published a reply. Pittenger raises question about Lewis's work—drawing on some of the more obscure patristic heresies (Docetism, Gnosticism, Apollinarianism, and Eutychianism) in his attack. Lewis, however, refutes the accusation and then proceeds to demolish Pittenger's Christology as dangerously "Liberal." Their differences come down to ontology and status: is Jesus Christ defined by the very nature of his being in and before God, or is *he* who *he* is because of humanely conferred status? Lewis comments that "If Dr Pittenger's 'may be called' means anything less or other than 'is,' I could not accept his formula." The Pittenger-Lewis debate relates closely to the christological issues that were hammered out by the Council of Chalcedon; in addition, Lewis's response, as does his presentation of Christ (and Aslan), raises questions about the λόγος ἄσαρκος–λόγος ἔνσαρκος (the *logos asarkos-logos ensarkos*). Nothing is written by chance or ignorance in Lewis's theology. Examining Pittenger's accusation and Lewis's response will allow us to consider in more detail how Lewis categorized his work in relation to the so-called experts, the professionals, but also how the debate exposed a fundamental fault-line between a "liberal" theological position and a traditional-orthodox one: Lewis's Christology was high; Pittenger's correspondingly low. The Pittenger-Lewis debate brings into sharp focus the distinction between an orthodox biblical-patristic Christology and a "Modern"/"Liberal" understanding of Jesus of Nazareth.

1. INTRODUCTION

In 1946 the University of St. Andrews, in Scotland, awarded C. S. Lewis an honorary Doctor of Divinity degree in recognition of his work in theology and apologetics. On June 27, 1946, Warnie and Jack travelled to St. Andrews for the award. At the degree ceremony on June 28, Lewis's promoter, the Dean of the Faculty of Divinity Professor D. M. Baillie commented:

> With his pen and with his voice on the radio Mr Lewis has succeeded in capturing the attention of many who will not readily listen to professional theologians, and has taught them many lessons concerning the deep things of God. For such an achievement, which could only be compassed by a rare combination of literary fancy and religious insight, every Faculty of Divinity must be grateful. In recent years Mr Lewis has arranged a new kind of marriage between theological reflection and poetic imagination, and this fruitful union is now producing works which are difficult to classify in any literary genre: it can only be said in respectful admiration that he pursues "things unattempted yet in prose or rhyme." It is not very frequently that the University confers its Doctorate of Divinity upon a lay theologian, but it may well be proud to give this acknowledgement to the work of C. S. Lewis.[1]

By the late 1950s, Lewis had published a considerable corpus of apologetics and theology and was widely regarded and acknowledged as a theologian and apologist. The Revd. Walter Robert Matthews, the Dean of St. Paul's Cathedral in London (at the heart, for many, of the Church of England establishment), had put forward Lewis's name for the Royal Air Force lectureship, where he toured RAF bases speaking on Christianity, to complement the BBC wartime radio talks. However, parts of the Anglican establishment had reacted to the BBC radio talks with characteristic criticism or aloof disdain: Lewis was deemed to be not qualified—he was not one of them. Some clergy within the Church of England regarded him as an outsider who had strayed into theology without being qualified to speak on the subject. He also had serious doctrinal critics amongst his contemporaries. Examples are Lewis' debate with leading Anglican bishops over the reductionist, demythologising approach to John's Gospel in the work of two Anglican clerics—Revd. Dr. Alec R. Vidler and Revd Dr Walter Lock—which centred upon questions of Christology and revelation, and resulted in heated exchanges in Oxford's common rooms; or the debate with the young philosophy don Elizabeth Anscombe, who in 1948 challenged Lewis's in a debate at the Oxford Socratic Club relating to the linguistic-philosophical nature of his arguments. However, there were also more public criticisms, outside the closed circles of Oxford. One example is the debate triggered by the apologist and process theologian William Norman Pittenger, who publically accused Lewis of christological heresy; and received a published reply from Lewis. What lay behind Pittenger's accusations, and how did Lewis respond? Their debate primarily concerned the nature of apologetics and how to communicate the gospel; however, at the heart of the Pittenger-Lewis exchange lay a fundamental principle of Christology: the nature and/or status of Jesus Christ. The debate hinged on ontology. What do we say about the very *nature* of *being* of this person Jesus of Nazareth? Is he defined by the very nature of his being in and before God (fully human

---

1 From *The St. Andrews Citizen* (June 29, 1946), quoted in, Hooper, *C. S. Lewis A Companion and Guide*, 43–44.

8. C. S. Lewis the Classical Philosopher Theologian III: Orthodoxy and Heresy

and fully divine) or is Jesus merely a human *seen as* divine by people (i.e., Jesus is only "god" due to humanely conferred status)?

The exchange exposed a fundamental dichotomy which has characterized the church since early times, and is perhaps more pertinent to churches today than even in Lewis's day. The *dichotomia* was epitomized by Jesus's question to Peter: "But who do you say that I am?" (Matt 16:15). This raises the question of whether it is *ontology* (the study of being or existence, of a thing's very nature) or *status* (whether humanly or divinely conferred) that tells us who Jesus is. The debate also exposes divisions in the understanding of the nature, status, and role of theologians, clergy, and lay Christians, and thereby the distinction between professionals and amateurs, or between a clerical elite and the so-called laity.

2. THE PITTENGER-LEWIS DEBATE

i. Orthodoxy and Heresy

The theologian, apologist and Process Theologian W. Norman Pittenger accused Lewis, publically, of christological heresy in the leading American weekly, *The Christian Century*.[2] Lewis answered Pittenger in reply published in the same publication.[3] Pittenger's critique was published in 1958, so almost all of Lewis's key works were available for him to read in forming his criticism; however, he clearly had not read some works and misquoted others (a point Lewis did not let him get away with in the reply!). Pittenger compliments Lewis on his ability to tell a story, but has much to say criticising the reception of Lewis's apologetics; therefore he appears, at times, to be attacking Lewis's readers more than Lewis, *per se*. When he turns to Lewis's serious theological writing, as he terms it, he comments that they "are not at all attractive."[4] He proceeds:

> Quite obviously he believes fervently in Christianity as he understands it; he writes in its defence with ease and charm; he is very much "up to date" in many of his ideas and in the way in which he approaches his contemporaries ... But having said all that, I can find little else that is good to say about Mr. Lewis as a Christian apologist and amateur theologian. It is my opinion that he has used his brilliant not to say coruscating style to commend a version of Christianity which is often not even "orthodox" (for what that is worth) and which in any event is frequently incredible ... I believe that he teaches a version of the Christian faith which is not only on occasion dubiously orthodox by the narrowest standards, but is also a kind of uncriticized "traditionalism" which is stated with such eloquence and brilliance that it deceives those who are not instructed and misleads many who are.[5]

---

2   Pittenger, "Apologist versus Apologist," 1104–7.
3   Lewis, "Rejoinder to Dr Pittenger," 1369–71.
4   Pittenger, "Apologist versus Apologist," 1104.
5   Ibid.

In criticising Lewis he cites a hundred years of "modern" academic biblical study, which, he claims, Lewis ignores; though it is important to remember that this secular academic Bible study was driven by a hermeneutic of suspicion that for many effectively destroyed the Bible, which is partly why Lewis ignored it. Much of Pittenger's thrust is against one book of Lewis: *Miracles*. However, he then moves on to try to demolish Lewis's reliance upon the principle of Vincentius of Lérins, by arguing that accepting or regarding as true the doctrines of church tradition leads Lewis to the assumption that authority is almost the basis of the Christian faith: "Lewis belongs to that modern school of thought which believes that if the catholic church has taught something long enough, then that something must necessarily be true, with the corollary that this superstructure will then establish the foundations upon which it is in fact based."[6] Pittenger then criticises Lewis's insistence that Jesus gave himself away as God, which then allows Pittenger to expose his own view of Jesus which, as we will see from Lewis's reply, is questionably "low," low enough to probably have been categorized as heretical by the patristic church. He also criticizes Lewis for supporting a "Pauline ethic based on man's sinfulness and helplessness."[7] Despite having criticized Lewis for over-relying on church tradition, Pittenger then accuses Lewis of rejecting history because of his skepticism of nineteenth- and twentieth-century philosophies and thought systems. In addition, he argues against Lewis's belief in the doctrine of original sin (ignoring all the evidence to the contrary that can be obtained by simply observing the willful state of fallen humanity). It is, however, when he turns to Lewis's Christology that he really denigrates Lewis's work: "Mr. Lewis's Christology, his doctrine of Christ, is outright Docetic, even Gnostic. It falls into at least two classical heresies: Apollinarianism in which the true human mind of the incarnate Lord is replaced by the divine mind, and Eutychianism in which the human nature as a whole is 'swallowed up' in the divinity of our Lord."[8] Pittenger does not go on to identify where and when Lewis is supposed to have committed these heresies, neither does he spell out what constitutes a Docetic or a Gnostic Christ. Lewis's Christ is not a spiritual apparition (Docetic); nor, for Lewis, is Christ accessed through special secret knowledge (Gnostic), therefore one is at a loss to understand what this charge relates to in Lewis's work. Pittenger acknowledged, to a degree, the subtle distinction between Apollinarianism and Eutychianism, both of which marginalized the humanity of Jesus Christ, but were not the same. (In addition, he does not seem to acknowledge the development of Eutychianism into Monophysitism and the subtle distinction between the two, and whether this relates to his charge.) Lewis was, in effect, placed in the position of Irenaeus who struggled long and hard against these early church heresies—in particular, Gnosticism. However, Pittenger is surprisingly unspecific for a professional theologian on what exactly it is in Lewis's writings that appeared to him to have marginalized the humanity of Christ.

---

6   Ibid., 1106.
7   Ibid.
8   Ibid., 1107.

8. C. S. Lewis the Classical Philosopher Theologian III: Orthodoxy and Heresy

In conclusion Pittenger succinctly, even simplistically, classifies Lewis as "a dangerous apologist and an inept theologian."[9]

ii. W. Norman Pittenger

Before we consider Lewis's published reply, we need to ask who Professor Pittenger was. William Norman Pittenger (1905–97) was a philosopher, apologist, and Process Theologian. Raised in Princeton, New Jersey, he attended Princeton University but left to work as a newspaper reporter in New York; he then went to The General Theological Seminary in Manhattan, where he graduated, taught, and became Professor of Christian Apologetics. He retired in 1966 and became an honorary senior member of King's College, Cambridge. In addition to work and writings in Christian apologetics and process theology, Pittenger wrote on human sexuality, attempting a defense of homosexuality. He was reputed to be one of the first theologians to argue for the open acceptance of homosexual relations.[10] Process theology is essentially associated with the University of Chicago Divinity School and is heavily reliant on "modern" philosophy and a "liberal" theological perspective. As a Process theologian, Pittenger regarded *becoming* as more important than *being*, and relied on a contemporary view of the world as continually changing, with the underlying principle that God is not immune from change. Pittenger, therefore, was more concerned with the *process* of becoming something else or someone other, the process of change and growth, than with what God may or may not have done for humanity *in Christ*. For Pittenger, theology was not necessarily about what God has done for us on the cross, but about how we change and *become* through being religious. Christianity, then, is a process of human development, and so, the argument goes, are other religions. Lewis had, of course, distanced himself from "modern" philosophy and "modern" theology, especially where they marginalized the reality that was attested in the creeds: the incarnation, cross, and resurrection. For Lewis, Jesus did not become who he was through being religious—he was the Christ, from all eternity through to all eternity. For Lewis, the fact that Jesus Christ died on the cross for our sins was more important than what we may term religious character development. This position was forensic and in many ways legalistic, and reflected Lewis' interest in, and the value he accorded to, Gustaf Aulén's seminal work on atonement, *Christus Victor*.

iii. Lewis's Reply

So what did Lewis say in reply? He concedes that the charge of Apollinarianism could be applicable to one statement about Christ in his very first work of apologetics—*The Problem of Pain*. That statement could be read as saying that the two natures within Christ were assimilated in his presentation so that the human side was deified forming

---

9   Ibid.
10   In terms of Christology and process theology, see: Pittenger, *The Word Incarnate*; Pittenger, *God in Process*; Pittenger, *Process-Thought and Christian Faith*; and Pittenger, *Christology Reconsidered*. In terms of his sexual ethics, see: Pittenger, *Making Sexuality Human*; Pittenger, *Time for Consent*; and Pittenger, *Love and Control in Sexuality*.

a new hybrid nature, which in turn marginalized or played down the humanity of Jesus Christ: specifically relating to the human mind of Jesus. Lewis commented that, "I must admit some truth in his charge of Apollinarianism; there is a passage in my *The Problem of Pain* which would imply, if pressed, a shockingly crude conception of the incarnation."[11] However, Lewis also notes that this point was corrected in a subsequent edition of the book, and that what is then presented in book 4 chapter 3 of *Mere Christianity* provides, Lewis argues, an antidote. What was this statement that Pittenger latched on to in *The Problem of Pain*? Lewis wrote: "I certainly think that Christ, in the flesh, was not omniscient—if only because a human brain could not, presumably, be the vehicle of omniscient consciousness, and to say that Our Lord's thinking was not really conditioned by the size and shape of his brain might be to deny the real incarnation and become a Docetist."[12] The implication is that the human limitations of Christ's human brain were submerged, swallowed up, to use Pittenger's phrase, by the divine. This is not really what Lewis is saying here; he is struggling to explain how the human brain-mind related to the traditional characteristics of God, in this case omniscience (to know all, simultaneously). However, Pittenger had also widened this accusation of christological heresy by also invoking Docetism, Gnosticism, and Apollinarianism. It is difficult to see whether he really understood what these were if he blindly invoked them all together. However, what he appears to be saying is that Lewis, *carte blanche*, presents a Christ who is more divine than human, that the humanity of Jesus Christ is played down, marginalized. In the symbolic narratives Lewis presents the Aslan-Christ in *The Chronicles of Narnia* as clearly very real, very feline, or lion-like; he bleeds, hurts, suffers, is real in terms of breath, paws, fur, and so on. Then throughout his apologetic work Lewis emphasizes the very real humanity of Christ in terms of flesh and blood and suffering, and that this is complemented by a very real complete human nature, a human character. There is a strong Platonic element to Lewis's writing—the universal Christ of eternity, co-eternal with the Father and the Spirit, coming down to earth to become one of us—but this is no spiritual visitation, the Son of God is incarnated in Lewis's work in flesh and blood. Lewis refutes these accusations, and fifty years on since Pittenger published, it is fair to say that such accusations of christological heresy have not risen since. It must be remembered that the charge of Apollinarianism and Eutychianism was leveled at Lewis's very first work of apologetics, that most theologians will make mistakes in their early work, and that even in their mature work, when they should be making fewer mistakes, they are still open to err, to straying from a balance between Christ's full humanity and full divinity, with two natures in one person (the Chalcedonian Creed).

Lewis then turns the attack onto Pittenger. Lewis did not to suffer fools gladly, particularly if they were professors of apologetics. Pittenger's deconstruction of Lewis's book, *Miracles*, is based on a misquote, a serious and fundamental misquote from the beginning of the book, which undoes all of Pittenger's subsequent argument. What Pittenger asserts Lewis said is not so! "I turn next to my book *Miracles* and am sorry

11   Lewis, "Rejoinder to Dr Pittenger," 1369.
12   Lewis, *The Problem of Pain*, 110.

8. C. S. Lewis the Classical Philosopher Theologian III: Orthodoxy and Heresy

to say that I here have to meet Dr Pittenger's charges with straight denials. He says that this book 'opens with a definition of miracles as the "violation" of the laws of nature.' He is mistaken. The passage (chapter 2) really runs: 'I use the word miracle to mean an interference with Nature by supernatural power.'"[13] However, Lewis concedes Pittenger's point that he does not use theological or biblical studies language:

> It is very true that I make no use of the different words (*semeia*, *terata* and the rest) which New Testament writers use for miracles. But why should I? I was writing for people who wanted to know whether the things could have happened rather than what they should be called; whether we could without absurdity believe that Christ rose from the emptied tomb. I am afraid most of my readers, if once convinced that he did not, would have felt it of minor importance to decide whether, if he had done so, this non-existent event would have been a *teras* or a *dunamis*.[14]

Pittenger is critical of Lewis's emphasis on God's transcendence, particularly the transcendent God that come down to us, though, as Lewis shows, there was in his day too great an emphasis on immanence, that is, God's action and presence in creation. Such a critique is to be expected of a thinker immersed in process theology, because, as Lewis notes, there is the ever-present risk of pantheism whereby God is identified with creation, or, as in panentheism, creation is seen as a part of God. Pantheism and panentheism are the ever-present risk with Liberal theology and, to a degree, process theology. The solution is, as ever with C. S. Lewis (and for that matter Karl Barth), to stress God's transcendence and freedom from creation but simultaneously *his* loving presence in coming down into creation to be incarnated for our salvation. Pittenger criticizes Lewis for this position but is merely stating the obvious! Lewis comments, echoing something of his own journey from idealism and pantheism (c. 1920–29) to theism (c.1929–31) and later to Christianity (1931): "I have stressed the transcendence of God more than his immanence. I thought, and think, that the present situation demands this. I see around me no danger of Deism but much of an immoral, naïve and sentimental pantheism. I have often found that it was in fact the chief obstacle to conversion." [15]

3. PITTENGER'S CHRISTOLOGY: "IS," OR "OF THE VALUE OF"?

After criticizing Pittenger's theology, Lewis moves on to his Christology exposing the theological "Liberalism" or "Modernism" in Pittenger's comments, derived very much from process theology. What is at stake here, Lewis argues, is the very core of the Christian belief in salvation: If Jesus of Nazareth was just an ordinary human being who had a heightened awareness of the "divine," and called this "divine" his "father," and was thus accorded the value of a "god" by his followers (in much the same way in which celebrities can be deified today, or Roman Emperors were fêted as divine two

---

13   Lewis, "Rejoinder to Dr Pittenger," 1369–70.
14   Ibid., 1370.
15   Ibid., 1370.

thousand years ago), then we are still lost, fallen, and in a perilous state.[16] For Lewis, the pertinent question is what Jesus Christ was or rather is—the very nature of his *being*—not the status accorded to him by his followers: Christ must be affirmed as an ontological reality rather than as possessing a humanly accorded status, or a unique value attributed by his followers.

i. An Ontological Distinction[17]

Lewis gets straight to the point and questions what exactly Pittenger means when he writes about the validity of Jesus Christ's unique place in the Christian faith as the one in whom God was highly active so that, he may be called g/God-man, stating that he, Lewis, is not quite sure about Pittenger's phrasing.[18] For Lewis, the problem is in Pittenger's use of the words, "may be called."[19] Lewis knows his theological history, that many theologians in the nineteenth century, in Central Europe (the theological Liberalism Karl Barth was reacting against) regarded Jesus of Nazareth as an ordinary human being who, because of his relationship with the "divine," came to be regarded as a "god" by his disciples and the whole apostolic Christian tradition that came after him, an understanding which was then codified and set into the religion we know as Christianity. Therefore, according to the theological Liberal tradition, originating to a degree in the late eighteenth century, people make a subjective judgment by which they give this man Jesus of Nazareth the value of a "god." Wrong, says Lewis, this man was more than that: he was the Son of God, therefore God incarnate. It is not our subjective personal opinions about this man that count, that make him what he *is*. In his reply to Pittenger Lewis wrote: "In other words, if Dr Pittenger's 'may be called' means anything less or other than 'is,' I could not accept his formula. For I think that Jesus Christ is (in fact) the only Son of God—that is, the only original Son of God, through whom others are enabled to 'become sons of God.' If Dr Pittenger wishes to attack that doctrine, I wonder he should choose me as its representative. It has had champions far worthier of his steel."[20]

---

16   "If there is no resurrection of the dead, then Christ has not been raised; and if Christ has not been raised, then our proclamation has been in vain and your faith has been in vain. We are even found to be misrepresenting God, because we testified of God that he raised Christ—whom he did not raise if it is true that the dead are not raised. For if the dead are not raised, then Christ has not been raised. If Christ has not been raised, your faith is futile and you are still in your sins. Then those also who have died in Christ have perished. If for this life only we have hoped in Christ, we are of all people most to be pitied." 1 Cor 15:13–19.

17   In theological terms this is about *ontology*, that is, that branch of metaphysics that is concerned with the nature of existence, the very nature of *being*: in modern Latin, *ontologia*, from the Greek ὤν, ὄντος, *ōn, ontos*, "that which is," "being," (from the verb εἰμί, *eimi*, pronounced *amy*, "to be"), and λογία, *logia*, "study, theorizing, science."

18   Pittenger, "Apologist versus Apologist," 1106.
19   Lewis, "Rejoinder to Dr Pittenger," 1369.
20   Ibid 1369–70.

8. C. S. Lewis the Classical Philosopher Theologian III: Orthodoxy and Heresy

---

C. S. Lewis: "If Dr Pittenger's *'may be called'* means anything less or other than *'is'*, I could not accept his formula."

W. NORMAN PITTENGER, **Key Proposition**	C. S. LEWIS **Key Proposition**
"may be called"	"is"
"consentient witness of all Christians"	"the only Son of God"
"But the validity of our Lord's unique place in Christian faith as that One in whom God was so active and so present that he may be called 'God-Man,' the incarnate Word, does not rest on any such mechanical grounds as Mr. Lewis advances, but on the total consentient witness of all Christians from the apostles' time that this Jesus is in very truth the Christ of faith, 'God in man-made manifest.'"	"Our Lord's actually unique place in the structure of utter reality, the unique mode as well as degree, of God's presence and action in Him, make the formula 'God-Man' the objectively true description of him . . . Jesus Christ *is* (in fact) the only Son of God—that is, the only original Son of God, through whom others are enabled to 'become sons of God.'"
W. Norman Pittenger, "Apologist versus Apologist: A Critique of C. S. Lewis as 'Defender of the Faith.'" *Christian Century* LXXV (1 Oct. 1958), 1104–7.	C. S. Lewis, "Rejoinder to Dr Pittenger." *Christian Century* LXXV (26 Nov. 1958), 1369–71.

Figure 7: Pittenger-Lewis—the fundamental distinction between a Liberal and a creedal-orthodox position on the very nature of Jesus Christ

ii. The λόγος ἄσαρκος–λόγος ἔνσαρκος

Being human is not the result of a value that is accorded to us; there is a deep core to us that is human, as distinct from animals and other creatures. Likewise being the God-man, Jesus Christ, is not simply about the value accorded to one human by another. What Lewis is talking about is the very being, the ontology, of Jesus Christ in relation to the uncreated divine nature: very man and very God, fully human and fully divine, and in his divinity co-eternal with the Father from eternity to eternity. If only the divine nature is uncreated this could be taken to apply only to the Father; asserting that the incarnate Son is uncreated appears to mingle the two natures—a concept that led to thousands of words being exchanged by theologians in the fourth to fifth centuries, a debate that was resolved through the Chalcedonian declaration, to a degree: that the two natures were equal—Jesus was equally fully human and fully divine. However, this raises questions about the λόγος ἄσαρκος–λόγος ἔνσαρκος (the *logos asarkos-logos ensarkos*, i.e., the logos, the Word of God unfleshed, *asarkos,* as distinct from enfleshed, *ensarkos*).²¹ Why is this relevant? Because an aspect of Lewis' Christology, which will be examined in depth when we consider Aslan and *The Chronicles of Narnia*, is that the Aslan-Christ (the feline, lionized, creator in *The Magician's Nephew*) is, yes, eternally begotten, uncreated, but appears to be *perpetually incarnate*, enfleshed; the Aslan-Christ does not appear to have had a time when he was the λόγος ἄσαρκος. Nothing is written by chance or ignorance in Lewis's theology and perhaps Lewis could see that this issue was to do with Platonic forms, temporality—or more pertinently a temporal paradox in the form of the relationship between eternity and our reality of time-space—and perhaps "the lamb that was slaughtered from the foundation of the world" (Rev 13:8). These issues are fundamental to the faith, they are at the heart of the biblical faith of the church—the "core" Lewis identified from his reading of Vincent of Lérins and Richard Baxter's "mere" (Lewis' methodological ground): the nature of Jesus of Nazareth, the Christ, is not the product of our subjective opinions or the value we might or might not accord to him.

iii. Lewis the Logician

What comes across from reading this debate after fifty years is how Lewis's sharp and incisive use of logic gives him the upper hand, particularly when responding to Pittenger's criticism of the very nature of Jesus Christ, but—also related to it—the value Lewis accorded to Scripture, in particular the status given to John's Gospel.²² Pittenger and Lewis are as different as chalk and cheese. They were never going to agree. Pittenger's colleagues even acknowledged that he seemed to regard Lewis as his adversary, his nemesis.²³ Neither of them was going to agree: Pittenger was in many ways an ethical and doctrinal Liberal who valued modern theology and modern philosophy; he was a child of the Age of Reason and the Enlightenment and came from a position that denigrated the tradition; Lewis was orthodox, he was patristic and biblical, and saw limited value in modern theology and philosophy. There was a similar debate between Karl Barth and Rudolf Bultmann in the early 1930s over the value of natural theology: Barth was fast becoming the champion of orthodoxy and, as such, his beliefs were diametric to Bultmann's. Barth commented of the whale and the elephant, of why the elephant can't have a meaningful conversation with the whale—"meeting with boundless astonishment on some oceanic shore. It is all for

---

21 The λόγος ἄσαρκος–λόγος ἔνσαρκος (*logos asarkos–logos ensarkos*): the Word of God unfleshed (*asarkos*), the pre-incarnate Word of God; and the word fleshed (*ensarkos*), incarnated. For those unfamiliar with the λόγος ἄσαρκος–λόγος ἔνσαρκος debate see, Gunton, *The Barth Lectures*, 167–70, which examines the issues involved and how Barth wanted to justify the λόγος ἔνσαρκος but found too many difficulties

22 Lewis, "Rejoinder to Dr Pittenger," 1370.

23 "[G]ossip was not his normal fare. More to his taste was the shooting off of epigrammatic one-liners at his theological foes, most of whom seem to have been named C. S. Lewis." Comment by Richard A. Norris, Jr. in the address given at The Memorial Eucharist for W. Norman Pittenger, Chapel of the Good Shepherd, The General Theological Seminary, The Feast of Lancelot Andrewes, 1997. Norris, "Memorial Eucharist for W. Norman Pittenger".
Online: http://findarticles.com/p/articles/mi_qa3818/is_199801/ai_n8791642/

8. C. S. Lewis the Classical Philosopher Theologian III: Orthodoxy and Heresy

Figure 8: C. S. Lewis and W. Norman Pittenger, pen and ink drawing, P. H. Brazier

nothing that one sends his spout of water high in the air. It is for nothing that the other moves its trunk in friendship and now in threat. They do not have a common key to what each would obviously like to say to each other in its own speech and in terms of its own element."[24] This also applied to the Pittenger-Lewis debate. It is important to remember that no one church or individual controls or owns the authority of the Holy Spirit: the Spirit moves where it will. Hindsight supports this: Pittenger's work has all but disappeared; Lewis's continues to be read and appreciated by millions.

4. PITTENGER-LEWIS: CONCLUSION

The Pittenger-Lewis debate brings into sharp focus the distinction between an orthodox patristic-biblical Christology, on the one hand, and a "Modern" and/or "Liberal" Christology, on the other. In the wider context of their work, it is fair to assert that Lewis' Christology was high and Pittenger's correspondingly low. This does not necessarily invalidate Pittenger's emphasis on the process of becoming: the Christian life is characterized by change, by sanctification. However, this process, as such, must be rooted in the life, crucifixion, and resurrection of God incarnate—in a Christ who

---

24 Barth, *Karl Barth-Rudolf Bultmann Letters 1922–1966*, 105.

"is." The debate between a high and a low Christology is ongoing and as relevant to the churches today as in Lewis's mid-twentieth-century Church of England.

If the Christian life is characterized by process then, despite Lewis' orthodox assertions, his rejoinder to Pittenger (1958) was issued on the eve of the most painful of his conversions: not the oft-discussed conversions as a young don first to theism (1929) and then to the gospel (1931), but the wrestling and frustration with, and initial rejection of the God manifested in, the suffering and death of his wife Joy Davidman from cancer on July 13, 1960. Lewis eventually capitulated and gave in to the Lord of Joy's affliction. This final conversion was a process, and initially meant that all the dogmatic and orthodox pride of C. S. Lewis the famous Christian apologist counted for naught.[25] The irony is that much that he outlined in his first work of apologetics more than twenty years earlier, *The Problem of Pain*, should have prepared him for what he went through; but practice was very different from theory. Advising people on the way of the cross, the pain they must go through in the process of sanctification, was very different from going through that pain, bereavement, and loss himself. Perhaps in some sense, it may be said that in the long run, Pittenger won the debate—that Lewis should have paid more attention to the motivations behind a process interpretation of the gospel and the Christian life, apart from statements about the nature of Jesus Christ. This raises an important doctrinal issue. Whatever we say or believe about Jesus of Nazareth, the Christ, none of it affects what he is, only our relationship to him. If we deny his divinity, this does not reduce him to a mere human. However, this does emphasizes the importance of faith (trust) as set out in the gospels by Jesus, irrespective of how confused our beliefs may be (*hominum confusione et Dei providentia?*[26]).

Apologetics is essentially about communication, and is not without risk: in meeting secular and multi-religious challenges, doctrinal content can become diluted, even corrupted. This is apparent in passages of both Lewis and Pittenger's work. However, Lewis exhibited a sharper intellect and use of logic than Pittenger, and also was able to communicate as an apologist through understanding his target audience in a way, it is fair to assert, that Pittenger did not. Lewis' Christology is in many ways Platonic and pneumatological. Lewis' invocation of *in mirabilibus supra me* is Platonic because it asserts that the truth is beyond us, in the other realm, eternity. We get glimpses, intimations; we can see shadows of the truth. But the real truth, the full revelation, is inherently beyond us. For Lewis, we must, in our knowledge of the Christ, rely on the accumulated wisdom of the developing church tradition: "Modern" Christological understanding, particularly on the question of the ontological reality of the Christ, must always be measured against this tradition. Theological talk about these matters is important, it guides us and keeps us on the right track—but must be kept in context—a faith context. Therefore, neither so-called "amateurs" such as Lewis, nor so-

---

25   Lewis' year-long struggle was recorded in a journal, published under a pseudonym: Clerk, *A Grief Observed*.

26   The confusion of men and the providence of God. Or, more pertinently, the church in what it says and proclaims, whether by theologians or priests/ministers (specifically Lewis and Pittenger), is perhaps ruled by uncertainty and bewilderment, yet it must, if it is to be of value, be governed simultaneously by and through God's providence: *hominum confusione et Dei providentia ecclesia regitur*.

8. C. S. Lewis the Classical Philosopher Theologian III: Orthodoxy and Heresy

called "professionals" such as Pittenger or the Anglican establishment that criticized the success of Lewis' war-time radio broadcasts, nor, for that matter, a Roman Catholic *magisterium*, are in a position to claim superiority over another's understanding simply by virtue of their education. Lewis was, in effect, a classical philosopher-theologian, a biblical-patristic apologist whose Christology, like Pittenger's, remains subject to

the scrutiny of the creeds and the patristic tradition, which culminated, in a sense, in Chalcedon. Lewis wrote as an apologist, *in mirabilibus supra se*, emphasizing the ontological reality of Christ, as distinct from the relativity of human-centered value judgments: Christ's status was not accorded to him by humanity, but results from his being in the triune God.

Part Three

C. S. Lewis—

Apologist, Broadcaster, and Public Figure

"The Church exists for nothing else than to draw men into Christ, to make them little Christs. If they are not doing that, all the cathedrals, clergy, missions, sermons, even the Bible itself, are simply a waste of time. God became man for no other purpose."

C. S. Lewis speaking in the wartime radio broadcasts—
The Fourth Series, *Beyond Personality: The Christian Idea of God* (1944).

9

Apologist and Defender of the Faith I: Revelation and Christology, 1931–44— The Early Works

SYNOPSIS:
Given what we have established about C. S. Lewis's methodology we can now examine Lewis's development as a Christian apologist and consider what he wrote. The early apologetic works are essentially some writings from the 1930s, and two major works: *The Problem of Pain* and the wartime *Broadcast Talks*. Lewis rose to public attention during the Second World War, essentially through the BBC radio broadcasts, initiated by James Welch and Eric Fenn, and the RAF lecture tour speaking on the basics of a "mere" Christianity. Lewis was part of the Inklings, a disparate group of writers, literati, and lay theologians in the mid-twentieth century, Christian, educated, indeed well read, but not official clerics. This group included J. R. R. Tolkien and Charles Williams amongst others. What did Lewis write about revelation and the Christ? What is Lewis's Christology, as evidenced in his works from this period? During the Second World War Lewis's understanding can be found, essentially, in *The Problem of Pain* (1940), Lewis's first foray into apologetics, considering the relationship between fallen humanity and God, and the place of suffering in the Christ event, into which all people are drawn, and *The Broadcast Talks* (1941–44)—the early version of Lewis apologetic summa—*Mere Christianity*. Lewis's understanding of revelation relates closely to his doctrine of God, and is both orthodox and original in identifying areas of study which return the faith to orthodoxy while opening up human religiosity to the Christ event. Lewis considers theodicy and human pain, how we approach God's justification in relation to affliction. This is seen to be rooted in the person and the office of Jesus Christ. Although written to be broadcast to the general public *The Broadcast Talks* provide the strongest insight into Lewis's technique as an apologist, grounded in *reductio ad absurdum*, and into his Christology and doctrine of revelation.

1. INTRODUCTION

We can now turn to an analysis of C. S. Lewis's Christology and doctrine of revelation, as evident from his numerous writings. Lewis's apologetics, philosophical theology, and other Christian writings can be broadly sub-divided according to how his work develops, the maturity of his faith, events in his life, and the approach he took to apologetics and philosophy. Therefore, for the purposes of this study we will identify three periods bounded by his conversion in 1931, and his death in 1963: the early works 1931 to 1944; the middle works 1941 to 1947 (a deliberate overlap is implied in these two periods); and the later works 1948 to 1963. The division between early and middle works is essentially defined by the wartime *Broadcast Talks* (1941–44); the middle from the later works by the Anscombe-Lewis debate (1948).

The Early Works: 1931–44

Lewis published *The Pilgrim's Regress* in 1933, two years after his final conversion to belief in Christ as the Son of God, the revelation of God. It was in some ways an intellectual apology for his conversion—his rejection of the various nineteenth- and twentieth-century philosophies and religious systems he had been seduced by. In 1936 he published an academic study—*The Allegory of Love*.[1] But all this time he was considering his vocation as an orthodox biblical and creedal Christian, evidenced by his correspondence. His witness in the common rooms of Oxford colleges led him, to a degree, to write his first Christian work—*Out of the Silent Planet* (1938). Further academic books in English literature followed, but it was not until 1940, at the suggestion of Ashley Samson of the Centenary Press, that he published a book that tackled one of the thorniest of subjects for one apologizing and defending the Christian faith: pain, affliction, and suffering. *The Problem of Pain* was published at the height of the blitz and the period when Britain was standing alone against Nazism.[2] The book was popular, and effectively launched Lewis's writing career as a Christian apologist, followed by the BBC radio broadcasts on the essence of the Christian faith.

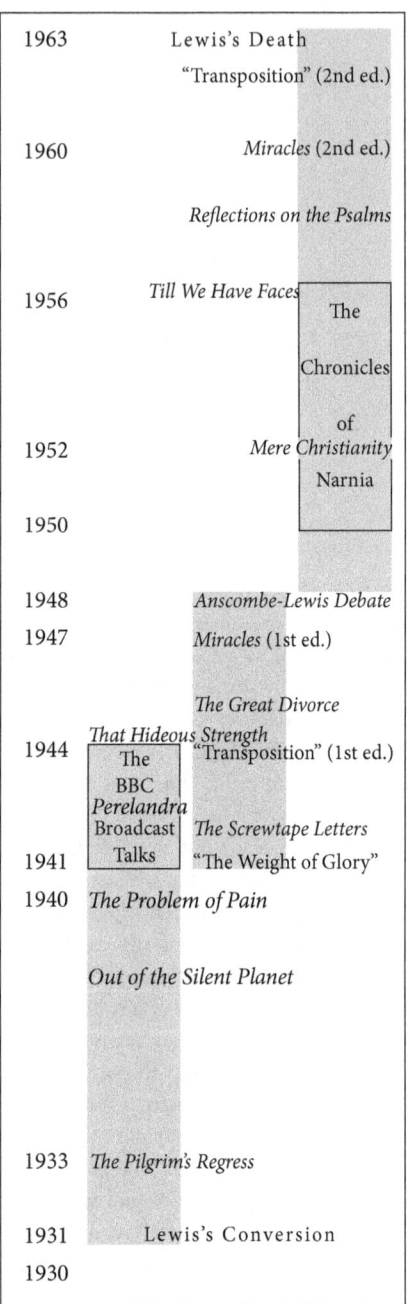

Figure 9 The Three Periods of Lewis's Apologetics and Theology

1   Lewis, *The Allegory of Love*.
2   Lewis, *The Problem of Pain*.

9. Apologist and Defender of the Faith I: Revelation and Christology, 1931–44

The Middle Works: 1941–47

The period of the middle works is where Lewis is arguably at his most productive and confident. This period overlaps the early period in that the radio broadcasts were initiated in 1941, and ran till 1944, but important works such as the sermon, "The Weight of Glory," and apologetic narratives such as *The Screwtape Letters*, which characterize the assertive confidence of the middle period works, originate from 1941, while Lewis was still working on the early broadcast talks. Before the radio broadcasts were over he had produced *The Great Divorce* and begun writing his seminal definition of the relationship between Platonism and the gospel in an address entitled, "Transposition" (delivered at Mansfield College just after the conclusion of the final series of broadcast talks). There are many essays and sermons that characterize the self-assured argumentative nature of Lewis's apologetics during this period, which culminates with the first edition of *Miracles*, still one of Lewis's most cogent arguments for the supernatural nature of the Christian faith.

The Later Works: 1948–63

In 1948 Lewis had what was to many a bruising encounter with a young philosophy don at the Oxford Socratic Club: Elizabeth Anscombe. An analysis of this rightly belongs later along with the nature of Lewis as a philosopher, and the complex issues the debate raised about naturalism and scientism, and about revelation and reason and the use of language. However, this debate, in effective, marks a slowly developing change in his work, with less of an emphasis on assertive apologetics. *The Chronicles of Narnia* are foremost in this later period, but also many more devotionally based works such as *Reflections on the Psalms* (1958), and the posthumously published, *Letters to Malcolm: Chiefly on Prayer* (1964). There is also a wealth of essays of philosophical theology, and important correspondence that contribute to his doctrine of Scripture, to consider. This later period is characterized essentially by "mere" Christology, and by Christlikeness.

2. REVELATION AND CHRISTOLOGY: THE EARLY PERIOD, 1931–44—THE KEY THEOLOGICAL AND PHILOSOPHICAL WORKS

What understanding of revelation and the Christ can we glean from Lewis's key theological works in the early period (1931 to 1944)? The early apologetic works are essentially some writings we have looked at from the 1930s; in addition, *Out of the Silent Planet* will be examined when we considered Lewis's use of narrative, including *The Chronicles of Narnia*, later in this series, as will *The Allegory of Love* when we examine Lewis's doctrine of atonement. However, this period is characterized and defined by two major works: *The Problem of Pain* (1940) and the wartime wireless/radio talks for the BBC: *The Broadcast Talks* (1941–42, 1943, and 1944).

C. S. LEWIS—REVELATION, CONVERSION, AND APOLOGETICS

i. Lewis the Broadcaster

Many readers born since 1960 would be surprised at the respect and position that was still accorded to the Church of England in the 1930s and 1940s. It was the established religion in a society still built upon deference and class. Lewis was, to a degree, the stranger—from Northern Ireland. The British Broadcasting Corporation (BBC)[3] was strictly controlled by the British establishment and although it transmitted religious programs, it acknowledged that religion was very much the preserve of the Church of England. In the early days of the BBC, in 1926, when it was planned to broadcast a service of choral evensong on a regular basis, a leading Church of England cleric objected, commenting that workingmen in pubs might listen to it with their shirt sleeves rolled up![4]

The BBC was the sole provider of radio stations in Britain, and when the Second World War broke out people relied on the radio for news—particularly when invasion was expected and was imminent. Eric Fenn, a Presbyterian minister and ecumenist, and James Welch, Director of Religious Broadcasting at the BBC, worked to improve the quality of religious broadcasting. Welch's desire was to get people to regard the church as more than a pious institution.[5] Most people in Britain were deemed to live their lives without any reference to God or to Christianity. Fenn and Welch saw that religious programs were part of the BBC and were also, to a degree, part of the national landscape, yet they were phrased in the language of the King James Bible, which, they believed, washed over the heads of most people. The BBC broadcaster, radio journalist, and writer, Justin Phillips, has shown how much work was done to achieve something real in terms of communicating the gospel in this arid spiritual landscape characterized by the BBC's broadcasting of repeats of church services.[6] However, James Welch saw this religious climate as promising:

> The situation also presented Welch with a golden opportunity. If religion was to compete in the broadcasting market-place against more popular programming, it had to become more accessible and less traditional. It had to explore new formats and to push out the boundaries. Why not religious drama? Why not produce more provocative programmes that captured the public imagination? Why not broaden the range of contributors to include those who could make religion more accessible? Welch felt strongly that the divisions of war did not diminish the relevance of the word of God or its direction. If anything, it made the gospel more important than ever.[7]

---

3   The British Broadcasting Corporation was founded on October 18, 1922, as the British Broadcasting Company, Ltd., by a consortium of radio manufacturers. It was granted a Royal Charter and became a state-owned corporation in 1927. Its news services are world renowned for attempting impartiality, particularly by listeners living under dictatorships. Its motto is "Nation Shall Speak Peace Unto Nation."

4   Choral Evensong was first broadcast by the BBC on Thursday October 7, 1926, live from Westminster Abbey and has been broadcast weekly (currently Wednesday afternoons, repeated Sunday afternoon) on BBC Radio (BBC R3) ever since.

5   Phillips, *C. S. Lewis at the BBC*, 23.

6   Ibid., 38–39.

7   Ibid., 37, see also 35.

9. Apologist and Defender of the Faith I: Revelation and Christology, 1931-44

Welch's genius was expressed in his decision to contact C. S. Lewis on the strength of his book, *The Problem of Pain*, to ask him to give talks that would address this situation. Lewis was not an establishment figure in the Church of England; he was a layman who could communicate. Although Welch initially suggested he might talk about Christianity and modern literature, Lewis, however, conceived of the series in broader terms. Welch wrote in early 1941 suggesting, "a series of talks on something like 'The Christian Faith as I see It—by a Layman': I am sure there is a need of a positive restatement of Christian doctrine in lay language."[8] Welch's response was cautious but positive. The first series of talks was broadcast later that same year. Running for four series, the talks were highly popular and later formed the basis of *Mere Christianity*. Building on the interest generated by the publication of *The Problem of Pain*, the radio talks established Lewis's career as a Christian apologist. Why Lewis? Because he complemented Welch's aims for broadcasting during the crisis of wartime. Writing in the BBC handbook for 1942, Welch wrote: "In a time of uncertainty and questioning it is the responsibility of the Church—and of religious broadcasting as one of its most powerful voices—to declare the truth about God and his relation to men. It has to expound the Christian faith in terms that can be easily understood by ordinary men and women, and to examine the ways in which that faith can be applied to present-day society during these difficult times."[9] From an interview with Walter Hooper, Justin Phillips recalls the way the talks were listened to by the ordinary man in the street; or, more pertinently considering the comment by an establishment bishop about the risk of working men in pubs listening to broadcasts of choral evensong, how people in public houses reacted:

> How did it go down with the listener? RAF officer John Lawler was in the officers' mess when someone had ordered a drink. The radio was on and Lewis came on the air as the barman was about to hand the drink back. "Suddenly everyone just froze listening to this extraordinary voice. And what he had to say. And finally they end up and there was the barman with his arm still up there and the other man still waiting for his drink. And they all forgot it, so riveting was that."[10]

Although Lewis's employment was in teaching English literature at Oxford, his apologetic work was more important to most people as it developed during the Second World War. The broadcast talks, as well as the Royal Air Force lecture tour, were fitted in around his responsibilities at Oxford. All of this had its genesis in 1941.

ii. A Professional Network and Context

What was the context of Lewis's apologetics? Was it rooted in his work, his professional status, teaching at Oxford? Lewis clearly saw himself in opposition to the "Liberal" and "Modern" apostate elements within the Church of England of his day—missionary

---

8   Welch writing to C. S. Lewis, Feb. 7, 1941. Ibid., 79–80.
9   Welch, writing in the BBC handbook for 1942, quoted in, Ibid., 35–37.
10   Phillips, *C. S. Lewis at the BBC*, 119. Phillips is quoting from an interview recorded with Walter Hooper on October 28, 1999.

to the priests of his own church was, as he asserted, an embarrassing role.[11] Many in the common rooms of the Oxford colleges sought religion in esoteric groups, philosophical sects; few identified with a missionary stance with regard to the mere core Lewis identified. Lewis is counted amongst a group of so-called lay theologians who wrote, published, and spoke on these matters in the mid-twentieth century. C. S. Lewis and J. R. R. Tolkien met on a regular basis—in a pub, the Eagle and Child, in the centre of Oxford. Self-styled as "The Inklings," this group met regularly and consisted of Lewis and his brother Warren Lewis (Warnie), also, Tolkien. Many were added to this group, which met from the mid-1930s to the mid-1960s: Owen Barfield, Charles Williams, Christopher Tolkien (Tolkien's son), Roger Lancelyn Green, Adam Fox, Hugo Dyson, Robert Havard, J. A. W. Bennett, Lord David Cecil, and Nevill Coghill. Other less frequent members included Percy Bates, E. R. Eddison, James Dundas-Grant, Colin Hardie, Gervase Mathew, R. B. McCallum, C. E. Stevens, John Wain and Charles Leslie Wrenn. The group was an informal literary gathering at which each would share passages from developing work.[12] Lewis therefore tested much of his apologetics on this group before sending it to the publisher. This contextual group complemented Lewis's character, for he was someone who was essentially private, who would share with a close group of trusted friends; he was a man whose communication with the outside world was effectively through a screen, a public persona, of talks and books. Conversation in the common rooms of Oxford colleges was of a more defensive nature—Lewis had to justify first his conversion, then his faith, then his Christian works. By comparison, he could share his work with like-minded writers and critics in the Inklings. However, although they shared his faith, aims, and motives, the other members of the Inklings did not allow Lewis to get away without a rigorous critical analysis.

What value was there to Lewis's involvement with the Inklings? Tolkien seems to have been against much of Lewis work, despite being instrumental in his conversion. Lewis would seek Tolkien's opinion even outside of the group's meetings. Therefore, it seems reasonable, given that Lewis did not change his work to accommodate Tolkien's criticisms (which were severe and dismissive with regard to *The Chronicles of Narnia*), to question what value there was to the Inkling meetings. Perhaps Lewis's work was forged not so much in the context of these meetings but as a thoughtful, contemplative, piercing intellect alone, absorbed in reading in the Bodleian Library.

3. THEODICY AND PAIN: GOD'S JUSTIFICATION

Lewis's first theological, or apologetic, work was commissioned by Ashley Sampson of the Centenary Press for the Christian Challenge series. The book was to be on the question of pain in relation to God: that is, a work of theodicy—how do you justify belief in a good God when there is so much pain and suffering in the world? The work

---

11   Lewis, "Modern Theology and Biblical Criticism," 166
12   See, Carpenter, *The Inklings*; see also, Green and Hooper, *C. S. Lewis: a Biography*, 2nd ed. 145–81.

9. Apologist and Defender of the Faith I: Revelation and Christology, 1931–44

was commissioned on the strength of *The Pilgrim's Regress* and *Out of the Silent Planet*. It was written in the second half of 1939 and read in installments to the Inklings, but especially to Tolkien, often in the latter's house.

i. Strengths and Weaknesses

The weakness of the book is essentially through its reliance on academically impartial philosophical and theological arguments (Plato, Aristotle, and Aquinas appear to be the names, so to speak, behind many of the arguments). This weakness is always the problem with theodicy—the arguments and objections often come from people who have not really suffered. However, what does the book tell us of Lewis's understanding of Christ and revelation?

Lewis opens with a quotation—opposite the contents page—from George MacDonald: "The Son of God suffered unto death, not that men might not suffer, but that their sufferings might be like his."[13] This is complemented by a proposition from Pascal in the opening pages denying nature as a basis for a doctrine of God—the apparent cold emptiness of the universe, the brutality of the natural world, is no basis for a sound understanding of God. We cannot go from the "course of events in this world to the goodness and wisdom of the creator," such a step would be "preposterous."[14] Nature does reveal something of God as creator, but it is no sound basis for a doctrine of revelation, for knowledge of God. Lewis asserts that the religious impulse in humanity is not there by accident; if we are to dismiss the explanation of anthropologists and psychologists then, for Lewis, there must be a divine origin, *in Christ*. Lewis posits three strands or elements to the religious impulse, then a fourth which is unique to Christianity. First, he cites the numinous, which he explains in relative detail, then concludes that if it is not an aberration in the human mind that serves no biological function and shows no tendency to go away, then we must see it as a direct experience of the supernatural, "to which the name revelation might be given."[15] The second strand or element is the moral ought, which is universal. Particular ethics might change but the desire, the compulsion, to do what is right, to judge that some things are wrong, is universal. This is not a logical inference from experience, asserts Lewis—"it is either an inexplicable illusion, or else revelation."[16] The third strand is to extrapolate to a moral guardian, a righteous judge—the origin of the moral ought is with the origin of the numinous. Lewis acknowledges that not all religions make this connection; there were and are non-moral religions as well as non-religious (or non-theistic) morality, but it was the Jews who were best at witnessing to this third element: "Once more it may be madness—a madness congenital to man and oddly fortunate in its results—or it may be revelation."[17] Therefore, Lewis asserts that

---

13 Lewis, *The Problem of Pain*, vi. Lewis credits MacDonald's first series; see, MacDonald, *Unspoken Sermons*.
14 Lewis, *The Problem of Pain*, 4.
15 Ibid., 8.
16 Ibid., 9.
17 Ibid., 10.

it is in the Abrahamic peoples generally that we truly find this, and specifically in the Jews who first identified the awful numinous haunting presence with the righteous Lord, the lover of righteousness. Therefore any religion of value will be revelatory; it is revelation that makes sense of the religious impulse. The fourth strand is then an historical event: the Christ event. Lewis asserts this with an early example of what is to become a key argument in his theology that Jesus is either mad, bad, or who he reveals himself to be. In this instance the proposition is dialectical—either Jesus is mad and evil, or he is who he reveals himself to be:

> There was a man born among these Jews who claimed to be, or to be the son of, or to be "one with," the Something which is at once the awful haunter of nature and the giver of the moral law. The claim is so shocking—a paradox, and even a horror, which we may easily be lulled into taking too lightly—that only two views of this man are possible. Either he was a raving lunatic of an unusually abominable type, or else he was, and is, precisely what he said. There is no middle way. If the records make the first hypothesis unacceptable, you must submit to the second. And if you do that, all else that is claimed by Christians becomes credible—that this Man, having been killed, was yet alive, and that his death, in some manner incomprehensible to human thought, has effected a real change in our relations to the "awful" and "righteous" Lord, and a change in our favour.[18]

ii. Suffering and the Christ Event

The Christ event is unique to Christianity, all that came before—the religious tradition of the Jews and intimations amongst other peoples and cultures—is summed up in Jesus Christ. Precisely how Christ's death atones, Lewis asserts, is beyond human comprehension, but it has changed us. Therefore, the Christ event is not the conclusion to a long philosophical debate spread out through centuries and cultures about whether there is a "god," neither is it speculative debate as to the origins of the universe and the meaning of life; it is, to use Lewis's word, "a catastrophic historical event following on the long spiritual preparation of humanity."[19] Therefore, the truth is open for us to know, to reason out; rebelling against or rejecting the numinous, the moral ought, the righteous guardian or Lord, is possible and is a path often taken, but if we rebel it makes the final step—the incarnation—the most difficult to accept for many.[20]

For Lewis the incarnation is trinitarian. For Lewis it is from the immanent Trinity—the loving relations between the three persons of the Trinity in eternity—that we will gain a true understanding of God and how God has revealed of God in Christ; only then will we truly understand the context and nature of pain: the key is that God is love. If God is love, then this is divine goodness, but our concept of goodness is at odds with God's—we don't want, writes Lewis, a Father in heaven, but a senile grandfather, a benevolent approval of all we do: "if God is love then our conception

---

18   Ibid., 10–11.
19   Ibid., 11.
20   Ibid., 12.

9. Apologist and Defender of the Faith I: Revelation and Christology, 1931–44

of love needs to change."[21] Christ calls people to repent, this is the primary response. Therefore, in the context of explaining pain before a God of love, we are faced with an intolerable compliment by Christ: he will change us, regardless of how uncomfortable that change may be. Coming to a right judgment about pain in relation to God is a form of revelation—such an understanding is revelatory. Such a right judgment is embedded in "the constant tenor of our Lord's teaching."[22] Therefore, Jesus Christ is not simply an object of study, of philosophical speculation, but the righteous Lord. Pain only becomes a problem if we attach a trivial meaning to *the* word "love." God does not need us, God does not experience a need for love—God loves *freely*. God does not change through loving us, but God's love changes us. This is in essence the contrast between altruistic gift love and egotistical love and is seen in the incarnation and cross: "When God becomes a Man and lives as a creature among his own creatures in Palestine, then indeed his life is one of supreme self-sacrifice and leads to Calvary . . . when God empties himself of his glory and submits to those conditions under which alone egoism and altruism have a clear meaning, he is seen to be wholly altruistic."[23] Therefore in the context of the cross and resurrection, Lewis's second element of religion, the moral ought, becomes a divine imperative. God wills our good, and our good is to love him, whatever it takes, and God has given the ultimate on the cross.

The root or origin for Lewis of our spiritual blindness and our rejection of this God of love because of pain and suffering lies in human wickedness and the fall. Accepting this is a problem for the "modern" mind, for Lewis notes how even when the apostles were preaching the gospel there was a real consciousness even amongst the pagans of deserving God's anger. Does not Christ take it for granted that people are inherently corrupted by original sin?[24] But what do we do about human guilt? The idea that time cancels out sin is regarded by Lewis as a strange illusion: "But mere time does nothing either to the fact or to the guilt of a sin. The guilt is washed out not by time but by repentance and the blood of Christ."[25]

iii. The Person and the Office

It is this more than anything else, which affirms that the difference between Jesus Christ and all the other religious leaders and teachers is not Christ's ethical teaching but the person and office: as we have seen from the Pittenger-Lewis debate, it is ontology not sermonizing that sets Christ Jesus apart, distinct, from all other human beings— Jesus as the second person of the Trinity, God from God through all eternity. It is not conformity to an external moral code that will save us, but Christ's sacrifice. Because of our fallen nature we cannot be good; Lewis restates the apostle Paul's assertion that obedience to the moral law is impossible—we cannot do the good we want to

---

21 Ibid., 26.
22 Ibid., 30, see also 23.
23 Ibid., 34–35.
24 Ibid., 40.
25 Ibid., 45–46.

(Rom 7:16–25). But neither does Lewis subscribe to a doctrine of total depravity; if we were *totally* depraved, he counters, we would not know ourselves to be so; the knowledge of our fallenness is the Spirit of Christ working in us.[26] Lewis relies often in *The Problem of Pain* on Augustine, for a doctrine of original sin. Sin for Lewis, drawing on Augustine, is characterized by pride and rebellion—paraphrasing Augustine, he describe pride as the movement whereby a creature—an essentially dependent being whose principle of existence lies not in itself but in another—tries to set up on its own, to exist for itself.[27] It is basic to human creaturely freedom that once such an individual becomes aware of God it can choose to focus on God or on self. Prior to the fall (i.e., prelapsarian) Lewis can assert that love, power, and joy descended from God to be gifted back by humanity as obedient love and ecstatic adoration, therefore men and women *were* truly the sons and daughters of God and as such were the prototype of Christ in obedience and self-surrender. Relating to a doctrine of original sin, Lewis did attempt to analyze how the self-emptying of the incarnation related to the confines of a human brain in terms of knowledge and understanding. For mere mortals our knowledge and understanding is conditioned by the fall. Thus Jesus of Nazareth's—if he was truly fully human and not just a Docetic apparition—would have been equally flawed.[28] From a sublapsarian perspective (i.e., after the fall) true knowledge is equated with true obedience and is only fully and completely seen in the cross; in Jesus the Christ, the obedient servant: "the filial self-surrender of our Lord enacted in the agonies of the crucifixion."[29] In quoting the Pauline statement that we all died in Adam and in Christ we are all made alive (1 Cor 15:22), Lewis can continue by asserting how we are also all included in Christ's sufferings.[30] "Martyrdom always remains the supreme enacting and perfection of Christianity. This great action has been initiated for us, done on our behalf, exemplified for our imitation, and inconceivably communicated to all believers, by Christ on Calvary. There the degree of accepted Death reaches the utmost . . . but the presence of the very Father to whom the sacrifice is made deserts the victim, and surrender to God does not falter though God 'forsakes' it."[31]

How does this work out? Christ's sacrifice echoes and repeats down though his followers (Lewis does not say through "the church"), through the ages: this may be simply an act of self-submission of intention, but equally may be the cruelest of martyrdoms: "the real problem is not why some humble, pious, believing people suffer, but why some do not."[32] Again drawing on Augustine's image that God cannot give us

---

26   Ibid., 50. A doctrine of total depravity is associated to a greater or lesser extent with all Protestant and Reformed churches, who draw on it from Calvin's teachings though it is in essence from Augustine's doctrine of original sin: through the fall all are enslaved to sin, therefore it is only through grace we may eventually choose and do the good, to accept salvation.
27   Ibid., 57. See, Augustine, *The City of God*, Pt. 2, bk. 14, chs. 14 and 15, 574f.
28   See, Lewis, *The Problem of Pain*, 110.
29   Ibid., 60.
30   Ibid., 67–68.
31   Ibid., 82.
32   Ibid., 82.

9. Apologist and Defender of the Faith I: Revelation and Christology, 1931–44

what we need because our hands are full with what we don't need, Lewis comments that our true good is in another world and our only real treasure is Christ. [33]

4 THE BROADCAST TALKS: A SUMMA?

The BBC radio broadcasts—the broadcast talks—made between 1941 and 1944 are probably one of the most underestimated of Lewis's works. The importance of these talks cannot be stressed enough. Yes, they are edited and rewritten, to a degree, by Lewis and re-published as *Mere Christianity* in the 1950s, but the original talks are crucial to understanding how and why Lewis went on to say and write what he did after the War and then through the 1950s towards his death in 1963. They were published after each series in three slim volumes to accompany the broadcasts. These talks published during the war included notes that were responses to listeners concerns and questions. What understanding of revelation and the Christ does Lewis present in the broadcast talks?

i. The First and Second Series—"Right and Wrong"
and "What Christians Believe"

Absolute Goodness

The first and second series (published together[34]) contain a brief statement of the value and importance of the Christ. Lewis noted in the preface that the second series of talks contained what was a summary of plain Christianity (it is not until 1944 that he uses the word "mere").[35] The first series of talks was essentially philosophical and it extrapolated an ethical basis for understanding the universe and for the existence of God; however, there is nothing uniquely *Christian* about this God—or, more pertinently, Lewis focuses on a philosophical speculation as to the existence of God, rather than going straight to Christian revelation. Lewis does, however, establish certain basis parameters for revelation—in particular that logically, from the universe, the religious view tells us that this God is more like a mind than a life force. This is leading to a "good" God, a God who can forgive: for only a person can forgive, not necessarily a life force—a some*one* not a some*thing*.[36] In this first series Lewis is speculating, philosophically, as to the existence of God, but ever-moving towards the idea of the Christ through ethical grounds—that is, the need for a redeemer, a forgiver, which must be grounded in the proposition that the universe is governed by absolute goodness. If this absolute goodness did not exist,

> then all our efforts are in the long run hopeless. But if it is, then we are making ourselves enemies to that goodness every day, and aren't in the least likely to do any better to-morrow, and so our case is hopeless again . . . God is the only

---

33   Ibid., 86.
34   Lewis, *Broadcast Talks*.
35   Ibid., 5.
36   Ibid., 30–32.

> ## THE BBC BROADCAST TALKS 1
>
> ### The First Series, 1941
> RIGHT AND WRONG
> Lewis delivered four live radio talks on the BBC Home Service entitled, Right and Wrong, on Wednesday evenings from 7:45 to 8:00 from Aug. 6 to Sept. 6 1941. An additional session answering questions from listener's letters was broadcast on Saturday Sept. 6.
>
> ### The Second Series, 1942
> WHAT CHRISTIANS BELIEVE
> Lewis delivered five live radio talks on the BBC Home Service entitled, What Christians Believe, from Sunday evenings from 4:45 to 5:00 on Jan. 11, to Feb. 15, 1942.
>
> These two series were published as–
> C. S. Lewis, *Broadcast Talks. Reprinted with some alterations from two series of Broadcast Talks Right and Wrong: A Clue to the Meaning of the Universe, and, What Christians Believe, given in 1941 and 1942.* London: Centenary, 1942.
>
> ### The Third Series, 1942
> CHRISTIAN BEHAVIOUR
> Lewis delivered eight live broadcast talks on the BBC Forces' Network entitled, Christian Behaviour, on consecutive Sunday afternoons from 2:50 to 3:00 pm from Sept. 20, to Nov. 8, 1942.
>
> This third series was published as–
> C. S. Lewis, *Christian Behaviour.* London: Centenary, 1943.
>
> ### The Fourth Series, 1944
> BEYOND PERSONALITY: THE CHRISTIAN VIEW OF GOD
> Lewis gave seven broadcast talks, three live (1, 3, 4, and 5), four pre-recorded (2, 6, and 7), on the BBC Home Service entitled, Beyond Personality: The Christian Idea of God, on consecutive Tuesday evenings from 10:15 to 10:30pm from Feb. 22, to Apr. 4, 1944.
>
> Each broadcast was published two days later in *The Listener*, the weekly magazine of the BBC; the fourth series was published complete as–
> C. S. Lewis, *Beyond Personality: The Christian Idea of God.* London: Centenary, 1944.

Figure 10: C. S. Lewis, the BBC Broadcast Talks 1941–44 (1)

9. Apologist and Defender of the Faith I: Revelation and Christology, 1931–44

The BBC Broadcast Talks 2

The First Series, 1941
RIGHT AND WRONG
First Talk
  1. "Common Decency,"
  Aug. 6, 1941
Second Talk
  2. "Scientific Law and Moral Law,"
  Aug. 13, 1941
Third Talk
  3. "Materialism or Religion,"
  Aug. 20, 1941
Fourth Talk
  4. "What Can We Do About It?"
  Aug. 27, 1941
Fifth Talk
  5. "Answers to Listeners' Questions,"
  Sept. 6, 1941

The Second Series, 1942
WHAT CHRISTIANS BELIEVE
First Talk
  1. "The Rival Conceptions
  of God" Jan. 11, 1942
Second Talk
  2. "The Invasion" Jan. 18, 1942
Third Talk
  3. "The Shocking Alternative"
  Feb. 1, 1942
Fourth Talk
  4. "The Perfect Penitent"
  Feb. 8, 1942
Fifth Talk
  5. "The Practical Conclusion"
  Feb. 15, 1942

For the publication of the third series Lewis noted that "Four sections have been added to bring in points which I had not time to deal with in the actual talks."

These sections were in the first, fourth and sixth talks, and are marked thus : §.

The Third Series, 1942
CHRISTIAN BEHAVIOUR
First Talk
  1. "The Three Parts" Sept. 20, 1942
  (§ "The 'Cardinal' Virtues")
Second Talk
  2. "Social Morality," Sept. 27, 1942
Third Talk
  3. "Morality and Psychoanalysis,"
  Oct. 4, 1942
Fourth Talk
  4. "Sexual Morality" Oct. 11, 1942
  (§ "Christian Marriage")
Fifth Talk
  5. "Forgiveness," Oct. 18, 1942
Sixth Talk
  6. "The Great Sin" Oct. 25, 1942
  (§§ "Charity" and "Hope")
Seventh Talk
  7. "Faith," Nov. 1, 1942
Eighth Talk
  8. "Faith," Nov. 8, 1942

The Fourth Series, 1944
BEYOND PERSONALITY: THE CHRISTIAN VIEW OF GOD
First Talk
  1. "Making and Begetting,"
  Feb. 22, 1944
Second Talk
  2. "The Three-Personal God,
  Feb. 29, 1944.
Third Talk
  3. "Good Infection," Mar. 7, 1944
Fourth Talk
  4. "The Obstinate Toy Soldiers,"
  Mar. 14, 1944
Fifth Talk
  5. "Let's Pretend," Mar. 21, 1944
Sixth Talk
  6. "Is Christianity Hard or Easy?"
  Mar. 28, 1944
Seventh Talk
  7. "The New Man," Apr. 4, 1944

Figure 11: C. S. Lewis, the BBC Broadcast Talks 1941–44 (2)

comfort, he is also the supreme terror: the thing we most need and the thing we most want to keep out of the way of. He is our only possible ally, and we have made ourselves his enemies.[37]

The Need for Forgiveness

Underlying this, Lewis admits, is the need for people to recognize that they have gone wrong and need forgiveness. If they don't see the need for repentance then Christianity has nothing to say to them. Only after acknowledging the existence of a moral law, and perceiving a "power" behind this moral law, then the perception comes that we are in the wrong relationship with this moral law and the righteous Lord that is the power behind it: then and only then does Christianity begin, in Lewis's words, to talk: "When you know you're sick, you'll listen to the doctor. When you have realized that our position is nearly desperate you'll begin to understand what the Christians are talking about."[38] Christians will tell you how God is at once an impersonal mind behind the moral law, yet also a person, and how we can never meet the demands of the moral law but "how God himself becomes a man to save man from the disapproval of God."[39] Underlying this is the fall—an orthodox-traditional doctrine of original sin and a doctrine of total depravity, which echo back to Augustine and Lewis's patristic reading. However, Lewis admits he is not necessarily trying to convert people—all he is doing is aiming to get people to face the facts, the questions which Christianity answers: *praeparatio evangelica*—this is Lewis's role in preparing for evangelism, for conversion. This is the conclusion of the first set of talks—which were a philosophical examination of the basis of reality from a Christian perspective—the "what if," a logical extrapolation of what follows if right and wrong really are a clue to the meaning of the universe.

A Dualistic Heresy

The second series of talks was entitled *What Christians Believe* and it is here that we begin to understand what Lewis taught in terms of revelation and the Christ. Having laid the philosophical groundwork through ethics, so to speak, Lewis now turns to the doctrinal basics of the Christian faith. Lewis straight away states that he is not asserting Christianity as right over and above all other religions; the truth is much more subtle than that—the truth is analogous to mathematics where there may be one right answer but many of the wrong answers are close to the truth in varying degrees. Therefore Lewis points towards an important proposition in his Christology—that there are elements of revelation in other religions and mythologies. However, he is critical of pantheism, of belief in a pantheistic "god" who is beyond good and evil; a "god" he particularly associates with the influential German nineteenth-century philosopher Hegel, a "god" that for many is ultimately to be seen as human consciousness. Christian doctrine speaks of a God who created the universe but is not part of it and is not tied

---

37 Ibid., 31.
38 Ibid., 32.
39 Ibid.

for his own divine existence to the universe—an artist is not the painting s/he creates, and the artist does not cease to exist if the painting is lost or destroyed.[40] Lewis is equally critical of dualism as an alternative revelation. Dualism, for Lewis, asserts that the dark power in the universe stands equal and uncreated in opposition to God. No, the evil one is created by God—not created evil, or to be evil, but we live within a reality that is in rebellion: "Christianity agrees with Dualism that this universe is at war. But it doesn't think this is a war between independent powers. It thinks it's a civil war, a rebellion, and that we are living in a part of the universe occupied by the rebel. Enemy-occupied territory—that's what this world is. Christianity is the story of how the rightful king has landed, you might say landed in disguise, and is calling us all to take part in a great campaign of sabotage."[41]

The Rightful King

So the very nature of reality—the universe—and the nature of good and evil is rooted in the Christ, who is at the heart of a sound orthodox doctrine of God: without Christ—the rightful king—any concept of God will be inherently flawed and will be, to a degree, human generated and inaccurate to varying degrees. We rely on revelation for any sound understanding of God, and this revelation is at its fullest in the Christ event. And revelation informs us that evil is real, tangible, personified—the devil, Satan, was a good power, created good, that has become so evil that it is now nothing but evil. And humanity exhibits the same potential though its misuse of free will.

Freedom and Happiness

Why have things gone wrong? Lewis placed the emphasis on free will—the freedom to be, the freedom that God imbues creation with. This freedom implies the ability to go wrong or right, and the dark evil one has set himself up as prince of this world in opposition to the rightful King, Christ. Christ has, however, landed—in disguise. Therefore, the pertinent question for Lewis is not, "Why does evil and suffering exist?," but, "Is this situation in accordance with the will of God?" In the context of what Christian revelation tells us about creation the answer must be yes: a God of absolute power creates freely with the potential to go wrong, yet stoops in humility to be incarnated as the creature, to redeem the creature and take the suffering on to God's-self—human religion could never have come up with such a story and solution: "The happiness which God designs for his higher creatures is the happiness of being freely, voluntarily united to him and to each other in an ecstasy of love and delight . . . And for that they've got to be free."[42]

The key to understanding reality and the human condition is in a doctrine of original sin, the fall (N.B., humanity fell, other species within creations may not have fallen).[43] Satan put the idea into the minds of our ancestors, wrote Lewis, that we could

---

40 Ibid., 39.
41 Ibid., 46.
42 Ibid., 47.
43 This is at the heart of Lewis's science fiction trilogy—as in the novel, *Perelandra*.

be like gods (Gen 3), that we could set up on our own, define our own happiness, our own morality. This attempt was hopeless and led merely to human history. A history, for Lewis, characterized by money and poverty, war and ambition, prostitution, the class struggle, empires and slavery. Lewis takes this further: original sin is the key to history. Civilizations and cultures grow up, often founded on sound principles; good laws are formulated, but something always goes wrong: "some fatal flaw always brings the selfish and cruel people to the top and it all slides back into misery and ruin."[44]

The Christ of Salvation History

It is here, at the end of the third talk ("3. The Shocking Alternative") of the second series, that we have the kernel of Christian doctrine, a simple *summa*, profound it its completeness and brevity. Lewis outlines the development of salvation history from the basic sense of a conscience, the perception of the moral law, in all people, but chiefly amongst the Jews, but balances the forging of a chosen people with the intimations of prefigurement of the incarnation-resurrection narrative amongst non-Jewish religious traditions and tribes. He then cites how amongst the Jews a man turns up talking as if he was God, because he claims to have existed always, he claims to be able to forgive people's sins, further, that he is coming to judge the world at the end of time. Claiming divine status was not unusual amongst pantheists, pagans, and in religious traditions from the Indian sub-continent, or in other world religious-mythological traditions, but coming from a man born and raised in the Jewish tradition this was something other. Lewis understood that the doctrine of God in the Jewish tradition was quite different from all other world religions at that time: "God, in their language, meant the Being outside the world who had made it and was infinitely different from anything else. And when you've grasped that, you will see that what this man said was, quite simply, the most shocking thing that has ever been uttered by human lips."[45] This man, Jesus, cannot simply be dismissed as just another religious human being, a guru or prophet, a religious teacher, with an enhanced sense of the divine. His words and actions claim that he is the divine, and in the context of a Jewish doctrine of God, this claim is to be God incarnate, the righteous Lord of Jewish salvation history, the ultimate being and source and creator of all. Therefore, the doctrine of God that is at the heart of Christianity is rooted in revelation, grounded in this man Jesus, and is different from a doctrine of God in all other religions and mythologies: because of Christology— i.e., what we say and believe about this man Jesus. Lewis then criticizes the opposite view as absurd, the opinion that Jesus was just a good moral teacher. Because of the way he acted and spoke Jesus did not leave this open to us. If he, in effect, marginalizes the role and value of Jesus as a teacher, Lewis then focuses in the fourth talk ("4. The Perfect Penitent") on the value of Jesus's death and resurrection— theories of atonement. However, here he explains that theories about Christ's death are not Christianity in itself, but are explanations about how the cross works: "The thing itself is infinitely more important than any explanations that theologians have

44 Lewis, *Broadcast Talks*, 49.
45 Ibid., 50.

produced ... no explanation will ever be quite adequate to the reality ... a man can accept what Christ has done without knowing how it works. We are told that Christ was killed for us, that his death has washed out our sins, and that by dying he disabled death itself. That's the formula. That's Christianity. That's what has to be believed."[46]

Lewis read and knew that most atonement theories varied on small details, yet these details had been enough for Christians at different times to kill each other, but more pertinently, all the atonement theories, so he asserted, were inadequate. This side of eternity we won't fully understand how Christ's death and resurrection achieves what it does. Lewis then deals with repentance. Repentance is our only legitimate response to what Christ has done for us: to repent in humility, turning to God in the light of what Jesus Christ has done for us, is our only response to the fall, our only way out of hell and back to God.

The Perfect Death

In the fifth talk ("5. The Practical Conclusion") Lewis moves into spirituality and the church. Christ's perfect death involves all humanity: "In Christ a new kind of man appeared: and the new kind of life which began in him is to be put into us."[47] This allows Lewis to speak on the sacraments, faith, and the church. Lewis has simply explained why he believed that Jesus was (and is) God;[48] what becomes important, echoing the Apostle Paul, is not necessarily theories of atonement but the Christ life—this is not a moral life or some mental process, but the indwelling of Christ's Holy Spirit in those who profess to be Christian. However, this does not produce, for Lewis, a closed religious sect. Simple knowledge about the Christ event does not lead to exclusivity. Lewis speaks of critics who claim that salvation based on knowledge of the Christ event is unfair: "Well, the truth is God hasn't told us what his arrangements about the other people are. We do know that no man can be saved except through Christ; we don't know that only those who know him can be saved through him."[49] Lewis then takes the concept of God *incognito* further. (Lewis's use of the word "disguise" relates, to a degree, to the Danish philosopher/theologian Søren Kierkegaard who wrote of Christ as *God incognito*.[50]) Lewis explains how the Christ event is a landing in disguise in enemy-occupied territory, which leads to the founding and creating of an underground force (the church) that will surely undermine the power and authority of Satan, but this is prior to the full invasion when God will come openly for all to see at the end of time, as all that we take for the world and reality dissolves away and we

46   Ibid., 52–53.
47   Ibid., 57.
48   Ibid., 58.
49   Ibid., 60.
50   Kierkegaard's thinking is shared by Lewis, though there is no evidence that Lewis knew of or had read Kierkegaard's work. For example, Søren Kierkegaard, *Einübung in Christentum*: Christ as "the paradox" (20, 25 and 57); the problem of the modern world and "contemporaneity," with Christ (ibid., 56–60); the "infinite qualitative distinction" (ibid., 124) between humanity and God; Kierkegaard's concept of the incarnation as the divine "incognito" (ibid., 112) is reminiscent of Lewis's picture of God landing in this world in disguise; and the realization of the impossibility of "direct communication" (ibid., 121–28) reflects, to a degree, Lewis's doctrine of transposition—that revelation is transposed.

perceive and know God without disguise. This will cause, "either irresistible love or irresistible horror into every creature. It will be too late then to choose your side . . . Now is our chance to choose the right side. God is holding back to give us a chance. It won't last forever. We must take it or leave it."[51]

ii. The Third Series—"Christian Behaviour"

A New Morality

The third series, as the title implies, is essentially about Christian ethics.[52] Though there is significantly less in terms of a doctrine of revelation and Christology, the talks are grounded throughout on, and with, references to the sayings of Jesus. This is not about rules of behavior; the implication for Lewis is that Christ wants servants with a child's simplicity of heart but with an adult's head.[53] God wants not obedience to a set of rules but people who have attained a certain *character*. Christ did not preach a new kind of morality because the golden rule ("Do as you would be done by," as Lewis terms it) of the New Testament sums up all that is in the Law in the Old Testament.[54] The third series of talks is essentially about the demands placed on us by Christ—the Christ as a reality beyond our own moral codes, our own preconceptions of how and why we should behave in a certain way. Therefore Lewis quickly nails on the head a dualistic morality that decries the body—the flesh is good, says Lewis, because the incarnation is good.[55] In case we are in any doubt as to the authority of how we should behave and the ontological reality in which ethics are grounded, Lewis asserts Christ's own words that a man and a woman become one flesh through marriage—that the Greek words used imply a single organism—therefore the very nature of being, of ontological existence of a woman and a man in Christ, changes.[56] That ethics is grounded in ontology is represented by Christ's revelation that for "Joy" (*Sehnsucht*) to live truly it must die:

> This is, I think, one little part of what Christ meant by saying that a thing won't really live unless it first dies. It's just no good trying to keep any thrill: that's the very worst thing you can do. Let the thrill go—let it die away—go on through that period of death into the quieter interest and happiness that follow and you'll find you are living in a world of new thrills all the time. But if you decide to live on thrills and try to prolong them artificially, they will all get weaker and weaker, and fewer and fewer, and you will be a bored, disillusioned old man for the rest of your life.[57]

---

51 Lewis, *Broadcast Talks*, 61–63.
52 Lewis, *Christian Behaviour*.
53 Ibid., 12.
54 Ibid., 16.
55 Ibid., 28.
56 Ibid., 30.
57 Ibid., 33.

9. Apologist and Defender of the Faith I: Revelation and Christology, 1931–44

Lewis is also cogent in his understanding of Scripture in relationship to death and ethics—unlike most writers he readily recognizes that the Greek word Christ uses when asserting that we should not "kill" is the word for *murder* (as also is the Hebrew word in the Pentateuch); not all killing is murder so there is no warrant for ethical pacifism.[58] We are therefore ever moving in our souls, within the very nature of our being, into either heavenly or hellish creatures.

The Great Sin

The first five talks in this the third series were in effect dealing with general Christian morality. From this point on ("6. The Great Sin") Lewis brings morality and ethics alongside and in relation to the incarnation, cross, and resurrection, the heart of Christian revelation: the sin at the centre of the fall, original sin. This is the pride that caused humanity's fall away from communion and safety with God; the pride that caused humanity to erect its own abilities proudly to go it alone. Unchastity, anger, greed, and drunkenness are, in comparison, minor—"it was through Pride that the devil became the devil: pride leads to every other vice: it is the complete anti-God state of mind."[59] Pride for Lewis equals power. It is at this point that Lewis draws on revelation in the context that the "god" many proud powerful people claim to believe in and worship, the "god" of people eaten up with pride, may not be the one true living God *revealed* in Christ Jesus. This, for Lewis, is a phantom "god": "I suppose it was of those people Christ was thinking when he said that some would preach about him and cast out devils in his name, only to be told at the end of the world that he had never known them. And any of us may at any moment be in this death-trap."[60] Therefore, the worst of vices can secrete itself into the very core of our religious life, worming (in a serpent-like manner) itself into us to cause in us this very "dictatorship of pride" which will alienate us from Christ.[61] The solution, so to speak, is the grace of God in Christ acting in us to bring about charity, which will cause us to forget about ourselves or see ourselves as truly without benefit or pride, as fallen and incapable of curing ourselves. Therefore faith, hope, and charity are for Lewis the three theological virtues. Because both good and evil advance exponentially, they "increase at compound interest,"[62] the little decisions we make each and every day are of "infinite importance."[63] If our minds are occupied with heaven we will sort out our earthly life.[64]

---

58   Ibid., 40. The sixth commandment, "Thou shalt not kill" (Exod 20:13) should be more accurately translated as "Thou shalt not commit an illegal killing." The Hebrew evokes an irrational act, an unmeasured response (the sin of Cain?). The nearest we have in English is the word murder: the Hebrew is *ratsach* (pronounced rah-tsakh)—a primitive root properly, to dash in pieces, i.e., to kill (a human being), especially to murder, put to death. In the Gospels, the word used is, φονεύω (*phoneuō*)—"murder," "put to death"; see, Matt 5:21; Mark 10:19; and Luke 18:20.
59   Ibid., 42.
60   Ibid., 45.
61   Ibid.
62   Ibid., 49.
63   Ibid.
64   Ibid., 51.

Grace Initiates—Works Respond

It is only, for Lewis, in attempting to fight the evil impulse that we can begin to understand its awesome strength. This is why grace is so important—through the cross Christ offers us something for nothing.[65] In this context Lewis examines the question of good works. The apparent dichotomy which has bedeviled many of the Protestant churches since the Reformation is solved for Lewis by asserting that *what comes first is faith in Christ*, the movement of the will to Christ, acceptance of what has been done on the cross; but *this should lead to so-called good works*. Motivation is the key—we cannot buy our way into heaven: "Faith in Christ is the only thing to save you from despair at that point: and out of that faith in him good actions must inevitably come."[66] Lewis continues that if what you call your faith in Christ doesn't involve taking the slightest notice of what Jesus Christ says or expects of you then it is no faith at all—perhaps it is some intellectual acceptance of a theory, but it lack the trust that is at the heart of faith. Lewis alludes to and paraphrases Paul's letter to the Philippians at this point near the end of the last talk in the series to show how the conflict between faith and good works comes together, where we are persuaded by Paul to work out our salvation, but to acknowledge that it is God working preveniently in us that is the origin of our deeds.[67]

iii. The Fourth Series—"Beyond Personality"

A Trinitarian Paradox

By the time Lewis came to write the fourth and last series in the winter of 1943–44, entitled *Beyond Personality*,[68] he was already formulating a clear understanding in his mind about a "Mere" core from his reading of Richard Baxter and Vincentius of Lérins, for he prefaces this series with the statement that "These talks attempt to put into simple modern language the account of God which, to the best of my knowledge, the vast majority of Christian churches have agreed in giving for a great many centuries."[69] Lewis is not attempting to be a systematic theologian and prove anything (if that is indeed what systematic theologians do) but to describe what Christians believe. Therefore his aim is to "apologize" for the Christian faith, his objective is to justify it through description. Lewis acknowledges that there will be people in different countries who question some of what he describes, but as we have seen, Lewis's aim was to present Mere Christianity not Mere Lewisianity—that which has been believed at "nearly all times and in nearly all countries."[70] The fourth series is much more infused

---

65 Ibid., 62.
66 Ibid., 63.
67 "Therefore, my dear friends, as you have always obeyed—not only in my presence, but now much more in my absence—continue to work out your salvation with fear and trembling, for it is God who works in you to will and to act according to his good purpose." Phil 2:12–13.
68 Lewis, *Beyond Personality: the Christian Idea of God*.
69 Ibid., 5.
70 Ibid.

9. Apologist and Defender of the Faith I: Revelation and Christology, 1931-44

by trinitarian theology and despite Lewis's claims of amateurism, his understanding is as nuanced and profound as most professional orthodox creedal theologians (probably because of the immense amount of patristic theology and medieval scholasticism he has read since his conversion over a decade earlier). Almost every talk deals with an attempt at explicating the paradox of the Trinity to a relatively uneducated audience without compromising theological cogency. Lewis knows he is dealing with doctrinal assertions and therefore opens with the analogy between faith and doctrine being comparable with a map of the Atlantic Ocean (attested to by hundreds of people's knowledge and experience) as compared to the individual experience of standing on the shore looking out to sea: the individual experience will seem more real than the map, but the map is immeasurably more accurate.[71] Lewis castigates again the idea that Jesus was just a good moral teacher; he gets straight to the heart of the faith—that is, the ontological status of Jesus as the Christ: "They say that Christ is the Son of God (whatever that means). They say that those who give him their confidence can also become Sons of God (whatever that means). They say that his death saved us from our sins (whatever that means)."[72] Series four of the Broadcast Talks is essentially a long discourse attempting an apologetic explanation to answer, "whatever that means." If Jesus of Nazareth is the Christ and if he is more than an ordinary human being then these questions about the nature of his being (ontology), his relationship to and in God (trinitarian), and his saving action that redeems us (soteriology— i.e., theories of salvation) are critical. Lewis acknowledges that these statements are difficult, but if we are to take our predicament seriously and if we are to take God seriously we cannot avoid these statements and the difficult questions that arise.

The Universal Christ

Lewis focuses in relative depth on the relationship between the nature of the Christ and our becoming sons and daughters of God. This allows him to extrapolate on the distinction between begotten and created/made, which he sustains throughout this series of talks: the universal Christ, the second person of the Trinity is begotten not created; we are created not begotten, yet are drawn into the trinitarian life through being enfolded into the Christ:

> To beget is to become the father of: to create is to make. And the difference is just this. When you beget, you beget something of the same kind as yourself. A man begets human babies . . . but when you make, you make something of a different kind from yourself. If he's a clever enough carver he may make a statue which is very like a man indeed. But, of course, it's not a real man; it only looks like one. What God begets is God; just as what man begets is man. What God creates is not God; just as what man makes is not man. That is why men are not Sons of God in the sense that Christ is.[73]

---

71   Ibid., 10.
72   Ibid., 11.
73   Ibid., 12-13.

Creation therefore involves difference; the Christ is eternally uncreated, the only begotten of the Father. We are created not begotten of God. The only begotten Son is all that the Father is; proceeding forth from and in the Father. Creation implies difference; the fall fractures this difference even further.

Lewis then moves into the second talk ("2. The Three-Personal God") where he deals with trinitarian theology. The Trinity is the single most unique element of Christian revelation; no pagan religion, however profound, could come up with such a doctrine of God. Lewis places great importance on holding to right ideas about God and life-after-death; such ideas will lead to a sound doctrine of God, which is trinitarian. Lewis initially deals with the question of "person" and "personality," through which the Christian conception of God is "*beyond personality*."[74] But contrary to other religious systems, "beyond personality" here, for Lewis, does not imply that God is impersonal. To be impersonal, Lewis asserts, is to be something less than personal: the trinitarian God is *supra*-personal: this makes the Christian doctrine of God unique, amongst religions.[75] This understanding is informed by Berkleyian Platonism: the real is *truly* real, it is *more* real; it is *supra*-real. Personality is more than we take for personality; it is more real, supra-real. The trinitarian three-personal life is *personality beyond personality*. Lewis appreciates that he is moving into the realm of paradox. This supra-real three-personal life is what we will be drawn into upon our death—we will not be absorbed, where absorption implies ceasing to exist.[76] What can we know of this?—"When you come to knowing God, the initiative lies on his side. If he doesn't show himself, nothing you can do will enable you to find him,"[77] which neatly brings Lewis's argument back to his conversion and his commission before the tri-personal God.

A Temporal Paradox: the Universal and Particular

Lewis takes the question of paradox further by fielding the question of time—time beyond time—and how this relates to the Trinity: God beyond time, God not in time, a trinitarian life that is not confined or characterized by moments of time, by sequentiality. God is characterized in relation to humanity by both universality and particularity (the incarnation): "When Christ died, he died for you individually just as much as if you had been the only man in the world."[78] Leading on from time Lewis asserts that God is one being who is three persons while remaining one being—he invokes the analogy of a cube containing six squares, and reiterates the distinction, now in the context of the non-sequential-time of the divine life, between begetting and making: the Son exists because the Father exists; but there never was a time before the Father begat the Son. The Son perpetually issues forth from the Father: "We must think of the Son always, so to speak, streaming forth from the Father, like light from

74 Ibid., 14.
75 Ibid., 15.
76 Ibid., 17–18.
77 Ibid., 18.
78 Ibid., 17–18.

9. Apologist and Defender of the Faith I: Revelation and Christology, 1931–44

a lamp, or heat from a fire, or thoughts from a mind. He is the self-expression of the Father—what the Father has to say. And there never was a time when he wasn't saying it."[79] God is love. Love exists between two persons; therefore if God was one, a monist singularity, then before anything was created God, asserts Lewis, could not have been love.[80] Lewis continues that God, the Christian doctrine of God, asserts that God cannot be a static thing, or even a single person, but ever dynamic, he uses the word "pulsating," a kind of drama.[81] Hence this union between the Father and the Son is such a live, concrete, supra-real thing that this union is also a person—the third person, the Holy Spirit. And this Spirit of God acts in and through us. Lewis invokes the "technical" language as he terms it of the Holy Ghost or the "spirit" of God. This, the third person of the Trinity, is going to be perceived by us as vaguer or more shadowy: "In the Christian life you aren't usually looking at him: He is always acting through you. If you think of the Father as something 'out there,' in front of you, and of the Son as someone standing at your side, helping you to pray, trying to turn you into another son, then you have to think of the third Person as something inside you, or behind you."[82] Lewis admits that many would prefer to start with the action and presence of the Holy Spirit, working towards the Son and the Father. Lewis noted often the importance of the action of the Holy Spirit in peoples and cultures widely dispersed and outside of the knowledge of salvation evident in Christians, for this is the Spirit of Love that from all eternity is a love existing between the Father and the Son, hence the three-personal life of God. Lewis does not indulge in technical theological language but we need to acknowledge a distinction in theology between the immanent Trinity (the triune life of love between the three persons in eternity, "beyond" and "before" the creation of space-time) and the economic Trinity (the action and presence of God *within creation*—governing the "economy" of the world, of creation). We are drawn by the Holy Spirit into Christ and thereby into the divine life in eternity—"Every Christian is to become a little Christ. The whole purpose of becoming a Christian is simply that: nothing else."[83] Furthermore, "The Church exists for nothing else than to draw men into Christ, to make them little Christs. If they are not doing that, all the cathedrals, clergy, missions, sermons, even the Bible itself, are simply a waste of time. God became man for no other purpose."[84]

"The Son of God became a man to enable men to become sons of God"

The fourth talk ("4. The Obstinate Toy Soldiers") asserts the reason for revelation: Christ descended to incarnation to raise us up to the life of God. What would have happened had humanity not rebelled, Lewis concedes, is speculation. Perhaps we would all have been *in Christ* and shared in the life of the Son. The fourth talk therefore deals with the nature of existence, the nature of being, the ontology of the second

79   Ibid., 25.
80   Ibid., 25.
81   Ibid., 26.
82   Ibid., 26–27.
83   Ibid., 28.
84   Ibid., 43.

person of the Trinity: the eternal being that created all became a fetus inside a woman's body; however, this one man becomes what all men and women were intended to be. Therefore there was one human in whom the created life was, in itself, to be completely and perfectly tuned into the begotten life. The natural human creature was taken up completely and fully into the divine life of the second person of the Trinity: humanity passes into the life of the Christ, the Son. Hence, for us, the natural life has to die to live. Lewis notes how Jesus chose an earthly career that involved the death of his human desires at every turn: "[This was] poverty, misunderstanding from his own family, betrayal by one of his intimate friends, being jeered at and manhandled by the Police, and execution by torture. And then, after being thus killed—killed every day, in a sense—the human creature in him, because it was united to the divine Son, came to life again. The Man in Christ rose again: not only the God."[85] Because of the interconnectedness of humanity, in one man all died (Adam) and in another all are raised up (Jesus).[86] We are part of this: "The Son of God became a man to enable men to become sons of God."[87] Therefore humanity, for Lewis, is already "saved" in principle; however, as individuals we have to appropriate this salvation. This does not mean we try to climb up into the spiritual life, for Christ has descended to us—all we need to do is lay ourselves open to the one man who was both real God and real man.

A doctrine of atonement is a theory about how this works. Lewis briefly tackles the question of atonement theories—for which he is often criticized for avoiding. Lewis observed that some of the fiercest divisions within Christianity (not just between denominations but in sub-groups within a particular church or denomination) came from disagreements resulting from competing doctrines of atonement. There is, it is fair to say, wisdom in what Lewis says in that he can see that agreement won't necessarily be reached and that a full and complete understanding of how atonement works is probably beyond humanity: Lewis notes that "God is no one but himself"; God's freedom implies that we will never fully know and understand this side of eternity how atonement works:

> Of course, you can express this [atonement] in all sorts of different ways. You can say that Christ died for our sins. You may say that the Father has forgiven us because Christ has done for us what we ought to have done. You may say that we are washed in the blood of the Lamb. You may say that Christ has defeated death. They're all true. If any of them don't appeal to you, leave it alone and get on with the formula that does. And, whatever you do, don't start quarrelling with other people because they don't use the same formula as you do. [88]

Although Lewis is often criticized for avoiding the difficulties and complexities in theories of how atonement works, our inability to understand fully how propitiatory reconciliation works will be the norm after the fall, this side of eternity: we are not the

---

85   Ibid., 30.
86   Lewis has a sound understand of the Apostle Paul on the relationship between sin, death, and resurrection through the one man: Rom 5:17 and 1 Cor 15:21; see also Rom 6 and 2 Cor 5:14.
87   Lewis, *Beyond Personality*, 28.
88   Ibid., 31.

9. Apologist and Defender of the Faith I: Revelation and Christology, 1931-44

author or subject of atonement, neither do we enact it—Jesus did on the cross; we are the object of atonement, the object of propitiatory reconciliation.

Carriers of Christ

The seventh talk ("7. The New Man") extends the theme of atonement into sanctification. In speaking the words of The Lord's Prayer we claim to be part of the trinitarian sonship ("Our Father . . ."), so we are attempting to put ourselves in the place of Christ; we should realize our inadequacy, yet we are ordered by Jesus to do this: "You see what's happening. The Christ himself, the Son of God who is man (just like you) and God (just like his Father) is actually at your side and is already at that moment beginning to turn your pretence into a reality . . . The real Son of God is at your side. He is beginning to turn you into the same kind of thing as himself."[89] The more we open ourselves to Christ the more we are changed, the more we are sanctified. Therefore for Lewis we are mirrors, or carriers, of Christ to other people. Church—or how we present Christ through the church—is thus of crucial importance. If we are "truly born again," says Lewis, if we are truly "putting on Christ," if "Christ is being formed in us," if we have "the mind of Christ," then we are the body of Christ.[90] This is more than merely following a teacher's teachings. This is about the nature of our being, but it is also about the judgment of God from the end of all things (eschatology): we are in some ways pre-judged if we are truly drawn into Christ's divine life. If all goes well, says Lewis, we will be turned permanently into a different sort of being; but, Lewis again asserts, we can do nothing of this: "it is God who does everything."[91] We are the grumbling, self-centered, rebellious, human animal that the "Three-Personal-God" sees, but in us he perceives the potential for change. Our consent, lowering our flag of rebellion, is all it takes.[92] This, for Lewis, is the whole of Christianity—it offers nothing else. It is therefore both hard and easy—Christ demands all, gives all, does all, but it is so hard for us to capitulate: at one time he says "take up your cross," then at another he says, "My yoke is easy and my burden light."[93] For Lewis this is encapsulated by the Apostle Paul's comments about putting on Christ.[94] Again, Lewis asserts the church exists for nothing else than to draw men into Christ—"God became man for no other purpose."[95] Should we count the cost? Are we nice people or a new creation in Christ? We should not count the cost, asserts Lewis, because of the command to be perfect.[96] But we may not be very nice as we are changed and transformed. Therefore, there may not be a clear distinction between Christians and non-Christians. Amongst Christians there will be people of varying degrees of perfection, and those who do

---

89 Ibid., 36.
90 Ibid., 38.
91 Ibid., 39.
92 Ibid., 39.
93 Ibid., 41. See: Matt 11:30 and 16:24; Mark 8:34; and Luke 9:23.
94 See, for example, Eph 4:24 and Col 3:10.
95 Lewis, *Beyond Personality*, 43.
96 Ibid., 48.

not accept the doctrines and teachings of the church to as full an extent as others and not necessarily any worse or better than those who can see and accept doctrinal statements—"many of the good Pagans long before Christ's birth may have been in this position . . . consequently it is not much use trying to make judgements about Christians and non-Christians in the mass."[97] Mere improvement is not redemption; it is transformation that is important: "Christ is the 'first instance' of the new man. But of course he is something much more than that. He is not merely *a* new man, one specimen of the species, but *the* new man. He is the origin and centre and life of all the new men. He comes into the created universe, of his own will, bringing with him the Zoe, the new life."[98] To be transformed into new men and women we must lose all that we consider ourselves. Once we turn to Christ and give ourselves up to him, we become new persons, and these truly new begin to have a real personality of their own.[99] There are no real personalities outside of the Trinity; therefore we can only truly exist in Christ, in the divine life. Lewis concludes the *Broadcast Talks* with this comment: "Keep nothing back. Nothing that you have not given away will ever be really yours. Nothing in you that has not died will ever be raised from the dead. Look for yourself, and you will find in the long run only hatred, loneliness, despair, rage, ruin, and decay. But look for Christ and you will find him, and with him everything else thrown in."[100]

---

97 Ibid., 50.
98 Ibid., 59–60.
99 Ibid., 63.
100 Ibid., 64.

9. Apologist and Defender of the Faith I: Revelation and Christology, 1931–44

C. S. Lewis: The Key Theological and Philosophical Works—The Early Period (1931–44) and The Middle Period (1942–47)

1933
— *The Pilgrims Regress: An Allegorical Apology for Christianity, Reason and Romanticism.*

1933
— *The Allegory of Love: A Study in Medieval Tradition.*

1938
— *Out of the Silent Planet.*

1940
— *The Problem of Pain.*

1941
— "The Weight of Glory."
A sermon preached at the University Church of St Mary the Virgin, Oxford, on 8 June 1941.

1942
— *Broadcast Talks.* Reprinted with some alterations from two series of Broadcast Talks *Right and Wrong: A Clue to the Meaning of the Universe* and *What Christians Believe* given in 1941 and 1942.
5 radio talks broadcast on BBC Home Service.
— *The Screwtape Letters.*
Originally serialised in the Anglo-Catholic newspaper, *The Guardian*, between May and November 1941.

1943
— *Christian Behaviour.*
8 radio talks broadcast on BBC Home Service.
— *Perelandra.*

1944
— *Beyond Personality: The Christian Idea of God.*
7 radio talks broadcast on BBC Home Service.
— "Transposition."
A sermon preached at Mansfield College Chapel, Oxford, Whit-Sunday, May 28, 1944.

1945
— *The Great Divorce: A Dream.* London: Macmillan, 1945.
— *That Hideous Strength. A Modern Fairytale for Grown-Ups.*

1947
— *Miracles. A Preliminary Study*

KEY WORKS—LETTERS 1931–47

— C. S. Lewis to Arthur Greeves, Feb. 28, 1916. *Collected Letters, Vol. I,* 167.
— C. S. Lewis to Arthur Greeves, Oct. 12, 1916. *Collected Letters, Vol. I,* 230–33.
— C. S. Lewis to Arthur Greeves, Aug. 4, 1917. *Collected Letters, Vol. I,* 333.
— C. S. Lewis to A. J. Lewis (father), Mar. 28, 1921. *Collected Letters, Vol. I,* 534–36.
— C. S. Lewis to Arthur Greeves, Sept. 22, 1931. *Collected Letters, Vol. I,* 969–72.
— C. S. Lewis to Arthur Greeves, Oct. 1, 1931. *Collected Letters, Vol. I,* 972–75.
— C. S. Lewis to Arthur Greeves, Oct. 18, 1931. *Collected Letters, Vol. I,* 977.
— C. S. Lewis to Arthur Greeves, Dec. 6, 1931. *Collected Letters, Vol. II,* 22–25.
— C. S. Lewis to Dom Bede Griffiths, Apr. 4, 1934. *Collected Letters, Vol. II,* 136.
— C. S. Lewis to Owen Barfield, Aug 1939. *Collected Letters, Vol. II,* 266–69.
— C. S. Lewis to Mrs Mary Neylan, Mar. 26, 1940. *Collected Letters, Vol. II,* 371–76.
— C. S. Lewis to W. H. Lewis (brother), Feb. 18, 1940. *Collected Letters, Vol. II,* 347–53.
— C. S. Lewis to W. H. Lewis (brother), Apr. 28, 1940. *Collected Letters, Vol. II,* 404–6.
— C. S. Lewis to Sr. Penelope CSMV, May 15, 1941. *Collected Letters, Vol. II,* 484–85.
— C. S. Lewis to the editor of The Spectator, Dec. 11, 1942. *Collected Letters, Vol. II,* 540.
— C. S. Lewis to Arthur Greeves, Jan. 30, 1944. *Collected Letters, Vol. III,* 1547–48.
— C. S. Lewis to H. Lyman Stebbins May 8, 1945. *Collected Letters, Vol. II,* 645–47.

A complete list of Lewis's works in this period can be found in the bibliography

Figure 12: C. S. Lewis: the Key Theological and Philosophical Works—The Early Period (1931–44) and the Middle Period (1931–47)

10

Apologist and Defender of the Faith II: Revelation and Christology, 1941–47— The Middle Works

SYNOPSIS:
Lewis's development as a Christian apologist was built on the success of the BBC radio broadcasts. The middle period of works, from 1941 to 1947, was probably Lewis's most intensely productive and assertively confident period. Lewis's understanding can be found, essentially, in *Miracles* (1947), but there is also valuable evidence in *The Screwtape Letters* (1942) and *The Great Divorce* (1945) as well as the many essays and other works where important evidence can be found. The key is, as ever with Lewis, in the person and the office of Jesus Christ. Revelation and reason: how does the revelatory "I Am," expose the fallacy of religion, popular human religion, referred to as "pantheism" by Lewis? How does the incarnation, "The Grand Miracle," relate to God's supranatural action within this reality, the world? In the *infinitum capax finiti* (the infinite capable of the finite) revelation defines what our understanding of God's infinity should be—the truly infinite capacity of God is also to be finite, specific, incarnated. This contradicts our religious expectations for a distant singular "god," an unknowable and unattainable "god," whereas transposition reveals the incarnation. In consequence, Lewis writes (drawing on the work of Thomas Erskine of Linlathen), that those who make "Religion their god," will not have "God for their religion." Because of our kingdom of religion, Christ is also hidden—he is the threatening Lord that intimidates and daunts Screwtape's machinations, yet he is the "bloody" charity that stands ever open to forgive people their stupid arrogant sins in *The Great Divorce*. The greatest understanding, arguably, of Lewis's development can be seen in two key essays/sermons from the period of the Second World War: "The Weight of Glory" (1941) and "Transposition" (1944). Likewise it is during this period that he formulates the ground for the patristic basis of what he identifies as "Mere" Christianity.

1. INTRODUCTION

In 1947 Lewis published a work entitled *Miracles*.[1] This was intended to be a serious apologetic, dealing with what Lewis and many perceived to be a chief objection to Christianity—the concept of miracles, the action of a supernatural being within what many academics and scientists considered to be a closed, single-level, universe.

---

1   Lewis, *Miracles*, 1st ed.

A primary objection to the concept of the miraculous was that the universe was fixed from the moment of creation, the big bang; further, that the universe was self-contained and hermetic, self-sustaining and autonomous. Lewis readily accepted the miraculous: "I have never found any philosophical grounds for the universal negative proposition that miracles do not happen."[2] The universal philosophical principle that Lewis cites is not a truism, simply an objection, however intellectually couched it may be. A secondary objection was the idea of that a "god" interfering with creation seemed preposterous. The book *Miracles* is essentially an apologetic discourse (drawing on Lewis's philosophical skills) in defense of miracles, and therefore of God's action within this world. We have encountered *Miracles* earlier in W. Norman Pittenger's criticism of Lewis's Christology. We need here to examine what Lewis tells us of his understanding of revelation and the Christ. This understanding can be found in two chapters: "XI. Christianity and 'Religion,'" and, "XIV. The Grand Miracle."[3]

2. THE REVELATORY "I AM," AND "THE GRAND MIRACLE"

i. Revelation over and against Religion

In, "Christianity and 'Religion,'" Lewis presents what is in effect a defense of revelation over and against religion—popular religion. The "god" of popular religion, Lewis asserts, could certainly not work miracles; therefore the question is whether such a popular religion is true: "I call it religion advisedly. We who defend Christianity find ourselves constantly opposed not by the irreligion of our hearers but by their real religion."[4] The problem, Lewis perceives, is in relation to a God who has purpose and performs actions within our reality: "The popular 'religion' excludes miracles because it excludes the 'living God' of Christianity . . . this popular 'religion' may roughly be called Pantheism."[5] Lewis proceeds to outline the roots of this popular religion in the Victorian Darwinian model of human evolution, which classified religion as a tribal human construct to a hostile world: "this imagined history of religion is not true."[6] According to this evolutionary model of religion tribal anthropomorphism—a "god" modeled on and projected from human fears—gradually evolves into a pure abstraction. All that is left is spirit, a spirit which is either divorced completely from this universe or, in pantheism, is aligned with everything. In terms of a psychological-Feuerbachian model, this divinity is then perceived as an illusion. Lewis classifies this popular religion as pantheism because it attempts a syncretistic fusion of all religions and human desires; it draws on the Darwinian evolutionary model, but pulls back

---

2   Lewis, *Reflections on the Psalms*, 94–95.
3   Lewis, *Miracles* 1st ed. 99–114 and 131–58.
4   Ibid., 99.
5   Ibid., 99–100.
6   Ibid., 100. Lewis does not mention Sir James George Frazer a Victorian anthropologist and religionist here, but this is the mind behind Lewis's criticism. Frazer's work and this model of religion, more pertinently the effect it had on the young Lewis, will be examined when we examine Lewis's respect for pagan North European myths and what they taught about the Christ.

10. Apologist and Defender of the Faith II: Revelation and Christology, 1941–47

from the Feuerbachian illusionary model—because there must be something, some sort of "god": "If 'religion' means simply what man says about God, and not what God does about man, then Pantheism almost is religion. And 'religion' in that sense has, in the long run, only one really formidable opponent—namely Christianity."[7] Lewis includes a footnote at the end of this sentence reflecting the policy of the post-war Labour government in seeking a broad non-Christian basis for religious education in British schools: "Hence, if a Minister of Education professes to value religion and at the same time takes steps to suppress Christianity, it does not necessarily follow that he is a hypocrite or even (in the ordinary this-worldly sense of the word) a fool. He may sincerely desire more 'religion' and rightly see that the suppression of Christianity is a necessary preliminary to his design."[8] What we find here is the origins of a form of dialectical thinking, as such, in Lewis's understanding—a dialectical opposition between *religions*, on the one hand, and *revelation*, on the other. Lewis criticizes such religion as artificial and false—in varying degrees—because what humanity conceives of and invents in terms of religious ideas about God ("what man says about God," as distinct from "what God does about man") may not be completely wrong, but may have degrees of truth amidst a plethora of falsity. Revelation is not to be seen as ideas people come up with about God, or the "gods," but what God does about the human predicament (the incarnation, and the cross-resurrection). In many ways this is an extrapolation of what Lewis said in the *Broadcast Talks*. Lewis is much more subtle and nuanced in this dialectic than many continental dialectical theologians because there is not a hard and fast division between religious ideas of human invention and what God reveals about God. The key questions is, "What is the extent to which some of these religious ideas are of human invention while others may be intimations from God, inspired in the mind by the Holy Spirit?" This leads to a second question: "What is the extent to which God puts into the imagination of diverse peoples some glimmer of understanding relating to the Christ event?"

What is it in revelation, or revealed religion, that is so distinct from this popular, pantheistic "religion" for Lewis? It is the Trinity. The pantheistic popular religion is too simple, too easy:

> God is present in a great many different modes: not present in matter as he is present in man, not present in all man as in some, not present in any other man as in Jesus ... God is super-personal. The Christian means by this that God has a positive structure which we could never have guessed in advance, any more than a knowledge of squares would have enabled us to guess at a cube. He contains "persons" (three of them) while remaining one God, as a cube combines six squares while remaining one solid body. We cannot comprehend such a structure any more than the Flatlanders could comprehend a cube. But we can at least comprehend our incomprehension, and see that if there is something beyond personality it ought to be incomprehensible ... at every point Christianity has to correct the natural expectations.[9]

7   Ibid., 101.
8   Ibid., 101, n. 1.
9   Ibid., 103–4.

ii. infinitum capax finiti: The Contradiction of our Religious Expectations

So, God is present in a great many modes, asserts Lewis; modes which at every point seem to contradict our religious expectations. It is here that Lewis gets the closest to a dialectical balance between religion and revelation. At the heart of the revealed knowledge of God is an understanding of the trinitarian nature of God that we could never has imagined for ourselves: the tri-personality, the Father, Son, and Holy Spirit. Knowledge of the Trinity is transposed—our feeble attempts at creating a mental model of God fail to get near the reality of God because God is beyond all we take for the reality that is God: "Christianity faced with popular 'religion' is continuously troublesome. To the large well-meant statements of 'religion' it finds itself forced to reply again and again, 'Well, not quite like that,' or, 'I should hardly put it that way.'"[10] A popular problem, Lewis identifies, paraphrasing the English philosopher and mathematician Alfred North Whitehead, is that we pay God too many ill-considered metaphysical compliments. Here we have something of a kernel of Lewis's doctrine of God, or more pertinently, the parameters of God as a being beyond being, more real than real but with a particular character

> We encourage ourselves to think of him as a formless "everything" about whom nothing in particular and everything in general is true . . . he is not "universal being," if he were there would be no creatures for a generality can make nothing. He is "absolute being"—or rather *The* "absolute being"—in the sense that he alone exists in his own right. But there are things which God is not. In that sense he has a determinate character. Thus he is righteous, not a-moral; creative, not inert.[11]

Lewis acknowledges that the Hebrew Scriptures have a better understanding of God, and maintain an admirable balance between finitude and infinitude. Better than what? Many of the attributes we give to God are derived from Greek philosophy—omnipotence, omniscience, omnipresence, infinitude, and so forth. This excludes, to a degree, the particular character of God as righteous Lord who shows both anger and favor with his chosen people. We will find this balance in the Hebrew Scriptures: "Once God says simply I AM, proclaiming the mystery of self-existence. But times without number he says, 'I Am The Lord'—I, the ultimate fact, have *this* determinate character, and not *that*. And men are exhorted to 'know the Lord,' to discover and experience this particular character."[12] Humanity in the form of this popular pantheistic religion will issue a compliment to God by asserting that he is no particular thing; asserting a particularity, it would be argued, would obliterate the immeasurability of God. Yet through revelation God shows God to be particular and universal—immeasurable yet specific. It is this compliment of *only* asserting immeasurability that denies the incarnation. If we say God is infinite, does that imply he cannot be finite, if God so wills? Lewis comments that if we have any sound understanding of what God is we

---

10 Ibid., 104.
11 Ibid., 106.
12 Ibid., 106–7.

should see that there is no question as to existence—it is impossible that God should not exist, God simply and entirely *is*. Yet once God creates, then there is the potential to be "other than," to be in some sense a particular thing. This does not lessen the immeasurability we attribute to God. But to say that God cannot be incarnated, that God cannot be finite, is to place limits on his infinite immeasurability. This reflects a concept we will come across again: *infinitum capax finiti*—God is infinite yet capable of being finite; God is boundless yet capable of limit. God's transcendence is boundless and infinite, unlimited, endless, yet he has the capacity to be contained, to be finite and restricted, defined; indeed must be also finite to be infinite. Why? To propose that God is *infinitum capax finiti* is to assert God's freedom to be immanent—God is and can be both immanent (existing or operating within the world) and transcendent (existing apart from and not subject to the limitations of the world). God is not so transcendent that he can't be within creation: God's transcendence means *God's capacity to become immanent*. If in asserting God's infinity you assert God cannot become finite, then God is not infinite. The key is christological: God demonstrates to human minds his transcendence by being incarnated a human being in Jesus. Incarnation does not deny transcendence. It is humanity's projection of immeasurability onto God that denies both immanence and transcendence; that creates false limits that we compliment God with. It is this compliment that denies revelation, so asserts Lewis: *infinitum capax finiti*—if God is truly infinite then God can encompass the finite without losing infinity.[13]

iii. Transposition and Analogy

If Lewis is expounding a degree of negation towards religion then the reason for this apophatic space is not that we should reduce our religious notions of God to nothing but that our notions of God should be re-clothed. If our idea of God is stripped of some of the puny (Lewis's term) concepts that we clothe it with, then the question arises, "With what do we re-clothe our idea of God?" We find that we "have no resources from which to supply that blindingly real and concrete attribute of Deity which ought to replace it."[14] From our perspective the result of the process of refining our idea of God is that our "god" becomes emptier and emptier, and we risk arriving at nothing and worshiping a nonentity: "The understanding, left to itself, can hardly help following this path. That is why the Christian statement that only he who does the will of the Father will ever know the true doctrine is philosophically accurate."[15] Furthermore, "The materials for correcting our abstract conception of God cannot be supplied by Reason: she will be the first to tell you to go and try experience—'Oh, taste and see!'"[16] Wisdom will, through reason, tell us that reason in itself will not give us the truth about God; it

---

13 Lewis does not use the Latin *infinitum capax finiti*, however, his comments reflect this proposition. See, Forsyth, *The Person and Place of Jesus Christ*.
14 Lewis, *Miracles*, 1st ed., 109.
15 Ibid., 109.
16 Ibid.

is revelation that will inform us and gives us true knowledge.[17] The space that the self-generated negation of our religious preconceptions opens up confirms transposition; that is why, as Lewis shows us, invoking the terms *incorporeal* and *impersonal* as attributes of God are misleading—*transcorporeal* and *transpersonal* would be more accurate. Lewis therefore invokes a word and concept that becomes a key to his work: *transposition*. "[Body and matter] should be regarded as the transposition into a minor key of, that creative joy which in him is unceasing and irresistible. Grammatically the things we say of him are 'metaphorical': but in a deeper sense it is our physical and psychic energies that are mere 'metaphors' of the real Life which is God. Divine Sonship is, so to speak, the solid of which biological Sonship is merely a diagrammatic representation on the flat."[18] Lewis first outlines a doctrine of transposition—which becomes the key concept for his understanding of how revelation is imparted and how we can understand the incarnation—in a sermon given in 1944.[19] Revelation is transposed, it changes, it becomes a diminution to a degree, as a symphony for full orchestra and choir is changed when transposed, re-scored, for solo piano. Therefore, and this is the form which flows from Lewis's doctrine of transposition, whatever we say about God, about Jesus Christ, all the theology we build, all is by analogy: we can speak about the Christian life, we can bear witness, we may write about God's revelation in apologetics and theology, but this is all analogical—we write and speak analogies. This is used by Lewis to great effect. His theological apologetic is, arguably, at its best when he explains a point using a picture or story—by analogy—for example, *The Screwtape Letters* and *The Great Divorce*. He uses this method to great effect in *The Space Trilogy* and *The Chronicles of Narnia*.

For Lewis *whatever* we say about God must, therefore, reflect a true authoritative living God. The crudest picture, writes Lewis, in the Old Testament of Yahweh as thunder and lightning or issuing out of dense smoke, is more accurate than philosophical abstraction or the compliments that restrict or reduce God to a distant impersonal universal force. In the Old Testament, "making mountains skip like rams, threatening, promising, pleading, even changing his mind, transmits that sense of living Deity which evaporates in abstract thought."[20] Our images of God must constantly stand in need of updating to reflect transposed revelation. We must never take God for granted. Humanity is reluctant to pass over from the concept of an abstract and negative deity to the living God. Moving over from the "god" of religion to the one true living God that your religion should serve is, for Lewis, like crossing the Rubicon.[21]

iv. Those that make religion their "god," will not have "God" for their religion

What is the context of Lewis's comments about Christianity and religion? It is significant that Lewis opened this essay on Christianity and religion with a quotation from the

17   John 1:29–51.
18   Lewis, *Miracles* 1st ed., 111.
19   Lewis, "Transposition," 1st ed., 9-20.
20   Lewis, *Miracles*, 1st ed, 111.
21   Ibid., 113–14.

10. Apologist and Defender of the Faith II: Revelation and Christology, 1941–47

work of Thomas Erskine of Linlathen that encapsulates this dialectical approach to revelation and religion: "Those who make religion their god will not have God for their religion."[22] Thomas Erskine was a nineteenth-century lay theologian, a trained lawyer and a Scottish laird and landowner, who devoted most of his time to studying and writing theology. He was often critical of the formality and rigidity of the Scottish Calvinism he had grown up in. His criticism of religion and church was countered by his growing acceptance of a doctrine of universal atonement. (The church in Scotland had become as frozen and formalized in its approach to Christ's atonement as the Roman Catholic church had in the late middle ages.) Though criticized for his approach to atonement by the Calvinist hierarchy, his universalism was in effect a declaration of the unconditional openness, the freeness, of the forgiveness laid out in the gospel: the cross was the centre of atonement, not primarily the incarnation. Erskine supported the Scottish theologian John McLeod Campbell in his declaration that Christ died to save *all* of humanity (McLeod was denounced as a heretic for this and expelled from ministry). This also has echoes with the rigid Ulster Calvinism, which Lewis was only too aware of in his childhood upbringing in Belfast. In quoting Erskine, and by default Erskine's endorsement of McLeod Campbell, Lewis is placing religion relative to the salvific actions of God in Christ.

v. The Incarnate God

The central miracle asserted by Christians, writes Lewis, is the incarnation.[23] All other miracles issue from and relate to the incarnation. If we follow this through logically then the incarnation-cross-resurrection is *the central event* in humanity's history; further, this event has cosmic implications given that death, which appears to have been written into the natural order of the universe since creation, is reversed. Lewis writes that, "As every natural event is the manifestation at a particular place and moment of Nature's total character, so every particular Christian miracle manifests at a particular place and moment the character and significance of the incarnation":[24] if this is so then the implication is that miracles as an intrusion or intervention within the natural order of creation are not "arbitrary interferences . . . The fitness, and therefore credibility, of the particular miracles depends on their relation to the Grand Miracle; all discussion of them in isolation from it is futile."[25] So what we observe of creation and the natural order is all intimately interconnected, and that very interconnectedness is christological: the universal Christ was/is the agent of creation and also of redemption. As Lord of creation it is only natural and fitting for him to work in and alter and change, to redeem, creation. Again, this contradicts the proposition of a closed universe, which had been foundational to Enlightenment and "Modern" philosophy, a proposition represented by the brutal logic that Lewis was

---

22 Ibid., Chp. XI "Christianity and Religion," 99. Quoting from Thomas Erskine, *Remarks on the Internal Evidence for the Truth of Revealed Religion* (Edinburgh: Waugh, Innes and Hamilton, 1820).
23 Lewis, *Miracles*, 1st ed., 131.
24 Ibid., 131.
25 Ibid.

immersed in on his return to Oxford after the First World War, a logicality derived from a literal interpretation of sense perception within the framework of a neo-Kantian concept of a closed, single-level, universe. By contrast Lewis's idealism contradicted, to a degree, the belief (even an article of faith?) amongst "modern" philosophers of the closed-off cosmos, the positivistic realism that asserted an accident of evolution as the source of all, and not a creator God (for the less assertive positivists, even if there was a God there was no perceivable connection or relationship between eternity and our reality). Wrong, asserts Lewis; what is more, creation as the work of Christ, the second person of the Trinity, is intimately interconnected with eternity—it issues from and is sustained from eternity.

vi. Fitness, Contingency, and Improbability

If all miracles within our reality can be judged in relation to the incarnation, we find it difficult to assign criteria to assess the incarnation itself: "it is very difficult to find a standard by which it can be judged."[26] Lewis continues that if it happened it is the central event in history: "the very thing that the whole story has been about. Since it happened only once, it is by Hume's standards infinitely improbable. But then the whole history of the Earth has also happened only once; is it therefore incredible? Hence the difficulty, which weighs upon Christian and atheist alike, of estimating the probability of the incarnation. It is like asking whether the existence of Nature herself is intrinsically probable."[27] Lewis refers to Hume's argument. The philosopher David Hume called into question the ability of reason to claim confidently, to be able to understand all of the laws of the universe. Hume's concern was to ground our claims to knowledge in experience and, pertinently, to the impressions which we receive. Hume's project led him to be skeptical about religious assertions—in particular claims about the miraculous—but also our claims to scientific knowledge: he criticized the doctrine of causality on which so much science rests, but also the concept of the miraculous upon which much religion relies. For Lewis, Hume argued that there is no verifiable evidence from sensory impression corresponding to a necessary connection between "cause" and "effect": events may be unrelated and happen by accident—apparently consecutive events may not be related. To deduce and assert a causal relationship there must be sequence, but also there must be a consistent concurrence of the two events, and that they consistently occur in temporal and spatial proximity (they occur in more or less the same place, at more or less the same time). A central criticism of science and religion is that both rely on inductive inference—which, in turn, is also a criticism of Hume's denial of the miraculous: too often in both science and religion we conclude not by examining exhaustively but by inference (no one has observed the entire natural world or examined every possible instance of the miraculous). This reliance on the inductive (a form of logic characterized by the inference of general laws from particular instances) weakens, for Lewis, scientific claims; but it also, for Hume, refuted

26   Ibid.
27   Ibid.

10. Apologist and Defender of the Faith II: Revelation and Christology, 1941–47

claims of the miraculous. Hume concludes that the claimed relation between cause and effect is no more than our propensity to form habits of expectation based upon repetition. Without repetition we would not be able to draw conclusions. Therefore the lack of repetition, indeed the very uniqueness, of the incarnation-resurrection disqualifies us from giving it any value, according of Hume's argument; from a strictly scientific viewpoint, Lewis concurs, that is, if Lewis is correct in his somewhat rigid interpretation of Hume's argument. Hume's objection to the miraculous supposes a predetermined and observable character to the miraculous and a complete understanding of the laws of nature as a foundational ground for a critical examination of claims of the preta- or supra-natural. Part of Lewis's concern with Hume's argument is that such a foundational ground is not possible; hence, Hume's argument falls back on inductive inference, which itself can be criticized as invalid.[28]

Lewis therefore comments that although, by Hume's standards, the incarnation is infinitely improbable, so is the possibility of the earth and life—which we cannot deny the existence of. Lewis writes that since the incarnation holds as fact a central position in the history of humanity, in the world, and in what we take for reality, and if we do not know from immediate sense perception and experience that it happened we fall back on analogy in understanding it.[29] If we come across a unique unpredictable passage that fits in with an already known book or novel, or a symphony, and if we find that this passage or chapter is crucial to the story, if it is fundamental to the whole plot of the novel, then do we dismiss it because it is unique, because it is a one-off event and was not part of the original story or score? We would not dismiss it, but would see whether the new passage did complete the story in ways we could not predict. If false the new passage, however attractive it may have been initially, will become progressively more difficult to reconcile with the work as a whole. But if genuine it will ring truer with time and elicit details in the whole work that were previously unrealized. Indeed, the new passage as key to the story or the symphony as a whole may perturb, may contains great difficulties in itself, it may upset our greatest preconceptions but it would still be genuine:

> Something like this we must do with the doctrine of the incarnation. Here, instead of a symphony or a novel, we have the whole mass of our knowledge. The credibility will depend on the extent to which the doctrine, if accepted, can illuminate and integrate that whole mass. It is much less important that the doctrine itself should be fully comprehensible. We believe that the sun is in the sky at midday in summer not because we can clearly see the sun (in fact, we cannot) but because we can see everything else.[30]

If it seems easy over a distance of two thousand years to dismiss the Gospel accounts of the incarnation-resurrection when we have neither the firsthand experience and observation to assert or deny, then we only have to consider how easy and spurious

---

28   For the original argument, rather than Lewis's interpretation, see, Hume, *An Enquiry Concerning Human Understanding*, VII "Of the Idea of Necessary Connection," 44–57.
29   Lewis, Miracles, 1st ed., 132.
30   Ibid., 132–33.

it was for the historian David Irving to question and dismiss the holocaust over a distance of half a century. David Irving, a military historian specializing in the Second World War, has produced controversial interpretations of the Nazis and the Third Reich; because of his involvement in the Holocaust denial movement his reputation as an historian has been discredited. Irving was convicted and imprisoned in Austria in 2006 under the Verbotsgesetz law ("for glorifying and identifying with the German Nazi Party").

The primary difficulty for Lewis is not the question of history, contingency, or the uniqueness of the event; the problem lies in the question, "What can be meant by God becoming man?" We are talking here about eternal spirit, fact-hood, combined with a natural human organism: in Jesus the "Supernatural Creator" is in union with humanity. It is here that most humanity finds difficulty: "The first difficulty that occurs to any critic of the doctrine lies in the very centre of it . . . I do not think anything we can do will enable us to imagine the mode of consciousness of the incarnate God. That is where the doctrine is not fully comprehensible."[31] At the heart of the paradox of the incarnation is the relationship between the natural and the supernatural, which we, with our feet of clay so to speak, cannot conceive of:

> The discrepancy between a movement of atoms in an astronomer's cortex and his understanding that there must be a still unobserved planet beyond Uranus, is already so immense that the incarnation of God himself is, in one sense, scarcely more startling. We cannot conceive how the Divine Spirit dwelled within the created and human spirit of Jesus: but neither can we conceive how his human spirit, or that of any man, dwells within his natural organism. What we can understand, if the Christian doctrine is true, is that our own composite existence is not the sheer anomaly it might seem to be, but a faint image of the Divine incarnation itself—the same theme in a very minor key.[32]

We take for granted the "discrepancy" between the mechanism of sensory observation (the movement of atoms that is sight), our conceptualization that something must be (the planet Uranus), and the conclusion about reality we arrive at; the paradox of the incarnation must be seen as not just equally immense but beyond. Analogy issuing from transposition is all that we can rely and trust in given our distance from the event.

vii. Three Paradigms: "Descent/Re-ascent," "Christological Prefigurement," and "Selectiveness and Vicariousness"

Lewis establishes three axiomatic paradigms that define the incarnation: first, the "descent/re-ascent" paradigm; second, "christological prefigurement"; and third, "selectiveness and vicariousness."

---

31   Ibid., 133.
32   Ibid., 134.

10. Apologist and Defender of the Faith II: Revelation and Christology, 1941–47

"Descent/Re-Ascent"

The "descent/re-ascent" paradigm illustrates the movement of God incarnate, and, coupled with the predicament issuing from the fall, becomes the "death-descent/ rebirth-re-ascent" paradigm. If the aim of the incarnation is the salvation of humanity, this paradigm defines the objective. God, the second person of the Trinity, descends to re-ascend with humanity: "In the Christian story God descends to re-ascend. He comes down; down from the heights of absolute being into time and space, down into humanity . . . He goes down to come up again and bring the whole ruined world up with him." [33] Lewis continues that in this descent and re-ascent everyone will recognize a pattern that is familiar—it is written into creation, in the natural world: "The doctrine of the incarnation, if accepted, puts this principle even more emphatically at the centre. The pattern is there in Nature because it was first there in God." [34]

"Christological Prefigurement"

The second paradigm is what may be termed "christological prefigurement"—this is the evidence in non-Christian religions and myths of echoes of the story of the incarnation-cross-resurrection. Numerous unrelated and diverse cultures, religions, and mythological systems of belief throughout the ancient world (whether pagan, Indo-European, Oceanic, or Norse and Celtic) gave rise to stories of "gods" descending, or dying to the benefit of the people and failing to be resurrected due to humanity's perverseness. Why is this so? Why are these stories there? If they are not competing myths or contradictions of the gospel then the question is raised of how they relate to the incarnation-cross-resurrection; how do they relate to revelation if they are not simply human-centered religion? For Lewis, *these stories-myths prefigure the actual Christ event*—the Gospel account is simply the reflection of the one true myth.

These first two paradigms are very important and they lie at the very centre of Lewis's Christology and thereby his doctrine of revelation; he writes at relative length on them and therefore they are of crucial understanding to this work.

"Selectiveness and Vicariousness"

Lewis rehearses and reiterates the relationship between salvation history and the incarnation: when all sound knowledge of God is lost one man from all humanity is chosen to bear witness to the truth—Abraham. And his witness leads to an uprooting and countless descendants to cover the earth. The process of forging a chosen people of God focuses onto "one small bright point like the head of a spear. It is a Jewish girl at her prayers [the Annunciation]. All humanity (so far as concerns its redemption) has narrowed to that."[35] This, coupled with an observation from the natural world raises the question, certainly for the modern mind, of selectiveness and vicariousness. The sheer wastefulness of nature, the vast size of the universe with the innumerable number of stars and planets, the sheer explosion of life on earth but with only a tiny proportion

---

33 Ibid., 135.
34 Ibid., 136.
35 Ibid., 140–41.

leading to rational intelligent life, this vicariousness is analogous, asserts Lewis, with the selectiveness of God—a chosen people, a single Jewish girl, Mary—which affronts modern sensibilities.[36] But, counters Lewis, this is not favoritism: "the chosen people are chosen not for their own sake (certainly not for their honor or pleasure) but for the sake of the unchosen."[37] It is in Abraham's seeds that all nations are blest; Israel suffers greatly for its chosen status, but this suffering heals others: "Her [Israel's] Son, the incarnate God, is a 'man of sorrows' . . . and certainly we have here come to a principle very deep-rooted in Christianity: what may be called the principle of Vicariousness."[38]

Therefore, a doctrine of the incarnation will, if we take it seriously, both effect and change our accepted modes of thought. If we do not take the incarnation seriously and allow it to change our innate selfish preconceptions it will be because we do not take the human predicament issuing from the fall seriously: "Throughout this doctrine it is, of course, implied that Nature is infected with evil."[39] But can a scientific analysis presupposing a closed-universe reveal this? The incarnation issues from outside of created reality; yet God is entering into and joining our reality in a new way. A scientific analysis will not reveal this; Lewis contradicts such a scientific presumption because nature is being illuminated by a light from beyond nature:

> Someone is speaking who knows more about her than can be known from inside her. Throughout this doctrine [the incarnation] it is, of course, implied that Nature is infected with evil. And this depravity could not be totally removed without the drastic re-making of Nature . . .
>
> Complete human virtue could indeed banish from human life all the evils that now arise in it from Vicariousness and Selectiveness and retain only the good: but the wastefulness and painfulness of non-human Nature would remain and would, of course, continue to infect human life in the form of disease. And the destiny which Christianity promises to man clearly involves a "redemption" or a "remaking" of Nature which could not stop at Man, or even at this planet. We are told that "the whole creation" is in travail.[40]

So the fall and the vicariousness of nature are intimately intertwined. Revelation tells us this, not reasoned scientific observation. And the Christ event has cosmic implication.

viii. Rebellion and Death

Why this situation? The sin of the angels and then humanity was possible because of God-given free will. God, for Lewis, surrendered part of his omnipotence. In so doing this leads to a divine death-like descending within the Godhead, though this proceeds ultimately to a deeper ascending happiness: "Because he [humanity] has fallen, God does the great deed; just as in the parable it is the one lost sheep for whom the

---

36 Ibid., 140f.
37 Ibid., 142.
38 Ibid., 142–43.
39 Ibid.
40 Ibid., 145.

10. Apologist and Defender of the Faith II: Revelation and Christology, 1941–47

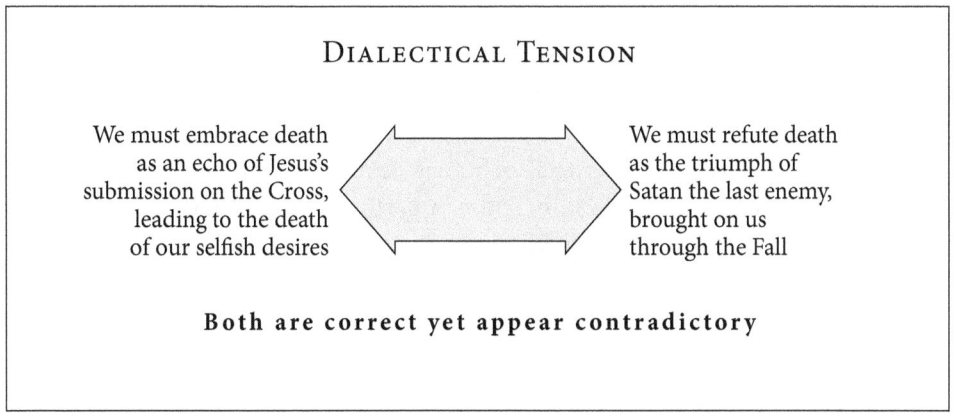

Figure 13: The Dialectical Tension in a Christian Doctrine of Death

shepherd hunts."[41] Lewis does admit that he presents the incarnation as engendered by the fall, but that this is not the whole purpose for many patristic theologians. There is a strong tradition, which Lewis is sympathetic to, that asserts that the descent of God into nature would have occurred *regardless of the fall*. The incarnation would have been for glorification and perfection, even if atonement and redemption had not been required: "The attendant circumstances would have been very different: the divine humility would not have been a divine humiliation, the sorrows, the gall and vinegar, the crown of thorns and the cross, would have been absent. If this view is taken, then clearly the incarnation, wherever and however it occurred, would always have been the beginning of Nature's re-birth."[42] So the paradigm of descent/re-ascent is written into creation; however, the character of the incarnation is envisioned by the fall. Is this leading to universal redemption? Will all eventually submit? Will all humanity, despite the threat and danger of hell, be saved? Lewis refuses, quite rightly, to answer this question. However, he does comment that the union between humanity and God in Christ admits no divorce: "God never undoes anything but evil . . . when spring comes it leaves no corner of the land untouched."[43] For Lewis, if there is a doctrine of universal redemption it leads out from humanity because of the incarnation. Lewis is therefore talking about the *potential* salvation of all humanity because of the interconnectedness of humanity. But whether all will submit to being saved is another matter. To proclaim universalism (that all are saved) is to ignore the seriousness of the human predicament, a seriousness that Lewis never ceases to declare. The predicament is death, which issues as the punishment from the fall. However, the very nature of the cross, whereby Christ submits to death so as to defeat death, illustrates how intimate and fitting is the

41 Ibid., 147.
42 Ibid., 148.
43 Ibid., 149.

relationship between the punishment and the redemption. To understand this we need to examine Lewis's Christian doctrine of death.

If the incarnation-cross-resurrection is intimately intertwined with the human predicament (the fall into original sin) and this predicament is scripturally defined by death then it is in "a Christian doctrine of human death"[44] that we can truly understand what the incarnation is. There is, therefore, a particular and unique understanding to the character and role of death from a Christian (i.e., incarnational) perspective. That God descends is in itself a form of divine death. This Christian-incarnational view of death is diametric to the approach to death common in both ancient and modern times. The Christian-incarnational view does not acquiesce—it does not give in to death, an approach epitomized for Lewis by the ancient Stoics, where death doesn't matter. But neither is the reality of death ignored, denied, or hidden from, as is common in the contemporary Western world. Christ neither negates nor affirms death. The Christian view is more nuanced. First, death must be seen before the gospel as "the triumph of Satan, the punishment of the Fall, and the last enemy"[45]—for this reason Jesus wept before Lazarus's tomb. Secondly, the paradox is that death is to be embraced—that is, the death of our selfish desires: "On the other hand, only he who loses his life will save it" because when we are baptized we are baptized into Christ's *death*, which is the remedy for the fall. There is, therefore, ambivalence, a paradox, it is both holy and unholy, writes Lewis; our supreme disgrace yet our only hope: "the thing Christ came to conquer and the means by which he conquered."[46] If death becomes dialectical after the cross, if death remains the ultimate punishment issuing from the fall, yet in apparent contradiction Christ embraces death as the way out for humanity, and if these two approaches to death stand in contradiction then this opposition will be reconciled in the eschaton—the last judgment. Only after our personal death and when we are raised from the dead will we understand how and why: "If the pattern of Descent and Re-ascent is (as looks not unlikely) the very formula of reality, then in the mystery of Death the secret of secrets lies . . . It is mercy because by willing and humble surrender to it Man undoes his act of rebellion and makes even this depraved and monstrous mode of Death an instance of that higher and mystical Death which is eternally good and a necessary ingredient in the highest life."[47] Satan produces human death, but in capitulating, giving in, acquiescing to death as part of the cross, humanity will be redeemed. Bodily death was once our enemy, indeed our enemy's greatest weapon; however, in the form of a blessed spiritual death it becomes our way out of the human predicament. If this is not enough, Lewis explains why Christ's death (because vicariousness is at the heart of reality) becomes our death.

---

44 Ibid., 152.
45 Ibid., 151.
46 Ibid.
47 Ibid., 151.

10. Apologist and Defender of the Faith II: Revelation and Christology, 1941–47

3. DOCTRINE... BY ANALOGY

If Lewis is correct in asserting in *Miracles* (1947), the relevant sections of which we reviewed above, that we, in effect, create a kingdom (or, more pertinently, a republic) of religion which to a greater or lesser degree excludes God's revelation *in Christ*, then we must conclude that Christ is to a large degree hidden from many people. The busyness of secular lives also exacerbates this spiritual void that people occupy. This apophatic space is not necessarily willed by God; it issues from our sin. It is caused partly by the efforts we put into creating a religious smokescreen; however this hiddenness is rooted in the fall. Prior to our eating the fruit of the tree of the knowledge of good and evil we "walked," according to the analogical picture in Genesis, with God in the cool of the evening. But God's coming forth now is veiled, hidden to most people. In coming forth, *in Christ*, God, for many who are unrepentant, is the threatening presence, the intimidating peril, the unapproachable fearful Lord.

i. Screwtape's Correspondence... and The Great Divorce

How does Lewis present this? In two short books published during the Second World War—contemporaneous to *The Broadcast Talks*—he paints pictures, word pictures, he uses narrative, analogy, even humor, to reveal some frightening truths about the human predicament in relation to the immensity of God's justice: *The Screwtape Letters* and *The Great Divorce*. There are no doctrinal statements relating to Christ nor a systematic analysis of revelation and the Christ event, however, both works are imbued with a sound Christology and an understanding of revelation. Christ is present throughout both works, though in many ways obliquely, yet he is a colossal and substantial presence that presses on both people and demons and influences them if they will allow this awesome and terrible holy presence to change them. We can "see" Christ just behind the shoulder of Screwtape, the senior devil, threatening his demonic plans and machinations; Christ fills him with loathing, for without Christ he would never have existed, and now without God he would cease to be or have anything to focus on or hate. The hidden Christ is also the "bleeding" charity that stands ever open to forgive people their stupid arrogant sins in *The Great Divorce*, if only they will have the courage—*post mortem*, for all this happens after death in a state of purgation; if only they would have the will, the audacity, the faith, but above all the courage, to step forth out of the hell they have created, to step beyond their tiny little republics where they believe they reign supreme and begin the pilgrimage, however painful it will be at first, towards and into the Christ.

The Screwtape Letters were initially published in serial form in thirty-one weekly installments from May 2 to November 28, 1941, in the Anglo-Catholic newspaper *The Guardian* (Lewis was paid £2 for each letter, and gave the money away to charity).[48] Screwtape being a senior devil expresses everything in a diabolical inversion—Satan

---

[48] *The Guardian* was a weekly newspaper for Church of England clergy, an Anglo-Catholic newspaper published in London by George Bell & Sons from 1846 to 1951. Lewis was a regular contributor.

is referred to as "our father below," Christ is seen as all that is bad and rotten and corrupt—from the perspective of Screwtape. In advising a junior devil by the name of Wormwood, Screwtape encourages it to try to get the patient—a young man on the verge of becoming a Christian whom the junior devil is *influencing*—to deny the reality beyond what we take for reality, to deny the supra- or preta-natural (in accordance with Enlightenment and modern philosophy). But Wormwood must be cautious: "Above all, do not attempt to use science (I mean the real sciences) as a defense against Christianity. They will positively encourage him to think about realities he can't touch and see."[49] The important thing for Wormwood to do is encourage the patient's involvement in churches that are modern, Liberal, and enlightened, and therefore subscribe to "Christianity *and* . . ."; that is, a diluted form of religion, independent of revelation.[50] Developing spiritual and religious pride is of great value here—advises Screwtape[51]—not disinterested love, which is all the enemy above can offer in reply to their diabolical inversion. If love is at the heart of the universe, if God is love and if Christ so loved us as to die for us on the cross, then Screwtape has absolutely no conception or understanding of this love, and therefore has no sound understanding, knowledge of, or relationship with the Christ. Above all Wormwood should get the patient to dismiss what he is going through as just a phase, a religious phase,[52] but never allow him to come into contact with the real existence and presence of God as Holy Spirit, the God who is by him and with him. Lewis, through Screwtape, is identifying a distinction between human "gods" and God. Wormwood must, insists Screwtape, encourage the "patient" to believe in the "god" of his own inventing. Therefore there is a distinction between the "god" he imagines—a composite object generated by his mind during his prayers—and the real presence of God, a revealed reality the patient can fly to immediately in prayer:

> You may even encourage him to attach great importance to the correction and improvement of his composite object, and to keeping it steadily before his imagination during the whole prayer. For if he ever comes to make the distinction, if ever he consciously directs his prayers "Not to what I think thou art but to what thou knowest thyself to be," our situation is, for the moment, desperate. Once all his thoughts and images have been flung aside or, if retained, retained with a full recognition of their merely subjective nature, and the man trusts himself to the completely real, external, invisible Presence, there with him in the room and never knowable by him as he is known by it—why, then it is that the incalculable may occur.[53]

The incalculable for Screwtape is conversion to and possession by Christ not by the devil; the incalculable is salvation. Above all Christ must not be seen as a real person; from the perspective of this diabolical inversion the Trinity must be mocked and belittled as an ancient superstition because for the devil to win religion must be human

---

49 Lewis, *The Screwtape Letters*, 3.
50 Ibid., 5, 16, and 97.
51 Ibid., 93.
52 Ibid., 35.
53 Ibid., 15–16.

10. Apologist and Defender of the Faith II: Revelation and Christology, 1941–47

centered. Conversely, when a human patient fails to dismiss the Trinity as absurd then the devil and all its schemes are threatened and there is a high risk of Wormwood failing to seduce and possess the patient. The portrait of Christ that we can read from *The Screwtape Letters* is of a person, a reality, that underpins and haunts all the activities of humans and demons alike and presses and influences, troubles, and disturbs. The reaction of humanity should be to change, to respond; or be damned. Humanity cannot avoid being influenced by Christ and his angels, or by demons: it is one or the other for we are not sealed off from the supra-natural; we are not sole masters of our fate. How humanity responds to the Christ is reminiscent, to a degree, of the process theology we encountered in the work of W. Norman Pittenger, amongst others. For example, "Though Lewis's personal theological perspective is rarely considered or studied in terms of Alfred North Whitehead's process philosophy, Lewis's portrait of 'the Enemy' (i.e., Jesus Christ) in *The Screwtape Letters* is more than a little similar to the rudiments of the christologies espoused by John Cobb, Peter Hamilton, and others. In short, 'the Enemy,' as presented in *The Screwtape Letters*, functions quite well in terms of process thought."[54] Above all Screwtape's advice to Wormwood is to prevent the young man, the "patient," having faith in, and trusting in the real Christ. This realization of the real presence is more important in some ways than religion or doctrinal assertions.

The Great Divorce was initially published in serial form between November 10, 1944, and April 14, 1945, in the Anglo-Catholic newspaper *The Guardian*. Christ is revealed in conversations between the redeemed from heaven coming to meet the damned from hell (though the terms are not as clear cut as may appear—if one of the damned chooses to leave the hell they sojourn in, then, for Lewis it was no hell at all but purgatory; the geography is not as fixed as it was in medieval models of hell-purgatory). Hell is the greatest compliment God can pay to humanity, to human free will, for God has waited all through a person's life for s/he to utter in prayer, "Thy will be done"; therefore, in the final reckoning—*post mortem*—God says to the rebellious, "Your will be done."[55] The damned can travel to the fringes of heaven, if they so desire, to converse with the redeemed who have travelled as far as it is "physically" possible towards the damned and their hell. In the resulting conversations they have the opportunity to change, to move into heaven, move deeper and deeper into Christ. Behind these conversations is the love that Screwtape is incapable of understanding— the disinterested, altruistic love; a love that ever gives, and in giving denies itself, yet through the denial it lives the greater life. And that love is the sacrifice of Christ on the cross: Lewis refers to this explicitly as the "bleeding charity."[56] The reality of Christ may be unknown to the damned—either they did not know of Christ or had the wrong idea about Christ, or the wrong relationship with him—but the greatest stumbling block appears to be their inability to go beyond themselves, to begin to love, truly to love, after the example of Christ the "bleeding charity." It is therefore the blood of Christ

---

54 Watkins, "The Screwtape Letters and Process Theism," 114.
55 Lewis, *The Great Divorce*, 58.
56 Ibid., 21.

that saves us, not necessarily the example, not the superb religious life Jesus led, but the sacrificial blood that cleanses us of sin—if we open ourselves to Christ.

For Lewis hell is a state of mind more than a physical geographic reality, and all turned in on themselves (though considering Lewis's childhood and his beliefs and isolation as a young adult there is something of the personal portrait here) are in hell; heaven by comparison is not a state of mind. Heaven is real; it is a fully real reality: therefore, for Lewis, there is still choice after death. It is not important whether we name this a state of purgation or identify something of a reality, partial and incomplete by comparison with heaven. What is important is the state of loss and regret that possesses the near to nothing existence that these damned souls must endure who languish outside of Christ. By comparison, the redeemed are those in whom flows an "abundance of life in Christ from the Father."[57] For Christ is the King of Justice and their High Priest.[58]

ii. Christian Atheism?

Atheism can only be defined by self-declaration. Another person can only be referred to as an atheist if s/he has declared her/himself to be an atheist. Religious atheists are, in effect, people who enjoy being religious, perhaps even deriving an income or status and power from being religious, while holding what they define as atheistic views. Religious atheism was, in many ways, Lewis's nemesis. This was often with specific reference to the Church of England: priests who published works denying Christ or God. We can identify a development within theology and the churches during the second half of the twentieth century, built upon the fruits of the Age of Reason and the Enlightenment. Such a system of belief asserts that Jesus of Nazareth was just an ordinary human being, admittedly with a super-religious consciousness, but, nonetheless, he was a man just like any other. This system of belief does not necessarily deny g/God, so it is not self-consciously atheistic; but because it denies that Christ is God incarnate it is therefore denying God in the context of revelation. Although these people deny the ground of orthodoxy Christian belief—the incarnation and resurrection—they will claim that being "Christian" is about believing in a super-religious ordinary human: Jesus of Nazareth; they will in all probability believe in some sort of "god", but this may be considered by some to be atheistic because it falls short of the reality of God revealed in the incarnation-cross-resurrection. Therefore if we must give this system of belief a name we can call it "Christian atheism" or perhaps "pseudo-Christian atheism?" This is not a term Lewis used but it was a system of belief Lewis identified—admittedly closeted—in the Church of England of his day, though this is by no means a phenomenon unique to Anglican circles (we will consider this in more depth later when we examine Lewis on Scripture). In the 1970s what we can now identify as a form of pseudo-Christian atheism came, so to speak, out of the closet and there were clergy and theologians who openly and proudly denied God's revelation

---

57   Ibid., 91.
58   Ibid., 87.

10. Apologist and Defender of the Faith II: Revelation and Christology, 1941–47

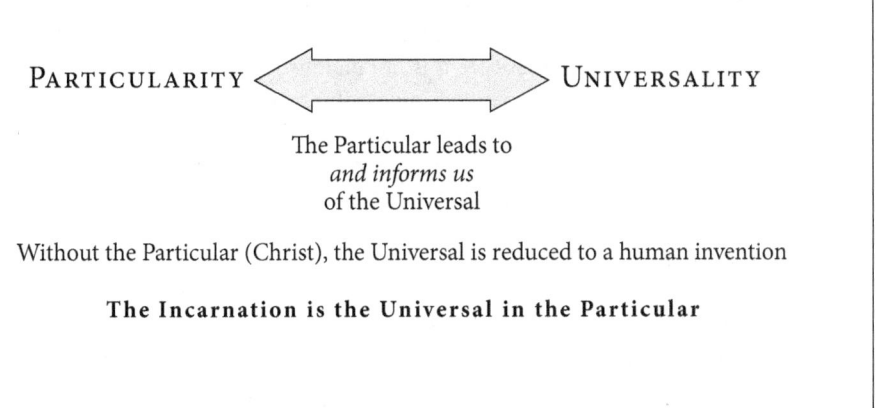

Figure 14: The Relation between the Universal and the Particular

in the Christ—who referred to the incarnation as "the myth of God incarnate." This approach was championed in the late 1970s by the religionist John Hick—whereby revelation was reduced to universal religiosity.[59] Hick's version of a Christ-denying religion was typical and became archetypal. It was John Hick to whom many attribute the phrase "the myth of God incarnate" (though it was half a century earlier that the German New Testament scholar Rudolf Bultmann called for a "de-mythologizing" of the gospel). Hick rejected any hierarchy of revelation; however, he does appear to assert a hierarchy of his own. This is not based on Christ or on what is taken to be revelation in orthodox circles—for an orthodox-traditional-creedal Christianity is considered inferior and inaccurate. Hick's hierarchy is derived from what he identifies as a democratic universal religious impulse in humanity (yet another case of humanity mistakenly paying "God" compliments by inaccurately asserting that all religions are equal). God, for Hick, is reduced to the concept of the transcendent. Externality (i.e., the supra- or preta-natural), for Hickians, is reduced to the ultimately Real. This ultimate Reality is, for Hick, available to all, but ironically Hick claim to have unique understanding of how the claims of particular religions relate to it. The problem is that this belief in a universal religion, which marginalizes specific Christian doctrine, is human-centered and is motivated by modern sensibilities about pluralism rather than the pursuit of truth. Hick's pluralism asserts that all religions are equally valid, yet simultaneously elevates Hick's own interpretation of religion as superior to that found in any actual religions (some understandings of religious truth, it seems, are more equal than others). Colin E. Gunton notes how many American scholars in the late twentieth century deconstructed this idea of pluralism by asserting that Hick was not identifying a plurality but simply asserting his particular point of view:

---

59   See, Hick, *An Interpretation of Religion: Human Responses to the Transcendent*.

> There is no such thing as pluralism, because pluralism is itself a particular position, a particular viewpoint. And that's right; Hick is taking up a position, a particular position, and therefore it is not pluralistic because Hick's position is just one among several competing, supposedly equally valid, positions . . . [his] very position is exclusive. Every position is exclusive, and that's right, logically it's right: if to say that "A" is true, it logically requires you to deny the truth of "not A," then you are being selective, you are excluding. So any thesis in that sense is exclusive.[60]

For Lewis, if we are to avoid the danger of a specific viewpoint masquerading as universal pluralism we must acknowledge revelation; further we must acknowledge that the initiative lies with God: Christ, the second person of the Trinity, reaches out to and into humanity (though the Holy Spirit intimates explicitly or implicitly in varying degrees God's saving purposes to diverse peoples and cultures spread throughout human history across the world, widely dispersed and often isolated). Lewis avoids the accusation of his theological apologetics being a personal position by asserting and acknowledging revelation, but accepting that there will be some personal element in what he identifies because he is human. Hence his doctrine of transposition, which asserted that truth is outside of us. However, through the faculties of imagination and reason we may intimate an understanding—inspired by the Holy Spirit—so that we can, to a greater or lesser degree, identify what this truth is in relation to God's saving actions. Therefore the universal is only accessible through the particular; the particular leads to and informs us of the universal. Without the particular (ultimately the Christ event) the universal is just a human invention. The Enlightenment opposition repudiated this particularity—ideas alone were universal; only the universal was considered true, the universal that was available to all humanity, not the particular enacted in the contingency of history. The idea that God could be incarnated human—that the universal could become temporal and finite, indeed all that was attested to in the Christ event was dismissed as the scandal of particularity by philosophers in the Age of Reason and the Enlightenment. Ironically the perception of this universal was only available to white, Western, cultured aristocratic intellectuals living in the particularity of eighteenth-century England, Germany, France, etc.

iii. The Denial of the Particular

So what does Lewis have to say in analogical narrative about what we may term Christ-denying-pluralistic-religious-professionals? There are two passages, one from *The Screwtape Letters* the other from *The Great Divorce*, which illustrate Lewis's understanding of this phenomenon.

Screwtape advises Wormwood that there is immense value in many "modern" Christian-political writers who are convinced that Christianity began going wrong early on—departing from the doctrine of the founder, Jesus of Nazareth, almost

---

60 Gunton, *Revelation and Reason*, 58. Gunton is referring to D'Costa, "The Impossibility of a Pluralist View of Religion," 232. See also: D'Costa, *Christianity and World Religions*, and, D'Costa, *Christian Uniqueness Reconsidered*.

10. Apologist and Defender of the Faith II: Revelation and Christology, 1941–47

immediately. This, of course, is a diabolical inversion and is very valuable from a demonic perspective! To assert that the early church got it wrong is the opposite of Lewis's assertion of a patristic core. According to Vincentius of Lérins, whom Lewis relied on, the early church was right, and was grounded in the Holy Spirit. Screwtape advises Wormwood that this early church misconception can be advanced by encouraging the "patient" to get involved in the study of the "historical Jesus" (i.e., the nineteenth-century biblical studies movement that emphasized Jesus as an ordinary human being), as a means of interpreting the Gospels—dig deep enough in the detail and you will be able to find the real human Jesus, asserts Screwtape. This involves clearing away the later "accretions and perversions" which characterize the Christian tradition:

> In the last generation we promoted the construction of such an "historical Jesus" on liberal and humanitarian lines; we are now putting forward a new "historical Jesus" on Marxian, catastrophic, and revolutionary lines. The advantages of these constructions, which we intend to change every thirty years or so, are manifold. In the first place they all tend to direct men's devotion to something which does not exist, for each "historical Jesus" is unhistorical. The documents say what they say and cannot be added to; each new "historical Jesus" therefore has to be got out of them by suppression at one point and exaggeration at another . . . In the second place, all such constructions place the importance of their historical Jesus in some peculiar theory he is supposed to have promulgated . . . We thus distract men's minds from who he is, and what he did. We first make him solely a teacher, and then conceal the very substantial agreement between his teachings and those of all other great moral teachers. For humans must not be allowed to notice that all great moralists are sent by the Enemy.[61]

Lewis is therefore advancing the idea that constructions such as the "modern" reinterpretation of Jesus are, in effect, the work of the devil. If this seems a little severe and judgmental then we must consider Jesus's reaction to Peter when Peter wanted to protect Jesus from the way of the cross. Jesus's immediate reaction was, "Get behind me Satan."[62] Lewis realizes that such a construct as the historical Jesus is not uniquely "modern" or "Liberal" because such a pursuit is relative and variable and the motives change—one generation follows "Liberal" or "humanitarian" aims, another Marxist or revolutionary lines. The diabolical aim for this is to cause perplexity—if Jesus from the Gospel records is deconstructed enough nothing is left except confusion. And from the confusion arises what to many increasingly becomes a personalized fictitious model of Jesus that is taken to be the true historical Jesus as distinct from the Christ of faith, the Christ attested to by the churches and the creeds. The foundational grounds for the study of the historical Jesus will be examined later.

Lewis was very specific, very direct, in his attack on such apostasy amongst Anglican clerics—particularly bishops. In *The Great Divorce* (1944), he creates one such character: a bishop theologian who resides in hell (though he does not realize he

---

61 Lewis, *The Screwtape Letters*, 90.
62 Matt 16:23; Mark 8:33.

is there). He has the chance to leave if he will only renounce his apostasy as represented by the academic books he published asserting Christ's humanity but denying Christ's divinity. Even when faced with Christ's forgiveness after his own death, he wishes to hang on to the grey nihilistic theories which he had invented and promoted, arguing he must be honest to himself; he is actually proud that he dared to write and publish the arguments while he was alive denying Christ's divinity and resurrection. He does not believe that there are real intellectual sins. (There is more than a touch of the old apostate atheistic C. S. Lewis in the portrait, which also in some ways reflects Lewis's theistic period from 1929 to 1931.) This bishop theologian wants to hide in obscure academic arguments and question the meaning of language—the words we use—refusing to give a definition of existence, repudiating still the idea of the supernatural, denying that there is a real heaven and a hell, refusing to see God as a fact. In a *post mortem* conversation with a former clergy colleague who had relinquished the "modern," "Liberal," views before his death, this apostate bishop, who has travelled to the fringes of heaven from hell, comments, "When the doctrine of the Resurrection ceased to commend itself to the critical faculties which God had given me, I openly rejected it. I preached my famous sermon. I defied the whole chapter. I took every risk." His colleague comments, "What risk? What was at all likely to come of it except what actually came—popularity, sales for your books, invitations, and finally a bishopric?" The conversation continues, "Dick, this is unworthy of you. What are you suggesting?" Dick replies,

> Friend, I am not suggesting at all. You see, I know now. Let us be frank. Our opinions were not honestly come by. We simply found ourselves in contact with a certain current of ideas and plunged into it because it seemed modern and successful. At College, you know, we just started automatically writing the kind of essays that got good marks and saying the kind of things that won applause. When, in our whole lives, did we honestly face, in solitude, the one question on which all turned: whether after all the Supernatural might not in fact occur? When did we put up one moment's real resistance to the loss of our faith?[63]

This bishop exists, subsists, in a monochrome hell of his own making, a thin world of near nothingness, when he could be really real by simply accepting he was wrong and allowing Christ to forgive him, to change him, because he has already been redeemed on the cross—the "bleeding charity." This bishop-theologian's Christian atheism (the denial of Christ's divinity, and the supernatural, leaving "god" as an idea) leads inevitably to a belief in a weak, personal, false "god," whereby he becomes seduced by his theories and imprisoned by them.

---

63   Lewis, *The Great Divorce*, 27–28.

4. REVELATION AND CHRISTOLOGY, 1941–47: THE KEY THEOLOGICAL AND PHILOSOPHICAL ESSAYS

i. *The Inconsolable Secret*

The period of the Second World War was one of the most theologically fruitful of Lewis's career—from *The Broadcast Talks*, through to the volume, *Miracles*, and the early analogical narratives, *The Screwtape Letters* and *The Great Divorce*. However, all these insights were encapsulated in the early years of the war in a sermon-essay preached in the University Church of St. Mary the Virgin, in the High Street, Oxford, on June 8, 1941: "The Weight of Glory."[64] Lewis notes how so many people regard a negative (unselfishness) as the highest of virtues when it is a positive (love) that is truly virtuous. Self-denial is part of the cross and the cross comes before heaven but this elevation of unselfishness, Lewis asserts, issues from "modern" philosophy in the form of Immanuel Kant and also from the Stoics. It is not so much that our desires are too great but that they are too weak, too insubstantial: "We are half-hearted creatures, fooling about with drink and sex and ambition when infinite joy is offered us . . . We are far too easily pleased."[65] Denial does, yes, lead to a greater reward but our desire for this reward, which is no mere bribe, is to lead to that which is the very consummation of our earthly desire. Somehow, somewhere, the idea has crept into the Christian faith that this desire for the glory of God is wrong (it can be argued, though Lewis does not do so, that this can be seen in many people as Protestant austerity). It is this sense in us (that desiring glory is not good) which Lewis tackles. In so doing he examines how and where *Sehnsucht* should generate in us this desire, a right desire, for God's glory given to us. *Sehnsucht* here is,

> The inconsolable secret in each one of you—the secret which hurts so much that you take your revenge on it by calling it names like Nostalgia and Romanticism and Adolescence; the secret also which pierces with such sweetness that when, in very intimate conversation, the mention of it becomes imminent, we grow awkward and affect to laugh at ourselves; the secret we cannot hide and cannot tell, though we desire to do both. We cannot tell it because it is a desire for something that has never actually appeared in our experience. We cannot hide it because our experience is constantly suggesting it, and we betray ourselves like lovers at the mention of a name. Our commonest expedient is to call it beauty and behave as if that has settled the matter.[66]

The danger, writes Lewis, which in some ways is a remembrance of his own wandering youthful apostasy is to mistake this desire for the thing in itself: "it is not in them, it

---

64   A sermon preached in the University Church of St Mary the Virgin on Jun. 8. 1941, initially published in, *Theology*, the Church of England-SPCK (Society for Promoting Christian Knowledge) journal. The sermon-essay was then reproduced as a pamphlet by SPCK: C. S. Lewis, *The Weight of Glory* (1942). It was later included in a volume of essays, C. S. Lewis, "The Weight of Glory," (1949), 21–33.
65   Lewis, "The Weight of Glory" (1949), 21.
66   Ibid., 23–24.

only came through them."⁶⁷ Thus the chief symptom, for many, that this desire for God exhibits is longing—that is, the inconsolable, piercing, longing of called *Sehnsucht*. Lewis therefore waxes poetic—it is the scent of an unknown flower, the echo of an unheard tune, news from a far-off distant country. This is revelation in us and we ignore it at our peril: "Almost our whole education has been directed to silencing this shy, persistent, inner voice; almost all our modern philosophies have been devised to convince us that the good of man is to be found on this earth. And yet it is a remarkable thing that such philosophies of Progress or Creative Evolution themselves bear reluctant witness to the truth that our real goal is elsewhere."⁶⁸ Thus we have the "heresy" of much that is proclaimed by "modern" or "Liberal" philosophers who decry the God-given, revealed desire for eternity—"Do what they will, then, we remain conscious of a desire which no natural happiness will satisfy."⁶⁹ Therefore, true to his understanding of *Sehnsucht*, Lewis is presenting the existence deep within the human psyche of a desire without, or uncertain of, its object and often directionless despite the intimation from the Holy Spirit that will guide it back to God. Sacred books, writes Lewis, will give us some guidance, or more pertinently, an account of the object, but it is important to note the symbolic—or transposed—nature of these accounts because heaven is outside of our experience and the intelligible descriptions relate to our experience: "The scriptural picture of heaven is therefore just as symbolical as the picture which our desire, unaided, invents for itself . . . the difference is that the scriptural imagery has authority. It comes to us from writers who were closer to God than we, and it has stood the test of Christian experience."⁷⁰ Hence Lewis's appeal to a patristic-based "mere" core, the tradition that his apologetics are grounded in.

So this is the promise of Scripture, which provides important clues, intimations, of the object that *Sehnsucht* should focus on, indeed, which trigger the experience of *Sehnsucht* (and the numinous) in us. Regarding the promise of Scripture, systematically, what does Lewis make of this, how does he classify this assurance, even, guarantee for the faithful? The promises of Scripture are primarily revelation:

First,
That we shall be with Christ

Second,
That we shall be like him

Third,
With an enormous wealth of imagery, that we shall have glory

Fourth,
That we shall, in some sense, be fed or feasted or entertained

---

67   Ibid., 24.
68   Ibid., 24.
69   Ibid., 25.
70   Ibid., 26.

10. Apologist and Defender of the Faith II: Revelation and Christology, 1941–47

Fifth,
That we shall have some sort of official position in the universe—
ruling cities, judging angels, being pillars of God's temple.[71]

Lewis does note that the subsequent promises are actually encapsulated in the first—to be with Christ is everything. The reason for the other promises is to be found in their symbolic nature—they "smuggle in ideas of proximity in space and loving conversation."[72] We err to ignore the very real, the supra-real nature of the fullness of reality that is eternity with and in Christ. The promises are couched in symbolic—or more pertinently analogical—imagery; the imagery is of our reality but should point us to and evoke eternity. Regarding these promises of Scripture, Lewis notes that each "is only a symbol, like the reality in some respects, but unlike it in others, and therefore needs correction from the different symbols in the other promises."[73] Nothing other than God is promised even though there is a multiplicity and variance of images: "a dozen changing images, correcting and relieving each other."[74]

Lewis then turns to the idea of glory. Lewis comments that there is no getting away from the fact that the idea of glory is central to and prominent within the New Testament and in early Christian writings: "Salvation is constantly associated with palms, crowns, white robes, thrones, and splendour like the sun and stars."[75] Lewis admits that he is "a typical modern" in that this jars with his mind-set, it makes no appeal to him, yet it must be regarded as revelation. "Glory suggests two ideas to me, of which one seems wicked and the other ridiculous. Either glory means to me fame, or it means luminosity. As for the first, since to be famous means to be better known than other people, the desire for fame appears to me as a competitive passion and therefore of hell rather than heaven. As for the second, who wishes to become a kind of living electric light bulb?"[76] However, Lewis then realizes that there is a strong Christian tradition that saw glory as appreciation by God—Lewis paraphrases Scripture for he comments that nothing we do or believe can diminish the divine accolade spoken to the righteous—"well done good and faithful servant," for "no one can enter heaven except as a child," a good child that exhibits pleasure in being praised, in doing the good.[77] It is this childlike acceptance of praise and glory from God that is so corrupted and tainted amongst adults so often driven by ambition so that the accolade is then self-generated. Glory is to be like the praise given to and accepted by a child, like a child before a parent, like a pupil before its teacher: for we are created to please the Creator. The language of Scripture may, therefore, be symbolic or more pertinently analogical, but we err to dismiss what is revealed if we redefine it in the jaded cynical terms of the ambitions of adults preoccupied with worldly concerns.

---

71 Ibid., 26.
72 Ibid.
73 Ibid., 26–27.
74 Ibid., 27.
75 Ibid.
76 Ibid.
77 Matt 25:21; also Mark 10:15 and Matt 18:2–6.

> Perfect humility dispenses with modesty. If God is satisfied with the work, the work may be satisfied with itself; "it is not for her to bandy compliments with her Sovereign." I can imagine someone saying that he dislikes my idea of heaven as a place where we are patted on the back. But proud misunderstanding is behind that dislike. In the end that Face which is the delight or the terror of the universe must be turned upon each of us either with one expression or with the other, either conferring glory inexpressible or inflicting shame that can never be cured or disguised.[78]

The implication here is that what God thinks of us is more important than what we think of ourselves and of God. Because of our fallen nature whatever we believe about ourselves and about God will inevitably be tainted and corrupted and therefore inaccurate. How God regards us is crucial; and if God so praises us and glorifies our righteousness who are we to diminish or deny the Almighty?

The promise of glory is the promise of Christ because it is won by and then conferred by Christ through the cross. The wonder is, for Lewis, that any of us shall survive that examination; that it is possible for *any* of us to please God. The key word therefore for Lewis in defining this glory is delight: "To be loved by God, not merely pitied, but delighted in as an artist delights in his work or a father in a son—it seems impossible, a weight or burden of glory which our thoughts can hardly sustain. But so it is."[79] Lewis therefore concludes that if we had stayed with our modern jaded dismissal of the authoritative and scriptural image of glory then we would have no real understanding *revealed to us* of God's desire and delight in us: by ceasing to consider my own wants, or my fallen and corrupted idea of my needs, we can truly appreciate what our needs are. The stab of *Sehnsucht* and the sense of the numinous are both important here because they should expose our false notion of what glory is and of what is praiseworthy. Lewis likens this to, quoting Keats, the journey homeward of the soul, those moments when we realize that we belong elsewhere, not to this world. The cynic will be convinced that this was an illusion, that such religious experiences are delusional. It is because of our mixed reception of this intimations, it is because of our sinful fallen nature that *Sehnsucht*, in particular, is characterized by the bitter-sweet: the astringent stab, the inconsolable longing, yet, the joy and delight of the promise.

We are on the outside, we are where we do not belong, but our condition does not befit us to where we truly belong. We believe we know about God when we should really listen to what *he* knows and how *he* regards us. The warning is there in Scripture, for some will come before him in judgment and will hear the terrible words, "You that are accursed, depart from me into the eternal fire prepared for the devil and his angels" (Matt 25:41). Our predicament outside becomes permanent. We must accept the desire of God to delight in us, to change us, to draw us up: Christ descended for to draw us up. Lewis therefore waxes lyrically Platonic.

> We do not want merely to see beauty, though, God knows, even that is bounty enough. We want something else which can hardly be put into words—to be

---

78 Lewis, "The Weight of Glory" (1949), 28.
79 Ibid., 29.

10. Apologist and Defender of the Faith II: Revelation and Christology, 1941–47

united with the beauty we see, to pass into it, to receive it into ourselves, to bathe in it, to become part of it. That is why we have peopled air and earth and water with gods and goddesses and nymphs and elves...

> For if we take the imagery of Scripture seriously, if we believe that God will one day give us the Morning Star and cause us to put on the splendour of the sun, then we may surmise that both the ancient myths and the modern poetry, so false as history, may be very near the truth as prophecy. At present we are on the outside of the world, the wrong side of the door. We discern the freshness and purity of morning, but they do not make us fresh and pure. We cannot mingle with the splendours we see. But all the leaves of the New Testament are rustling with the rumour that it will not always be so. Someday, God willing, we shall get in.[80]

When we have become as perfect as possible in voluntary obedience, then God will confer that glory which is delight. But, warns Lewis, the cross comes before the crown, and our neighbor now becomes a holy object presented to our senses, because Christ is hidden in him or her, the true glory is hidden: "for in him also Christ *vere latitat*—the glorifier and the glorified, Glory himself, is truly hidden."[81]

ii. Revelation and Transposition

Towards the end of the Second World War Lewis gave what is in many ways the most important essay/paper he ever gave—entitled "Transposition."[82] Revelation is communicated without one-to-one correspondence. There is a varying degree of change, dilution, or more pertinently diminution—a reduction or alteration, transformation, to a degree. We noted how Lewis applied this to music (a work for full orchestra changes but is still "true" when re-scored for solo piano), but he also invoked drawing—pencil lines on paper, or oil paint on canvas, is not in reality the object, but holds something of its truth. Revelation is subject to a doctrine of transposition, what we can say or know about God is by analogy. The essay "Transposition" was originally preached as a sermon on Whit-Sunday in Mansfield College Chapel, Oxford, on May 28, 1944. The thinking behind it therefore belongs in this rich seam of wartime development in Lewis the apologist, philosopher, and theologian. At the heart of revelation is incarnation—the second person of the Trinity incarnated as a human is a form of transposition. What does Lewis say here? What does he mean? This doctrine of transposition and the implications for Lewis's Christology and doctrine of revelation will be examined in depth when we examine Lewis on Scripture, revelation, and reason. It is this doctrine of transposition—itself Platonically transposed—that, it can be argued, forms the key to all of Lewis's work.

Transposition as a key is developed in Lewis's thinking at the same time as he develops his understanding of the dual core of Christian doctrine—the "mere" core or ground derived from Richard Baxter and Vincentius of Lérins. This "mere" core was

---

80 Ibid., 31.
81 Ibid., 33.
82 Lewis, "Transposition," 1st ed., 9-20.

first named as such by Lewis in the introduction he wrote for Sr. Penelope's translation of Athanasius's *de incarnatione verbi Dei* (*The Incarnation of the Word of God*):[83] "Mere Christianity," was a name, as we have seen, derived from the seventeenth-century Puritan Richard Baxter.

Picking out Lewis's ecclesiology—his doctrine of the church—is to be achieved by sifting through his writings. If the church is to be considered the body of Christ, however, there is a profound statement of the nature of the church, and the legitimacy of the Church of England that Lewis presented during the war as part of The Clark Lectures given in Cambridge in 1944. Perhaps what this shows us is that Lewis had a keen and profound understanding of Reformation history and how none of the churches or denominations, post-Reformation could claim the authority that the early or patristic church once claimed.[84]

---

83 Lewis, "Introduction." In, Athanasius, *The Incarnation of the Word*, 5–12.
84 C. S. Lewis, "Introduction: New Learning and New Ignorance," part of The Clark Lectures, delivered at Trinity College Cambridge, 1944, later to form the "Introduction" to *English Literature in the Sixteenth Century*. See in particular p. 32f.

11

Apologist and Defender of the Faith III: Revelation and Christology, 1948–63— The Later Works: Mere Christology

SYNOPSIS:
What is Lewis's Christology, as evidenced in his works from the period 1948 through to his death in 1963? Reason is still central to Lewis, but the method of analogical narrative increasingly assumes a greater role in his thinking. Are these later works generally orthodox? What flaws are there in, for example, Lewis's *summa*—the publication of the war-time broadcasts in a single volume—*Mere Christianity* (1952)? Is it broadly creedal? Critics assert that he marginalizes the role of the cross and resurrection. Is this a fair criticism? It is important here to consider the criticisms of the biblical theologian N. T. Wright. Lewis's understanding of the cross, however, appears to be focused on the nature of atonement that issues from the death of Jesus of Nazareth, the Christ, and how this repays the debt generated by humanity through sin, even though Lewis eschews atonement theories, or at least the contradictory nature of them. Does this marginalize the place of punishment? Or is punishment subservient to the debt repaid through the Christ's life blood spilt? It is the blood of the lamb, Jesus the Messiah, slain for our salvation, that is the key to Lewis's understanding of the cross, not necessarily the means (crucifixion) of his death; this is confirmed by the Hebrew categories defining the relationship between blood and atonement. Why blood?—because the ancient Hebrews conceptualized the very life force of an individual as being in, with, contained by, but essentially part of the blood: people bled to death. To understand this, and Lewis's presentation, we need to consider not the general religious ideas about life after death across world religions but the true reality revealed from the Hebrew tradition. It is this tradition that paints a true picture of the human predicament, *post mortem*, the situation Jesus was born into. It is important to remember the Jewish background to sacrifice where blood is key to the apparent validity of sacrifice in the Old Testament. This can be read from *Mere Christianity*, but is stated explicitly in *The Chronicles of Narnia*; for example the resurrection of King Caspian in *The Silver Chair*, enacted by a drop of Aslan's blood. This focus on the critical value of the blood of the sacrificial lamb, the crucified Christ, achieves a greater place in Lewis's mature work.

C. S. LEWIS—REVELATION, CONVERSION, AND APOLOGETICS

1. REVELATION AND CHRISTOLOGY, 1948–63: THE KEY THEOLOGICAL AND PHILOSOPHICAL WORKS

Theology by analogy is a method Lewis uses consistently throughout his work from the late 1930s. We may call this method analogical narrative—theologically charged stories, which are neither fiction nor non-fiction. These analogical narratives are usually considered to be four works, chronologically, *The Space Trilogy* (1938, 1943, 1945), *The Screwtape Letters* (1942), *The Great Divorce* (1945), and *The Chronicles of Narnia* (1950–56). Lewis also uses this method and technique in his apologetics; for example, he often presented a seemingly complex theological point in, for example, *The Broadcast Talks* or in *Miracles*, as a word picture. A systematic study of the figure of Christ in Lewis's analogical narratives rightly occurs later, as a topic in its own right. The question here is, "What do these works tell us of Lewis's developing understanding of Christ in the context of his theology?" Lewis could have written a systematic theological analysis of Christ—a doctrine of Christ, a Christology. What he did in the 1950s was, from his skill as a lecturer and professor in literature, write theologically charged stories where the method is analogy: this word picture tells us something about what Christ is. This method is shown in all of his analogical narratives and is often considered as being in many ways more successful than philosophical disputation. Lewis is working in a long allegorical tradition. For example, Dante's *Divine Comedy* and Bunyan's *Pilgrim's Progress*, although there is an important distinction here between allegory and analogy; the difference is to do with one-to-one correspondence—Aslan may be similar or dissimilar by analogy, by comparison, to Christ, but he is never an allegory of Christ; Aslan cannot be interpreted as being a hidden Christ. In terms of method Lewis writes directly from the voice of the character that analogically "re-presents" Christ so that the reader makes a decision—yes, this is like Christ, or no, this is not like Christ. The decision should not be subjective, the opinion of the reader should be governed by revelation and reason: that is, to what extent does Lewis's picture of Christ (Aslan in *The Chronicles of Narnia*), or Christ-likeness (*Ransom in The Space Trilogy*), or the judgment of Christ (as in *The Great Divorce*), or the eschatological reality we face all the time before the hidden Christ (as in *The Screwtape Letters*) represent in some ways but not others what we understand to be Christ from Scripture, from revelation, from deductive reasoning and from church tradition. Christ, "in" Aslan, is "presented" as holy and just, awesome and powerful, yet loving and submissive. On the other hand, for the senior demon Screwtape, this righteousness is perceived as deeply troubling and threatening, something to be avoided. Are not both word pictures accurate according to the understanding we have of Christ from Scripture and revelation, from reason and deduction, and in accordance with developed church tradition? This orthodox understanding could be presented discursively, a written description, couched in theological and philosophical language, which draws on accepted cultural norms in terms of the meaning and use of words; therefore, as such, a theological discursive description about the nature and work of Christ would not be very different to Lewis's analogical narratives, but with one

11. Apologist and Defender of the Faith III: Revelation and Christology, 1948–63 (1)

exception—Lewis's analogical narrative are often considered to be clearer and more accessible than theological and philosophical writing. Aslan is written for children, yet is valued by adults the world over, particularly by thinking Christians.

2. ANSCOMBE-LEWIS

But this analogical approach is not exclusive; reason is still important to Lewis, reason as the reason of God. *The Broadcast Talks* were reissued in one volume, re-edited, and became Lewis's *summa*—the oft-cited *Mere Christianity*. It is, therefore, still important for Lewis during this period to assert a reasoned justification for the incarnation-cross-resurrection. This is no more so than in the re-edited material that forms *Mere Christianity*: Logos as reason is fundamental to this analogical approach. However, Lewis's understanding of revelation and reason changes with his mature work. But this change is gradual: it can be seen, in genesis, in his theologically charged stories from as early as the late 1930s, but in 1948 Lewis has what to many is a bruising confrontation with Elizabeth Anscombe: on February 2, 1948, a young philosophy don, G. E. M. Anscombe, presented a paper to The Oxford Socratic Club deconstructing Lewis's argument against naturalism. Whatever the truth and effect of the debate at the Oxford Socratic Club, Lewis appeared profoundly affected by the encounter. Or does he? The ensuing debate became seminal. The exchange and the issues involved continue to generate interest because of the relationship between religion and the question of philosophical naturalism and scientism (which has seen a fresh airing due to the publication of the work of many of the so-called New Atheists). The Anscombe-Lewis debate was about the fundamental philosophical concepts that underpin Christianity, and was noted for its impact on Lewis by supporters and detractors alike. But how does it affect the development of Lewis's mature work? The issues involved here are complex and are closely related to Lewis's formation in the 1920s and his work as a philosopher, and will form a thematic focus for us later: Lewis the philosopher on causation and naturalism, revelation and reason.[1]

3. AN ORTHODOX CHRIST: MERE CHRISTIANITY

i. Mere Christology?

The BBC *Broadcast Talks* from the 1940s were re-published in a single volume in 1952 under the title *Mere Christianity*. Although they were essentially the same, being restructured into a single volume, there were subtle though important changes. For example, Lewis extends the argument of some points, and added emphasis on others so that the whole reads, to a degree, as a single developing argument. Therefore, the work is often cited as a basic defense for the Christian worldview. Does *Mere Christianity* give an accurate introductory picture of Jesus Christ? The picture Lewis presents is the same as we examined earlier in our analysis of *The Broadcast Talks*, with subtle changes

---

1   See: Brazier, "C. S. Lewis and the Anscombe Debate." The debate will be examined in-depth in the third book in this series.

to add to the cohesion of the whole picture as a single volume; however, Lewis's Jesus must be seen as a personal picture, to a degree, despite the claims of the volume to be an orthodox introduction to Christianity. Is Lewis's picture of Jesus Christ creedal, is it orthodox? Very few people would say no; the answer in general terms is yes. However, there are critics. Obviously, self-confessed atheists or religionists (people who believe all religions are equally valid and point to the same unknowable "god") would refute Lewis's picture, but that is only to be expected. But there are also some critics of Lewis who write from an orthodox perspective; for example, the Bible scholar and theologian N. T. Wright.

The Historical Jesus?

Wright acknowledges the great debt he and many others owe to Lewis's writings, in particular *Mere Christianity*; works that nurtured them as young Christians when, Wright argues, the established churches failed them. But, asserts Wright, there is the criticism that "the Christianity offered by Lewis both was and wasn't the 'mere' thing he made it out to be. There is a definite spin to it."[2] This as a criticism can and should be applied to every theologian's writings (including Wright's). Lewis would have freely admitted that he knew there was a "mere" core to the Christian faith and that he, to a greater or lesser degree, identified it. Lewis is writing not as a disinterested, neutral, and impartial academic but as "a direct report from the front line."[3] Wright acknowledges that Lewis correctly asserts that faith is more important than feelings, which contradicts the Romanticism of the West in the twentieth century; further that falsehood is unmasked and understood from the perspective of truth, not from the relativity of falsehood. However, there are deeper criticisms that are christological: Wright finds Lewis's understanding of resurrection, and therefore heaven and immortality, vague and insufficient; therefore he concludes that this is too Platonic. This leads Lewis, so Wright asserts, to a poor, vague, and insufficient treatment of Jesus of Nazareth as a historical person. This is, to a degree, true: *Mere Christianity* and *The Broadcast Talks* do not give what some theologians and philosophers would like to have seen as a picture of the historical Jesus and the Christ of faith, a picture that reflects their personal studies. Wright commented: "I am well aware that some in our day, too, see the historical context of Jesus as part of what you teach Christians later on rather than part of how you explain the gospel to outsiders. I think this is simply mistaken."[4] Neither the apostles nor the patristic theologians were overly concerned with an analysis of the historical Jesus, and however correct Wright may be to emphasize the Jewishness of Jesus, what was incarnated was the universal Christ, the second person of the Trinity; hence, to Lewis and most patristic theologians, Jesus was a manifestation of a Platonic universal form. It was taken for granted by the apostles and the early church that Jesus was a historical person, because the early disciples had seen him: seen him with their eyes, heard with their ears, and perceived and knew him!

2   Wright, "Simply Lewis: Reflections on a Master Apologist After 60 Years". Online: para. 6.
3   Ibid. Online: para. 14.
4   Ibid., Online: para. 46.

11. Apologist and Defender of the Faith III: Revelation and Christology, 1948–63 (1)

C. S. LEWIS: THE KEY THEOLOGICAL AND PHILOSOPHICAL WORKS—THE MATURE PERIOD (1948–63)

1950
— *The Chronicles of Narnia. The Lion the Witch & the Wardrobe.*
— "What Are We to Make of Jesus Christ?"

1951
— *The Chronicles of Narnia. Prince Caspian. The Return to Narnia.*
— "Christian Hope—Its Meaning for Today."

1952
— *The Chronicles of Narnia. The Voyage of the Dawn Treader.*
— *Mere Christianity.*
— "Is Theism Important? A Reply."

1953
— *The Chronicles of Narnia. The Silver Chair.*

1954
— *The Chronicles of Narnia. The Horse and His Boy.*
— "De Descriptione Temporum."
— "Introduction: New Learning and New Ignorance." In *English Literature in the Sixteenth Century Excluding Drama.*

1955
— *The Chronicles of Narnia. The Magician's Nephew*
— *Surprised by Joy.*

1956
— *The Chronicles of Narnia. The Last Battle*
— *Till We Have Faces.*

1957
— "The Psalms".

1958
— *Reflections on the Psalms.*
— "Rejoinder to Dr Pittenger".

1959
— "Modern Theology and Biblical Criticism".
— "Screwtape Proposes a Toast".

1960
— *Miracles* (2nd edition).
— *The Four Loves.*
— "It All Began with a Picture...".
— "The Efficacy of Prayer".

1961
N.W. Clerk (pseudonym), *A Grief Observed.*

1962
— "Transposition"
(a reworked and extended edition).

1963
— (with Sherwood E. Wirt), "I was Decided Upon", and, "Heaven, Earth and Outer Space."
— "We Have No 'Right to Happiness.'"
— "Must Our Image of God Go?".

1964
— *Letters to Malcolm: Chiefly on Prayer.*

KEY WORKS—LETTERS 1948–63

— C. S. Lewis to the Editor, *The Church Times*, CXXXV, Feb. 8, 1952. *Collected Letters Vol. III*, 164.
— C. S. Lewis to Genia Goelz, Mar. 18, 1952. *Collected Letters Vol. III*, 172.
— C. S. Lewis to Dom Bede Griffiths, May 28, 1952. *Collected Letters Vol. III*, 195.
— C. S. Lewis to Genia Goelz, June 20, 1952. *Collected Letters Vol. III*, 204–5.
— C. S. Lewis to Mrs Johnson, Nov. 8, 1952. *Collected Letters Vol. III*, 245–48.
— C. S. Lewis to Emily McLay, Aug. 8, 1953. *Collected Letters Vol. III*, 356–57.
— C. S. Lewis to Mr Allcock, Mar. 24, 1955. *Collected Letters Vol. III*, 587–89.
— C. S. Lewis to Janet Wise, Oct. 5, 1955. *Collected Letters Vol. III*, 652–53.
— C. S. Lewis to Corbin Scott Carnell, Oct. 13, 1958. *Collected Letters Vol. III*, 978–80.
— C. S. Lewis to Lee Turner, July 19, 1958. *Collected Letters Vol. III*, 960.
— C. S. Lewis to Mrs Hook, Dec. 29, 1958. *Collected Letters Vol. III*, 1004–5.
— C. S. Lewis to Clyde S. Kilby, May 7, 1959. *Collected Letters Vol. III*, 1044–46.
— C. S. Lewis to Vera Gebbert, Oct. 16, 1960. *Collected Letters Vol. III*, 1198.
— C. S. Lewis to Mrs Green, Jun. 18, 1962. *Collected Letters Vol. III*, 1353.

A complete list of Lewis's works in this period can be found in the bibliography

Figure 15: C. S. Lewis: the Key Theological and Philosophical Works—
The Mature Period (1948–63)

Perhaps Wright, despite his excellent orthodox biblical credentials, is too much of a hostage to modernism in this concern with the human Jesus and his Jewish heritage? Was *Mere Christianity* meant to be a comprehensive Christological treatise? Probably not, despite the fact that it is often feted as such by some Evangelicals. However, its reception and use since its publication has proved its worth, and the intervening years have proved its Catholic-Evangelical credentials. *Mere Christianity* is orthodox, creedal, and traditional in its Christology, but it is *not* a complete christological *summa* and neither does it accommodate the somewhat obscure interests of many academics with regard to the historical Jesus, as if it is at all possible to re-create an absolutely accurate portrait of someone who lived two millennia ago.

Salvation and Sanctification

Wright is critical of Lewis's soteriology in *Mere Christianity*—that is, his understanding of salvation. He criticizes Lewis for asserting that we can do nothing for ourselves, we cannot save ourselves, hence the priority of grace, yet, Wright asserts, Lewis speaks of us becoming gradually good through Christ in us:

> At this point, of course, we come up against Lewis's implied soteriology... Several times he insists, effectively, on the priority of grace: We can't save ourselves, but God does it, takes the initiative, rescues those who couldn't rescue themselves. But equally often he speaks as though it's really a matter, as with Aristotle, of our becoming good by gradually learning to do good things, and with Jesus coming alongside, and indeed inside, to help us as we do so. Salvation, and behaviour, are caught by infection, by our being in Christ and his being in us.[5]

Wright mistakenly sees these two concepts as mutually exclusive. However, Lewis is drawing on an Augustinian concept of prevenient grace, which held that we are too corrupted by original sin to help or save ourselves, yet the Holy Spirit, issuing from the grace of God (grace as the free undeserved love and forgiveness of God for humanity exercised in the cross), will act on us to generate whatever good there is in us. This is prevenient (*preceding, prior*) grace that predisposes the human heart to seek God prior to any initiative on the part of the human. Prevenient grace asserts that any good we do comes from the prevenient (i.e., prior) action of the grace of God through the Holy Spirit working in and through us. This relates closely to the incarnation and cross whereby Jesus's Spirit will *preveniently* change us—this is what sanctification is about. Therefore, for Lewis, sanctification must be seen as gradual: as we stand in our sins with feet of clay. This gradual process is biblical and can be seen in the early church, and specifically the Apostle Paul's Epistles and the Letter to the Hebrews. This gradual process is also asserted by the Roman Catholic and Orthodox churches. For Lewis—and this is clearly evident from *The Broadcast Talks* that we analyzed earlier, and many times over in subsequent works—if grace is the free unwarranted forgiveness of God for humanity, and if this grace is primarily exhibited in the procession of God to save humanity, descending (incarnation), crucified (the cross, to atone), to be raised-up

---

5   Ibid., Online: para. 24.

11. Apologist and Defender of the Faith III: Revelation and Christology, 1948–63 (1)

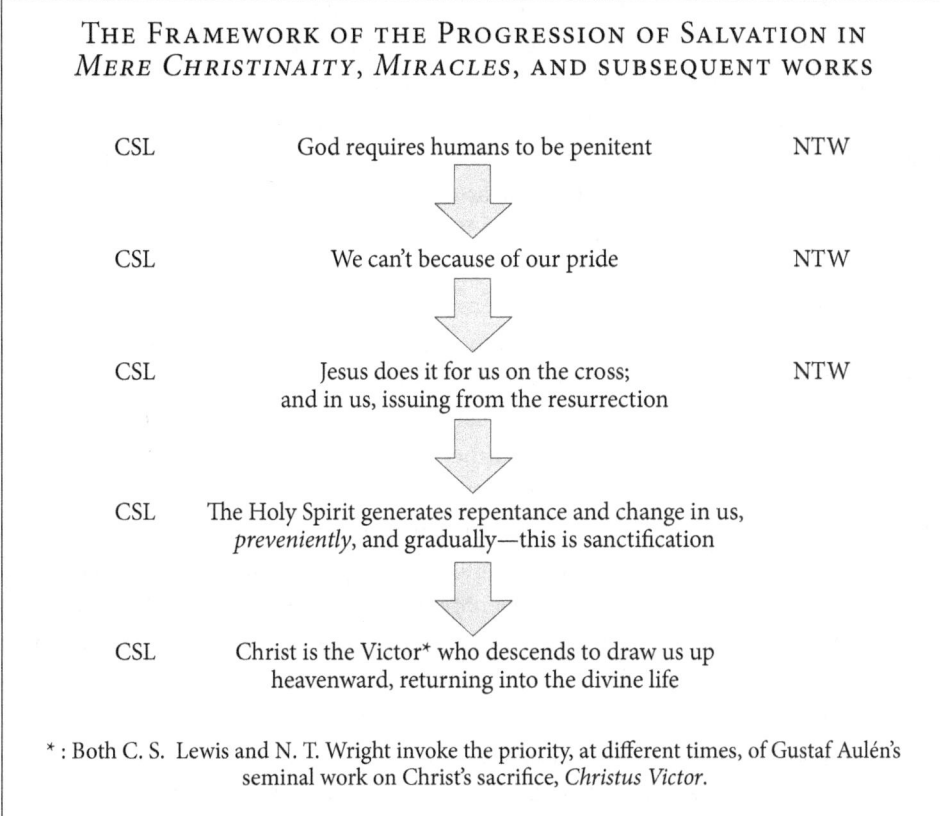

Figure 16: The Framework of a Doctrine of Salvation from *Mere Christianity*

(resurrection and ascension) to draw humanity with Christ into the divine life, then grace is also, *secondarily*, the work of the Holy Spirit in changing us, re-birthing us (John 3), acting prior to our corrupted will, recreating us, in effect restoring the *imago Christi* (the image of Christ, ultimately the *imago Dei*, the image of God) in us. This is consistently found in Lewis's writings, and in the work of patristic theologians.

ii. The Death of Jesus of Nazareth

The Cross

N. T. Wright takes Lewis to task on his treatment of the cross in *Mere Christianity*; here, Wright appears to be on more solid ground in the sense that Lewis's treatment and coverage does not superficially appear to be as comprehensive as one would expect from the perspective of certain Protestant-Evangelicals, or Roman Catholics for that matter. Wright has devoted much academic study to understanding Jesus as a Jew, claiming that this is the proper historical context for understanding Jesus: "Judaism's incarnational principle doesn't undermine the eventual claim, nor does it short-circuit it. It places it in its proper historical context and enables it to be at once nuanced into a proto-Trinitarian framework, employing and appropriately transcending the messianic category 'Son of God,' which simultaneously settles down into first-century Judaism and explodes beyond it. Lewis's overconfident argument, by contrast, does the opposite: it doesn't work as history, and it backfires dangerously when historical critics question his reading of the Gospels."[6] So Lewis's "picture" of Jesus is incomplete from an academic perspective. Lewis by contrast grounds his Jesus in the universal Christ of all eternity, the second person of the Trinity who is transposed in incarnation, who—as demonstrated in Philippians (the christological kenotic hymn, Phil 2:5–11)—restrains his divine attributes in becoming human. Yes, the Logos did assume a Jewish humanity, but in becoming the new Adam, the primary evidence for Lewis for the Christ is in the immanent Trinity (see John 1:1–18); the secondary evidence is in Jesus the Jew, the focus and locus of incarnation. Christ was incarnated a Jew, born into the Hebrew religious tradition, and therefore much that he was and did is to be understood in this Jewish context. But as the universal Christ the Holy Spirit reveals something of an understanding of Jesus, for Lewis, through other religions, or for that matter, through non-religious culture or music. To emphasize and move the secondary to the primary is very modern and very Liberal (Lewis's twin "enemies"). That Lewis presents Jesus as the perfect penitent is, according to Wright, correct; likewise that differing or competing theories of atonement are not necessarily to be seen as a flaw—"Christians are not committed to one single way of understanding the meaning of the cross,"[7] because looking at the cross as God's love and forgiveness is "sufficient" at the beginning of the Christian pilgrimage. However, Wright again criticizes the focus in Lewis's soteriology: is it Christ on the cross that does everything (Wright's view) or do we do something for our salvation (Wright's understanding of Lewis's view)? Wright correctly identifies the order of salvation in *Mere Christianity*, which is coherent with the rest of Lewis's works, but he then claims that Lewis *overvalues repentance*, arguing that for Lewis salvation is God doing something *in* us, rather than *extra nos* (outside of us). However, a comprehensive reading of Lewis's works from the 1930s to the late 1950s shows that he held to both—with the primacy locus of salvation *extra nos* (in this instance, the cross), and secondarily God generating repentance as a valid response in us (preveniently).

For Wright, the cross as God's action *extra nos* appears to be minimized in Lewis's work; he therefore comments—invoking Gustaf Aulén's seminal work on Christ's sacrifice—that this reduces the *Christus victor* theme.[8] However, this is a particular narrow and selective reading; Lewis invokes, acknowledges, and refers to Aulén's work, and stresses the importance and primacy of God's action on the cross, *extra nos* so it appears that Wright's interpretation of Lewis here is, at best, ungenerous.[9]

---

6   Ibid., Online: para. 50
7   Ibid., Online: para. 51.
8   Ibid., Online: para. 52.
9   Lewis writing to Corbin Scott Carnell Oct. 13, 1958. *Collected Letters Vol. III*, 980. Aulén, *Christus Victor*.

11. Apologist and Defender of the Faith III: Revelation and Christology, 1948-63 (1)

The Death

What does Lewis say about the death of Jesus in *Mere Christianity*? What value does he place on Jesus's death—torture, punishment, and crucifixion—at the hands of the Romans and the Jewish religious authorities? Lewis comments on the importance for the disciple to take up the cross,[10] furthermore, that, "It costs God nothing, so far as we know, to create nice things: but to convert rebellious wills costs him the crucifixion"[11]; indeed the world's reaction is diametric to the crucifixion: "Its [the world's] first disappointment was over the crucifixion. The Man came to life again."[12] What value does Lewis place on the *death* of Jesus? Lewis notes how there are stories scattered through religions about a "god" who dies and comes to life again, but, importantly, this death, imparts new life. Furthermore, consider the following quotes: "as soon as you look into the New Testament or any other Christian writing you'll find they're constantly talking about something different—about his death and his coming to life again."[13] If "the central Christian belief is that Christ's death has somehow put us right with God and given us a fresh start," then we must ask why and how.[14] We've noted already Lewis's justified skepticism as to the multiplicity and range and diversity of atonement theories; however, although we cannot fully explain how atonement works, Jesus's death is important and central—"Theories about Christ's death aren't Christianity: they're explanations about how it works."[15] Lewis places cosmic importance on the death of Jesus of Nazareth, the Christ; we may not be able to fully explain why and how, but this does not mitigate or underestimate the central importance of his death:

> We believe that the death of Christ is just that point in history at which something absolutely unimaginable from outside shows through into our own world. We are told that Christ was killed for us, that his death has washed out our sins, and that by dying he disabled death itself. That's the formula. That's Christianity. That's what has to be believed. Any theories we build up as to how Christ's death did all this are, in my view, quite secondary: mere plans or diagrams to be left alone if they don't help us, and, even if they do help us, not to be confused with the thing itself, All the same, some of these theories are worth looking at.[16]

This involves the perfect surrender and humiliation undergone by Jesus; the perfection, asserts Lewis, issues from the very nature of the incarnation: "perfect because he was God, surrender and humiliation because he was man."[17] This relates closely to discipleship on a pneumatological level: the Holy Spirit will "pick us up" when we fall, those owned by Christ will be changed as we repent; this enables us "to repeat (in some

---

10   *Mere Christianity*, 197.
11   Ibid., 212-14, see also, Bk. 3 ch. 12, 147; Bk. 4 ch. 3, 169-70; Bk. 4 ch. 11, 222. See also, *Beyond Personality*, 53, and, 22. Also, *Christian Behaviour*, 62.
12   *Mere Christianity*, Bk. 4 ch. 11, 222; *Beyond Personality*, 60.
13   *Mere Christianity*, Bk. 2 ch. 4, 53. *Broadcast Talks*, 51.
14   *Mere Christianity*, Bk. 2 ch. 4, 54. *Broadcast Talks*, 52.
15   *Mere Christianity*, Bk. 2 ch. 4, 54-54. *Broadcast Talks*, 52-53.
16   *Mere Christianity*, Bk. 2 ch. 4, 55. *Broadcast Talks*, 53-54.
17   *Mere Christianity*, Bk. 2 ch. 4, 60. *Broadcast Talks*, 56.

degree) the kind of voluntary death which Christ himself carried out."[18] Thus, writes Lewis, this is part of what Jesus Christ meant by saying that a thing won't really live unless it first dies, we must go through such a period of death.[19] Therefore, through death Jesus of Nazareth as very God and very Man has defeated death as the Messiah.[20] If we follow Christ he invites us to take up the cross, and despite the implications he asserts that his yoke is easy and his burden is light.[21] This is where humanity is crucified, when we turn to God:

> Make no mistake, he [Christ] says, "If you let me, I will make you perfect. The moment you put yourself in My hands, that is what you are in for . . . Whatever suffering it may cost you in your earthly life, whatever inconceivable purification it may cost you after death, whatever it costs Me, I will never rest, nor let you rest, until you are literally perfect—until my Father can say without reservation that he is well pleased with you, as he said he was well pleased with me."[22]

The Debt

Lewis's own atonement theory relates to "debt." If we consider that we have been let-off because Jesus volunteers to bear a "punishment" instead of us then we may ask why God could not simply have let us off in the first place. But also there is raised a much more pertinent, valid, and awkward question—what possible point could there be in punishing an innocent person instead of the guilty person? Punishing the one truly innocent human only makes the situation worse. Lewis therefore asserts "debt" rather than (or in addition to) punishment as the central reason for the passion of the Christ: "On the other hand, if you think of a debt, there's plenty of point in a person who has some assets paying it on behalf of someone who hasn't . . . When one person has got himself into a hole, the trouble of getting him out usually falls on a kind friend . . . It means killing part of yourself, undergoing a kind of death."[23] But what is the connection between cancelling debt, repayment by a perfectly good person, and the repentance needed? "Only a bad person needs to repent: only a good person can repent perfectly. The worse you are the more you need it and the less you can do it. The only person who could do it perfectly would be a perfect person—and he would not need it."[24] Hence only the perfectly good person could make the ultimate sacrifice to wipe the slate clean, to cancel the debt accumulated through centuries, millennia, of sin. The death by Jesus Christ on the cross for our benefit must therefore be echoed in us, however imperfectly, to complete the cancellation. This, for Lewis, must be a death to ourselves which we must undertake in relation to Jesus's death, but not necessarily the means of his death (crucifixion)—"Remember, this repentance, this willing submission to

18 *Mere Christianity*, Bk. 2 ch. 5, 61. *Broadcast Talks*, 59.
19 *Mere Christianity*, Bk. 3 ch. 6, 111. *Christian Behaviour*, 33.
20 *Mere Christianity*, Bk. 4 ch. 5, 182. *Beyond Personality*, 31.
21 *Mere Christianity*, Bk. 4 ch. 8, 197. *Beyond Personality*, 41.
22 *Mere Christianity*, Bk. 4 ch. 9, 202. *Beyond Personality*, 45.
23 *Mere Christianity*, Bk. 2 ch. 4, 56. *Broadcast Talks*, 54–55.
24 *Mere Christianity*, Bk. 2 ch. 4, 57. Lewis, *Broadcast Talks*, 55.

11. Apologist and Defender of the Faith III: Revelation and Christology, 1948–63 (1)

humiliation and a kind of death, isn't something God demands of you before he'll take you back and which he could let you off if he chose: it's simply a description of what going back to him is like."[25] By repaying the debt, though his death on the cross, through the shedding of blood, we are talking about something quite different from popular religion, precisely because "they say that his death saved us from our sins."[26]

Crucifixion is more than the cross, it is the combined effect of the outsidership foisted onto Jesus, the rejection, the scourging and torture, the humiliation, the carrying of the cross to Golgotha, and finally the nailing of human flesh with the splintering of bone and the severing of sinews to a wooden cross, and being *raised up*, dehydrated, traumatized, bleeding, struggling to get every breath, before all humanity—to die. But the central element of crucifixion, leastwise in the death of Jesus, is the shed blood of the Jewish Messiah: the crown of thorns, the piercing of hands and feet/ankles, and finally the abdomen split by spear. But this is *Jewish blood*: "Guilt is washed out not by time but by repentance and the blood of Christ."[27]

iii. Jesus the Jew

Wright has noted, and quite accurately, that Lewis makes one glaring omission— Easter is not mentioned once (either in *The Broadcast Talks* or in *Mere Christianity*), also, neither, the word "resurrection," or the phrase, the "kingdom of God." Yes, the importance of Easter, the centrality of resurrection, and the lordship of the kingdom of God is implicit in *Mere Christianity*, and most of Lewis's apologetics, but not to mention them explicitly in relation to Jesus of Nazareth, the Christ, is to be considered a serious omission by Lewis: "This is less surprising, though still regrettable, because, to be frank, the Western church in the middle of the twentieth century simply didn't understand what the kingdom of God in Jesus' teaching was all about—again, at least in part, because of its relentless de-Judaizing of the whole story."[28] That twentieth century (Western) theology is guilty of de-Judaizing is true, to a degree, but this applies to Lewis only as an *inadvertent* omission. The Judaistic elements to the Jesus event are of primary importance, but surely not to the exclusion of the salvific efforts of Christ now working through the Holy Spirit, the universal Christ, part of the economic Trinity, who is not to be identified by human culture, religion, or race, but is perhaps best invoked by the Book of Common Prayer language of "the Holy Ghost" the righteous haunter of humanity, invisible, unknowable in human cultural terms.

Wright does conclude that *Mere Christianity* as an introduction is a "fine but leaky building,"[29] and Lewis deserves credit where credit is due; what is more *The Broadcast Talks*, and their subsequent editing into *Mere Christianity* were never meant to be perfect or complete. The late twentieth century is littered with Western theologians attempting to produce a complete and balanced systematic theology and failing,

---

25　*Mere Christianity*, Bk. 2 ch. 4, 57. Lewis, *Broadcast Talks*, 55.
26　*Mere Christianity*, Bk. 4 ch. 1, 156. Lewis, *Beyond Personality*, 11.
27　Lewis, *The Problem of Pain*, 45–46.
28　Wright, "Simply Lewis." Online: para. 54.
29　Ibid., Online: para. 56, see also paras. 57–59.

including for that matter, biblical studies scholars who persistently get confused by the relationship and balance between elements of Christian doctrine. For many patristic theologians, Scripture, though of fundamental importance, was secondary to doctrine issuing from the witness of those (the disciples and apostles) who knew and saw and heard the Christ. "Lewis himself would have been the first to say that of course his book was neither perfect nor complete, and that what mattered was that, if it brought people into the company, and under the influence (or "infection") of Jesus Christ, Jesus himself would happily take over—indeed, that Jesus had been operating through the process all along, albeit through the imperfect medium of the apologist."[30] Is *Mere Christianity* creedal? Does it generally conform to and reflect the revealed truth of the creed? Broadly speaking the answer is yes, although it is flawed on its degree of emphasis. Given that at the heart of the Apostle's Creed and *Mere Christianity* is Jesus of Nazareth, the Christ, the second person of the Trinity, the revelation of our *Lord* and *Savior*, the measure must be Christological

First, *Mere Christianity* may be taken as a *summa*, a comprehensive account of the Christian faith, but Lewis never intended it as such. The aims and objective goes back to the inception of *The Broadcast Talks* in 1941: James Welch, Director of Religious Broadcasting at the BBC, requested, from Lewis, "a series of talks on something like 'The Christian Faith As I see It—by a Layman': I am sure there is a need of a positive restatement of Christian doctrine in lay language."[31] Given the wartime context of the talks they therefore have a much more existential context rather than the oeuvre of a calm, disinterested, dispassionate, academic study and presentation: turn to Christ, the salvation of God, before the Nazis rape, kill, and destroy all you are and hold of value, or the Soviets flood the West with Marxist atheism!

Second, does this work measure up to the Apostle's Creed in its balance and treatment? The answer is yes, it does; although individuals might be critical of the emphases or the weight given to certain clauses. Yes, Lewis, in *Mere Christianity*, certainly believes in "God, the Father almighty, creator of heaven and earth," likewise in "Jesus Christ, his only Son, our Lord." For Lewis, the Christ "was conceived by the power of the Holy Spirit and born of the Virgin Mary." However, some will argue that Lewis gives scant acknowledgement and reference to Mary (Roman Catholics will argue this; yet will Evangelicals applaud the marginalization of Mary?). It is clear from *Mere Christianity* that Jesus "suffered under Pontius Pilate, was crucified, died, and was buried." Does Lewis give sufficient emphasis on, "He descended into hell"? Certainly, for Lewis, "on the third day he rose again, he ascended into heaven, and is seated at the right hand of the Father." Likewise Lewis cannot be accused of downplaying the risk of eschatological judgment: "He will come again to judge the living and the dead." Lewis in *Mere Christianity* can see the action of the Holy Ghost, the haunter and troubler of humanity, the raiser-up of the fallen, the redeeming Spirit, the life of the churches, and the influence of the community of those who have passed over: "I believe in the Holy

---

30 Ibid. Online: para. 60.
31 Welch to C. S. Lewis, Feb. 7 1941. Phillips, *C. S. Lewis at the BBC*, 79–80.

11. Apologist and Defender of the Faith III: Revelation and Christology, 1948-63 (1)

> ### THE APOSTLES' CREED
>
> *I believe in God, the Father almighty,*
> *creator of heaven and earth.*
> *I believe in Jesus Christ, his only Son, our Lord.*
> *He was conceived by the power of the Holy Spirit*
> *and born of the Virgin Mary.*
> *He suffered under Pontius Pilate,*
> *was crucified, died, and was buried.*
> *He descended into hell.*
> *On the third day he rose again.*
> *He ascended into heaven*
> *and is seated at the right hand of the Father.*
> *He will come again to judge the living and the dead.*
> *I believe in the Holy Spirit,*
> *the holy Catholic Church,*
> *the communion of saints,*
> *the forgiveness of sins,*
> *the resurrection of the body,*
> *and the life everlasting.*
> *Amen.*

Figure 17 : The Apostles' Creed

Spirit, the holy catholic church, the communion of saints." Perhaps he can be accused of laying too little emphasis on "the forgiveness of sins, the resurrection of the body" but certainly not, "the life everlasting."

4. THE BLOOD OF THE LAMB

Wright's criticisms raise several questions about Lewis's Christology, and consequently his doctrine of salvation. This is a major subject and will be examined in later parts of this work. It is assumed often that Wright stands against Lewis's Platonism—as do many who are broadly considered to be Evangelical, Reformed or Low Church. Platonism is fundamental to Lewis's work and in particular to his understanding of revelation and Christology and relates to his doctrine of transposition, which will be examined as part of his understanding of Scripture. However, how do we address this criticism of Lewis's apparent marginalizing of the cross in *The Broadcast Talks* and *Mere Christianity*?

i. Death, and New Life—A Means to an End?

Critics will assert that Lewis does not emphasize the cross to the degree they expect from an orthodox theologian, but while it can be said that Lewis does not have an overly masochistic interest in the cross and the suffering entailed, neither does he deny the cross. Indeed, Lewis's understanding of how salvation works does not negate the cross, although he is essentially neutral towards all the multifarious doctrines of atonement. However, what Lewis does emphasize is the blood of the lamb. The means of death—crucifixion—is not necessarily specific. Yes Jesus died on a cross and it was crucifixion, the Roman form of execution *par excellence*, but there is nothing essential to the means by which Jesus suffered and died other than the spilling of blood. The prophesies that he would be crucified are circular: because Jesus was crucified, the Holy Spirit gave intimations of the means of death to the prophets, whispered into the minds of the prophets, *prior to the event*—this is how prophecy works, this is why what was written was prophetic. Therefore what is important to Lewis is the blood of the lamb, spilled, Jesus' lifeblood poured out. This is by default a very Hebraic concept and is reminiscent of atonement and sacrifice in the Old Testament: the sacrificial lamb that dies to redeem the Jews from their sins. The lamb, spotless and true, was to have its blood shed and sprinkled on the altar in the temple to redeem, to cleanse the people of their sins; and in Exodus blood from the Passover meal, the sacrificed lamb, painted on the door frames ensures the spirit of death, that the world justly deserves, passes over (Exod 12:7). If indeed crucifixion is more than execution on a cross, if the effect of being *raised-up* outside the city walls, if the rejection, the scourging and humiliation are all part of the ultimate sacrifice as the Messiah's head is pierced to bleed by the crown of thorns (the crown of thorns as a symbol of his Lordship issues blood), his limbs pierced to bleed by nails, and his spear-split side bleeds blood and water, then what role does the blood of the lamb have in Lewis's developing understanding of atonement?

Not long after his final capitulation to Christ (the conversation in Addison's Walk with Tolkien and Dyson recounted earlier) he wrote to his friend Arthur Greeves that his difficulties and doubt, his perturbations and puzzlement, with Christian truth was centered on the doctrine of redemption. In part this was because he had an inbuilt fear of doctrine, but also he could not understand how or in what sense the life and death of this one person, Jesus the Christ, somehow saved humanity. He could see that this was more than the example of one good person. The example Jesus sets us is not irrelevant, but it is not what atonement is about, it is not at the heart of the Christian faith because, as Lewis notes, "right in the centre of the Gospels and St Paul, you keep on getting something quite different and very mysterious expressed in those phrases I have so often ridiculed ('propitiation'—'sacrifice'—'the blood of the Lamb') . . . the idea of a god sacrificing himself to himself."[32] The full understanding of this was to occupy Lewis over the next thirty years.

What does Lewis have to say about the blood of the lamb? The spilling of the blood is the key to Lewis's concept of the movement of atonement, the procession: God turns to us, Christ, the second person of the eternal Trinity, descends into incarnation, dies, spills his blood through *sacrificial execution* (crucifixion), to bequeath new life,

---

32   Lewis writing to Arthur Greeves, Oct. 18, 1931. *Collected Letters Vol. I*, 976.

11. Apologist and Defender of the Faith III: Revelation and Christology, 1948–63 (1)

then to re-ascend drawing humanity up through resurrection, ascending, before us, to heaven and eternity.

The blood shed is the key, the moment of turning as Jesus dies on the cross. N. T. Wright is in many ways a low church Anglican, even Evangelical; he notes Lewis's downplaying of the cross in atonement but overlooks the emphasis on the blood spilled. Lewis is, by comparison with Wright, Anglo-Catholic; some would argue more and more Roman Catholic as he matured. This emphasis on the centrality of the blood of the lamb spilled is central to Lewis's Anglo-Catholic thinking.

ii. A Hebrew Concept

Why blood? Because the ancient Hebrews conceptualized the very lifeforce of an individual as being in, with, contained by, but essentially part of the blood; people bled *to death*. Cain murdered Abel in a passion of religious self-righteousness, thus he spilled blood; this was sin: "The LORD said, 'What have you done? Listen! Your brother's blood cries out to me from the ground. Now you are under a curse and driven from the ground, which opened its mouth to receive your brother's blood from your hand'" (Gen 4:10–11). It is important to remember that blood is key to the apparent validity of sacrifice in the Old Testament. For the ancient Hebrews blood sacrifices were in three groups—Olah sacrifices (burnt offerings, the whole animal burnt), guilt offerings (part burnt), and peace offerings (part burnt). However, often sacrifice is considered of lesser value as compared to prayer and contrition (as often exampled in the Book of the Psalms). The blood of the lamb does not deny the need for or negate the cross, but it does, certainly for Lewis, marginalize the *sole* need for punishment. The mechanism of blood spilt, the lifeblood of the one perfect, does make sense, though not as a punishment in the place of the guilty but rather as a debt repaid on behalf of the many who cannot repay. Also, it negates the need for absolute punishment because the debt is cleared. However, secondarily, the means of death (crucifixion) assuages the righteous anger (evident in the Old Testament where God's love is turned to anger by humanity's sinfulness). Jesus therefore literally bled to death—the lifeforce left him, was extinguished—poured out onto the ground for the atonement of humanity.

To understand this, and Lewis's presentation, we need to consider not the general religious ideas about life after death across world religions but the true reality revealed from the Hebrew tradition. It is this tradition that paints a true picture of the human predicament, the situation Jesus was born into. This is not a picture of disembodied souls wafting around in some sort of spiritual afterlife where everybody is happy and ethereal. The true reality was revealed by the beliefs about death the ancient Hebrews held.

- Both religious and secular people hide from the truth of the reality humanity is in.
- Eternal life, immortality, is a gift from God, a promise to all humanity, a yet-to-be-fulfilled promise.

- The situation we are in issues from the fall, humanity is infected with death due to original sin.

- Death follows on from the fall; it is our innate reward for rebellion (Gen 3).

- Death led to a diminished existence; this was the thin near-to-nothingness of the person's continued life after death in the Hebrew Sheol, or the Greek Hades.

- Resurrection restores the unity of body and soul; we are not a disembodied soul in the *post mortem* state.

This true reality is attested to in The Letter to the Hebrews

> And what more shall I say? I do not have time to tell about Gideon, Barak, Samson, Jephthah, David, Samuel and the prophets, who through faith conquered kingdoms, administered justice, and gained what was promised; who shut the mouths of lions, quenched the fury of the flames, and escaped the edge of the sword; whose weakness was turned to strength; and who became powerful in battle and routed foreign armies. Women received back their dead, raised to life again. Others were tortured and refused to be released, so that they might gain a better resurrection. Some faced jeers and flogging, while still others were chained and put in prison. They were stoned; they were sawed in two; they were put to death by the sword. They went about in sheepskins and goatskins, destitute, persecuted and mistreated—the world was not worthy of them. They wandered in deserts and mountains, and in caves and holes in the ground. These were all commended for their faith, yet none of them received what had been promised. God had planned something better for us so that only together with us would they be made perfect.
> Heb 11:32–40

The Apostle Paul, in his Letter to the Colossians, asserts the new life that replaces this perilous situation of the human condition: fullness of life issues from the supremacy of Christ—"For in him all the fullness of God was pleased to dwell, and through him God was pleased to reconcile to himself all things, whether on earth or in heaven, by making peace through the blood of his cross" (Col 1:19–20). Therefore, together all humanity now has the potential for the fullness of real resurrection through the blood of the Lamb, shed on the cross.

Essentially, a theology of the blood of the lamb can be read from Hebrews chapters 9–13. The High Priest enters the inner sanctuary annually so as to offer a blood sacrifice on behalf of the sins the people had committed in ignorance (Heb 9:7); because without the shedding of blood there is no forgiveness (Heb 9:22); but without Christ's sacrifice this will not atone. Therefore Jesus suffered outside of the city walls to make the people holy, through the shedding of his lifeblood (Heb 13:12). Any earthly

11. Apologist and Defender of the Faith III: Revelation and Christology, 1948–63 (1)

sacrifice is at best an imitation, a copy (Heb 9:24), it is impossible for human generated sacrifice to remove the stain of sin (Heb 10:3).[33]

Ultimately what does the phrase, or idiom, "the blood of the lamb" mean contextually? The context must be that used by the writers of the Hebrew Bible, but pertinently, by the writers of the New Testament who, importantly, were raised in a Jewish religio-cultural context. They are not talking about a young sheep, whose throat was slit so it bled to death (though the phrase *bled **to** death* is important in a literal context). If Jesus willingly submitted himself to the atoning sacrifice of scourging, humiliation, crucifixion, and death, then we are talking about the *will* to submit to the *will* of God: the meaning and value of this was prefigured in the spotless lamb sacrificed on the Hebrew altar. Therefore this submission of will means, in a Judeo-religio-cultural context, the *"will to do the will of God."*[34] Consider Jesus's mental wrestling prior to his arrest: "Father, if you are willing, take this cup from me; yet not my will, but yours be done" (Luke 22:42; also Mark 14:36, 26:39).

iii. An Haematological Perspective?[35]

"The Blood of our Lord Jesus Christ, which was shed for thee . . ."

Lewis's churchmanship revolved around the Holy Communion service in *The Book of Common Prayer* (1662). This was often a simple service, said not sung, often early in the morning. At the distribution of the communion, the bread is offered to the communicant with the words: "THE BODY of our Lord Jesus Christ, which was given for thee, preserve thy body and soul unto everlasting life. Take and eat this in remembrance that Christ died for thee, and feed on him in thy heart by faith with thanksgiving." The means of execution is not mentioned. When the chalice is offered to each worshipper, the words, spoken to each as a prayer, recount the central importance of the life blood of the Messiah to each and every individual: "THE BLOOD of our Lord Jesus Christ, which was shed for thee, preserve thy body and soul unto everlasting life. Drink this in remembrance that Christ's Blood was shed for thee, and be thankful."[36] Whether in his local parish church on a Sunday morning, or the almost daily remembrance at an 8:00am said Holy Communion in one of the College chapels in Oxford, Lewis, from the point of his conversion on, was hearing this as a prayer, and as a personal command. What was Lewis's response? What does Lewis say? How

---

33   In general terms see Heb 2:14; 9:7–12, 18–25; 11:28. In terms of the impossibility of human generated sacrifice, see, Heb 10:4, 19–29. In terms of the value of the blood for humanity see, Heb 12:4; 12:24; 13:11–12.

34   "Hebrew Idioms and Blood of Lamb." www.ccel.org/node/4938, para. 6.

35   Haematology (from the Greek, αἷμα, *haima*, "blood") is the branch of medicine concerned with the study and treatment of the blood. Hamartia is from the Greek(ἁμαρτία, *harmatia*) and is often used to refer to sin in the New Testament. Its original ancient Greek form referred to "deliberate wrong-doing", as also, "missing the mark", "mistaken ignorance" and "accidental wrongdoing."

36   "The Order of the Ministration of Holy Communion." *Book of Common Prayer*, 1662, 275–76. The sentence accompanying the chalice has now been replaced in the average Church of England Eucharist with the staccato phrase, "The Blood of Christ," repeated with speed as the chalice moves hastily along the row of communicants.

important is the invocation of the shed blood in *Mere Christianity*? He comments, "You can say that Christ died for our sins. You may say that the Father has forgiven us because Christ has done for us what we ought to have done. You may say that we are washed in the blood of the Lamb. You may say that Christ has defeated death. They're all true."[37] In a late work of apologetics, in relation to the Hebrew perception that, *post mortem*, humanity faced a diminished existence, a disintegration of soul and body, to become a "witless psychic sediment,"[38] Lewis comments, "If so, Homer's idea that only a drink of sacrificial blood can restore a ghost to rationality would be one of the most striking among many Pagan anticipations of the truth."[39]

An Haematological Sacrifice

But this goes beyond apologetics and is expressed at its most profound in Lewis's analogical narratives. The true value and importance of the execution and shedding of Jesus's blood can be seen in *The Chronicles of Narnia* (1950–56) and in *The Great Divorce* (1945). Aslan, the Christ-figure, in *The Lion, the Witch and the Wardrobe*, is not crucified; atonement is achieved through his being stabbed through the heart—the nexus of the lifeblood. As Aslan dies—bound, shaven, on a stone altar—the blood (like the blood of Abel) seeps out from him onto the ground. This is an explicit analogy with the death of Jesus of Nazareth in our reality. The means of execution is the stone knife, on the stone table. After Aslan's resurrection, the stone knife is missing; however, with the return of the four Pevensie children to our reality after many years as kings and queens, the Narnians make a religious cult out of the stone table and Aslan's sacrifice. During the period before the arrival of the Telmarines (*Prince Caspian*), the stone table is preserved and idolized, worshipped, a mound called Aslan's How is raised hundreds of feet over it: a religious cult evolves. But the stone knife, the means of death, is missing. The knife turns up in *The Voyage of the Dawn Treader*. It is at the centre of a table, a table filled with all manner of sumptuous food and wine—a banquet, on a scale no one could imagine. The banquet is renewed each and every day. Those who have travelled thus far across uncharted oceans, encountered many strange islands and lands with creatures beyond imagining, those who have thus traversed life and creation, are welcomed at this banquet, with the place of honor reserved for the means of the new life that issued from the shedding of Aslan's blood: the stone knife. Aslan's feast, the new life, the utter generosity of the Aslan-Christ cannot be separated from the means of death, the sacrifice, which led to the new life—resurrection:

> Lucy now noticed something lying lengthwise on the table which had escaped her attention before. It was a knife of stone, sharp as steel, a cruel-looking, ancient-looking thing . . .
>
> "What is this Knife of Stone?" asked Eustace.
>
> "Do none of you know it?" said the girl.

---

37 Lewis, *Mere Christianity*, Bk. 4 ch. 5, 182. Lewis, *Beyond Personality*, 31.
38 Lewis, *Reflection on the Psalms*, 32.
39 Ibid., 32.

11. Apologist and Defender of the Faith III: Revelation and Christology, 1948-63 (1)

> "I—I think," said Lucy, "I've seen something like it before. It was a knife like it that the White Witch used when she killed Aslan at the Stone Table long ago."
> "It was the same," said the girl, "and it was brought here to be kept in honour while the world lasts."[40]

Therefore, there is an indelible connection between the means of sacrifice and the new life that issues from the sacrifice—a voluntary sacrifice, the single altruistic sacrifice from the holy one. The means (the stone knife) is removed to prevent idolatry, but the relationship, the connection, can never be erased: the sacrificial means (the cross) is eternally part of the new life (resurrection): the connection, the nexus is in the blood shed.

The importance of the shed blood, the relationship between sacrificial blood and the new life, is at its most profound and explicit in *The Silver Chair*. Jill and Eustace, with the dead King Caspian, find themselves in Aslan's country. Caspian's old body lies in a stream.

> [T]he children looked into the stream. And there, on the golden gravel of the bed of the stream, lay King Caspian, dead, with the water flowing over him like liquid glass. His long white beard swayed in it like water-weed. And all three stood and wept. Even the Lion wept: great Lion-tears, each tear more precious than the Earth would be if it was a single solid diamond. And Jill noticed that Eustace looked neither like a child crying, nor like a boy crying and wanting to hide it, but like a grownup crying . . .
>
> "Son of Adam," said Aslan, "go into that thicket and pluck the thorn that you will find there, and bring it to me."
>
> Eustace obeyed. The thorn was a foot long and sharp as a rapier.
>
> "Drive it into my paw, Son of Adam," said Aslan, holding up his right forepaw and spreading out the great pad towards Eustace.
>
> "Must I?" said Eustace.
>
> "Yes," said Aslan.
>
> Then Eustace set his teeth and drove the thorn into the lion's pad. And there came out a great drop of blood, redder than all redness that you have ever seen or imagined. And it splashed into the stream over the dead body of the King . . . And the dead King began to be changed.[41]

Caspian is not a disembodied spiritual being; Caspian is not distinct from his body, there is no dualism between body and soul. Caspian is raised up, resurrected, directly by the blood of the lion—the Narnian equivalent of the blood of Jesus (is the thorn driven into Aslan's paw analogous with the crown of thorns pressed into Jesus's head?). This is no mere resuscitation. This is bodily resurrection. Caspian stands before Jill and Eustace as alive as when he was a young man.

> "But," said Eustace, looking at Asian. "Hasn't he—err died?"

---

40 Lewis, *The Voyage of the Dawn Treader*, 152–53.
41 Lewis, *The Silver Chair*, 187–88.

> "Yes," said the Lion in a very quiet voice almost (Jill thought) as if he were laughing.
>
> "He has died. Most people have, you know. Even I have. There are very few who haven't."
>
> "Oh," said Caspian. "I see what's bothering you. You think I'm a ghost, or some nonsense. But don't you see? I would be that if I appeared in Narnia now: because I don't belong there any more . . ."
>
> A great hope rose in the children's hearts. But Aslan shook his shaggy head. "No, my dears," he said. "When you meet me here again, you will have come to stay. But not now. You must go back to your own world for a while."[42]

An orthodox doctrine of atonement does not get more explicit than this: The Aslan-Christ declares he has died (sacrificed on the stone table; crucified in our reality), his blood has been shed for new life. Critics will assert that there is an insufficient emphasis on the cross-resurrection in *Mere Christianity*, but this is not so when applied to Lewis' work generally. The one true sacrifice of the only good and pure person through the shedding of lifeblood leads to new life, as the debt of sin is cancelled. We must all die if we are to be truly alive; Lewis notes that this is what is at the heart of the ultimate atonement sacrifice, but it is also woven into nature. This is a pattern seen in creation—all life must descend to re-ascend, the seed must die to be born again, therefore there are myths and stories spread widely of death and rebirth within nature: "The doctrine of the incarnation, if accepted, puts this principle even more emphatically at the centre. The pattern is there in nature because it was first there in God."[43] Death and rebirth is fundamental in the move towards eternity because it is inscribed into reality.[44] The real story is in the gospel;[45] though imitations of Christ are written into the natural world.

Critics, such as N. T. Wright, might claim that "Easter," "resurrection," even "the cross" are not given the sort of treatment they expect in *Mere Christianity*, and although this is true as far as it goes as a criticism of that one book, across Lewis's *corpus* this pattern of death-rebirth and the central motif of the blood of sacrificial lamb is paramount. Indeed, the new life issuing from the death and resurrection of the Christ is often criticized for being too real. For example, the very tangible and material, corporeal, existence after death in *The Last Battle* is but one example. Likewise there is the dangerously real existence in *The Great Divorce*, where the visitors from hell, on the fringes of heaven, find even the grass too hard and sharp to walk on: the condemned in their diminished existence (an existence matching the Hebrew *Sheol* in many ways) shy away into the slim, miniscule near nothingness of their existence away from the super-real joyous existence of heaven. The blood from Jesus's sacrifice is the key to atonement (forgiveness and new life). This is for Lewis, the "bleeding charity."

---

42   Ibid., 188–89.
43   Lewis, *Miracles*. 1st ed. 1947, 118.
44   Specifically, ibid., ch. 14, 112, and 125. See also, Lewis, *Mere Christianity*, 154–55; and, Lewis, *The Screwtape Letters*, 147.
45   Lewis, *Miracles*. 1st ed. 1947, 130.

11. Apologist and Defender of the Faith III: Revelation and Christology, 1948–63 (1)

In *The Great Divorce* the "bleeding heart" of Jesus is set-off against self-righteousness, individuals trying to justify each and every self. One inhabitant of hell, who fails to see why he has condemned himself simply by rejection of the forgiveness of Christ, complains that a fellow workmate, who was convicted of murder, is in heaven, when he is in hell. The man comments, "'What I'd like to understand,' said the Ghost, 'is what you're here for, as pleased as Punch, you, a bloody murderer, while I've been walking the streets down there . . . That's just what I say. I haven't got my rights. I always done my best and I never done nothing wrong. And what I don't see is why I should be put below a bloody murderer like you.'" The work colleague invites him to taste of heaven: "Who knows whether you will be? Only be happy and come with me." The bitter man answers: "What do you keep on arguing for? I'm only telling you the sort of chap I am. I only want my rights. I'm not asking for anybody's bleeding charity." In fast response the work colleague retorts, "Then do. At once. Ask for the 'Bleeding Charity.' Everything is here for the asking and nothing can be bought." But the bitter man is trapped in his own pseudo-religious self-righteousness: "That may do very well for you, I daresay. If they choose to let in a bloody murderer all because he makes a poor mouth at the last moment . . . I don't want charity. I'm a decent man."[46] The key is the blood of Christ, the "bleeding charity"—all we have to do regardless of all we hold dear or claim in righteousness is to accept what has been shed for us. This is taken further in *The Great Divorce* where Lewis presents an atheistic apostate bishop who speculates on what Jesus would have been like had he not been crucified—had he not died he would have gone on to become a profound and wise religious philosopher (atonement and salvation is therefore nothing to do with Jesus's life and mission). The crucifixion was just a terrible accident that should not have happened, according to this atheistic apostate, who laments that Jesus died so young, before his true mission and life's work could be perceived and achieved.

---

46   Lewis, *The Great Divorce*, 20–21.

12

Apologist and Defender of the Faith IV: Revelation and Christology, 1948–63— The Later Works: Christlikeness

SYNOPSIS:
What is Lewis's Christology, as evidenced in his works from the period 1948 through to his death in 1963? Lewis's understanding of Christology and revelation in the 1950s is less focused, though more nuanced, and spread across many books and essays. Chief amongst them, employing this method of analogical narrative, are *The Chronicles of Narnia* (1950–56); though the value of reason is still present, for example in the revised second edition of *Miracles* (1960). This mature period of Lewis's work also sees his spiritual autobiography, *Surprised by Joy* (1955), published, along with *The Four Loves* (1960) and *A Grief Observed* (1964), which brings in the personal side of Lewis's theology—his conversion to and acknowledgement of the God of suffering in and behind the Christ. Lewis's theological works take on what appears to many to be a different method from the one used in the 1940s, as evidenced in *Reflections on the Psalms* (1958), and the posthumously published, *Letters to Malcolm: Chiefly on Prayer* (1964). A salient theme in these and other later works is "Christlikeness," where Lewis, like the Russian writer Fyodor Mikhailovich Dostoevsky, translates Christ into ordinary human mortals—the characteristic being the ability to sustain altruistic love as seen in *Till We Have Faces*, in the person of Psyche, as compared to her sister Orual. This raises importance questions about the *imago Christi* (the image of Christ), which relates closely to the *imitatio Christi* (the imitation of Christ), though the two are not synonymous. How does the Holy Spirit *recover* the image of Christ buried deep within us? Our feeble halting imitation, if it is conscious, can only, perhaps, be Christlike when it involves self-denial, and leads us to self-sacrifice, which every fiber of our being rebels against, yet we must submit gracefully. In addition there are important essays which illustrate Lewis's developing understanding. For example, "What Are We to Make of Jesus Christ?" (1950) and "Is Theism Important? A Reply" (1952). The introduction to Lewis' history of English literature in the sixteenth century provides valuable insights into Lewis's understanding of the church, dealing, as it does, with the period of the Reformation. Lewis's mature critical apologetics are exhibited in two seminal essays. The "Rejoinder to Dr Pittenger" and "Modern Theology and Biblical Criticism." Both represent a criticism of a "Liberal-Modern" establishment, and illustrate how his understanding of the Christ event relates closely to his doctrine of God: the God who reveals of God to humanity. These essays are an original re-presentation of orthodoxy, critically valuing religiosity but cautious as

to its often human-centeredness: Lewis points to the primacy of the Christ event, always. In the last year of his life Lewis responds to the growing dominance of "Liberalism" in the Church of England in his response to J. A. T. Robinson's controversial book, *Honest to God*, by simply and succinctly reasserting a doctrine of the Trinity where God is not just an entity, a being, a mono-"god," or even just one person, but where the apparent individuality in communion of the triune God (within and without of the immanent and economic Trinity) is, in Lewis's words, taken to mean "a person and more as in an orthodox doctrine of the Trinity."

1. CHRISTLIKENESS

Lewis's apologetic work is concluded, in many ways, with the publication of the revised edition of *Miracles* in 1960. However, the mature Lewis uses, more and more, an imaginative re-presentation of the truths of Christology. Often this is by exposing the flaws in humanity, and thereby establishing the theme of Christlikeness. This builds on the character of Ransom in *Perelandra* (1943) and the "good," or redeemed, people in *The Great Divorce* (1945).

i. The Lord and Haunter of Creation

Lewis finally published an account of his conversion in 1955. We have looked at this spiritual autobiography earlier so as to chart and understand Lewis's developing relationship with the Christ, but what picture does *Surprised by Joy* give us of the second person of the Trinity? The picture Lewis gives is essentially pneumatological—that is, God as Holy Spirit, as the Holy Ghost, the "haunter" of Lewis the apostate who dragged his feet, silently almost with a whimper, into the kingdom. Eventually, at the behest of Hugo Dyson and J. R. R. Tolkien, he was forced to accept through pressured argument the reality behind what he had experienced—that God had descended to earth to be incarnated as a human, to suffer and die for Lewis's sins, yes, to echo, to become concrete, in reality what had been intimated in story and myth across numerous other world religions. How Lewis then squared this discursive narrative with what he had been experiencing became a lifetime's work. If *Surprised by Joy* is not a conventional autobiography but a charting of the journey of the discovery of the meaning of *Sehnsucht* (for Lewis "Joy"), then where is Christ in this? Admittedly, and Lewis does lay this out clearly in the last two chapters, he begins to realize that his search for a repetition of "Joy" is almost idolatrous, and that these pangs of longings are essentially from God in the truth of the gospel. So are we to conclude that Lewis's elusive pangs of longing, these stabs of "Joy," swiftly departing never to be conjured-up by him, were ultimately the action of the Trinity seeking his conversion and salvation? Yes; but *Sehnsucht*, generally regarded as a literary wistful longing, is to be seen, from a christological perspective as an intimation of the Holy Spirit convicting us, anonymously, haunting and troubling us, perhaps even generating a sense of eschatological judgment. This is, to a degree, how Lewis responded, but he had to accept the "road map," the truth of the gospel narrative, the incarnation-cross-resurrection, so that what he had experienced made sense. Therefore Lewis's *Sehnsucht*/"Joy" is

12. Apologist and Defender of the Faith IV: Revelation and Christology, 1948–63 (2)

essentially the action of the resurrected and ascended Christ Jesus acting on him in and through the Holy Spirit. We noted earlier how Lewis's conversion was not a once and for all Damascus Road experience and encounter, a single event, but rather how there were four distinct encounters/events (the bus journey; the capitulating don; the critical conversation; and the motorcycle journey). Lewis sensed that a fact about himself was being presented to him; he was aware that he was holding something at bay, shutting something out, he was being given a free choice but then he gives in and kneels in his rooms at Magdalen, acknowledging the real personal God, becoming, in his own words, the most dejected of converts, but this had to be followed by the crucial conversation with Dyson and Tolkien in Addison's Walk, which exposed Lewis to doctrinal truths, which prepared the ground for his final acceptance, the journey on his brother's motorcycle, which generated the realization that truth was outside of Lewis's intellectual ego: Jesus Christ died for our sins on the cross. Therefore *Surprised by Joy* is a journey into Christ. He had to accept how God had acted unilaterally; God in and through Christ had sought and courted, haunted and changed Lewis: "Every step I had taken, from the Absolute to 'Spirit' to 'God,' had been a step towards the more concrete, the more imminent, the more compulsive."[1]

But is this a forgiving Christ? How much did Lewis make a connection between Christ's passion as a truth statement, atonement for humanity, and his own personal conversion? It is clear from his subsequent work in apologetics and philosophical theology that he saw atonement as such, that the wider corporate mission of the churches was in some ways consequent upon personal salvation. In his mature work, "His attention was directed towards the salvation of the individual soul rather than to the solution of communal problems."[2] However, there still appears to be a disjuncture between any sense of individual forgiveness emanating for Lewis from the passion of the Christ in the account given in *Surprised by Joy*. Are Lewis's sins essentially intellectual and does he see repentance as adopting a correct intellectual approach? There does seem to be an element of God as an oppressive divine, a force outside of Lewis, the transcendental interferer, whom Lewis reluctantly has to acknowledge the existence of. *Surprised by Joy* is in many ways a portrait of the action within humanity of the Lord and haunter of creation.

If there is a troubling fierceness to the God Lewis eventually perceives and gives in to in *Surprised by Joy* then perhaps this is not surprising. Karl Barth commented that God's love takes the form of wrath when it is rejected. This is obvious in human form—the wife betrayed for a young mistress. However, when humanity rejects the love of God then it takes the form of wrath, or more pertinently will not humanity *perceive* God in wrathful terms? "When it is resisted God's love works itself out as death-dealing wrath. If Jesus Christ has followed our way as sinners to the end to which it leads in outer darkness then we can agree with the passage from the Old Testament, Isaiah 53."[3] Does this explain something of Lewis's cold-hearted apostasy?

---

1   Lewis, *Surprised by Joy,* 229.
2   Carpenter, *The Inklings*, 207.
3   Barth, *Church Dogmatics*, Vol. IV/1, §59.2, 253. See also, Gunton, *The Barth Lectures*, 176–77.

Does this explain the marginalizing of a forgiving God in his protracted conversion? If so, then this is a wrathful judgment that is still out of love as it leads to pardon. It is simply that this pardon takes a long time to work out in Lewis.

ii. The imago Christi

Surprised by Joy focuses this concern with Christlikeness—the person before and in Christ, and how the Holy Spirit will change and mould, break and rebuild the person on an individual and communal level. This process may take time. Lewis had already commented in *The Broadcast Talks* how the whole point of the church was to make people into little Christs.[4] In effect, this is the drawing out of the *imago Christi* within people, more pertinently the *recovery* of this *image of Christ*, tarnished and buried deep, but not lost. Christlikeness can be seen in other religions, but only the person and office of Christ subsist in the Christian religion. If we speak of "image" we must avoid the contemporary Western obsession with personal appearance, with projecting a lifestyle image. The *imago Christi*—the image of Christ—is not an affectation we project for the benefit of others, it does not issue from our vanity, it is the essential nature and character that is deep within us, it is the ground from which everything that constitutes us emerges. Prior to the fall (Gen 3) this image was complete and untainted—we were as God intended. After the fall, it becomes corrupted, tarnished, prey to evil, self-justifying in its corruption. But it is not lost completely. Christlikeness, issuing from the atonement wrought for us by the blood of the lamb, will gradually restore us by drawing out the *imago Christi*: "And all of us, with unveiled faces, seeing the glory of the Lord as though reflected in a mirror, are being transformed into the same image from one degree of glory to another; for this comes from the Lord, the Spirit" (2 Cor 3:18). What are the salient characteristics of Christlikeness generally, and specifically for Lewis? Incarnation is defined by the apparent self-emptying of God, that is, kenosis (Phil 2:7). Jesus the Christ is characterized by beauty of character, graceful, exuding self-denying love; he gives joy, light, and he is compassionate. His words and actions are characterized by Messianic authority. In suffering he takes-on death voluntarily, for the sake of others—for love my Savior now is dying. Clearly there are certain characteristics that are unique to the Christ, to his absolute nature as the second person of the Trinity—only Christ as the one perfect human can offer the perfect sacrifice for sin, only he can atone. However, people can in a haltingly limited way, through being in-Christ, begin to be drawn into Christlikeness: beauty of character, graceful compassion, self-denying, altruistic love, joyous yet suffering, humble but self-effacing, they may radiate an inner Christlikeness despite manifold difficulties and oppression. The *imago Christi* relates closely to the *imitatio Christi* (the imitation of Christ), though the two are not synonymous, indeed often the *imitatio Christi* issues from the *imago Christi*, however any imitation of Christ must be unself-conscious, or it is likely to be a feign. Imitation if it is conscious can only, perhaps, be Christlike when it involves self-denial, and leads us to do something (self-sacrifice?)

---

4   Lewis, *Beyond Personality*, 28.

12. Apologist and Defender of the Faith IV: Revelation and Christology, 1948–63 (2)

which every fiber of our being rebels against, but we still go ahead with it. If we submit gracefully this will often be the work of the Holy Spirit in us rather than our innately fallen and selfish will that initiates.

Lewis sees this Christlikeness evident in North European pagan and Middle Eastern myths, and in Greek mythology (Balder, Adonis, Osiris, Plato's suffering servant, Homer's assertion about sacrificial blood we noted earlier), but Christ is clearly more than all of these. (The extent to which a Christlike figure is in other religions is a large and complex subject and will be dealt with later.) Lewis wrote in *The Broadcast Talks* of how we are changed into Christlike people; likewise he clearly asserts in his apologetics the reality of original sin and the fall in forming our present state. In his mature works he states this doctrinal reality through Christlike people building on what was established in *The Space Trilogy* and *The Great Divorce* (and inversely, the nihilistic absence of Christlikeness in *The Screwtape Letters*). As a storyteller and mythmaker Lewis recasts doctrinal truth in his analogical narratives. In effect he interprets Christ into ordinary mortals.

The most prominent example of this developing absorption with Christlikeness is, in many ways, the character and person of Aslan. Aslan is not simply a picture of Christ, or a Christlike figure. He is the Christ, or more pertinently, he is an imaginative answer to the question, what would Christ be like if he died and was resurrected for the salvation of people in another reality? "Aslan is the deity; it is an extraordinarily original achievement . . . Aslan has divine qualities of awe, power and authority, yet he exudes love and is himself somehow intensely lovable, so lovable that it is possible for children to want to embrace him, to put their arms about his neck and kiss him."[5] This is an orthodox analogy of Christ, who exudes Christlikeness because he is the incarnate deity. Aslan is not, therefore, exactly what we are talking about—this Christlikeness manifests itself in ordinary mortal humans whom the Spirit of Christ will change, reform, towards redemption. Christlikeness was central a decade earlier in *The Space Trilogy*. Elwin Ransom is not Christ; he is an ordinary, extremely mortal, human. Neither is he divine; but he is Christlike because of the manner in which he remains wedded to the good, specifically in the way he responds and reacts to specific situations and challenges, difficulties and questions, as compared to Weston who is demonic in that he considers his perception of events and the world to be superior to all others, and himself to be, in effect, lord over all creation. Satan believed he could challenge God in divinity; Weston acts as if he were God—*eritis sicut Deus*. Therefore for Ransom to be Christlike is to be existential—the essential characteristics of the image of Christ in humanity are part of existence, the characteristic of Christlikeness become real in how we respond to situations. However, this is a movement towards true Christlikeness and leaves us vulnerable—as indeed Ransom is. The real Christ figure (not merely a Christlike one) in *The Space Trilogy* is Maleldil-the-Young (the

---

5   Comments from *Beyond Personality—A memoir of C. S. Lewis*, a documentary broadcast on BBC Radio 4, Sunday December 18, 1988, compiled by Ann Bonsor. (Programme not subsequently published; comments from own tape recording of the programme.)

Son), whereas Maleldil is God (the Father), but we only know them in reference, they are referred to by the inhabitants of Malacandra and Perelandra.

How are these people and characters Christlike? Because of the incarnation. God has shared our humanity through the taking of human flesh. If we are deemed Christlike it is not because we can imitate Jesus; rather, there is unselfconsciousness about these characters. Indeed we will see how in many instances they do not perceive of themselves as necessarily Christlike. Therefore this is not about producing a list of the salient features of Jesus Christ and then ticking the boxes off; this is not salvation through works. It is about how the Holy Spirit changes people, drawing them into this Christlikeness: the incarnation leads to the pneumatological re-ordering of the individual.

2. TRANSLATING CHRIST

i. Till We Have Faces

Steven P. Mueller uses the term "translates" for when Lewis presents Christlike figures in his stories, drawing on Lewis's own aims and objectives in writing these stories and noting Lewis's comment that if "real" theologians had undertaken this task of translation in the nineteenth century (when they began to lose touch with ordinary Christians) there would have been no work for him to undertake.[6] Lewis, as Mueller notes, does more than merely dress-up characters in an appearance of Jesus: something of the *reality* of Christ is *recast* in the form of ordinary people. Elwin Ransom (*Out of the Silent Planet*), therefore, translates something of Christ to us, likewise the character of Psyche in *Till We Have Faces*, published in 1956.

In *Till We Have Faces* Lewis resituates and re-tells the Greek myth of Cupid and Psyche, only this is from the viewpoint of Orual, Psyche's sister, who perceives herself ugly by comparison with Psyche's beauty; however, Psyche's beauty is more than skin deep—she captivates all who behold her in appearance, in her mind, and in her goodness of character. Orual is, however, somewhat obsessive in her love for her sister. Psyche is sacrificed to the pagan god of the mountain for the benefit of the people. Orual in an attempt to rescue her sister fails; however, for one brief moment she recognizes the castle in which her sister lives, after her sacrifice, but she regards this as a momentary illusion. She finds Psyche alive and gloriously happy, visited nightly by a god—Cupid. Against Cupid's wishes Orual urges Psyche to look at her husband when he visits as she believes he is a monster. Using a smuggled lantern she does look on him—and the god of the mountain exiles her to a barren and difficult life, which Psyche submits to gracefully. Orual ascends to the throne of Glome and is widely recognized as a just and righteous queen. However, she is secretly racked by guilt because she (unintentionally,

---

6 Mueller, "Christology in the Writings of C. S. Lewis," 280–81, 283, 286, 293, 296–97, and 299. Mueller is referring to Lewis's comments in Lewis, "Rejoinder to Dr Pittenger," 1369–71; Lewis was responding to Pittenger, "Apologist versus Apologist: a Critique of C. S. Lewis as 'Defender of the Faith,'" 1104–7.

so she believes) wrecked her sister's happiness. Orual hears of a tale (gossip) depicting her deliberately destroying her sister's happiness for envy; her response is to write *this* tale. Orual wrestles with the truth of the perception of her motives, ending in an inner desperation. She is in receipt of mysterious visions relating to the assignments undertaken by Psyche after her expulsion by the god of the mountain. In her dream Orual petitions the gods, however, she perceives that her love for Psyche, was tainted and possessive, and that jealousy drove her. This enables reconciliation with Psyche.

anima naturaliter Christiana

Psyche is widely acknowledged as a Christlike figure:[7] as a child and as an adult she loves altruistically, always helping others, putting others first; her beauty is deep within her person, not just her appearance. She heals people, taking their diseases away, often to her own loss; she willingly allows herself to be sacrificed for the good of others; she is doomed, dying on a tree, her sacrifice leads to her being named blessed. She is seen, *post mortem*, by her sister, who only just manages to perceive the castle she lives in (Orual's eyes are still too tainted with self-interest). Quoting Lewis's acknowledgement that the link between Christ and Psyche was intentional, Stephen P. Mueller asserts, further, that Psyche was more than a comparison:

> The character of Psyche, like Ransom, is not meant to be Christ but nonetheless parallels and exemplifies him. In a letter to Clyde Kilby Lewis wrote: Psyche is an instance of the *anima naturaliter Christiana* making the best of the Pagan religion she is brought up in and thus being guided (but always "under the cloud," always in terms of her own imaginations or that of her people) to the true God. She is in some ways like Christ because every good man or woman is like Christ. What else could they be like? ... Lewis stated that Psyche is like Christ because of her goodness, but the similarities are far deeper. Her entire life is parallel to his. Psyche is richly evocative of Christ and further translates Christ to the reader.[8]

So is Lewis talking about naturally occurring Christlikeness (*anima naturaliter Christiana*:[9] the soul is naturally Christian)? Where is grace in this? Is it truly possible for a fallen human being to be naturally Christlike? Is Lewis overlooking the often-strong assertion of the corruption of the human through original sin? Lewis, however, writes that his real interest is Psyche's sister: "Orual is an instance, a 'case,' of human affection in its natural condition: true, tender, suffering, but in the long run, tyrannically possessive and ready to turn to hatred when the beloved ceases to be its possession."[10] Furthermore, Lewis asserts, this is often the case when a family member becomes a Christian (for example, joining a religious community, or becoming a missionary—others feel cheated, suffer outrage).

---

7 For example, Mueller, "Christology in the Writings of C. S. Lewis," and, Gibson, *C. S. Lewis, Spinner of Tales*.

8 Mueller, "Christology in the Writings of C. S. Lewis," 295–96, quoting, Lewis to Clyde S. Kilby, Feb. 10, 1957. *Collected Letters Vol. III*, 830–31.

9 A phrase originally used by the patristic theologian Tertullian (c. 160–220).

10 Lewis to Clyde S. Kilby, Feb. 10, 1957. *Collected Letters Vol. III*, 831.

Psyche and Orual may respectively be an example of Christlikeness and fallenness in pre-Christian pagan religion, and as such this has implications for the state of post-Christian Western society, as Jon Balsbaugh has shown.[11] However, regardless of the state of acknowledgement of the unique revelation of God in Jesus Christ within post-Christian societies, this does have greater implications for theological anthropology in terms of the human condition before God. If the reality of Christ is recast in the form of ordinary people, this is something that the nineteenth century Russian writer and prophet Fyodor Mikhailovich Dostoevsky undertook in his novels. Like Lewis, Dostoevsky presents the complexity of the human condition before God, a condition caused by the fall, but intensified by the incarnation.

In Dostoevsky's *The Idiot*,[12] Prince Myshkin is a young man, an epileptic, who has been in a clinic in Switzerland for years receiving treatment that, like the woman with a hemorrhage in Mark's Gospel, has failed.[13] Myshkin is the Christlike figure; he tries to save Nastasya Filippovna who has been severely sexually abused as a child and teenager, who hates herself and exhibits a self-destructive tendency, and is amoral, save that which benefits her. Myshkin fails in his efforts to save her because he is human and not divine. Yet his efforts are beyond the normally human; he is characterized by clumsiness and a fearlessness, which become an offence to the world of social convention; therefore the one who understands the meaning of this life as a denial before God will be seen as a fool, as weak, as sickly, to be tolerated as a social outcast (except in Myshkin's case where he is of wealthy nobility, and attracts those seeking social status and wealth). The problem with Christlikeness, from a worldly perspective (whether exhibited in Myshkin or Psyche), is that the stumbling foolishness of the holy fool[14] judges and negates the success of this world. Dostoevsky was concerned throughout the 1870s with Christlikeness in relation to religious belief; this is a dialectical tension that can only be resolved in God. Myshkin may be *Christlike* but he is not *the Christ*. Psyche, though pre-Christian (whereas Myshkin is after the Christ event), exhibits something similar. She cares for the poor and diseased, taking their disease upon herself; she exhibits none of the guile and cunning of this world that would have questioned her sister's advice about unveiling Cupid's face, ignorant as she was of the dangers involved. Any attempt at Christlikeness will fail because we are mere mortals, as happens to Prince Myshkin in *The Idiot*. This is paradoxical considering how we are called to follow Christ. Furthermore, Dostoevsky's daring is to make Christ pass as an idiot in society and the real understanding of him begin with a harlot (Nastasya) and a murderer (Rogozhin), who truly see the *Christlikeness* in Myshkin, but perhaps that is because they are outside of the polite bourgeois norms that fail to perceive Christlikeness. The polite religious bourgeoisie in St. Petersburg

---

11   Balsbaugh, "The Pagan and the Post-Christian," 191–210.
12   Dostoevsky, *The Idiot*, 218.
13   Mark 5:25–26.
14   In Dostoevsky's Russian Orthodox tradition this is the юродивый (*iurodivyi*—holy fool, or God's fool), people who exhibit юродство (*foolishness*, in Christ); this applies to people that transcend the cognitive limits of conventional religious knowledge and behavior, and thereby witness to God's forgiveness through altruistic love.

dismiss Myshkin for his lack of social convention; Psyche is, likewise, something of an outsider. By contrast Orual exhibits the almost schizophrenic cunning and guile that characterizes Myshkin's enemies.

The Paradox of Christlikeness

Both Dostoevsky's *The Idiot* and Lewis's *Till We Have Faces* are parables about the paradox of Christlikeness; both Psyche and Myshkin exhibit unworldliness. Myshkin never partakes in the games of status, power, and sexual politics that other people do, and he eventually returns to the asylum as the result of *status epilepticus* (continuous epileptic seizures) having effectively been destroyed by the people he was trying to save. Does not Psyche end up suffering, enduring for years as a result of her naïve foolishness (while her sister reigns as Queen, though Orual's conscience is troubled by her treatment of Psyche)? We will not know and understand God in our haltingly human manner through the understanding gained solely from this world. Therefore, Myshkin and Psyche are seen as Christlike archetypes in relation to our knowledge of God. Job is righteous before God because of his honesty, but also through his acceptance of the mystery of God as compared to his so-called comforters.[15] No amount of systematization in theology and philosophy will close the paradox between God and humanity, between suffering in this life and the resolution, reconciliation, to come. The incarnation simply exacerbates, heightens, the paradox. In many ways this is a Christian tragedy—but we are wrong to interpret such Christlike worldly failure as wrong before God, for was not Christ himself forced outside of the formal respectable religion of his day, only to die a criminal's death outside the city walls, an apparent failure? Ultimately Christlikeness is to be seen as evidence of a transcendent holiness, as Lewis so often emphasized, in cultures and societies, religions and myths, outside of the Judaeo-Christian.

Psyche, being pre-Christian has no conscious knowledge of the Christ event; ironically, Dostoevsky presents Myshkin, who has been raised within a supposedly Christian culture and religion, as likewise having no knowledge; however, this issues in part from the fact that his brain has been damaged by lifelong epileptic seizures and when questioned by Rogozhin as to whether he believes in God or not, Myshkin answers obliquely and enigmatically. Myshkin answers (like Jesus of Nazareth when questioned) with a parable—an analogical narrative![16] The parable is about four people, and illustrates the relative value of religious belief. Simply declaring belief in God is not enough, likewise issuing a denial of God's existence is not irrefutably damning (particularly as it raises the question of which particular "god" a person does or does not believe in). To Myshkin (and therefore Dostoevsky) holiness and sanctification are what is important. The first character is a man who passionately claims atheism but lives an apparently good Christian life, kind and altruistic. The second character is a poor but devout Christian who is so beguiled by a friend's silver watch and chain that he creeps up behind his friend, raises his eyes to heaven, crossing himself, crying out,

---

15   Job 38–42.
16   Dostoevsky, *The Idiot*, 218–21.

"God forgive me, for Christ's sake!" as he cut his friend's throat like a sheep, and took the watch; the third character is an old drunken soldier who cons Myshkin into buying what he claims is a solid silver cross on a chain but is really only cheap tin. Myshkin buys it, laments that the old soldier has probably gone off to drink the proceeds but comments, "I thought, 'I will wait awhile before I condemn this Judas. Only God knows what may be hidden in the hearts of drunkards.'"[17] The fourth character defines Myshkin's answer: a poor Russian peasant woman, carrying a child, a baby of some six weeks old who for the first time smiles up at her, in response the young woman crosses herself in thanks to God—Myshkin comments, "Exactly as is a mother's joy when her baby smiles for the first time into her eyes, so is God's joy when one of his children turns and prays to him for the first time, with all his heart! . . . such a deep, refined, truly religious thought it was—a thought in which the whole essence of Christianity was expressed in one flash—that is, the recognition of God as our Father, and of God's joy in people as his own children, which is the chief idea of Christ."[18] Myshkin does not answer Rogozhin's question with a doctrinal assertion, but by analogy, through parable, a story. Rogozhin is left confused by the story, yet fully aware of Myshkin's Christlike simplicity. Neither Psyche nor Myshkin are assertively dogmatic, yet both are in Christ.

Does Lewis take the paradox of Christlikeness in Psyche as far as Dostoevsky does with Myshkin? Probably not, though it is difficult to tell because the story is recounted by Orual and as such she is retelling the events from her perspective and does not give the fullness of the paradox that Dostoevsky presents; despite Myshkin's witness, despite wrecking his health by racing here and there trying to change people, draw them away from the selfish evil that is engulfing them, those who surround Myshkin fail to see the Christlikeness within him—save for Rogozhin the murderer and Nastasya the harlot (but the perception does not *change* them, only Christ's Holy Spirit can)! Orual is trying to counter another version of her story (court gossip?) where she is to blame for Psyche's suffering. Although Lewis was faced with this paradox when his wife Joy Davidman died of cancer after a long illness, he failed to see the immediacy of the paradox of Christlikeness in her suffering. Is Orual's love essentially of the anti-Christ? Lewis comments on Orual's selfish love, but also how this is a slowly developing understanding of love in *Till We Have Faces*, how eventually she must perceive that her ability to love was not in freedom, but in the desire to possess the object of love, where human affection is initially true and tender, but in the long run becomes tyrannically possessive, turning to hatred when the beloved ceases to be its possession. Did Lewis fail to see this in himself, did he fail to realize this upon Joy's death?[19]

---

17   Ibid., 219–20.
18   Ibid., 220–21.
19   Lewis to Clyde S. Kilby, Feb. 10, 1957. *Collected Letters Vol. III*, 831.

12. Apologist and Defender of the Faith IV: Revelation and Christology, 1948–63 (2)

ii. "We are Christians not Stoics"

Later works of Lewis's stress the comfort of christological truths having established the veracity of the doctrine in his earlier apologetic works. This comfort is often seen in the consolation of sharing with Christ's passion through personal suffering. So does suffering equate with Christlikeness? What of our own moral responsibility if this suffering is self-inflicted? Is Lewis's doctrine of suffering different in the 1950s (*Reflections on the Psalms* and *Letters to Malcolm: Chiefly on Prayer*) as compared to the earlier, *The Problem of Pain*? The salient characteristics of Christlikeness, where the hallmarks of the Christ are beauty and holiness, suffering and sacrifice, may be exhibited by people as they struggle against evil and fallenness, human error and frailty, but they will fail without the Holy Spirit.

The Cry of Prayer

In *Reflections on the Psalms*, published in 1958, Lewis presents Christ as the compassionate Lord of judgment—we must pin all our hopes on the mercy of God and the work of Christ, not on our goodness.[20] This leads to questions regarding the salvation of pre-Christian peoples, though any answer is not as cut-and-dried as we might like it to be.[21] Psalm 49, for Lewis, refers to the redeeming work of Christ, achievable by no mere human: "The price of salvation is one that only the Son of God could pay."[22] The comfort and consolation we may receive comes because "Our life as Christians begins by being baptized into a death . . . centred upon the broken body and the shed blood."[23] In the context of "bad people" who have suffered as a consequence of their actions (as distinct from "very bad people who are powerful, prosperous and impenitent"[24]) Lewis asserts that the judgment of Christ is judgment in forgiveness, if we are prepared to accept the consolation of forgiveness issuing from the change repentance presages; the woman taken in adultery (John 8:1–11) is an example— this does not condone adultery, but points to the consolation of repentance.[25] The important concept that Lewis notes in depth is the second meanings that we can read from the Psalms—there is much which after the Christ event we can see as presaging the atonement issuing from Christ's sacrifice.[26] The Psalms contain second or hidden meanings concerned with the "central truths of Christianity, with the Incarnation, the Passion, the Resurrection, the Ascension, and with the Redemption of man."[27] To this end much of the Old Testament is a prophetic announcement not only for Lewis but orthodox Christian scholars for millennia: "They ought to have known from their

---

20 Lewis, *Reflections on the Psalms*, 11. (See also, Lewis, "The Psalms," 114–28.)
21 Ibid., 23.
22 Ibid., 30. This also relates to the salvation of the soul in, as Lewis terms it, the Christian sense, ibid., 33.
23 Ibid., 45.
24 Ibid., 58.
25 Ibid., 58; see also, 60–61.
26 See, Brazier, "C. S. Lewis & Christological Prefigurement," 742–75.
27 Lewis, *Reflections on the Psalms*, 85.

Bibles that the anointed one, when he came, would enter his glory through suffering."[28] And within this is consolation and comfort if we are prepared to tread the path with Christ.[29]

"There is Danger in the very Concept of Religion"

The relationship between the redeemed individual and the church occupies Lewis's thought more and more in his mature years. He does make the bold statement in *Reflections on the Psalms* that our worship fails: "For our 'services' both in their conduct and in our power to participate, are merely attempts at worship, never successful, often 99.9% failures, sometimes total failures"[30] In *Letters to Malcolm: Chiefly on Prayer*, published posthumously the year after Lewis's death, this concern is even more on Lewis's mind.[31] If *Reflections on the Psalms* focused, to a degree, on the perception of the actions of Christ outside of the life and death of Jesus of Nazareth, and how this related to the individual *in Christ*, Lewis explores the relationship between the individual Christian and the church, in the context of prayer, and the validity-invalidity of our prayer, indeed the very nature of our prayer: *Letters to Malcolm* essentially poses the question, "What is the acceptability of our prayer before the resurrected and ascended Christ?" Lewis presents several questions and answers and paradoxes about prayer, essentially doctrinal issues, but these are presented through analogical narrative—a correspondence exchanged between two individuals, Lewis and an imaginary questioner named Malcolm. If prayer is petitionary then the entreaty—the supplication, even the plea, however much born of frustration, anger, or love—must not be for personal gain, nor even to suffer the will of God patiently, but, "In the long run I am asking to be given 'the same mind which was also in Christ.'"[32] Inevitably this leads Lewis into a criticism of religion and the church. This is at its most acerbic when arguing against John Henry Newman's assertion that heaven is like a church because both offer one single sovereign subject, named, religion—Newman forgets, comments Lewis, that there is no temple in the New Jerusalem; further, Newman "has substituted religion for God . . . even in this present life there is danger in the very concept of religion."[33] To dialectically counter this criticism of the church Lewis affirms the passion of the Christ, and it is here that he stresses the comfort drawn from suffering aligned with Christ's sacrifice; we may *in Christ* be near Jesus on the cross, our small haltingly feeble way of coping with pain and suffering, rejection and affliction, we may endure, but "the servant is not greater than the master. We are Christians not Stoics."[34] The prayer of Jesus in the Garden of Gethsemane illustrates that the anxiety is not diminished by the will of God and the consolation and strengthening is equally part of human destiny. The prayer of anguish in Gethsemane is not granted, but the

28   Ibid., 101; see also, 94f., and 97.
29   Ibid., 101–3.
30   Ibid., 82.
31   Lewis, *Letters to Malcolm: Chiefly on Prayer*, 81f.
32   Ibid., 23, quoting Phil 2: 3–11.
33   Ibid., 27–28, this criticism continues throughout ch. 6.
34   Ibid., 40.

12. Apologist and Defender of the Faith IV: Revelation and Christology, 1948-63 (2)

strength is given to endure.[35] Christ brought the church into existence (by gathering the disciples) yet at his moment of greatest need it abandons him, essentially because as a human agency it is created in freedom:

> If God will create, he will make something to be, and yet to be not himself. To be created is, in some sense, to be ejected or separated. Can it be that the more perfect the creature is, the further this separation must at some point be pushed? It is saints not common people who experience the "dark night." It is men and angels, not beast, who rebel. Inanimate matter sleeps in the bosom of the Father. The "hiddenness" of God perhaps presses most painfully on those who are in another way nearest to him, and therefore God himself, made man, will of all men be by God most forsaken?[36]

Lewis therefore is pointing towards, though he does not systematically define, a dialectic between Christlikeness and religion, which can also be perceived in spirituality.[37] There is something of a tension and conflict, an antinomy that is unresolved, between Psyche and her sister Orual, but also between Psyche and the Priest of Glome—Arnom; this is dialectical and can only be resolved in the eschaton—the last judgment—of which none of the characters in *Till we have Faces* is aware of in their conscious mind. Only after death will we be known for the Christlikeness, which others may or may not have perceived when we were alive. Therefore Lewis can confidently affirm that there is a Christlike potential in all people.[38] If we are to criticize religion where it fails then we should look to the religion Jesus taught.[39] Any religious image that does not draw us into the failure of religion is suspect, and the failure of religion is defined by the cross (that is if we can bear to contemplate the full horror of what was foisted onto Jesus).[40] How can we, if we face the historic reality of the crucifixion, not be swept up by humility and repentance? If we are to acknowledge the importance of the shed blood, then this raises questions, often marginalized by Evangelical and low Protestant churches, of the Eucharist, Holy Communion, and transubstantiation.[41] It is *here*, writes Lewis, that the veil between the worlds is at its thinnest, yet also so opaque to the intellect (which struggles to understand what is happening in the Eucharist): "Here a hand from the hidden country touches not only my soul but my body ... the command, after all was 'Take eat': not 'Take, understand.'"[42] This points to enigma and, according to the standards of this world, apparent contradiction: "the paradox of Christianity."[43] This paradox, indeed all apparent contradictions and dialectics, are

---

35 Ibid., 40–41.
36 Ibid., 41–42.
37 Ibid., 61–62.
38 Ibid., 71.
39 Ibid., 81.
40 Ibid., 82.
41 Ibid., 98–101.
42 Ibid., 100–101.
43 Ibid., 110.

resolved in the eschaton: the four last things—death judgment, heaven, and hell. In Christ we are resurrected to new life.[44]

What appears to drive Lewis's understanding of the church and religion (and their relationship to the universal resurrected and ascended Christ), in his late works is a difference—a dialectic—between what we take to be the church before us (the people, the buildings, and the traditions), and the reality—invisible to most—of the body of the redeemed in Christ, in eternity. To argue otherwise raises the question, "Is Jesus responsible for the sins of the churches?" This is a classic distinction between the visible and the invisible church—the *ecclesia visibilis-ecclesia invisibilis*. It is important to understand this dialectic and how it is present, more and more, in Lewis's mature work; however, to fully understand it means analyzing it in depth later.

Comfort and Consolation

What Christlike comfort and consolation did Lewis gain in his late years from the love of God? In *The Four Loves* he exhibits a sound orthodox understanding of what the love of God is as compared to human love in its manifold forms. Along with *The Allegory of Love* this forms a sound doctrine of love, but, does he reflect this understanding in his life and faith? Lewis struggled in his late years, following the death of his wife Joy Davidman from cancer in 1960. They married in 1956 after her first diagnosis, she then appeared miraculously healed, only for the cancer to return and kill her four years later. There is a disjuncture between the theologian and philosopher who has a highly orthodox and sound understanding of pain and suffering, grief and loss, and altruistic love on the one hand, as compared to the inherently selfish love engrained into humanity after the fall. In his personal life Lewis rebels against the human condition, and displays the selfish need for his wife Joy. *A Grief Observed*, initially published under a pseudonym, charts this struggle, eventually to regain the light of Christ in a true understanding of himself, his love for Joy, and the will of God in their lives. In the early pages of *A Grief Observed* Lewis almost seems a parody of the characterization of twisted love he analogically projected onto characters in *The Great Divorce*, who emerged from hell to be given the opportunity to move beyond themselves, out of themselves, into the light—however much it hurt—only to return to the grey nihilistic bickering hellish world that they felt safe in,[45] or the characterizations in *The Four Loves* that read so accurately of the way relationships can turn sour with one partner preying on the hard-pressed other, exploiting and wearing down in the name of love.[46] But Lewis did not fail this final test; he struggled on and through the demons that beset his mind, his thoughts, he realized that the love of God was ultimately greater than anything he could imagine and that the real enemy was his selfish desires. Only then did true comfort and consolation come, the succor, solace, and support that came from being *in Christ*.

---

44   Ibid., 116f.
45   Lewis, *The Great Divorce*, ch. 4, especially 9f.
46   Lewis, *The Four Loves*, 40–49, especially "Mrs Fidget," 46–48.

12. Apologist and Defender of the Faith IV: Revelation and Christology, 1948–63 (2)

As the American Christian philosopher Nicholas Wolterstorff notes, Lewis's understanding of human suffering, certainly as presented in and from *The Problem of Pain* (1940), "takes the traditional form of a theodicy."[47] This, however, does not sit easily with his account of personal suffering in *A Grief Observed*. This traditional theodicy (i.e., how can God be good when there is so much evil in the world?[48]) is grounded in a patristic understanding—essentially, according to Wolterstorff, in the work of Irenaeus, that is, soul-making theodicy, whereby suffering and pain does us good. There is, therefore, a disjuncture of sorts between Lewis's soul-making theodicy from *The Problem of Pain* and his wrestling with pain in *A Grief Observed* twenty years later. Or, as, Wolterstorff notes, "suffering becomes for him no longer a problem to be discussed with the leisure of the scholar but the existential condition into which he has been plunged."[49] This is intrinsically bound up with how we understand love, and in particular the relationship between God's love, and the human response we call love for God and others. This raises questions: Is our kindness merely the desire to alleviate suffering? Is our feeble response to God's love ever altruistic? Are we ever looking to ourselves and our own concerns when we claim to love God, or another? Both *The Four Loves* and *A Grief Observed* begin to tackle these sorts of questions, as compared to the God's megaphone (in *The Problem of Pain*) whereby God shouts at the world, through pain and suffering, to wake humanity up from its dreamlike stupor. If we were created to receive the love of God, and in return love God, and if we do not, given that humanity before God is now defined by the fall into original sin, if we love ourselves and not God, then we perhaps are in no position to complain. Reorientation will, as Lewis asserted, be painful; however, "suffering sometimes makes the sufferer a worse rather than a better person, and often has no effect one way or the other."[50]

Does the crucifixion change the value and importance of all questions and objections? Does Lewis give enough reference and ground to the cross in his writings on suffering and pain? Wolterstorff thinks not. This is an echo of N. T. Wright's criticism that we encountered earlier, and perhaps within *The Problem of Pain* there is insufficient reference to the cross for broadly Protestant philosophical sensitivities. Nevertheless, the criticism is countered by Lewis's assertion that it is the shed blood of Jesus that is of ultimate value: "guilt is washed away . . . by repentance and the blood of Christ."[51] To paraphrase comments by the French existential Jewish philosopher and convert to Christianity, Simone Weil, the extreme greatness of Christianity lies in the fact that it does not seek a supernatural *remedy* for suffering, but a supernatural *use* for

47   Wolterstorff, "C. S. Lewis on the Problem of Suffering," 3.
48   Theodicy, noun (plural theodicies): the vindication of divine providence in view of the existence of evil (OED). The word is from the eighteenth century French, *théodicée*, devised by the philosopher and mathematician, Gottfried Leibniz, from the Greek θεος (*theos*, God) and δικη (*dikē*, justice), for the title of a book of his purporting to answer the question. Theodicy can relate to suffering and pain in the world: How do you justify belief in a good God when there is suffering, badness, evil? Theodicy is not primarily about pain and suffering, but, these questions are related. To what extent do we connect bad things with evil, and why is justice so uneven?
49   Ibid., 3–4.
50   Ibid., 14.
51   Lewis, *The Problem of Pain*, 41.

it. This belief was also manifest in the work of George MacDonald, quoted by Lewis at the opening of *The Problem of Pain*, whereby the Son of God suffered not so that we should escape suffering but so that our sufferings might be like Jesus's.[52] If we are truly orientated to Christ we will not cease to suffer, but our pain and affliction will be given meaning by comparison with Christ, through being drawn into Christ, but ultimately because of the atonement wrought by Christ on the cross.

After Joy's death and the wrestling with God that is *A Grief Observed*, the right judgment that emerges in Lewis's beliefs is shown in the posthumously published *Prayer: Letters to Malcolm*, where he has learned to accept affliction and suffering, anguish and pain, in relation to the cross of Christ. The passion of Christ does not ease or belittle the suffering but it does give it meaning and use. Afflictions, then for Lewis, become "our share in the Passion of Christ."[53] If knowledge and meaning is withdrawn from Jesus in the Garden of Gethsemane, then like us, we may not fully understand our pain and suffering, our afflictions. "We all try to accept with some sort of submission our afflictions when they actually arrive. But the prayer in Gethsemane shows that the preceding anxiety is equally God's will and equally part of our human destiny."[54] Our sharing in the passion of Christ is where our comfort and consolation lies, but this is experienced not as friendship but as rejection and isolation (hence the Christlikeness of Psyche and Myshkin and their lot in life). Lewis may be criticized for an apparent marginalization of the cross but he does see the pattern of the cross as the passion of Christ in the lives of Christians today. While in the passion we may feel lost, rejected, and we may not find the comfort of God, we only appear to ourselves abandoned (hence the very real abandonment he felt after Joy's death, despite the intellectualization of *The Problem of Pain*). It is worth noting here Lewis's systemization of this abandonment in Christ's passion.

> Does not every movement in the Passion write large some common element in the sufferings of our race? First, the prayer of anguish; not granted. Then he turns to his friends. They are asleep—as ours, or we, are so often, or busy, or away, or preoccupied. Then he faces the Church, the very Church that he brought into existence. It condemns him. This is also characteristic. In every Church, in every institution, there is something which sooner or later works against the very purpose for which it came into existence. But there seems to be another chance. There is the State; in this case, the Roman state. Its pretensions are far lower than those of the Jewish church, but for that very reason it may be free from local fanaticisms. It claims to be just, on a rough, worldly level. Yes, but only so far as is consistent with political expediency and *raison d'etat*. One becomes a counter in a complicated game. But even now all is not lost. There is still an appeal to the People—the poor and simple whom he had blessed, whom he had healed and fed and taught, to whom he himself belongs. But they have become overnight (it is nothing unusual) a murderous rabble shouting for his blood. There

---

52   Ibid., vi. Lewis credits MacDonald's first series; see, MacDonald, *Unspoken Sermons*.
53   Lewis, *Letters to Malcolm: Chiefly on Prayer*, 39.
54   Ibid., 40.

12. Apologist and Defender of the Faith IV: Revelation and Christology, 1948–63 (2)

is, then, nothing left but God. And to God, God's last words are, "Why hast thou forsaken me?"[55]

Jesus did not gain any support or solace, comfort or consolation, from his closest friends, the Jewish religious authorities, the State, or the general population; neither, at the end, from God, because the distance was at its greatest. And yet, in this was the will of God. Therefore is not the implication of what Lewis is saying that when we are most at one with the will of God we are most at distance from our religious concepts of God? It is important to remember that much of the church, though not all of it, rejected Lewis's marriage to Joy Davidman because she was a divorcee. Though ironically from a strict interpretation her first marriage did not count because her first husband himself had been a divorcee; also it was a secular marriage. All this would not have counted in the eyes of Rome as an impediment *if* they had been Roman Catholics. So Lewis knew what it meant to be abandoned by the Church (of England).

This, of course, makes Lewis, as he terms it, "A Job's comforter. Far from lightening the dark valley where you now find yourself, I blacken it."[56] But perhaps it is in this honesty that he does the greatest credit to the cross, even if it is not named as such. Ultimately the question of comfort and consolation, pain and suffering, revolves on a doctrine of creation: under what conditions and for what purpose was humanity created? Here we may just begin to find an answer to the question, "Why do good people suffer?," or more pertinently, "Why do *apparently* good people suffer?"—for goodness lies in the judgment of God. At least Lewis begins to realize that if God creates, creation must subsist in freedom:

> Is it that God himself cannot be Man unless God seems to vanish at his greatest need? And if so, why? I sometimes wonder if we have even begun to understand what is involved in the very concept of creation. If God will create, he will make something to be, and yet to be not himself. To be created is, in some sense, to be ejected or separated. Can it be that the more perfect the creature is, the further this separation must at some point be pushed? It is saints, not common people, who experience the "dark night." It is men and angels, not beasts, who rebel. Inanimate matter sleeps in the bosom of the Father. The "hiddenness" of God perhaps presses most painfully on those who are in another way nearest to him, and therefore God himself, made man, will of all men be by God most forsaken?[57]

Writing here near the end of his life, Lewis is coming to understand the centrality of these questions in a doctrine of creation; ironically he did express something of this understanding twenty to twenty-five years earlier in *The Problem of Pain* where he commented, often quoted, that "A man can no more diminish God's glory by refusing to worship him than a lunatic can put out the sun by scribbling the word 'darkness' on the walls of his cell."[58] Therefore if God wills creation to be, God creates in freedom; some suffering and pain will be self-inflicted, some will be willed by God

---

55 Ibid., 41–42.
56 Ibid., 42.
57 Ibid., 41–42.
58 Lewis, *The Problem of Pain*, 41.

on the creature for correction (Lewis's analogy of God's megaphone), in other cases the inherent freedom in creation may cause pain and suffering inadvertently on the creature—accidents happen, we may be subject to the vagaries and verisimilitudes of random genetic mutations, which can afflict, likewise we may be subject to injury from our neighbor.

3. REVELATION AND CHRISTOLOGY, 1948–63: THE KEY THEOLOGICAL AND PHILOSOPHICAL ESSAYS

i. fides—Faith and Religion

In terms of the late works, Lewis's thinking represents similar interest to his early and middle works which were centered on the person and figure of Jesus Christ. The question of revelation and reason is now seen in relation to religion. The importance of Jesus Christ is not primarily "religious," as we can see from a paper Lewis presented to the Socratic Club in 1952 in reply to Professor H. H. Price.[59] Price argued that theism was not necessarily central to or important to religion; further, he appeared to argue for a multiplicity of "gods" and therefore freedom of religion. Lewis's response initially systematizes this into two forms of religious faith:

> (a) A settled intellectual assent. In that sense faith (or "belief") in God hardly differs from faith in the uniformity of Nature or in the consciousness of other people. This is what, I think, has sometimes been called a "notional" or "intellectual" or "carnal" faith.
>
> (b) A trust, or confidence, in the God whose existence is thus assented to. This involves an attitude of the will. It is more like our confidence in a friend. It would be generally agreed that Faith in sense A is not a religious state.

Faith-B is closer to faith in a personal God, of accepting God's will in one's life, or seeking to know this God as one knows a friend, relation, or for that matter a lover. In terms of conversion Faith-B usually (but not always) follows on from Faith-A, which may take the form of speculation as to the existence of this or that "god": "The devils who 'believe and tremble' have Faith-A. A man who curses or ignores God may have Faith-A. Philosophical arguments for the existence of God are presumably intended to produce Faith-A."[60] Lewis is beginning to develop a skepticism towards philosophical arguments for the existence of God. For example, "Of course Faith-A usually involves a degree of subjective certitude which goes beyond the logical certainty, or even the supposed logical certainty, of the arguments employed. It may retain this certitude for a long time, I expect, even without the support of Faith-B. This excess of certitude in a settled assent is not at all uncommon. Most of those who believe in Uniformity of Nature, Evolution, or the Solar System, share it."[61] Nonetheless faith, *true* faith, not

---

59   Lewis, "Is Theism Important? A Reply," 138–42. This is a reply to a paper read to the Oxford Socratic Club by H. H. Price, "Is Theism Important?," 39–47.
60   Lewis, "Is Theism Important? A Reply," 139.
61   Ibid., 139–40.

12. Apologist and Defender of the Faith IV: Revelation and Christology, 1948–63 (2)

merely religious assertions that are often syncretistic, will move through these stages: trust, confidence, issues from the will, and follows on from assent to the existence of God. If we must see this as religious then it is the hallmark of true religion. Lewis is then drawing a distinction between all of our religious feelings and ideas, which are often human-generated, and God. If Lewis is drawing a distinction between religion and faith, on the one hand, and the actions of God within our reality, on the other, then these actions are more usually called the economic Trinity and focus on what has happened within history, salvation history, two thousand years ago. Faith-B is more usually, in its genuine or authentic state, a *gift* from God: preveniently, the Holy Spirit will have been influencing, subtly, our minds as we *decide* grounds for Faith-A, leading us to the gift of Faith-B. Therefore Lewis can assent to Price's proposition that philosophical proofs of the existence of God do not logically lead to Faith-B; Lewis will argue that the philosophical concept that there might just be a "god" does not lead to Faith-B. No, it is the prevenient action, influence, of the Holy Spirit that leads us from Faith-A to Faith-B. However, the actions of the economic Trinity are not simply confined to the prevenient influence of the Holy Spirit on people's minds. These actions are evident in salvation history. Lewis starts with the numinous; somehow these "quasi-religious experiences," though not faith in themselves, lead to *fides quaerens intellectum*—faith seeking understanding. The numinous may be more akin to awe, even fear, Lewis asserts, but the "numinous or awful is that of which we have this, as it were, objectless or disinterested fear."[62] But what we take to be religion transforms this awe; but this religion is not of itself generated, there is a strong moral element in it and it is the realization of actions outside of ourselves, culminating in the incarnation-cross-resurrection. Lewis continued:

> But even in the higher Paganism, I do not think this process led to anything exactly like *fides*. There is nothing creedal in Paganism. In Israel we do get *fides* but this is always connected with certain historical affirmations. Faith is not simply in the numinous Elohim, nor even simply in the holy Jahweh, but in the God "of our fathers," the God who called Abraham and brought Israel out of Egypt. In Christianity this historical element is strongly re-affirmed. The object of faith is at once the *ens entium* [being of beings] of the philosophers, the Awful Mystery of Paganism, the Holy Law given of the moralists, and Jesus of Nazareth who was crucified under Pontius Pilate and rose again on the third day.[63]

The mistake is to regard all religions, all religious experiences, all ideas of the holy and the numinous, as equivalent so as to subject them all to analysis and control at a distance (as academics often do). The actions of the economic Trinity in and through Jesus of Nazareth, the Christ, are the focus of true religion and the pinnacle of God's actions towards humanity. So often we confuse this with our own religious inventions. What is important is not Price's theories about religion and faith, or even Lewis's systematizing of his criticism of religion, what is important is this action of the Trinity

---

62   Ibid., 140.
63   Ibid., 141.

in the event and person of Jesus of Nazareth—in this lies our salvation out of a perilous predicament whatever our religious beliefs may be.

In terms of revelation, and how we receive and perceive of God, the key address he gave in 1944 is re-published in a second edition, an extended form—"Transposition."[64] In many ways this is his most important writing because it contains the key to his work. In terms of the incarnation this is Lewis's contribution to the doctrine of the incarnation. Building on his word picture of God landing in this world in disguise, leads us to perceive the impossibility of direct communication,[65] which in itself illustrates a degree of transposition—that revelation is transposed Sonship (God the Son, the second person of the Trinity) is, so to speak, the solid of which biological sonship (Jesus) is merely a diagrammatic representation on the flat.[66] We have seen this already: revelation is transposed, it changes, it is diminuted, in varying degrees, as—using analogy—a symphonic work is transposed for solo instrument. Therefore all theology is by analogy. Therefore this revised and extended essay on transposition comes conveniently towards the end of his work, indeed published a year before his death. It is built on his life's work and beliefs—that truth is outside of us, yet, through the faculties of imagination and reason we may intimate through the Holy Spirit, just as a drawing is not the object depicted but re-presents something of its truth.

In terms of a doctrine of Scripture the key work is "Modern Theology and Biblical Criticism," an address given at Westcott House, Cambridge, May 11, 1959[67] (published after Lewis's death) to a relatively unsympathetic audience of academics and students who were enamored with the hermeneutic of suspicion and the reduction of the Bible to something resembling myth. Lewis takes to task this "Liberal"/"Modern" reductionist method of form criticism because of its presence in so many Church of England training colleges.[68] This methodology raises serious question about the nature of Scripture, a doctrine of inspiration, and what is meant when we call the Bible the word of God when Jesus Christ is the Word of God. Lewis was also highly critical of the supposed expertise of "modern" New Testament scholars in their understanding of genre and literary types, particularly when such criticism was based on the mistaken notion of historical superiority, a denial of supernaturalism, and an attempt to place the text in the life and times when they were, which, by and large, Lewis believed failed and could not be verified: the writer of Mark's Gospel is dead, he is not around to question, or to refute the skepticism of the critics. Lewis held to an orthodox view of the credibility of Scripture; however, questions remain about his view of the nature

---

64   Lewis, "Transposition." 2nd ed. 166–82.
65   Ibid., 121–28.
66   Lewis, *Miracles*. 1st ed. 111.
67   Lewis, "Modern Theology and Biblical Criticism."
68   Westcott House, an Anglican theological college established in 1881, was named after its first President and then Regius Professor of Divinity at the university (and later Bishop of Durham), Brooke Foss Westcott. The college has always stood in the broad, liberal tradition characterized by Westcott's detailed study of the New Testament, and thus would have been out of step with Lewis's rather traditional view of literary criticism. Lewis was invited to speak at the college by the Principal, Kenneth Carey (later Bishop of Edinburgh).

12. Apologist and Defender of the Faith IV: Revelation and Christology, 1948–63 (2)

of Scripture as revelation and mediation. This along with Lewis's doctrine of the w/Word of God (Scripture and the Christ), and his doctrine of transposition, and the implications for Lewis's Christology and doctrine of revelation will be examined later.

ii. Eschatology and Pelagianism: A Lewisian Perspective

Identity

A little known short paper of Lewis's published in 1950 contains the kernel of his preoccupations and his Christology. This is what we may term the ontology of Jesus of Nazareth—that is, who or what is he? This preoccupation goes back to the late night conversation with J. R. R. Tolkien and Hugo Dyson in Magdalen water meadows, along the tree-lined Addison Walk twenty years or so earlier. It was this conversation that forced Lewis to confront the question of the identity of Jesus, his human and divine natures united in one person. The paper entitled, "What Are We to Make of Jesus Christ?"[69] deals with what Jesus is if he is not divine. It is centered on a proposition that preoccupied Lewis all his Christian life: *aut Deus aut malus homo*—either God or a bad man. We cannot attribute the recorded sayings and actions of Jesus to a sane or good man, if he is merely human. In terms of his popular apologetics Lewis phrased this as a trilemma—Mad, Bad, or God. There was no room for compromise: as he commented in *The Broadcast Talks*; for Lewis this is a stark decision—we must choose: either this Jesus was and is eternally the Son of God, or he was a madman or worse.[70] Lewis is directing his readers to important christological questions—What or who is this Jesus if he was not God incarnate? What can we say about this man if he was not divine? Does the record, written under threat of persecution, testify to Jesus's divinity? What we have here are the critical issues: how do we deal with the historical problem in the recorded sayings and acts of Jesus? Considering the shrewdness and depth, the clear cool lucidity of Jesus' moral teaching, how do we balance this with his theological assertions, which are the utterances of a megalomaniac ego defined by messianic pretences. Only God is defined by such utterances and actions towards humanity, or one suffering delusions. In addition, those around Jesus did not regard him as a good honest and decent teacher: Jesus was never regarded as a mere moral teacher—"He produced mainly three effects—hatred - terror - adoration. There was no trace of people expressing mild approval."[71] There are many issues in this assertion, *aut Deus aut malus homo*, which are centered in Lewis's paper, "What Are We to Make of Jesus Christ?" issues that will be analyzed in depth subsequently.

Judgment

A salient point Lewis makes in this paper is that it is not so much what we make of Jesus Christ, but *what he makes of us*! This prioritizes: Jesus himself poses the

---

69   Lewis, "What Are We to Make of Jesus Christ?," 49–53.
70   Lewis, *Broadcast Talks*, 50–51.
71   Lewis, "What Are We to Make of Jesus Christ?," 50.

question implicitly and explicitly to us—"Who do you say that I am?"[72] The disciples are questioned by Jesus, Simon Peter specifically, and their answer is important; Peter recognizes Jesus for what he is—"You are the Messiah, the Son of the living God"[73] What is important is that Peter came to this conclusion himself, but preveniently, by the Holy Spirit: "flesh and blood has not revealed this to you, but my Father in heaven."[74] This is eschatological, it is of the last judgment: it is crucial for our salvation that we come to understand and to recognize Jesus for who and what he is. Lewis understood this and realized that many will face this decision after death—he presented this admirably in *The Great Divorce*, where many turn away and cannot face the cost of accepting what Jesus the Christ has done for them. Therefore, the importance of Jesus lies initially in what we make of him, but then the question is turned around, turned on us—what does Jesus make of us, sitting as he will be in judgment on us? The older Lewis became, the more his mind turned, naturally, to the eschaton: the end. Central to this is hope—Christian hope.

These christological issues were dealt with at the same time as the writing of "What Are We to Make of Jesus Christ?" in the early 1950s, in an article contemporaneous with the early *Chronicles of Narnia* novels entitled "Christian Hope—Its Meaning for Today."[75] The eschaton, is about judgment. The implication is that an external divine force operates on us, decides on us. This is not a Buddhist nirvana where ultimately our hope is that we can extinguish ourselves, achieve self-annihilation. Many liberals would like to believe that only the righteous experience life after death (annihilationists). Scripture does not necessarily support these ideas; we are to face judgment after death, judgment on ourselves, what we have become, what our lives were. In the reprint of this essay in 1960, the title is changed to "The World's Last Night." Lewis is writing against the backdrop of contemporary scientific opinion epitomized by the concept of the steady-state universe, exemplified by the scientist and astronomer, Sir Fred Hoyle.[76] The steady state theory asserts that the universe has always existed and always will, *everything* was not created at a point from nothing, *everything* always existed, always was, and it will not end, it will continue into infinity. Christian theology has always acknowledged a point of creation and a Creator—the universe being created *ex nihilo* (out of nothing). Exponents of the steady-state theory, dominant in the post-war period, used their theory to mock religious belief, in particular a doctrine of creation. Most scientists now accept that the universe had a beginning (the so-

72   Matt 16:15, c.f. Mark 8:27–30 and Luke 9:20–21.
73   Matt 16:16b.
74   Matt 16:17.
75   Lewis, "The World's Last Night," 93–113. Lewis drew upon a poem, *Holy Sonnet XIII: What If This Present Were The World's Last Night?*, by the Anglican poet and churchman John Donne (1572-1631).
76   Sir Fred Hoyle FRS (1915-2001), an astronomer, cosmologist, and mathematician who worked in the fields of stellar nucleosynthesis, was somewhat controversial because of his position on various scientific matters. He rejected the big bang theory and developed the steady state theory, along with Thomas Gold and Hermann Bondi, in the late 1940s. The big bang theory, asserting a point of creation, is the model that currently dominates cosmology and the steady state theory has been more or less abandoned.

12. Apologist and Defender of the Faith IV: Revelation and Christology, 1948–63 (2)

called big bang theory); however, scientists may still claim this beginning was self-generated. Orthodox Jews and Christians will disagree: the universe was created and will at some point in the future end. Those who subscribed to the steady state theory often subscribed to the myth of cultural progress, but also they denied the idea of catastrophe—evolutionary time with its gradual changes denied these sudden catastrophic events. In Lewis's time the dominant position was that change happened very, very slowly, over eons of unimaginable time; Christians by comparison expect and "reckon with sudden interruption from without—at any moment"[77] Scientists of all persuasions think differently now, the West is to a degree preoccupied with the threat of sudden catastrophic events from asteroids to climate change.[78]

The question of creation aside, Lewis argues that the importance about the doctrine of the world's end is not simply because of the destruction of all we take for reality but because of the return of Jesus Christ to judge:

> It seems to me impossible to retain in any recognizable form our belief in the Divinity of Christ and the truth of the Christian revelation while abandoning, or even persistently neglecting, the promised, and threatened, return. "He shall come again to judge the quick and the dead," says the Apostles' Creed. "This same Jesus," said the angels in Acts, "shall so come in like manner as ye have seen him go into heaven." "Hereafter," said our Lord himself (by those words inviting crucifixion), "shall ye see the Son of Man . . . coming in the clouds of heaven."[79]

Lewis asserts that there is general "modern embarrassment" over the doctrine of the eschaton—the world's end is denied (or was, in the academy of Lewis's day), the second coming rebutted, judgment, heaven and hell conflated into a comfortable heaven. However, he also noted how this embarrassment extended to clergy for two reasons: first is the theological over-emphasis of the eschaton in some quarters; second, the delayed parousia (i.e., the second coming of Jesus Christ). The disciples and apostles expected Christ's return soon after the ascension. As Lewis notes, the delayed parousia is an embarrassment; why has Jesus not yet returned? This problem revolves around the question of time—how long constitutes a delay. Scripture is ambiguous: Jesus commented on the eschaton that "this generation will certainly not pass away until all these things have happened" (Matt 24:34), yet, as Lewis notes,

> It is certainly the most embarrassing verse in the Bible. Yet how teasing, also, that within fourteen words of it should come the statement "But of that day and that hour knoweth no man, no, not the angels which are in heaven, neither the Son, but the Father." The one exhibition of error and the one confession of ignorance grow side by side. That they stood thus in the mouth of Jesus himself, and were not merely placed thus by the reporter, we surely need not doubt. Unless the reporter were perfectly honest he would never have recorded the confession of ignorance at all; he could have had no motive for doing so except a desire to tell the whole truth. And unless later copyists were equally honest they would never have preserved the (apparently) mistaken prediction about "this generation"

---

77 Lewis, "The World's Last Night," 110–11.
78 Ibid., 100–101.
79 Ibid., 93.

> after the passage of time had shown the (apparent) mistake. This passage and the cry "Why hast thou forsaken me?" together make up the strongest proof that the New Testament is historically reliable.[80]

This raises questions about the knowledge and understanding Jesus as the Son of God had: omniscience, an attribute of God, would surely have denied Jesus's full humanity? The orthodox answer, as Lewis notes, is that "the God-Man was omniscient as God, and ignorant as Man."[81] However, Lewis develops this by speculating on the nature of Jesus's consciousness and the unconsciousness of Christ in sleep, or for that matter the dawn of reason in his infancy. If this seems paradoxical and contradictory, if we can barely begin to conceptualize the implications of God become man, then we need only look, comments Lewis, to the paradoxical assertions of the physical sciences—cosmology and quantum mechanics offer much that our minds find extraordinarily difficult to conceptualize, or much that our belief systems cannot imagine: "A generation which has accepted the curvature of space need not boggle at the impossibility of imagining the consciousness of incarnate God. In that consciousness the temporal and the timeless were united. I think we can acquiesce in mystery at that point, provided."[82] The paradox with the incarnation lies in the relationship between the temporal and the timeless: the eternal locked into the finite, subject to the vagaries and verisimilitudes of this reality. Therefore the incarnation must be seen as beyond time; it is not simply an episode in the "life" of God, Christ is incarnated, suffers on the cross, and is resurrected throughout eternity because God is eternal. The implications for this have preoccupied theologians for centuries, with precedent in Scripture (Rev 13:8), and Lewis is only too aware of this.[83] Does this begin to solve the quandary about the delayed parousia? To a degree, yes. Was Jesus referring to the new life and relationship with God that humanity would experience following on from his own resurrection? The generation he spoke of, and addressed, did not pass away until this new life issued from the cross and resurrection. But often theologians appeal to Jesus's human ignorance, which is not ideal. Lewis perhaps is loath to leave the question open simply because he feels the need to give an apologetic answer to skeptics. Perhaps we have simply misunderstood the meaning of Jesus's words on this matter.

Lewis's perception is that the doctrine of the second coming, the teaching that the world will end and that we will be judged, teaches us that we do not and cannot know when this is to be; the curtain, as he puts it, may be rung down at any moment. We must live in this tension. There is no way the parousia can be dated; many have foolishly tried. Lewis asserts that the doctrine of the second coming is summarized by three propositions: first, that Christ will certainly return; second, we must live in ignorance as to when; third, that we must live our lives planning for the future, yet must be ready at any given moment for Christ's return in judgment.[84] The salient

---

80   Ibid., 98.
81   Ibid.
82   Ibid., 99.
83   Ibid., 100.
84   Ibid., 107.

12. Apologist and Defender of the Faith IV: Revelation and Christology, 1948–63 (2)

characteristic of the second coming is judgment; Lewis does not find the pictures of the physical catastrophe that will usher in the *eschaton* to be disturbing as much as "the naked idea of judgment."[85]

Lewis argues well for the unknowable and immediate nature of the end of the world, but he doesn't tackle the question of the imagery used in the Bible—is this metaphorical, allegorical, or literal? Liberal skeptics will claim that the imagery of being lifted up into a cloud is not to be taken literally? Lewis should have tackled this skepticism because it erodes the authority of the Bible. As a generation that accepts the curvature of space baulks at the incarnation, likewise a generation that thinks it is only a matter of time until Star Trek transporters are realized scorns the ascension; such a people need to examine why they hold such beliefs. Skeptics reject the miracle at Cana (water into wine) yet happily drink wine—where agriculture has turned water into wine through propagating vines, tending and harvesting, pressing and fermenting and bottling! Miracles such as Cana and the ascension are not so much a denial or usurpation of the laws of nature (as we understand them) but a question of time and mechanics: the miracle at Cana achieved in mere seconds what a farmer takes years to achieve. Most people in the West accept and wait for the day when Star Trek transporters can dematerialize matter and reassemble it elsewhere, yet baulk at the traditional imagery in the ascension story: people will accept what humanity can do, but reject it when God does it; this is about control—humanity wants to control its destiny, it does not trust God to govern!

A Theological Perspective

As we saw with *Letters to Malcolm: Chiefly on Prayer* (1964) Lewis considers prayer from a christological perspective. A precursor to this is seen in a paper published in *The Atlantic Monthly*, on the efficacy of prayer.[86] There is inevitably an existential focus in this paper: why do we pray, how does it work, why do its results appear random, and, pertinently, why is prayer so essential to the human condition, why can we not avoid it? Lewis avoids questions about the "strength" of prayer, or praying in the right spirit (questions he did allude to in *Surprised by Joy*); he now assumes that prayer is nothing else than a devout setting of the will towards God.[87] Words, language, and meaning are unambiguous, linguistic analysis won't help our relationship with the Lord because before we utter a word in prayer our will, our stance, our determination and resolve, betray us. Lewis therefore demonstrates that there is an immediacy of relationship through Christ when we pray. Lewis does not try to ground this paper in an academic, disinterested, seemingly impartial, analysis. He starts straight away with the paradoxical miracle and prayer for his wife Joy who was healed of cancer, but died a few years later from secondary tumors: bone eaten away by cancer in a middle aged woman was miraculously restored as tumors throughout her body disappeared, but remission was for only a few years. The question, Lewis asserts, is why the pattern; it

---

85 Ibid., 113.
86 Lewis, "The Efficacy of Prayer," 3–12.
87 See Wolters, *The Cloud of Unknowing and Other Works*, §.39, 106.

clearly was miraculous but short-lived; this raises questions about our expectation and how much our desires correlate with the will of God, but also the role of suffering in the Christian life.

> But once again there is no rigorous proof. Medicine, as all true doctors admit, is not an exact science. We need not invoke the supernatural to explain the falsification of its prophecies. You need not, unless you choose, believe in a causal connection between the prayers and the recovery. The question then arises, "What sort of evidence would prove the efficacy of prayer?" The thing we pray for may happen, but how can you ever know it was not going to happen anyway? Even if the thing were indisputably miraculous it would not follow that the miracle had occurred because of your prayers.[88]

We need look no further than Jesus in the Garden of Gethsemane to see the difference between request and compulsion, between motive and aims; can we ever prove with scientific certainty a causal connection between the asking and the getting. Or as Lewis then emphasizes, the question "Does prayer work?" is the wrong question from the outset, because prayer is primarily personal contact between flawed, incomplete persons and the utterly concrete and complete person, more real than we can conceive of with our feet of clay. If this is not so, the prayer is sheer illusion. Prayer is no illusion; prayer is real, it is our contact with ultimate reality, a contact that issues from God's revelation.[89] In advancing the idea that results are not necessarily the primary aim of prayer Lewis comments, quoting Blaise Pascal, that God instituted prayer so as to lend his creatures dignity; but what does Lewis make of the biblical injunction to pray for the right things, and biblical claims about prayers answered? Lewis in effect grants God the freedom to allow creation to look after and care for itself. So why then did not Joy die with the first round of cancer? There must have been some reason for a Christian to recover? Here we come close to a theological reality that perhaps Lewis, still reeling from her death, was reluctant to pursue, after all, as Lewis comments, "Prayer is not a machine. It is not magic."[90] The answer relates to the Christian life—does God forsake those closest to him. This resonates with Jesus's cry from the cross. "And I dare not leave out the hard saying which I once heard from an experienced Christian: 'I have seen many striking answers to prayer and more than one that I thought miraculous. But they usually come at the beginning: before conversion, or soon after it. As the Christian life proceeds, they tend to be rarer. The refusals, too, are not only more frequent; they become more unmistakable, more emphatic.'"[91] In his waning years Lewis's understanding of prayer is perhaps overlooked in an attempt to find assertive apologetics.

---

88 Lewis, "The Efficacy of Prayer," 4.
89 Ibid., 8.
90 Ibid., 10.
91 Ibid., 10.

12. Apologist and Defender of the Faith IV: Revelation and Christology, 1948–63 (2)

History: Teleology and Meaning

Not being afraid to place our relationship with Jesus Christ, risen and ascended, at the heart of theology, Lewis constantly answers skepticism and asserts the truth of the gospel, however lowly or lofty a publication and its audience may have been. Therefore he was not afraid to challenge the religious public holiday, characterized by obligation and indulgence, that was Christmas, in a society that considered itself to be nominally Christian.[92] Lewis tackled, in apologetic terms, the fascination in the late 1950s and early 1960s with the potential of sending a man into space, and the fear amongst ordinary Christians that the exploration of space would destroy their image of God.[93]

Late in his career Lewis tackles the question of an intellectual control over time, that was prevalent amongst elements of academia at Oxford in the 1920s. In "*De Descriptione Temporum*" (literally, "From the Delineation of the Times"),[94] Lewis's inaugural lecture given on taking up the position of Professor of Medieval and Renaissance Literature at Cambridge in November 1954, he deconstructs the ability in academics to categorize and compartmentalize history into periods, which in effect further criticizes the intellectual snobbery (Lewis's term) that he writes about disentangling himself from in *Surprised by Joy* and *The Pilgrim's Regress*.[95] Lewis extends the proposition established earlier that Western humanity falsely believes that it is progressing higher and higher, to a better and better way of living, that progress is always upwards and onwards. Lewis criticizes various intellectual positions that assert the dawn of enlightenment and advancement, and draws an apparent causal connection between the reduction of child abuse and the Copernican revolution: "as if a new hypothesis in astronomy would naturally make a man stop hitting his daughter about the head."[96] Useful though the categorization of history into periods is, this is ultimately a vain glorious exercise; quoting the Cambridge historian, G. M. Trevelyan, Lewis comments, "Unlike dates, periods are not facts."[97] If periods are retrospectively imposed on past events they create a false picture, to a degree: nothing is that new, no efforts by humanity lead inevitably to progress. It is academia's desire to give the past some kind of structure that is the problem, and this is also true with church history or so-called Christian history: to what extent then is this classification "largely a figment of humanist propaganda"[98] This leads to an even greater existential understanding of the gospel, that humanity is the same now as when it fell into original sin, that we can do nothing to improve our lot, only Christ's atoning sacrifice can help—human

---

92   Lewis, "What Christmas Means to Me," 253–54.
93   Lewis, "Religion and Rocketry," 83–92.
94   Lewis, "De Descriptione Temporum," 9–25.
95   Lewis, *Surprised by Joy*, 207. Along with Owen Barfield and J. R. R. Tolkien, Lewis would then raise the question of why did a particular thought system cease to be fashionable, and whether it was ever refuted, and if so, how. See also, Lewis, *Mere Christianity*, ch. 7; also, the first volume of the space trilogy, Lewis, *Out of the Silent Planet*, where the anti-heroes, Devine and Weston, assume all ideas that have gone before are inferior and flawed, even in relation to alien species on another planet.
96   Lewis, "De Descriptione Temporum," 10
97   Ibid., 11.
98   Ibid.

progress, humanity as the measure of all things, will not. Intellectuals, by and large, during the Age of Reason and the Enlightenment rejected a religious perspective substituting with what they saw as humanity's innate capacity to deal with life from its own strength through the faculty of reason; in this was progress, advancement that asserted that humanity could improve, that past ideas were innately obsolete, thereby echoing the ancient Greek pre-Socratic philosopher Protagoras, this eighteenth-century white Western male oligarchic elite, confidently proclaimed that man was the measure of all things.[99] Therefore Lewis writes that, "About everything that could be called 'the philosophy of history' I am a desperate sceptic. I know nothing of the future, not even whether there will be any future. I don't know whether past history has been necessary or contingent. I don't know whether the human tragi-comedy is now in Act I or Act V; whether our present disorders are those of infancy or of old age."[100] What this is about is theological anthropology; that is, the human condition before God. The idea of inventing historical periods somehow softens the human reality, makes the human condition nicer and more acceptable, but above all masks the true reality behind a smoke screen. The key to understanding reality and the human condition is in a doctrine of original sin, the fall. Satan put the idea into the minds of our ancestors that we could be like "gods" (Gen 3), that we could set up on our own, define our own happiness, our own morality. This attempt was hopeless and led merely to human history, with its historical categories. Historical periods, and the inevitable philosophy of history, is defined according to Lewis by poverty amidst wealth, warring tribalism and ambition, sexual deprivation, struggle, empires and enslavement, and the dehumanization of those classified as "enemies." Lewis takes this further. Original sin is the key to history: civilizations and cultures grow up, often founded on sound principles, good laws are formulated, but *something always goes wrong*. "[This is] the long terrible story of man trying to find something other than God which will make him happy . . . some fatal flaw always brings the selfish and cruel people to the top and it all slides back into misery and ruin."[101] Historical periods and the myth of progress hide this, the delineation and classification of time into these periods erects a smoke screen; if the truth of our predicament were acknowledged humanity would have two choices: desperation, or faith in Christ's atoning sacrifice. Part of the problem is that history is written and categorized by the winners, and it may fairly be postulated that the winners serve the spirit of this world, the *Zeitgeist*, rather than Christ: Christ was crucified by the spirit of this world. In this context Lewis notes how if there is any sense in the delineation of historical time then the shift from a pagan to early

---

99   "Man is the measure of all things: of things which are, that they are, and of things which are not, that they are not." See, Hermann Alexander Diels (1848–1922), a German classical scholar known for his work compiling a collection of quotations from and about Pre-Socratic philosophers. Protagoras's statement that humanity (ἄνθρωπος) is the measure of all is summarized and reiterated by Plato in his *Theaetetus*, §152a, however, a full quotation is given by Sextus Empiricus (c. 2nd–3rd C. BC) in *Adversus Mathematicos* (*Against the Mathematicians*), §7.60: πάντων χρημάτων μέτρον ἐστὶν ἄνθρωπος, τῶν μὲν ὄντων ὡς ἔστιν, τῶν δὲ ὄντων ὡς οὐκ ἔστιν. See Plato, *Theaetetus*, §152a, 169.

100   Lewis, "De Descriptione Temporum," 12.

101   Lewis, *Broadcast Talks*, 49.

12. Apologist and Defender of the Faith IV: Revelation and Christology, 1948–63 (2)

Christian Europe is less than the shift from supposedly Christian Europe to the post-Christian Europe: "The christening of Europe seemed to all our ancestors . . . a unique, irreversible event. But we have seen the opposite process. Of course the un-christening of Europe in our time is not quite complete."[102] Lewis observes that this is, in part, because "Christians and Pagans had much more in common with each other than either has with a post-Christian."[103] Skeptics have existed for centuries, but, a great sea change has swept through the West certainly in the last third of the twentieth century. So is this an artificial categorization? Or is there some sense in the flawed human attempt to delineate human history if we dismiss any belief in progress?

Pelagianism and Prevenient Grace

Lewis's critique of the intellectual imposition of structure onto time and the artificial classification of history into periods raises questions of Pelagianism. The position Lewis is criticizing and dismissing relates closely to the Pelagian heresy. Pelagius (c. 354–430 AD) was a Romano-British churchman, orator, and ascetic who denied the doctrine of original sin and was declared a heretic by the church, his beliefs becoming known as Pelagianism. Essentially Pelagianism taught that individuals could achieve salvation purely by their own efforts, through good works. Pelagius's teachings are essentially a contradiction of the doctrine of original sin, formulated by Augustine of Hippo and grounded in Scripture (Gen 3; Rom 5). According to Pelagianism, original sin did not taint human nature; therefore people are still capable of choosing good or evil without the influence of God through the Holy Spirit in the form of divine grace. The sin of Eve and Adam was merely a bad example to follow. The action of original sin did not, according to Pelagianism, have a changing effect on the rest of humanity—the very nature of humanity was not changed, corrupted, dis-graced, by the actions of Eve and Adam. The view of Pelagius is that Jesus is setting a good example for humanity to follow. Therefore humanity has full control and therefore full responsibility for obeying or disobeying Jesus' teachings. Grace is essentially to be considered superfluous and unnecessary. Pelagius's beliefs have led to the comment that Pelagianism is about humanity trying to raise itself up by its own boot laces, pull itself up by its own efforts. In the twentieth century neo-Pelagianism has been prevalent; furthermore there is an emphasis in many of the world's religions on merit and personal effort. In the West, to a degree, this emphasis on good works is seen in contemporary "spirituality" in the emphasis on self-definition and self-identification. In Lewis's day the ability to control time (through the definition of history) by academics was a form of neo-Pelagianism: the past was defined and controlled and in exchange people were given to believe that they were innately good, were getting better, that progress was in effect saving them. In the early twenty-first century this has developed into lifestyle identity: "I make myself better, I improve, I fulfill myself through my lifestyle and identity, by self-definition I can to attain nirvana, heaven." Prevenient grace is the grace of God that comes before any good in the human; prevenient (preceding, prior) grace predisposes the human

---

102 Lewis, "De Descriptione Temporum," 13.
103 Ibid., 14.

heart to seek God prior to any initiative on the part of the human. Any good we can do does not come from our own strengths, our own initiative, but is the Holy Spirit working in and through us prior to any efforts of our own initiative. Prevenient grace issues from the decision by God, the free unwarranted grace that forgives humanity, which then, through the Holy Spirit, raises up humanity. We cannot achieve this for ourselves but God can achieve good through us: grace initiates, works respond

What did Lewis have to say? The key, for Lewis, is love bestowed out of sheer grace; the saved through and after conversion loves, does a work of love, because s/he is saved. This is not a work that guarantees salvation; the work of love issues from salvation, proceeding in and through the human by the prevenient action of the Holy Spirit.

> All the initiative has been on God's side; all has been free, unbounded grace. And all will continue to be free, unbounded grace. His [the converts] own puny and ridiculous efforts would be as helpless to retain the joy as they would have been to achieve it in the first place. Fortunately they need not. Bliss is not for sale, cannot be earned. "Works" have no "merit," though of course faith, inevitably, even unconsciously, flows out into works of love at once. He is not saved because he does works of love: he does works of love because he is saved. It is faith alone that has saved him: faith bestowed by sheer gift.[104]

The ability of humanity to go it alone and believe it can change the condition of humanity through its own monumental efforts is a form of twentieth century neo-Pelagianism, issuing, to a degree, from the Age of Reason and the Enlightenment: from the French Revolution to the Communist Revolution in Russia, through the Nazi definition of humanity in its own image: these efforts have failed. The delineation of time, as Lewis terms it, the categorization of the past, is part of this ability to aid humanity in its own efforts.

iii. Analogy and Apologetics

Story, Analogy, and Pictures

In his later years Lewis reflected about the method of his analogical narratives. In a short article written for *The New York Times*, Lewis describes the relationship between the creative process and his faith.[105] He explains how ideas seem to "bubble up" in his mind but the impulse to write, to compose, will only happen if the idea of a form offers itself—poem or narrative, play or short story. If this impulse is a desire, then aspiration and longing will see the idea take form. Therefore analogical narratives such as *The Chronicles of Narnia* started with an image coming into Lewis's mind—"a faun carrying an umbrella, a queen on a sledge, a magnificent lion. At first there wasn't even anything Christian about them; that element pushed itself in of its own accord."[106]

---

104 Lewis, *English Literature in the Sixteenth Century*, 33.
105 Lewis, "Sometimes Fairy Stories may say best what's to be said," 35–38. See also: Lewis, "On Three Ways of Writing For Children," 22–34.
106 Lewis, "Sometimes Fairy Stories," 36.

12. Apologist and Defender of the Faith IV: Revelation and Christology, 1948–63 (2)

The form was dictated by the content, Christian analogy (rather than allegory). The aim was given by Lewis's realization that as a child he had been paralyzed by religion, failing to feel as he was expected to feel about God, or the sufferings of Christ: "An obligation to feel can freeze feelings . . . [religion] was associated with lowered voices; almost as if it were something medical."[107] Therefore Lewis wanted to steal past the Sunday School teachers he regarded as "watchful dragons" by transposing the Christ event into an imaginary world. But these became more than children's stories—for Lewis the form is "The Fantastic or Mythical."[108] The gestation of the Narnia books was over several decades. The initial picture in his mind of a faun carrying an umbrella and walking through a snowy wood had been in his mind since he was sixteen years. The decision to put the idea into a form came when he was around forty years of age: "At first I had very little idea how the story would go. But then suddenly Aslan came bounding into it."[109] The presence of the lion Aslan (the Christ figure) pulled the entire story, and series, together.

Apologetics and Witness

As reasoned argument attempting to justify a belief system, a theory or doctrine, in the face of contradictory belief systems, apologists will argue and confront the apparent disagreements and divergences that are evident between competing belief systems. This is perhaps best illustrated by the often-acrimonious debate between Darwinian evolutionists and creationists. Christian apologetics are written to defend the truth of the gospel when confronted with the arguments of atheists, scientists, philosophers, for that matter, any one that denies the heart of the Christian faith. Lewis's arguments and emphasis in "The World's Last Night" illustrate a fundamental weakness in the method and nature of apologetics. With apologetics the truth of the gospel is represented in such a way that the content may appear changed in reaction to a contradictory belief system or perceived threat, the apologetic content may actually be defined by the threat. The emphasis and space devoted by Lewis to a rebuttal of Sir Fred Hoyle's steady state theory is an example of this. Much of Lewis's essay is therefore anachronistic precisely because he is arguing against the mind-set of a steady state theory when scientists and cosmologists no longer, in general, accept Hoyle's theory. All Lewis had to do was quote the authority of the Book of Genesis—that the universe *was* created.

Towards the end of his life Lewis was even more out-of-step with the liberalization of theology in Britain, especially in the 1960s. He was required to write a response to the "Honest to God" debate. The Bishop of Woolwich, John A. T. Robinson, had written a book—*Honest to God*[110]—that had stirred controversy before it was published.[111]

---

107 Ibid., 37.
108 Ibid., 38.
109 Lewis, "It All Began with a Picture . . . ," *The Radio Times, Junior Section* (July 15, 1960).
110 Robinson, *Honest to God* (London: SCM Press, 1963). See also, Edwards, The Honest to God Debate, specifically, 91–92.
111 Robinson was interviewed for the Sunday newspaper, *The Observer*, in which he outlined his challenge to traditional ideas about God: Robinson, "Our Image of God Must Go" (Mar. 17, 1963), 21–22, 39–40.

C. S. LEWIS—REVELATION, CONVERSION, AND APOLOGETICS

Robinson's central proposition was that we needed to change, to reappraise and modernize, our ideas about God; we needed to reject the traditional concept of God as "up there," or "out there." These were, to Robinson, an old fashioned and out-of-date idea about the nature of divinity: he preferred the concept, borrowed from the American theologian Paul Tillich, of God as *the ground of our being*. Robinson was attempting to bring theology into the public arena; as such this may be considered to be apologetics. Lewis, as an apologist, was approached to add his comments into the debate.[112] What was Lewis's response? Lewis writes as a "Christian layman," emphasizing the distinction between ordinary orthodox believers and this high-ranking cleric, though he notes how Robinson is likely to upset ordinary orthodox believers less than he hoped.

> We have long abandoned belief in a God who sits on a throne in a localized heaven. We call that belief anthropomorphism, and it was officially condemned before our time. There is something about this in Gibbon. I have never met any adult who replaced "God up there" by "God out there" in the sense "spatially external to the universe." If I said God is "outside" or "beyond" space-time, I should mean "as Shakespeare is outside The Tempest"; i.e., its scenes and persons do not exhaust his being. We have always thought of God as being not only "in," "above," but also "below" us: as the depth of ground. We can imaginatively speak of "Father in heaven" yet also of the everlasting arms that are "beneath." We do not understand why the Bishop is so anxious to canonize the one image and forbid the other.[113]

Lewis is speaking of the intimate connection between language and concept, and how the words we use cannot be separated from what we believe (doctrine) and how we behave (ethics); we may try to compartmentalize, but we do the same with God. Robinson appears to be working with an ancient Greek idea of God (which itself can be argued is no more than a reflection of the privileged education he had received), whereas Lewis, albeit briefly, is clearly working with a trinitarian concept, biblically given. Robinson questions whether God "exists" in the way he "exists" as a person, then asking whether ultimate reality is personal (on the assumption that God is ultimate reality—a concept borrowed from the Greek philosophers, not from the Bible). Whereas most of the media and the public simply rejected *Honest to God* because it challenged their stereotypical idea of God; Lewis noted how a triune doctrine of God was the key to any criticism of Robinson's book: "Does the Bishop mean that something which is not 'a person' could yet be 'personal'? Even this could be managed if 'not a person' were taken to mean 'a person and more'—as is provided for by the doctrine of the Trinity. But the Bishop does not mention this."[114] Orthodoxy demands that any discussion of God must be in a trinitarian context; this is one of the things that is unique to Christian revelation, and it is this triune "nature," the three persons in one, that overcomes Robinson's problems with "person," "spatiality" and

---

112 Lewis, "Must Our Image of God Go?" (Mar. 24, 1963), 14.
113 Ibid., 91
114 Ibid., 92

12. Apologist and Defender of the Faith IV: Revelation and Christology, 1948–63 (2)

"existence." Any talk about God is bound to be qualified by revelation. What does God reveal of God?—that God is triune: three person in one, uniquely co-existing. Without this there are two problems: first, the risk of deism (total situated separation whereby God has nothing to do with creation and "exists" utterly outside of creation); second, panentheism (where creation is identified as a part of God). There is a degree of confusion with the mono-"god" that Robinson appears to talk of—situated here, and there, then over there? Such a risk is countered by a doctrine of the Trinity: the Father is separate; the Son situated through incarnation yet ascended; the Holy Spirit is active in the world, yet is not in it. The doctrine of three persons equally co-existing denies the risk of deism and panentheism that the idea of God as a singularity does. Lewis understood this and it is evident in his reply to Robinson, but it is also there throughout his writings after his conversion. To say otherwise, even if a small degree of theoretical triunity is acknowledged, runs the risk of modalism (that God is the Father, then God *becomes* [a movement in space-time] the Son, then God *becomes* [a movement in space-time] the Holy Spirit, but is not all three coexisting simultaneously in triune unity). Through revelation God is revealed as a three-fold "structure," of three persons: God then can love in freedom—God loves humanity unto death on the cross yet is not tied to the creation. The failure of so much twentieth-century theology during Lewis's lifetime was that it either denied the Trinity (such theology formulated a doctrine of a mono-"god") or was not trinitarian enough (such theology reflected a conception of the Trinity that did not give full weight to the personhood of the Father, the personhood of the Son, and the personhood of the Holy Spirit). The way out of Robinson's angst over God-talk is, as Lewis shows, in a doctrine of the Trinity where God is not just a person, but where the apparent individuality in communion of the triune God is, in Lewis's words, taken to mean "a person and more as in an orthodox doctrine of the Trinity."[115] Fortunately since Lewis's death there has been a revival of the doctrine of the Trinity in the West; at the time Lewis was active he was, to a degree, a prophet speaking in the wilderness of post-war "l/Liberalism." Therefore he was prepared to make a stand. We have seen already how Lewis was not shy of courting controversy, or in answering his critics, as attested to by the Pittenger-Lewis debate.[116] It seemed that the gulf between Lewis's orthodoxy and the "Modern" and "Liberal" developments within the Church of England widened so as to make dialogue as difficult as trying to conduct a conversation from one shore of a lake to another.

4. TOWARDS DEATH

The *Honest to God* debate was in the last year of Lewis's life. Shortly afterwards he was interviewed by Sherwood E. Wirt for the American periodical *Decision*, which we examined in the early chapters of this book, in particular how the mature Lewis reflected on his life, his conversion, and his relationship with God.[117] The crucial

---

115 Ibid., 92
116 Lewis, "Rejoinder to Dr Pittenger," 1369–71.
117 Wirt and Lewis, "Cross-Examination," 215–21.

concept in this interview is, as we saw earlier, that Lewis came to realize the importance of the prevenient action of God in his life: he had not chosen Christ, Christ had chosen him; therefore he had been decided upon. All humanity can do is respond to Christ, whether Christian, or not, whether religious, or not. The last piece Lewis wrote before his death, published posthumously, dealt with the craving of humanity for happiness, but how this was focused on earthly pleasure and worldly satisfaction to the extent that the universality of the given moral order was compromised. In "We have no 'Right to Happiness,'"[118] though not explicitly theological, Lewis reasserts the truth of natural law in the face of the growing moral relativity that would culminate in what became known as the permissive Sixties. If humanity is to claim a right to happiness, how is that to be done when a right is a freedom guaranteed by law, and if natural law is an eternal truth given by God, then how do we frame such happiness? Without a natural, God-given, law, the statutes of the nation state become a tyranny; whatever the state decrees becomes an absolute. Without natural God-given law, the laws passed by a parliament are considered higher than morality: "Without it [Natural Law], the actual laws of the state become an absolute, as in Hegel. They cannot be criticized because there is no norm against which they should be judged."[119] So often people—and law makers—do not consider the issues from this perspective; so often they are talking, Lewis asserts, about sexual happiness (hence Lewis uses the divorce laws for the context of his criticism) with no thought for the implications within the family, within the community, or, more pertinently, before God. Is there no longer such a thing as a morality that is higher than humanity's laws? Where is the will and judgment of Christ in this? To talk of the moral *ought* is to speak of Christlikeness; our ultimate happiness lies with being in and for Christ. Lewis died, on November 22, 1963, shortly after writing this piece; perhaps, had he lived, he would have developed the ideas into a book.

---

118 Lewis, "We Have No 'Right to Happiness,'" 265–69.
119 Ibid., 266.

Conclusion
Apologist and Defender of the Faith

Lewis was orthodox in that he presented a high Christology; indeed, for many of his "modern" and/or "Liberal" contemporaries, particularly those who were part of the clerical establishment in the Church of England, this was embarrassingly too high. Many of his contemporaries wanted a low, or much lower, Christology so as to accommodate contemporary academic doubts about Jesus, but also to acknowledge, or allow space for, a range of religions and religious opinions. For Lewis, Jesus either is or is not who he gave himself away to be. The highest form of revelation is Jesus Christ; and revelation is seen as the revealing of God by God; that is, God giving of or about God—that is as much as our fallen human condition can cope with. But knowledge and understanding is only secondary. Revelation and the Christ are intimately intertwined with our need for salvation. All other revelation issues from or relates to Christ as universal and ascended, even transcended. No one is potentially beyond receiving some form of transposed intimation from God through Christ; how they respond is another matter. Therefore, Christ as God may be hidden from people—he is hidden from the visiting sinners on the fringes of heaven in *The Great Divorce*; he is a threatening inversion to Screwtape and his manifold legions—yet Christ generates the highest of loving desire in us, granting intimations of what will be to those who love him. Like Jesus' parables, pictures and analogy tell us more than attempting one-to-one correspondence. This is what Lewis often did in writing about revelation and the Christ.

The period of the Second World War was, as we have seen, an intense phase of development in Lewis's thinking, a period where he formulated and wrote down the philosophical basis of his theology, the parameters of his doctrine, and the ground for his ministry as an apologist. Much of the depth to his philosophical theology can be found in a significant number of essays in this period; however, perhaps he was, in many ways, too "busy." Lewis made no attempt to see how his work systematically cohered; how all the essays and works he wrote held together. There is, however, an astonishing breadth to his work: analogical picture stories, such as *The Great Divorce*, a layperson's guide to Christian belief in the broadcast talks, and academically astute papers and essays on philosophical, theological, and literary topics. Despite the breadth and the acknowledged flaws, does all this work portray something of the essence of the Christian faith? Perhaps Lewis over-relied on what appears to be an unimpeachable model of reason. His work developed along characteristically different lines, though not exclusively, in the 1950s with a much greater use of analogy. Much that follows on, that is published in the post-war period is based on these developments

During the 1930s Lewis, having been brought to accept that Jesus of Nazareth was the Christ, that Christ was Lord and God, read deeply; he drank in the Christian tradition focusing more and more on the pre-modern, pre-Enlightenment period, the first 1700 years, so to speak, of the Christian era. Many of his contemporaries saw his broad rejection of contemporary thinking as a fatal flaw in his work. However, much of this "modernist" and "Liberal" agenda is now—from a postmodern perspective—seen as flawed and of limited value. Despite what many see, rightly or wrongly, as the superficial shallowness of the broadcast talks, they are still accepted as a relatively accurate *summa* of the Christian faith. That is, with the exception of Lewis's avoidance of the minefield of atonement theories.

Lewis was an avid reader who could absorb even ancient texts with ease. Whilst focusing more and more on the patristic roots of the doctrinal ground of the faith he continued to write, broadcast, and preach, in particular against the background of wartime Britain. We know the outcome of the Second World War but Lewis and his readers/audience didn't. And there is nothing like war to focus the mind on the meaning and value of life, and wider questions about what may or may not lie beyond this life. Lewis was the man for the moment, the time. However, was this "fame" good for him and the development of his work? His doctrine and apologetics were sound, orthodox, though like all theologians, he needed others occasionally to keep him within the tramlines of orthodoxy, and the ever watchful eye of the Inklings to assess, rigorously, his work (in particular, J. R. R. Tolkien). The period of the Second World War, and the immediate post-war years was in many ways the most fruitful in Lewis's orthodox apologetics.

As Lewis matured, his wisdom on matters relating to the Christ event deepened; however, he began to be more and more out of step with the post-war spirit of the age, the brave new, never-had-it-so-good, world of Britain in the 1950s and 1960s. This difference was in many ways summed up by Humphrey Carpenter in his biography of the Inklings. John Wain, a former pupil of Lewis's, was invited as a junior research fellow to join the Inkling meetings. However, in the early 1950s, Wain developed away from the old school represented by Tolkien, Lewis, *et al.* Wain held Lewis in great admiration but he developed away from the Romantic basis of their work; he became associated with "The Movement," a group of writers who eschewed Romanticism and worked towards what was described as the "New Form." These writers included Kingsley Amis, Philip Larkin, Elizabeth Jennings, and Thom Gunn. "The Movement" was more interested in the world of politics and social change. Wain learnt from the Inklings the serious importance of literature as communication, but he was a modern realist who rejected their conservative socio-cultural beliefs, likewise their interest in what was mistakenly termed "fantasy" writing. The new realists firmly believed in the post-war Labour government and the welfare state as the final solution to humanity's ills and problems. Carpenter notes how Wain admired Lewis and the Inklings greatly but it was clear he failed to share their principles.[1] They were, to Wain, politically conservative, in many ways reactionary, High Anglican or Roman Catholic, and hostile to the spirit of modernism and liberalism: Lewis started to find himself out of touch with the post-war generation of undergraduates, many of whom, like John Wain, were beginning to be politically aware and to take the state of society rather more seriously than their predecessors had done. Lewis lamented this. "The modern world is so desperately serious," he remarked to Arthur Greeves.[2] Lewis found he was distanced, out of sympathy, with Oxbridge dons:

> It might or might not be true to say that Christians were in the minority in the senior common rooms of Oxford; but certainly those dons who did profess Christianity generally kept their religion to themselves, attending their college chapel or parish church but, not making any display of the fact, and certainly not writing popular books in the hope of converting others to their beliefs. Lewis, in fact, had offended against Oxford etiquette not by becoming a Christian, but by making a public matter of his conversion. He had refused to adopt the detached irony which Oxford has always regarded as an acceptable manner of cloaking one's true beliefs. He had indeed guyed this ironical detachment in the character of "Mr Sensible" in *The Pilgrim's Regress*.[3]

However, Carpenter also noted that although he could expose the irony and cloaked hypocrisy of academia successfully, he offered no critically ironic portrait of himself.

Lewis, the person, underwent a protracted conversion over a relatively long period (certainly compared to the seemingly instantaneous conversion of Paul); he did eventually give in to the Holy Spirit that brought him to accept Jesus as the Christ, as the self-revelation of the one true living God. This conversion affected every aspect of his life and changed him. Early on he started to write about what had happened to him—*The Pilgrim's Regress* (1933)—but soon found himself drawn into apologetics: writing to defend the Christian faith (*The Problem of Pain*, 1940). This became a career when he was invited to give *The Broadcast Talks* during World War Two. His "fame" developed, he published more; he had his detractors, but his work was received and valued by more and more. Professionally Lewis was an Oxford fellow—in English Literature; theologically he was, strictly speaking, an amateur. As a Christian apologist he valued this amateur status, which gave him a degree of independence from a clerical elite whom he often castigated as "modern" and/or "Liberal." But Lewis was more than an apologist; he was in effect a classical philosopher theologian. Underlying his work was a systematic theology, though incomplete. He had a well thought-out method—derived from Vincentius of Lérins and the seventeenth-century Puritan Richard Baxter—whereby he defined and asserted a "mere" core of orthodoxy: that which had been held by all during the patristic era; a "mere" core that developed in the early centuries of the church, which neither the Age of Reason, the Enlightenment, or "modern" and "Liberal" developments could undermine.

1 Carpenter, *The Inklings*, 206–7.
2 Ibid., 207.
3 Ibid., 207–8.

Although essentially unfinished as a systematic exposition of the Christian faith, and although framed most often as popular apologetics, given what we have established of Lewis methodology, the value he accorded to revelation and reason, and given the context we have established for his work against, in many ways, the "modern" tendency generally in Western Christianity, specifically in the Church of England of his day, Lewis's theology and philosophy is nonetheless cogent, convincing, biblical, and orthodox, while being original, imaginative, and of value. Therefore, in the second book in this series, we will turn to examine in depth certain aspects and themes of Lewis's work, which constitute elements of a systematic theology, which were the measure of the man and his faith: first, Lewis's doctrine of Scripture, that is, his understanding of the relationship between revelation and the Bible, and the gestation of his doctrine of transposition, which is the key to all his work. Second, what is often termed Lewis's trilemma, the "Mad, Bad, or God" argument for Christ's divinity: what did Lewis write and what was the history of this argument in *aut Deus aut malus homo* (either God, or a bad man)? Third, what we may term his doctrine of christological prefigurement, his understanding of the intimations God gave to people outside of the Judaeo-Christian tradition in the form of myths about incarnate, dying, and resuscitated "gods."

Select Bibliography

LETTERS AND ARTICLES BY C. S. LEWIS

Lewis, C. S., "Avant-Propos a l'édition Française." In *Le Problème de la Souffrance*, translated by Marguerite Faguer, 11–12. Paris: Desclée de Brouwer, 1950.

———. "Christian Apologetics." Paper read at the Carmarthen Conference for Youth Leaders and Junior Priests, Church of Wales, at Carmarthen, Easter 1945. In *Undeceptions: Essays on Theology and Ethics*, 64–76. London: Bles, 1971.

———. "Cross-Examination." In *Undeceptions: Essays on Theology and Ethics*, 215–21. London: Bles, 1971.

———. "De Descriptione Temporum." In *They Asked for a Paper: Papers and Addresses*, 9–25. London: Bles, 1962.

———. "The Efficacy of Prayer." In *The World's Last Night and Other Essays*, 3–12. New York: Harcourt, Brace, and World, 1960.

———. "God in the Dock." In *Undeceptions: Essays on Theology and Ethics*, 197–201. London: Bles, 1971.

———. "Introduction. New Learning and New Ignorance." In *English Literature in the Sixteenth Century*, 2–65. Oxford: Clarendon, 1954.

———. "Introduction." In George McDonald, *Phantastes*, v–x. Grand Rapids: Eerdmans, 2000.

———. "Introduction." In *St. Athanasius: The Incarnation of the Word. Being the Treatise of St. Athanasius, De incarnatione Verbi Dei*. Translated by Sr. Penelope CSMV, 5–12. London: Centenary, 1944.

———. "Is Theism Important?" In *Undeceptions: Essays on Theology and Ethics*, 138–42. London: Bles, 1971.

———. "Is Theology Poetry?" In *They Asked for a Paper: Papers and Addresses*, 150–65. London: Bles, 1962.

———. "It All Began with a Picture . . ." *The Radio Times, Junior Section*, CXLVIII (15 July 1960).

———. "Letter to Arthur Greeves, Dec. 6, 1931." In, *Collected Letters, Vol. II: Books, Broadcasts and War 1931–1949*, edited by Walter Hooper, 22–25. San Francisco: Harper, 2004.

———. "Letter to the Arthur Greeves, Oct. 18, 1931." In *Collected Letters, Vol. I: Family Letters 1905–1931*, edited by Walter Hooper, 975–77. San Francisco: Harper, 2004.

———. "Letter to the Arthur Greeves, Sept. 22, 1931." In *Collected Letters, Vol. I: Family Letters 1905–1931*, edited by Walter Hooper, 969–72. San Francisco: Harper, 2004.

———. "Letter to the Church Times, Feb. 8, 1952." In *Collected Letters, Vol. III: Narnia, Cambridge and Joy 1950–1963*, edited by Walter Hooper, 164. San Francisco: Harper, 2007.

———. "Letter to Clyde S. Kilby, Feb. 10, 1957." In *Collected Letters, Vol. III: Narnia, Cambridge and Joy 1950–1963*, edited by Walter Hooper, 830–31. San Francisco: Harper, 2007.

———. "Letter to Corbin Scott Carnell, Oct. 13, 1958." In *Collected Letters, Vol. III: Narnia, Cambridge and Joy 1950–1963*, edited by Walter Hooper, 978–80. San Francisco: Harper, 2007.

———. "Letter to Dom Bede Griffiths, Apr. 4, 1934." In *Collected Letters, Vol. II: Books, Broadcasts and War 1931–1949*, edited by Walter Hooper, 133–37. San Francisco: Harper, 2004.

———. "Letter to H. Lyman Stebbins, May 8, 1945." In *Collected Letters, Vol. II: Books, Broadcasts and War 1931–1949*, edited by Walter Hooper, 645–47, 1–12. San Francisco: Harper, 2004

———. "Letter to Mrs Emily McLay, Aug. 3, 1953." In *Collected Letters, Vol. III: Narnia, Cambridge and Joy 1950–1963*, edited by Walter Hooper, 354–55. San Francisco: Harper, 2007.

———. "Letter to Warren Lewis, Apr. 28, 1940." In *Collected Letters, Vol. II: Books, Broadcasts and War 1931-1949*, edited by Walter Hooper, 401-6, 1-12. San Francisco: Harper, 2004.

———. "Letter to Warren Lewis, Feb. 18, 1940." In *Collected Letters, Vol. II: Books, Broadcasts and War 1931-1949*, edited by Walter Hooper, 347-53. San Francisco: Harper, 2004.

———. "Lewis to Sister Penelope CSMV, May 15, 1941." In *Collected Letters, Vol. II: Books, Broadcasts and War 1931-1949*, edited by Walter Hooper, 484-85. San Francisco: Harper, 2004.

———. "Modern Theology and Biblical Criticism." Paper delivered at Westcott House, Cambridge, 11 May 1959. In *Christian Reflections*, 152-66. London: Bles, 1967.

———. "Must Our Image of God Go?" The Observer, March 24, 1963, 14.

———. "On Three Ways of Writing for Children." In *Of Other Worlds*, 22-34. London: Bles, 1966.

———. "The Poison of Subjectivism." In *Christian Reflections*, 72-81. London: Bles, 1967.

———. "Preface to the Third Edition." In *The Pilgrim's Regress: An Allegorical Apology for Christianity, Reason and Romanticism*. 3rd ed., ix-xx. London: Bless, 1944. (Note in some American reprints this "Preface" is placed at the end of the book and called an "Afterword.")

———. "The Psalms." In *Christian Reflections*, 114-28. London: Fount, 1967.

———. "Rejoinder to Dr Pittenger." Christian Century LXXV (26 November 1958) 1369-71.

———. "Religion and Rocketry." In *The World's Last Night and Other Essays*, 83-92. New York: Harcourt, Brace and World, 1960.

———. "Sometimes Fairy Stories May Say Best What's to be Said." In *Of Other Worlds*, 35-38. London: Bles, 1966.

———. "Transposition." 1st ed. A sermon given in Mansfield College, Oxford on Whit Sunday, 28 May 1944. In *Transposition and Other Addresses*, 9-20. London: Bless, 1949.

———. "Transposition." 2nd ed. In *They Asked for a Paper*, 166-82. London: Bles, 1962.

———. "We Have No 'Right to Happiness.'" In *Undeceptions: Essays on Theology and Ethics*, 265-69. London: Bles, 1971.

———. "The Weight of Glory." In *Transposition and Other Addresses*, 21-33. London: Bles, 1949.

———. "What Are We to Make of Jesus Christ?" In *Asking Them Questions* (Third Series), edited by Ronal Selby Wright, 49-53. Oxford: Oxford University Press, 1950.

———. "What Christmas Means to Me." *Undeceptions: Essays on Theology and Ethics*, 253-54. London: Bles, 1971.

———. "The World's Last Night." In *The World's Last Night and Other Essays*, 93-113. New York: Harcourt, Brace, 1960.

BOOKS BY C. S. LEWIS

Lewis, C. S., *The Allegory of Love: A Study in Medieval Tradition*. Oxford: Clarendon, 1936.

———. *Beyond Personality: The Christian Idea of God*. London: Centenary, 1944.

———. *Broadcast Talks: Reprinted with some alterations from two series of Broadcast Talks 'Right and Wrong: A Clue to the Meaning of the Universe' and 'What Christians Believe' given in 1941 and 1942*. London: Centenary, 1942.

———. *Christian Behaviour*. London: Centenary, 1943.

———. *Christian Reflections*. London: Fount, 1967.

———. *The Chronicles of Narnia: The Voyage of the Dawn Treader*. London: Bles, 1952.

———. *The Chronicles of Narnia: The Silver Chair*. London: Bles, 1953.

———. *Collected Letters, Vol. I—Family Letters 1905-1931*. Edited by Walter Hooper. San Francisco: Harper, 2004.

———. *Collected Letters, Vol. II—Books, Broadcasts and War 1931-1949*. Edited by Walter Hooper. San Francisco: Harper, 2004.

———. *Collected Letters, Vol. III—Narnia, Cambridge and Joy 1950-1963*. Edited by Walter Hooper. San Francisco: Harper, 2007.

———. *English Literature in the Sixteenth Century*. Oxford: Clarendon, 1954.

———. *The Four Loves*. London: Bles, 1960.

———. *The Great Divorce: A Dream*. London: Macmillan, 1945.

——— (writing as N. W. Clerk). *A Grief Observed*. London: Faber and Faber, 1961.

———. *Letters to Malcolm: Chiefly on Prayer*. London: Bles, 1964.
———. *Mere Christianity: A revised and amplified edition, with a new introduction, of the three books Broadcast Talks, Christian Behaviour and Beyond Personality*. London: Bles, 1952.
———. *Miracles: A Preliminary Study*. 1st ed. London: Bless, 1947.
———. *Miracles*. 2nd ed. London: Bless, 1960.
———. *Of Other Worlds*, 22–34. London: Bles, 1966.
———. *Out of the Silent Planet*. London: Bodley Head, 1938.
———. *Perelandra*. London: Bodley Head, 1943.
———. *The Pilgrim's Regress: An Allegorical Apology for Christianity, Reason and Romanticism*. 1st ed. London: Bless, 1933.
———. *The Pilgrim's Regress: An Allegorical Apology for Christianity, Reason and Romanticism*. 3rd ed. London: Bless, 1944.
———. *The Problem of Pain*. London: Centenary, 1940.
———. *Reflections on the Psalms*. London: Bles, 1958.
———. *The Screwtape Letters*. London: Centenary, 1942.
———. *Selected Literary Essays*. Cambridge: Cambridge University Press, 1969.
———. *Surprised by Joy: The Shape of my Early Life*. London: Bles, 1955.
———. *They Asked for a Paper: Papers and Addresses*. London: Bles, 1962.
———. *Till We Have Faces*. London: Bles, 1956.
———. *Transposition and Other Addresses*. London: Bles, 1949.
———. *Undeceptions: Essays on Theology and Ethics*. Edited by Walter Hooper. London: Bles, 1971. (Published in the USA as, God in the Dock: Essays on Theology and Ethics. Grand Rapids: Eerdmans, 1970.)
———. *The Weight of Glory*. Series: Little Books of Religion, no. 189. London: SPCK, 1942.
———. *The World's Last Night and Other Essays*. New York: Harcourt, Brace, 1960.

OTHER BOOKS AND ARTICLES

Adam, Karl. "Die Theologie der Krisis." *Hochland* XXIII (1926) 271–86.
Alexander, Samuel. *Space, Time and Deity—The Gifford Lectures 1910-1918. Volumes I and II*. London: Macmillan, 1920.
Anselm of Canterbury. *The Proslogion*. In Brian Davies and G. R. Evans, *Anselm of Canterbury: The Major Works*. Oxford: Oxford University Press, 1998.
Augustine. *The City of God*. Edited by David Knowles, translated by Henry Bettenson. Harmondsworth, UK: Pelican, 1972.
———. *Confessions*. Translated by Henry Chadwick. Oxford: Oxford University Press, 1991.
———. *Sancti Aurelii Augustini Retractationum libri II*. Edited by Almut Mutzenbecher. Turnholti: Brepols, 1984.
Aulén, Gustaf. *Christus Victor: An Historical Study of the Three Main Types of the Idea of the Atonement*. London: SPCK, 1931.
Balsbaugh, John. "The Pagan and the Post-Christian: Lewis's Understanding of Diversity Outside the Faith." In *C. S. Lewis Light Bearer in the Shadowlands*, edited by Angus J. L. Menuge, 191–210. Wheaton, IL: Crossway, 1997.
Balthasar, Hans Urs von. *Karl Barth, Darstellung und Deutung seiner Theologie*. Köln: Hegner, 1951.
Barth, Karl. *The Church Dogmatics*. 14 Vols. Translated and edited G. W. Bromiley and T. F. Torrance. Edinburgh: T. & T. Clark, 1936–77.
———. "Concluding Unscientific Postscript on Schleiermacher." In *The Theology of Schleiermacher: Lectures at Göttingen, Winter Semester 1923-4*. Translated by Geoffrey Bromiley, 261–79. Grand Rapids: Eerdmans, 1982.
———. "Evangelische Theologie im 19. Jahrhundert." An address delivered at the meeting of the Goethegsellschaft in Hanover, 8th January 1957. In *Evangelische Theologie im 19. Jahrhundert*. Zürich: Zollikon, 1957.
———. *Fragments Grave and Gay*. London: Collins, 1971.
———. "Die Gerechtigkeit Gottes." In *Das Wort Gottes und die Theoligie*, 1–17. München: Kaiser, 1925.

———. *Karl Barth–Eduard Thurneysen Briefwechsel Band II 1921–1930*. Zürich: Theologischer, 1973.

———. *Karl Barth–Rudolf Bultmann Letters 1922–1966*. Translated and edited G. W. Bromiley. Edinburgh: T. & T. Clark, 1971.

———. "Kriegszeit und Gottesreich." In *Glaube und kommunikative Praxis*, edited by Herbert Anzinger, 120–22. München: Kaiser, 1991.

———. *Die Menschlichkeit Gottes*. Zürich: Zollikon, 1956.

———. "Nachwort." In *Schleiermacher-Auswahl*. Series, edited by Siebenstern Taschenbuch 113–14. München: Siebenstern Taschenbuch, 1968.

———. *Natural Theology: Comprising "Nature & Grace" by Professor Dr Emil Brunner and the reply "No!" by Dr Karl Barth*. Translated by John Baillie. 1934. Reprint. London: Centenary, 1946.

———. *Predigten 1913*. Gesamtausgabe, Band.8, Predigte, 4. Mai 1913. Zürich: Theologischer, 1994.

———. "Der römische Katholizismus als Frage an die protestantische Kirche." In *Die Theoligie und die Kirche Evangelischer*, 329–63. Zürich: Zollikon, 1928.

Baxter, Richard. *Church-History of the Government of Bishops and their Councils*. London: Simmons, 1680.

———. "What History is Credible, and What Not." In *Church-History of the Government of Bishops and their Councils*, ix–xviii. London: Simmons, 1680.

Brazier, P. H. *Barth and Dostoevsky: A Study of the Influence of the Russian Writer Fyodor Mikhailovich Dostoevsky on the Development of the Swiss Theologian Karl Barth, 1915–1922*. Milton Keynes, UK: Paternoster, 2008.

———. "Barth and Rome: A Critical Engagement." *The Downside Review*, 12.431 (2005) 137–52.

———. "Barth and Rome—II: Socialism, the Church and a Theocratic Illusion." *The Downside Review*, 124.434, (2006) 61–78.

———. "C. S. Lewis and Christological Prefigurement." *The Heythrop Journal*, 48.5 (2007) 742–775.

———. "C. S. Lewis and the Anscombe Debate: from *analogia entis* to *analogia fidei*." *The Journal of Inklings Studies*, 1.2 (2011), 69–123.

———. "C. S. Lewis: A Doctrine of Transposition." *The Heythrop Journal*, 50.4 (2009) 669–88.

———. "C. S. Lewis on Revelation & Second Meanings: A Philosophical & Pneumatological Justification." *The Chronicle of the Oxford University C. S. Lewis Society*, 7.1 (2010) 18–35.

———. "C. S. Lewis on Scripture and the Christ, the Word of God: Convergence and Divergence with Karl Barth." *Sehnsucht*, 4 (2010) 89–109.

———. "The Pittenger–Lewis Debate: Fundamentals of an Ontological Christology." *The Chronicle of the Oxford University C. S. Lewis Society* 6.1 (2009) 7–23.

———. "Why Father Christmas Appears in Narnia." *Sehnsucht* 3 (2009) 61–77.

Brumley, Mark, "The Relevance and Challenge of C. S. Lewis." Ignatius Insight website, November 29, 2005. No pages. Online http://www.ignatiusinsight.com/features2005/print2005/mbrumley_relcslewis_nov05.html.

Bullock, Karen O'Dell, *Shepherd's Notes: Writings of Justin Martyr*. Nashville, TN: B. & H., 1999.

Busch, Eberhard, "God is God: The Meaning of a Controversial Formula and the Fundamental Problem of Speaking about God." *Princeton Seminary Bulletin* 7.2 (1986) 101–13.

———. *Karl Barths Lebenslauf: nach seinem Briefen und autobiographischen Texten*. München: Kaiser, 1975.

Calvin, John. *Institutes of the Christian Religion*. Edited by John T. McNeill. Library of Christian Classics. Louisville, KY: Westminster John Knox, 2006.

Carpenter, Humphrey. *The Inklings: C. S. Lewis, J. R. R. Tolkien, Charles Williams and their Friends*. London: Allen & Unwin, 1978.

Chesterton, G. K. *The Everlasting Man*. London: Hodder & Stoughton, 1925.

———. *Orthodoxy*. New York: Doubleday, 2001.

Clerk, N. W. *A Grief Observed*. London: Faber and Faber, 1961.

Cranmer, Thomas. "The Order of the Ministration of Holy Communion." *The Church of England Book of Common Prayer, 1662*, 256–81. Oxford: Oxford University Press, 1995.

D'Costa, Gavin. *Christian Uniqueness Reconsidered: the Myth of a Pluralistic Theology of Religions*. Maryknoll, NY: Orbis, 1990.

———. "The Impossibility of a Pluralist View of Religion." *Religious Studies* 32 (1996) 223–32.

———. *Christianity and World Religions: Disputed Questions in the Theology of Religions*. Chichester, UK: Wiley-Blackwell, 2009.

Davidman, Joy. "The Longest Way Round." In *These Found the Way: Thirteen Converts to Protestant Christianity*, edited by David Soper, 13–26. Philadelphia: Westminster, 1951.

Dearborn, Kerry. *Baptized Imagination: The Theology of George MacDonald*. Ashgate Studies in Theology, Imagination and the Arts. Aldershot UK: Ashgate, 2006.

Derrick, Christopher. *C. S. Lewis and the Church of Rome: A Study in Proto-Ecumenism*. San Francisco, CA: Ignatius, 1981.

Dorsett, Lyle W. *And God Came In: The Extraordinary Story of Joy Davidman, Her Life and Marriage to C. S. Lewis*. New York: Macmillan, 1983.

Dostoevsky, Fyodor Mikhailovich. *The Idiot*. Translated by Richard Pevear and Larissa Volokhonsky. London: Everyman's Library, 1993.

Edwards, Mark. "C. S. Lewis and Early Christian Literature." In *C. S. Lewis and the Church: Essays in Honor of Walter Hooper*, edited by Judith Wolfe and Brendan N. Wolfe, 23–39. London: Continuum, 2011.

Edwards, David L. *The Honest to God Debate: Some Reactions to the Book 'Honest to God' with a New Chapter by its Author, J. A. T. Robinson, Bishop of Woolwich*. London: SCM, 1963.

Erskine, Thomas. *Remarks on the Internal Evidence for the Truth of Revealed Religion*. Edinburgh: Waugh, Innes, and Hamilton, 1820.

Feuerbach, Ludwig. *The Essence of Christianity*. Gesammelte Werke, Vol. 5. Edited by W. Schuffenhauer. Berlin: Akademie, 1973.

Forsyth, Peter Taylor. *The Person and Place of Jesus Christ: The Congregational Union Lecture for 1909*. London: Hodder & Stoughton, 1910.

Fox–Genovese, Elizabeth. "The Way of Conversion." *Crisis* 20.6 (2002). Online: http://www.catholicity.com/commentary/genovese/08018.html.

Gerrish, Brian A. "Feuerbach's Religious Illusion." *Christian Century* 114 (1997) 362–65, 67.

Gibson, Evan K. *C. S. Lewis, Spinner of Tales: A Guide to his Fiction*. Washington DC: Christian College Press, 1980.

Green, Roger Lancelyn, and Walter Hooper. *C. S. Lewis: A Biography*. 2nd ed. London: Harper Collins, 2002.

Gunton, Colin E. *The Barth Lectures*. Transcribed and edited by P. H. Brazier. London: T. & T. Clark, 2007.

———. *Revelation and Reason: Prolegomena to Systematic Theology*. Transcribed and edited by P. H. Brazier. London: T. & T. Clark, 2008.

Hamilton, Clive. *Dymer*. London: Dent, 1926.

———. *Spirits in Bondage*. London: Heinemann, 1919.

"Hebrew Idioms and Blood of Lamb." *The Christian Classics Ethereal Library Website*. Online: http://www.ccel.org/node/4938.

Heck, Joel D. "Praeparatio Evangelica." In *C. S. Lewis, Light Bearer in the Shadowlands*, edited by Angus J. L. Menuge, 235–57. Wheaton, IL: Crossway, 1997.

Herrmann, Wilhelm. *The Communion of the Christian with God*. Philadelphia: Fortress, 1971.

Hick, John. *An Interpretation of Religion: Human Responses to the Transcendent*. Basingstoke, UK: Macmillan, 1989.

Hooper, Walter. *C. S. Lewis: A Companion and Guide*. London: Harper & Collins, 1996.

Hume, David. *An Enquiry Concerning Human Understanding and Other Writings*. Edited by Stephen Buckle. Cambridge: Cambridge University Press, 2007.\

Jenson, Robert. *Systematic Theology Vol. 1: The Triune God*. Oxford: Oxford University Press, 1997.

Johnson, Aaron P. *Ethnicity and Argument in Eusebius' Praeparatio Evangelica*. Oxford: Oxford University Press, 2006.

Kierkegaard, Søren. *Einübung in Christentum*. Halle: Fricke, 1878.

MacDonald, George. *Phantastes, a Faerie Romance*. Grand Rapids: Eerdmans, 2000.

———. *Unspoken Sermons: Series I, II and III*. Charleston, SC: Biblio Bazar, 2007.

Macquarrie, John. *Christology Revisited*. Harrisburg, PA: Trinity, 1998.

———. *Jesus Christ in Modern Thought*. London: SCM, 1990.

Markos, Louis. *From Achilles to Christ: Why Christians Should Read the Pagan Classics.* Downers Grove, IL: InterVarsity, 2007.
McCormack, Bruce. *Karl Barth's Critically Realistic Dialectical Theology: Its Genesis and Development 1909-1936.* Oxford: Clarendon, 1995.
McGrath, Alister. *Christian Theology.* Oxford: Blackwell, 1994.
Mueller, Steven P. "Christology in the Writings of C. S. Lewis." In *C. S. Lewis, Light Bearer in the Shadowlands,* edited by Angus J. L. Menuge, 279–302. Wheaton, IL: Crossway, 1997.
Nicholi, Armand. *The Question of God: C. S. Lewis and Sigmund Freud Debate God, Love, Sex and the Meaning of Life.* New York: Free, 2002.
Norris, Jr., Richard A. "Memorial Eucharist for W. Norman Pittenger, Chapel of the Good Shepherd, The General Theological Seminary, The Feast of Lancelot Andrewes, 1997." *The Anglican Theological Review* (Winter 1998). Online: http://findarticles.com/p/articles/mi_qa3818/is_199801/ai_n8791642/.
Nygren, Anders. *Agape & Eros (Part 1: A Study of the Christian Idea of Love and Part II: The History of the Christian Idea of Love, in One Volume).* Translated by Philip S. Watson. London: SPCK, 1957.
Pearce, Joseph. *C. S. Lewis and the Catholic Church.* San Francisco: Ignatius, 2003.
Phillips, Justin. *C. S. Lewis at the BBC: Messages of Hope in the Darkness of War.* London: Harper Collins, 2002.
Pittenger, W. Norman. "Apologist versus Apologist: A Critique of C. S. Lewis as 'Defender of the Faith.'" *Christian Century* LXXV (1958) 1104–7.
———. *Christology Reconsidered.* London: SCM, 1970.
———. *God in Process.* London: SCM, 1967.
———. *Love and Control in Sexuality.* Philadelphia: United Church, 1974.
———. *Making Sexuality Human.* Philadelphia: United Church, 1970.
———. *Process Thought and Christian Faith.* New York: Macmillan, 1968.
———. *Time for Consent: A Christian's Approach to Homosexuality.* London: SCM, 1970.
———. *The Word Incarnate: A Study of the Doctrine of the Person of Christ.* London: Harper, 1959.
Plato. "Theaetetus." In *Plato Complete Works,* translated by M. J. Levett, revised by Myles Burnyeat, and edited by John M. Cooper, 157–234. Indianapolis, IN: Hackett, 1997.
Price, H. H. "Is Theism Important?" *The Socratic Digest* 5 (1952) 39–47.
Robinson, J. A. T. *Honest to God.* London: SCM, 1963.
———. "Our Image of God Must Go." *The Observer,* March 17, 1963, 21–22, 39–40.
Schama, Simon. *The American Future: A History.* New York: Ecco, 2009.
Sibley, Brian. *Shadowlands: The True Story of C. S. Lewis and Joy Davidman.* London: Hodder & Stoughton, 1985.
Stellars, J. T. *Reasoning beyond Reason.* Eugene, OR: Pickwick, 2011.
Tegnér's, Esaias. "Drapa." In *The Seaside and the Fireside,* edited by Henry Wadsworth Longfellow. Boston, MA: Ticknor, Reed, and Fields, 1849. Online: http://www.thehypertexts.com/Tegner's%20Drapa%20Translation.htm.
Thompson, Francis. *The Hound of Heaven.* London: Burns Oates & Washbourne, 1900.
Traupé, A. "Saint Augustine." In *Patrology: The Golden Age of Latin Patristic Literature, Vol. 4,* edited by Johannes Quasten and Angelo Di Berardino, 56–84. Westminster, MD: Christian Classics, 1986.
Tyrrell, George, S.J. *Christianity at the Cross-Roads.* London: Longmans Green, 1909.
Vincent of Lérins. *The Commonitory of Vincent of Lérins, for the Antiquity and Universality of the Catholic Faith against the Profane Novelties of all Heresies.* Translated by C. A. Heurtley, edited by Philip Schaff and Henry Wace, 207–60. In *The Nicene & Post-Nicene Fathers, Second Series, Vol. 11, Sulpitius Severus, Vincent of Lerins, John Cassian.* Grand Rapids: Eerdmans, 2002.
Watkins, Duff. "The Screwtape Letters and Process Theism." *Process Studies,* 8.2 (1978) 114–18.
Webster, John. *Barth.* London: Continuum, 2000.
Weil, Simone. *First and Last Notebooks.* Translated by Richard Rees. Oxford: Oxford University Press, 1970.
———. *On Science, Necessity, and the Love of God.* Edited by Richard Rees. Oxford: Oxford University Press, 1968.
———. *The Simone Weil Reader.* Wakefield, RI: Bell, 1977.

Bibliography

———. *Waiting on God*. Translated by Emma Crauford from *L'Attente de Dieu* with an introduction by Fr. J. M. Perrin. London: Routledge & Kegan Paul, 1950.

Welch, James. Letter to C. S. Lewis, Feb. 7, 1941. In *C. S. Lewis at the BBC: Messages of Hope in the Darkness of War*, edited by Justin Phillips, 79–80. London: Harper Collins, 2002.

Wirt, Sherwood E., and C. S. Lewis. "I was Decided Upon." *Decision* II (September, 1963) 3.

———. "Heaven, Earth and Outer Space." *Decision* II (October, 1963) 4.

Wolters, Clifford. *The Cloud of Unknowing and Other Works*. Translated with an Introduction by Clifford Wolters. London: Penguin, 1978.

Wolterstorff, Nicholas. "C. S. Lewis on the Problem of Suffering." *The Chronicle of the Oxford University C. S. Lewis Society* 7.3 (Michaelmas 2010) 3–20.

Wright, N. T. "Simply Lewis: Reflections on a Master Apologist After 60 Years." In *Touchstone Magazine* 20.2 (March 2007) 39–40. Online: http://www.touchstonemag.com/archives/article.php?id=20-02-028-f.

Index of Names

Abraham 187–88, 245
Adam (Old Testament) 49, 74, 154, 158, 172, 212, 223, 255
Adam, Karl 74
Addison's Walk 39, 43, 218, 229, 247
Adonis 231
Alexander, Samuel 35, 254
America, United States of 54, 60, 78
Amis, Kingsley 262
Anscombe, Elizabeth 134, 150–51, 207
Anselm of Canterbury 90–91, 115, 126
Anzinger, Herbert 84
Aquinas, Thomas 72, 74, 113, 155
Aristotle 116, 155, 210
Arnold, Matthew 95, 127
Aslan (The Chronicles of Narnia) 16, 23, 92, 133, 138, 143, 205–6, 207, 222–24, 231, 257
Athanasius 107, 204
Athens 116
Augustine of Hippo 6, 31, 65, 69, 70–71, 80, 93, 113, 115, 121–22, 158, 162, 255
Aulén, Gustaf 113, 137, 211–12
Austen, Jane 107

Balder 24, 231
Barfield, Owen 154, 175, 253
Barth, Karl 12, 20, 65, 72–94, 96–99, 104, 128–29, 139–40, 143–44, 229
Bates, Percy 154
Baxter, Richard 13, 103, 107–9, 111, 113, 115–16, 121–22, 126, 128, 143, 168, 203–4, 263
BBC (British Broadcasting Corporation) 13, 107–9, 134, 149, 150–53, 159–61, 175, 177, 207, 216, 231
Beethoven, Ludwig Van 10
Bennett, J. A. W. 154
Beowulf 107
Berlin 76
Berne 76
Bethlehem 110
Blumhardts, Christoph and Johann 81, 87

Bonhoeffer, Dietrich 92
Bultmann, Rudolf 144, 195
Bunyan, John 48, 206
Busch, Eberhard 74, 85–86, 88–90, 92, 104

Calvin, John 72, 95, 158
Campbell College 25
Carpenter, Humphrey 154, 229, 262–63
Caspian, Prince (The Chronicles of Narnia) 205, 209, 222–24
Cecil, Lord David 154
Chaucer 107
Chesterton, G. K., 34–35, 104, 115, 127
Coghill, Nevill 34, 154
Constable, John 10, 126
Council of Trent, The 78

Damascus 39, 46, 48, 70, 229
Dante 34, 107, 113, 206
David (Old Testament) 2, 55, 57, 154, 184, 186, 220
Davidman, Joy 12, 15, 51, 54–55, 57–61, 63, 65–66, 68, 70–71, 87, 90, 93, 94, 97–99, 123, 145, 240, 243–44
D'Costa, Gavin 196
Dearborn, Kerry 52
Dostoevsky, Fyodor Mikhailovich 40, 78, 80, 86–87, 227, 234–36
Dundas-Grant, James 154
Dyson, Hugo 35, 37, 39, 43, 45, 47, 49, 63, 154, 218, 228–29, 247

Eddison, E. R., 154
Eliot, T. S., 104
Erskine, Thomas, of Linlathen 177, 183
Europe 9, 42, 54, 70, 78, 108, 114, 140, 255
Eustace (The Chronicles of Narnia) 222–23

Fenn, Eric 149, 152
Fessio, Fr. S. J., 11

273

Feuerbach, Ludwig 66, 67, 93, 98
Fillipovna, Nastasya, (The Idiot) 234, 236
Fox, Adam 34, 69, 154
Frazer, Sir James George 178

Garden of Gethsemane 238, 242, 252
Gideon (Old Testament) 220
God 1-9, 12-15, 17, 19, 20-22, 24-32, 34-35, 36-37, 39, 40-43, 45-48, 50-63, 65-78, 81-99, 104, 106-7, 110, 112, 114-17, 119-22, 124-26, 128-31, 133-34, 136-41, 143-45, 147, 149-50, 152-73, 175, 177-84, 186-96, 198, 199-4, 207, 209-21, 224, 227-35, 238-48, 250-61
    Christ 1-10, 12-16, 19-23, 25, 29-30, 37, 39-43, 45-53, 55-63, 65-79, 82-83, 86-88, 90-99, 103-6, 109-10, 112-13, 115-7, 119-28, 131, 133-34, 136-41, 143-45, 147, 149-51, 155-59, 162-74, 177-79, 181-84, 187-98, 200-18, 220-22, 224-25, 227-42, 244-51, 253-55, 257-58, 260-61
    Father, God the 11, 15-16, 19-20, 25, 43, 74, 84, 89, 93, 117, 131, 138, 141, 156, 158, 170-73, 180-81, 194, 214, 216-17, 221-32, 236, 239, 243, 248-49, 258-59
    Holy Spirit 4, 14-15, 19, 22, 30-32, 34-35, 37, 40, 42, 45, 47, 51-53, 56-58, 61-62, 67-71, 81, 86-90, 97-98, 104-5, 117, 123, 128, 131, 144, 165, 171, 179-180, 192, 196-97, 200, 210-13, 215-16, 217-18, 227-32, 236, 245-46, 248, 255-56, 259-60, 263
    Jesus 1, 3-6, 8, 10, 12-15, 19-22, 29, 31, 37, 39, 40-43, 45, 47-48, 53, 59, 61, 63, 65, 67, 72, 74-75, 77-79, 83-84, 87-88, 90, 95-96, 98-99, 109, 106, 109-10, 112, 120-22, 124, 131, 133-34, 136-38, 140-41, 143-45, 149, 156-58, 164-69, 172-73, 177, 179, 181-82, 186, 189-90, 193-94, 96-97, 205, 207-9, 214, 216-17, 221, 125, 227, 229, 230, 232, 234-35, 238, 244, 246-49, 252-53, 255, 261-63
    m/Messiah 1-3, 14, 124, 205, 214-15, 218, 221, 248
    Nazareth, Jesus of 1-4, 7, 9, 14-15, 20, 76, 79, 106, 133-34, 139-40, 143, 145, 158, 169, 194, 196, 205, 208, 211, 213-16, 222, 235, 238, 245-47, 262
Graham, Billy 73, 95, 127
Green, Roger Lancelyn 21, 26, 154, 209

Greeves, Arthur 27, 39, 43, 45, 49, 117, 175, 218, 263
Gresham, William Lindsay 51, 55, 60, 63, 64, 68
Griffiths, Dom Bede 106, 175, 209
Gunn, Thom 262
Gunton, Colin E., 7, 73, 81, 86-87, 143, 195-96, 229

Hamilton, Revd. Thomas R., 21, 52
Hardie, Colin 154
Harper, Annie 23
Havard, Robert 154
Headington (Oxford) 35, 46, 47
Headington Hill 35, 46
Hegel, Georg Wilhelm Friedrich 86, 98, 162, 260
Herbert, George 84, 113
Herrmann, Wilhelm 76, 78, 84-86
Hick, John 195, 196
Hooker, Richard 34, 113
Hooper, Walter 21, 26, 106, 134, 153-54
Hoyle, Sir Fred 248, 257
Hume, David 184-85
Husserl, Edmund 71

Inklings, The 104, 149, 154-55, 229, 262-63
Irving, David 186
Israel 2, 104, 188, 245

Jennings, Elizabeth 262
Jenson, Robert 66-67
Jill (The Chronicles of Narnia) 223-24
John (New Testament) 24, 26-29, 31, 39-40, 43, 46, 48-50, 72, 87, 92, 117, 123-24, 134, 144, 153-54, 182-83, 193, 195, 211-12, 237-38, 248, 257, 262-63
Joseph (New Testament) 11, 54, 67, 126

Kant, Immanuel 12, 76, 86, 199
Keats, John 10, 98, 202
Kierkegaard, Søren 78, 80, 165
Kirkpatrick, William T. 26, 31, 41, 53
Kutter, Hermann 81, 86-87, 104

Larkin, Philip 262
Lazarus (New Testament) 24, 190
Leatherhead 33, 51-52, 56-57, 98
Lewis
    Lewis, Flora Augusta, née Hamilton 21, 24-25, 48, 52, 183, 193
    Lewis, A. J. (Albert James) 24, 26

Index of Names

Lewis, C. S. (Clive Staples, "Jack") 1, 3–12, 14–20, 21, 22–31, 33–50, 52–72, 73–99, 103–10, 112–17, 119–31, 133–41, 143–45, 147, 149–75, 177–219, 221–25, 227–33, 237–64
Lewis, W. H. (Warren Hamilton, "Warnie") 21, 23–27, 46, 48, 133, 154
Lion of Judah (Old Testament) 62
Lock, Revd Dr. Walter 134
Longfellow, Henry Wadsworth 10, 24
Lucy (The Chronicles of Narnia) 222–23
Luke (New Testament) 63, 68, 110, 112, 167, 173, 221, 248
Lyman Stebbins, H., 116–17, 175

MacDonald, George 12, 33–34, 51–53, 59, 96, 155, 242
Magdalen College 37, 39, 43, 46, 52, 61, 86, 229, 247
Malvern 25–27
Manhattan 54–55, 137
Marburg 76
Mark (New Testament) 22, 52, 63, 68, 110, 112, 114, 127, 131, 167, 173, 197, 201, 221, 234, 246, 248
Martyr, Justin 119, 124, 125
Marx, Karl 59, 72
Mary (New Testament) 1, 39–40, 67, 117, 121, 175, 188, 199, 216–17
Mary Magdalene (New Testament) 39–40
Mathew, Gervase 154
Matthew (New Testament) 42, 62, 68, 94–95, 110, 127
McCallum, R. B., 154
McGrath, Alister 66
McLeod Campbell, John 183
Milton, John 23, 34, 107, 113
Monreale 15
Mozart, Wolfgang Amadeus 72, 73, 126
Myshkin, Prince (The Idiot) 234–36, 242

New Atheists, The 207
Newman, John Henry 238
New York 51, 54–57, 64, 71, 98, 137, 256
Nicodemus (New Testament) 31, 46
Nygren, Anders 113

Origen 119, 125
Orual, (Till We Have Faces) 227, 232–36, 239
Osiris 231
Overbeck, Franz 80

Oxford 6, 8, 11, 12, 15, 21, 25, 29, 34, 39, 40–43, 47, 50, 52–53, 72–73, 91, 98, 104, 125, 130, 133–34, 150–51, 153–54, 175, 184, 199, 203, 207, 221, 244, 253, 263

Pascal, Blaise 34, 155, 252
Paul (New Testament) 45, 48, 66, 69, 70, 72, 74, 94, 110, 126, 134, 157, 165, 168, 172–73, 210, 218, 220, 258, 263
Pearce, Joseph 11–12, 126–27
Pelagius 255
Penelope, Sr. 107, 122, 175, 204
Perrin, Fr. 70–71
Peter (New Testament) 11, 20, 39, 40, 86, 92, 94, 135, 193, 197, 248
Pevensie children, The (The Chronicles of Narnia) 222
Phillips, Justin 152–53, 216
Picasso, Pablo 126
Pittenger, W. Norman 13, 133–41, 143–45, 157, 178, 193, 209, 227, 232, 259–60
Pius X, Pope 74
Plato 7, 34, 116, 155, 231, 254
Protagoras 254
Psyche, (Till We Have Faces) 227, 232–36, 239, 242

Rackham, Arthur 27
Ragaz, Leonard 81
Ransom, Elwin (Out of the Silent Planet) 206, 228, 231–33
Ritschl, Albrecht 76, 78, 81
Robinson, J. A. T., 228, 257–59
Rogozhin, Parfyon Semyonovich (The Idiot) 234–36
Rubicon, The 36–37, 62, 65, 73, 87, 93, 97, 182

Safenwil 75, 79–81, 84
Sampson, Ashley 154
Samson (Old Testament) 150, 220
Samuel (Old Testament) 35, 220
Satan 163, 165, 189–91, 197, 231, 254
Sayers, Dorothy 104
Schleiermacher, Friedrich 81–82, 86, 98
Scott Carnell, Corbin 113, 209, 212
Screwtape (The Screwtape Letters) 60, 150–51, 175, 177, 182, 191–93, 196–97, 199, 206, 209, 224, 231, 261
Shakespeare, William 63, 258
Spenser, Edmund 113
Stein, Edith 65, 70–72, 90
Stevens, C. E. 154

Stoics, The 124, 190, 199, 237–38
Surrey 26, 33, 53

Teresa of Avila 71–72
Thompson, Francis 51, 60–62
Thurneysen, Eduard 86–87
Tolkien, Christopher 154
Tolkien, J. R. R. (Ronald Reuel Tolkien) 15, 33, 35, 37, 39, 43, 45, 47, 49, 63, 104–5, 149, 154–55, 218, 228–29, 247, 253, 262
Traherne, Thomas 113
Tübingen 76
Turner, Joseph Mallord William 10, 209
Tyrrell S. J., George 79

University of St. Andrews 133

Valhalla 32
Vidler, Revd. Dr. Alec R., 134
Vincentius of Lérins 13, 103–7, 114, 116, 121, 136, 168, 197, 203, 263

Wagner, Richard 10, 27, 33
Wain, John 154, 262–63
Weil, Simone 65, 70–71, 90, 241
Welch, James 149, 152–53, 216
Whipsnade Zoo 45, 47, 49
Whitehead, Alfred North 180, 193
Williams, Charles 104, 149, 154
Wirt, Sherwood E. Wirt 95, 127, 209, 259
Wolterstorff, Nicholas 241
Wordsworth, William 10, 98
Wrenn, James 154
Wright, N. T., 3, 11, 205, 208, 211, 224, 241
Wynyard School 25–26, 29, 47

Index of Subjects

academic 5–6, 11, 20, 27, 83, 128–30, 136, 150, 177, 198, 208–12, 216, 245–46, 251, 255, 261
actuality 75, 91
aesthetic 22–23, 30, 36, 41, 56
affliction 13, 144, 149–50, 238, 242 *see: pain, suffering*
Age of Reason 6–7, 9–10, 65–66, 78, 98, 113–14, 120, 124, 142, 194–96, 254–56, 263
agnostic 70–71 *see: Enlightenment*
allegory 47–48, 53, 206, 257
    allegorical 31, 47–48, 206, 251
analogy 26, 98, 169–70, 181–83, 185–86, 191, 203, 206, 222, 231, 236, 244, 246, 256–57, 261, 262
    analogical 5, 182, 191, 196, 199, 201, 205–207, 222, 227, 231, 235–38, 256, 261
    analogically 206, 240
Anglican 3–4, 20, 23, 73, 75, 79, 98, 103–4, 107, 110, 116–20, 122, 127, 130, 134, 145, 194, 197, 219, 246–48, 263 *see: church*
Anglo-Catholic 25–26, 103–5, 120, 175, 191, 193, 219 *see: church*
anima naturaliter Christiana 233
anointed/anointing 1–2, 238

anthropology 66, 73, 234, 254
anthropomorphism 178, 258
antiecclesiastical 43 *see: church*
Apollinarianism 133, 136, 137, 138
apologetic(s) 1, 5, 8, 12–16, 25, 68, 92, 103, 112–14, 119–21, 123, 127, 130–35, 137–38, 144–45, 149–54, 169, 177–78, 182, 196, 200, 206, 215, 222, 227–29, 231, 237, 247, 250–53, 256–58, 262–64
apologist(s) 5, 8, 10–14, 21, 40, 73, 91, 99, 119, 124, 131–37, 140–41, 144–47, 149, 177, 203–205, 208, 216–17, 227, 232, 257–58, 259, 261
apostasy 27, 197–99, 229
    apostate 12, 23, 42–44, 63, 106, 153, 198, 225, 228
a posteriori 2
apostle(s) 2–3, 7–8, 11, 76–78, 106, 109, 115–17, 127, 141, 157, 208, 216–17, 249 *see: disciples*
    apostolic 7, 117, 140
    sub–apostolic 7
ascension 2, 211, 237, 249, 251
    ascended 15, 30, 39, 47, 58, 61, 66–67, 72, 216–17, 229, 238–40, 253, 259, 261

Index of Subjects

aseity 36, 84–86, 88–89, 91, 97
atheism 20–21, 27, 29, 31, 36, 40–41, 47, 54–57, 59, 62, 66, 68, 75, 119–20, 194, 198, 216, 235 *see: theism*
    atheist(s) 8, 12, 20, 26, 28, 36, 40–41, 51, 54–55, 57–58, 59–61, 63, 66–67, 88, 91, 119–20, 184, 194, 208, 257
    atheistic 10, 21, 23, 27–30, 33, 36, 41, 44–47, 54, 57, 68, 70, 104, 106, 119–20, 194, 198, 225
    atonement 14–15, 44, 75, 78, 137, 151, 164–65, 172–73, 183, 189, 205, 212–14, 218–19, 222, 224, 229–30, 242–43, 225 *see: salvation*
    aut Deus aut malus homo 247, 264

Baptist 3, 104, 123
    baptized 12, 21, 46, 51–53, 57, 63, 71, 86–87, 104, 112, 129–31, 190, 237
beauty 10, 16, 22–23, 30–32, 51, 56–59, 74, 93, 199, 202–203, 230–33, 237
Bible 3, 8, 11, 26, 30, 59, 75, 79, 81, 86–87, 105, 112, 127, 130, 136, 147, 152, 171, 208, 221, 246, 249, 251, 258, 264 *see: Scripture*
    biblical 8, 12, 74, 83, 86–87, 104, 110, 119–21, 126, 130–33, 136, 139, 142–43, 145, 150, 197, 205, 210, 215, 252, 252, 253
blood 14, 44, 66, 138, 157, 172, 193–94, 205, 215, 218–25, 230–31, 239–42, 248
    blood of the lamb 14, 205, 218–21, 230
broadcast(s) 13, 40, 107–109, 123, 131, 145–47, 149–53, 159–61, 164, 166, 169, 175, 177, 179, 191, 199, 205–10, 213–17, 230–31, 247, 254, 261–63
    Broadcaster 13, 147, 152

Calvinistic 74, 96
Catholic-Evangelical 4–5, 119, 210
Chalcedonian 138, 141
childhood 19, 21–23, 27, 29, 31, 39, 42, 55, 61, 68, 75, 129, 183, 194
Christianity 3, 4, 10, 11, 13–14, 28, 33, 41–45, 47–48, 55, 61, 66, 69, 75, 79, 81–83, 92–93, 103–7, 109–10, 112–30, 134–35, 137–38, 139–40, 149–50, 152–59, 161–65, 168, 172–73, 175, 177, 178–80, 182, 188, 192, 195–97, 204–17, 221–22, 224, 236, 239, 241, 245, 253, 254, 263, 264
    Christian(s) 1–16, 19–21, 25–28, 33–34, 37, 40–42, 44, 46–49, 52–53, 55, 59–63, 65–66, 70–80, 83–84, 86, 91–92, 98–99, 101–19, 122–31, 133, 135–37, 139, 140–41, 143–44, 147, 149, 150–51, 153–54, 156, 159–68, 170–77, 179, 181–83, 184, 186–87, 189–90, 194–204, 207–9, 212–14, 216, 218–19, 230, 232–35, 237–38, 241–42, 247–49, 252–53, 255–59, 260–63
Christlike 227, 230–40
    Christlikeness 14, 114, 151, 227–28, 230–39, 242, 260
christocentric 86, 88
christological 13–14, 53, 65, 74–76, 79, 123, 133–35, 138, 144, 181–83, 186–87, 208–10, 212, 216, 228, 237, 247–48, 251, 264
Christology 3–5, 13–20, 42, 74–90, 114, 124–25, 133–39, 142,–45, 149, 151, 162, 164, 166, 177, 187, 191–92, 199, 203–7, 210, 217–18, 227, 232–33, 244, 247–48, 261
Christus Victor 113, 137, 211–12
Church(es) 1–11, 13, 19–21, 25–31, 39, 42–48, 52, 63, 65, 70–79, 83, 84, 86, 88, 89, 91, 92, 96–98, 101, 103–17, 119–31, 134–36, 142–44, 147, 152–54, 158, 165, 168–75, 183, 191–92, 197, 199, 204, 206, 208–10, 215–19, 221, 227–30, 238–43, 246, 253, 255, 259, 261, 263–64
    churchmanship 43, 83, 126, 221
clergy 79, 85, 105, 112, 119, 129, 130–35, 147, 171, 191, 194, 198, 249
    clerical 104, 125, 130, 135, 261–63
communion 44, 167, 216–17, 221, 228, 259
communism 51, 59–60, 62
    communist 51, 55, 59–60, 62, 70–71, 256
conversion(s) 1, 4–6, 9, 12–21, 25, 30–49, 51–58, 61–71, 73, 75–76, 80, 82–83, 86–88, 90–99, 101, 106–8, 113, 122–27, 139, 144–45, 149–50, 154, 162, 169–70, 192–93, 221, 222, 230, 244–45, 252–53, 256–57, 259 *see: salvation*
    accept(ed) (conversion) 7, 15, 26, 39–40, 47–48, 52, 62–63, 73, 78, 87, 90, 94, 95, 99, 106, 121, 133, 140–141, 156, 158, 165, 174, 178, 185, 187, 188, 201, 202, 206, 225, 224, 228–29, 237, 242, 248, 250–51, 257, 262–263
    acceptance (conversion) 4–6, 12–17, 39–40, 47, 90, 93, 137, 168, 183, 201, 229, 235
correspondence 27, 39, 80, 106–7, 150–51, 203–6, 238, 261
creation 8, 14–15, 39, 42, 51, 56–58, 69, 93, 96, 105, 163, 170–71, 173, 178, 181–84, 187–89, 222–24, 228–29, 231, 243–48, 249, 252, 259

277

creative 52, 53, 58, 180, 182, 256
Creator 52, 186, 201, 248
creed(s) 3-4, 8, 9, 11, 15, 42-43, 65, 78, 79, 105, 109-10, 112-13, 120, 127, 131, 137-38, 145, 197, 216-18, 249
    creedal 9, 12, 14, 41, 47, 65, 73, 75, 79, 83, 98, 104-5, 110, 141, 150, 169, 195, 205, 208, 210, 216, 245
cross, the 2, 12, 14-15, 17, 19, 25, 43, 47-48, 59, 61-62, 71, 72-73, 78-79, 95-98, 120, 122, 127, 137, 144, 157, 158, 164, 167, 168, 173, 179, 183, 187, 189, 190-94, 197-99, 202-7, 210-15, 217-20, 223-24, 228-29, 236, 238-45, 250, 252, 259
    crucified 8, 25, 37-39, 40, 67, 127, 205, 210, 214, 216-18, 222, 224-25, 245
    crucifixion 8, 14, 19-20, 42, 44, 112, 143, 158, 205, 213-15, 218-19, 221, 225, 239, 241, 249

death 8, 12, 14-15, 19, 24-26, 29, 33, 41-43, 46, 55, 58, 62, 68, 71-72, 75, 85, 95-96, 99, 101, 104, 121-22, 144-45, 149, 150, 155-56, 158-59, 164-72, 183, 187-91, 198, 205, 211-15, 217-22, 224-25, 227, 229-30, 235-36, 238-42, 246, 248, 252, 259, 260
    dead 24, 33, 40, 140, 174, 190, 216-17, 220, 223, 246, 249
de incarnatione verbi 107, 204
Deism 39, 78, 139
    deist(ic) 12, 19
denomination(s) 4, 6, 103-12, 116-17, 128, 127-29, 172, 204 *see: church*
Deus absconditus 81
Deus dixit 76, 81, 97
dialectic(al) 15, 156, 179, 180, 183, 190, 234, 239 *see: paradox*
    antinomy 239
    diastasis 84
disciples 2, 20-21, 39-40, 78, 140, 208, 216, 239, 248, 249 *see: apostles*
divine 2, 3, 14, 42, 46-47, 60, 66, 76-89, 124, 135-36, 138-41, 155-57, 163-65, 170-74, 188-90, 201, 211-12, 229-31, 234, 241, 247-48, 255-56
    divine life 2, 14, 170-74, 211
    divinity 9, 42, 63, 74, 77, 120, 133-38, 141, 144, 178, 198, 231, 246-47, 249, 258, 264
Docetism 77, 133, 138
doctrine(s) 3-6, 8, 13, 26, 43-44, 65-67, 72-73, 76, 79, 80-85, 96-97, 103-106, 112, 114, 116-17, 122, 128-131, 136, 140, 149, 151-55, 158, 162-66, 169-74, 180-90, 195-96, 203-4, 216-18, 224-25, 227-28, 240, 243, 246-50, 254-55, 257-62, 264 *see: theology*
    doctrinal 9, 82-84, 88, 108, 120, 134, 142, 144, 162, 169, 174, 191-93, 229, 231, 236-38, 262

Easter 59, 215, 224
ecclesiastical 21, 123 *see: church*
ecclesia visibilis–ecclesia invisibilis 240
ecumenical councils 11, 78
elect 96, 121
    election 95-96, 121
encounter 3-7, 23-25, 39, 40, 42, 45-47, 51, 56-58, 61-63, 65-66, 71, 97-98, 121-22, 124, 151, 207, 229
Enlightenment 6, 7, 9, 12, 47, 48, 65, 66, 78, 83, 98, 113, 114, 115, 120, 124, 142, 183, 192, 194, 196, 254, 256, 262, 263 *see: Age of Reason*
eschaton 8, 190, 239-40, 248-49, 251
    eschatological 31, 206, 216, 228, 248
    eschatology 87, 173
eternity 14-15, 27, 57, 75-77, 117, 119, 126, 128-129, 131, 137-138, 141-142, 144, 156-157, 165, 171-172, 184, 200-201, 212, 218, 224, 240, 250
ethics 5, 9, 54-55, 81, 84, 105-106, 114-116, 120, 137, 155, 162, 166-67, 258 *see: moral*
    ethical 9, 63, 78, 87, 112, 120, 142, 157, 159, 167
Eutychianism 133, 136, 138
Evangelical(s) 3-7, 11, 13, 73, 78, 103-107, 110, 112, 119-23, 125, 210-11, 216-19, 239 *see: church*
    Evangelicalism 21
    evangelism 122, 162
    Evangelist 26
evil 61, 66, 87, 96, 121, 156, 162, 163, 167, 168, 188, 189, 191, 230, 236, 237, 241, 255
existence 14, 28, 36, 42, 45-46, 49, 50, 76, 85-87, 114, 121-22, 135, 140, 158-59, 162-163, 166, 171, 180-81, 184-86, 192, 194, 198, 200, 220, 222, 224, 229, 231, 235, 239, 241-42, 244, 245, 259
    exist 32, 67-69, 77-78, 84-85, 89, 121, 158, 159, 163, 170, 174, 181, 197
    existed 41-42, 53, 56, 116, 164, 191, 248, 255
    existential 31, 35, 49, 216, 231, 241, 251-53
    existentialism 50
experience 12, 15, 21-24, 28, 30-34, 36, 39, 41, 45, 51, 53, 56-57, 58, 61-63, 65-67, 70-71, 78, 81, 83-84, 94, 97, 121, 155-57, 169,

180–81, 184–85, 199–201, 229, 239, 243, 248, 250

faith 3–6, 8, 11–14, 20–21, 24, 27, 31, 32, 36–37, 46, 52, 54–55, 59, 60, 62–63, 67, 69, 75, 78–79, 83, 88, 90–91, 93–94, 97–98, 103–8, 110, 112, 114, 116, 119, 120, 122–28, 130, 135–36, 140, 141–44, 149, 150, 151, 153–54, 162, 165, 167, 168–69, 191–92, 197–99, 208, 216, 240, 218, 220, 221, 244–45, 254, 256–58, 261–64, 50
    faithful 52, 108, 112, 127, 200–201
    fides 90, 244, 245
fall, the 8, 23, 27, 30, 44–45, 88, 96, 98, 105, 157–58, 162–65, 167, 170–72, 185–88, 189, 190–91, 213, 219–20, 230–31, 234, 240–41, 254 *see: original sin*
    fallen 15, 49–50, 53, 60–61, 65, 68, 79, 84, 94, 98, 136, 140, 149, 157, 163, 167, 188, 202, 216, 231–33, 261
    fallenness 86, 158, 234, 237
finite 13, 33, 177, 180–81, 196, 250
forgiveness 16, 73, 90, 120, 127, 161–2, 183, 198, 210, 212, 217, 220, 224–25, 229, 234, 237
    forgiving 22, 73, 229–30
foundational 86, 98, 114, 183, 185, 197
Four Last Things 8, 105 *see: eschaton*
freedom 9, 15, 33, 52, 75, 83–84, 94, 97, 139, 158, 163, 172, 181, 236, 239, 243–44, 252, 259–260
    free will 45, 63, 94, 96, 163, 188, 193

glory 19, 25, 51, 98, 157, 199–203, 230, 238, 243
Gnosticism 27, 34, 76–77, 133, 136–38
God-man 3, 110, 112, 140–41
gospel 4, 7–8, 11, 13, 28, 31, 37, 40–42, 44, 46–47, 53, 61–63, 73–74, 79–81, 84, 91–92, 98, 107–8, 110, 114–15, 119, 123–24, 126, 128–29, 134, 144, 151–52, 157, 167, 183, 187, 190, 195–97, 208, 212, 218, 224, 228, 253, 257 *see: Bible, Scripture*
grace 19, 22, 44, 48, 55–56, 63, 69–70, 75, 94, 96–7, 158, 167–68, 210–11, 233, 255–56 *see: prevenience*
    gracefully 227, 231, 232
grief 24–25, 68, 240
    Haematological 221–22
    Haematology 221
    harmatia 221

haunted 58, 229
    haunter 156, 215–16, 228–29

heaven 4, 8, 25, 31, 40, 48, 53, 55–59, 84, 92–93, 125–26, 131, 156, 167–68, 193–94, 198–202, 208, 216–18, 220, 224–25, 238, 240, 248–49, 255, 258–59
Hebrew 1–3, 14, 40, 86, 89, 125, 167, 180, 205, 212, 219–22, 224 *see: Jew, Israel*
Hegelian 12, 20, 34, 36, 42, 70, 78, 80, 84, 88–91, 93, 97
    Hegelianism 34, 35, 48
hell 8, 31, 46, 48, 53, 96, 125, 165, 189, 191, 193–94, 197–98, 201, 216–18, 224–25, 240, 249
heresy(ies) 13, 14, 76, 133–36, 138, 162, 200, 255
hiddenness 89, 91, 99, 191, 239
history 3, 5, 10, 12, 16, 78, 81, 84, 86, 89, 103, 107, 109–12, 114–16, 119, 122, 124, 136, 140, 164, 178, 183–87, 196, 203–4, 212–13, 227, 245, 253–55, 264
historical 3, 5, 12, 78–79, 110, 114, 124, 156, 197–98, 208–10, 211–12, 245–47, 254–55
holiness 15, 34, 235, 237
hominum confusione et Dei providentia 128–29, 144
human 2–4, 6–9, 11, 13, 16, 19–21, 27–28, 30, 36, 41–42, 44, 46, 49–50, 52–54, 56, 57, 58, 61–62, 65–68, 71–73, 75–79, 85–96, 98, 104, 112, 114, 120, 124, 128, 134–41, 144–45, 149, 155–58, 162–64, 167, 169, 172, 173, 177–79, 181, 185–97, 200, 203, 205, 210, 212, 214–15, 219–20, 227–28, 229–42, 245, 247, 250–51, 253–54, 255–56, 261
    humanism 48
    humanist 48, 78, 253
    humanity 1–3, 5, 7, 8, 12, 14–16, 19, 20, 30, 32, 35–36, 50, 3, 66–67, 76–78, 81, 83–84, 90, 92, 94, 98–99, 112, 114–15, 136–38, 145, 149, 155–56, 158, 163–65, 167, 170–72, 179, 181, 183, 185–87, 189, 190–91, 193, 195–98, 205, 210, 214–16, 218–20, 222–23, 227–29, 231, 240, 241, 243, 245, 247, 250–51, 253–54, 255–57, 259, 260
humble 15, 158, 190, 230
    humility 15, 53, 55, 67, 71, 75, 90–91, 108, 163, 165, 189, 202, 239

idealism 34, 39, 41–42, 48, 70, 80, 84, 97, 139, 184 *see: Hegelian*
    idealist 20, 78
idolatry/idolatrous 30–31, 228
illuminate 19, 65, 83, 108, 185
imagination 12, 22, 36, 51–53, 57, 87, 134, 152, 179, 192, 196, 246 *see: understanding*

image 15, 35–36, 45, 52–53, 57, 79, 116, 158, 182, 186, 192, 201–202, 211, 227, 230–31, 239, 253, 256, 258
  imaginative 53, 228, 231, 264
  imagining 72, 222, 250
imago Christi 211, 227, 230
imago Dei 15, 211
imitatio Christi 227, 230
immediacy 4, 44, 84, 121, 127, 236, 251
incarnate 4, 14–15, 20, 25, 37, 43, 67, 136, 140–43, 164, 186–88, 194, 195, 231, 247, 250, 264
  incarnation 2, 6, 8, 9, 13–15, 19–20, 36–37, 39, 42, 44, 52, 61, 74, 89, 91, 105, 107, 112, 114–15, 137–38, 156–58, 164–67, 170–71, 177, 179, 180–90, 194–95, 203–4, 207, 210, 212–13, 218, 224, 228, 230, 232, 234–35, 237, 245–46, 250–51, 259
  incarnational 190, 211
individual 4, 6, 11, 16, 30–31, 45, 50, 65–66, 68–71, 83, 85, 91, 94, 98, 115, 119–20, 131, 143, 158, 169, 205, 219–21, 228–29, 230, 232, 238
  individualism 104, 228
  individualistic 30, 46, 85
  individuality 77, 96, 228, 259
infinite 13, 27, 33, 61, 83, 89, 93, 165–67, 177, 180–81, 199
infinitum capax finiti 13, 177, 180–81
in mirabilibus supra me 119, 130–31, 144
inspiration 246
  inspire 247
intellect 6, 26, 41, 44, 51–53, 55, 65, 70–71, 86, 88, 125, 129, 130, 144, 154, 239 *see: mind*
  intellectual 11, 12, 20, 22, 28, 29–30, 32, 39–42, 44, 46–47, 51, 58, 65, 68–69, 72, 78, 83, 87, 95–97, 104, 114–15, 125, 129, 150, 168, 198, 229, 244, 253, 255
intimation(s) 30–31, 36, 51–52, 62, 57, 119, 131, 144, 145, 156, 164, 179, 200–201, 218, 228, 261, 261, 264
invisible 121–22, 192, 215, 240
Israel 2, 104, 188, 245 *see: Hebrew, Jew*

Jew(s) 2, 42, 54, 57, 59, 63, 70, 72, 79, 155–56, 164, 211–12, 215, 218, 249 *see: Hebrew, Israel*
  Jewish 2–3, 9–10, 15, 51, 54–55, 59, 63, 70–71, 164, 187–88, 205, 210, 212–13, 215, 221, 241–42, 243
  Judaism 1, 51, 54–55, 70, 211–12

Joy 12, 15, 19, 21–24, 26–27, 30–32, 34–36, 39, 42, 44, 46–52, 54–63, 66, 68, 70, 87–88, 91, 93–95, 97–99, 121, 123, 144–45, 166–67, 209, 227–30, 236, 240, 242–45, 251–53, 255 *see: Sehnsucht*
Judge(d) 24, 74
  judgment 8, 15–16, 31, 53, 62, 68, 72, 76, 78, 96, 140, 157, 173, 190, 202, 206, 216, 228, 230, 237, 239–40, 242–43, 247–49, 250–51, 260
justice 54–55, 84–85, 191, 220, 241

kingdom of God, the 22, 53, 78, 86, 215
knowledge 1, 15, 19–20, 34, 42, 45, 58, 60–62, 68, 70, 85–86, 88, 99, 106, 112, 136, 144, 145, 155, 158, 165, 168–69, 171, 179–80, 182, 184–85, 187, 191–92, 234–35, 242–43, 250 *see: understanding*

language 6, 20, 44, 49, 58, 89, 95, 108, 126, 139, 151–53, 164, 168, 171, 198, 201, 206, 215–16, 251, 258
l/Liberal 4, 9, 13, 47–48, 65, 73, 75–76, 79, 80–82, 84, 86, 91, 103, 105, 114–15, 119–20, 130, 133, 137, 139, 140, 142–44, 153, 192, 197–98, 200, 212, 227, 246, 251, 259, 261–62, 263 *see: modern*
  l/Liberalism 9, 33, 73–76, 79, 82, 96–98, 119–20, 139–40, 228, 259
literature 10, 25, 32, 34, 53, 59, 91, 103, 107, 113–14, 126, 150, 153, 206, 227, 262–63
  literatus 103
logic 26, 41, 63, 130, 142, 144, 183–84
  logician 26, 125
Logos 77, 124–25, 207, 212
  logos asarkos–logos ensarkos 133, 141
  Logos Spermatikos 124
Lord 4, 5, 25–26, 36–37, 39–40, 45, 47–49, 57, 68–69, 74–75, 83, 88, 90, 98, 104, 124, 127, 136, 138, 141, 144–45, 154, 156, 157–58, 162, 164, 173, 177, 180, 183, 191, 216, 218, 221, 228–29, 230, 237, 249–51, 262
  lordship 60, 74, 215
love 4, 14–16, 19–24, 27–28, 32, 35, 41, 46, 53, 57–59, 60–61, 70–71, 75, 83, 89–90, 92, 113, 131, 156–58, 163, 166, 171, 192–93, 199, 210, 212, 219, 227, 229–34, 236, 238, 240–41, 256, 259, 261
Lutheran 66, 85–86, 109

Manichaeism 70
martyr 72

martyrdom 72, 125
Martyrdom 158
Marxism 60, 70, 91, 115
Medieval 34, 103, 109, 113–14, 175, 253
meer/mere
    meer 109
    Mere Christian 3, 13, 103, 106–7, 109
    Mere Christianity 3–4, 13, 14, 103, 105–7, 109–10, 112–13, 115, 125, 127, 129–30, 138, 149–50, 153, 159, 168, 204–5, 207–8, 210–17, 221–22, 224, 253
Messiah(s) 1–3, 14, 124, 205, 214–15, 218, 221, 248
    messiahship 1–3
    messianic 2, 212, 247
    Messianic 230
Methodist 3, 110, 122
mind(s) 9, 15, 22, 29, 31, 34–37, 42, 44–45, 47, 51–53, 56–57, 60–62, 66, 68–70, 79–80, 83, 87–88, 98, 131, 136, 138, 155, 157, 159, 162–63, 167–68, 171, 173, 178–79, 181–82, 187, 192, 194, 197, 201, 218, 232, 238–40, 245, 248, 250, 254, 256–57, 262 *see: intellect*
miracle(s) 24, 81, 93, 136, 138, 139, 150–51, 175, 177–78, 181–85, 191, 199, 206, 209, 211, 224, 227–28, 246, 251, 252
    miraculous 63, 120, 178, 184–85, 252
missionary 42, 105, 122–23, 130, 153–54, 233
modalism 76, 259
m/Modern 6, 8, 13, 41, 48–49, 69, 72, 74–75, 81–82, 103, 107, 109, 113–14, 116–17, 119, 124, 130–33, 136–37, 142, 144, 153, 157, 165, 168, 184, 187–88, 190, 192, 195–203, 246, 249–50, 261–63 *see: liberal*
    m/Modernism 6, 9, 12, 83, 103, 114–15, 117, 120, 130, 139, 210, 263
    modernist 4, 9, 63, 74, 120, 262
    modernity 76
moral 12, 14, 51, 62, 76, 78, 122, 155–57, 162, 164–66, 169, 180, 197, 237, 245, 247, 260 *see: ethics*
    morality 9, 54–56, 67, 69, 155, 164, 166–67, 254, 260
mystical 21, 29, 31–33, 35, 46, 70–71, 92–93, 97, 190
mysticism 27, 78, 97
myth(s) 9, 24, 27–28, 32, 34, 43–44, 91–92, 178, 187, 195, 203, 224, 228, 231–32, 235, 246, 249, 254, 264 *see: narrative*
    mythological 28, 47, 164, 187
    mythology 10, 27, 32, 47, 98, 231

Narnia 14–16, 23, 33, 53, 92, 138, 142, 150–51, 154, 182, 205–6, 209, 222–25, 227, 248, 256–57
narrative(s) 5, 15, 16, 98, 114–15, 138, 151, 164, 191, 196, 199, 205–7, 222, 227–28, 231, 235, 238, 256
naturalism 151, 207
natural law 260
nature 2, 3, 7, 13–15, 27–28, 30, 41, 50, 56, 74, 77–78, 83, 86, 90, 95, 98–99, 103, 113, 126, 129, 133–36, 138–39, 140–42, 144, 151, 154–57, 163, 166–67, 169, 171, 173–74, 180, 183–85, 187–89, 200–4, 205, 224–25, 238, 244, 246, 250–51, 255, 257, 258
New Testament 2–3, 6, 8, 63, 95, 112, 117, 127, 139, 166, 195, 201–3, 213, 221, 246, 250
nihilism 115
    nihilistic 26, 58, 68, 115, 198, 231, 240–41
    nothingness 35, 198, 220, 224
Norse 10, 24, 27, 32, 187
Northernness 25, 27, 28, 41, 44
    northern 24
novum mysterium 75
numinous 155–56, 200, 202, 245

object 7, 17, 20, 29, 30–32, 35–36, 61, 65, 89, 95, 157, 173, 192, 200–201, 203, 236, 245–46 *see: subject*
Old Testament 2, 54, 72, 89, 115, 166, 182, 205, 218–19, 229, 237
omnipotence 67, 94, 180, 188
omnipresence 67, 180
omniscience 67, 138, 180, 250
omniscient 138, 250
ontology 13, 133–35, 140–41, 157, 166, 169, 171, 247
    ontological 140, 144–45, 166, 169
oremus pro invicem 130
original sin 8, 22, 30, 94, 98, 136, 157–58, 162–64, 167, 190, 210, 219, 231, 233, 241, 253–55 *see: fall, the*
o/Orthodox 1, 3, 5, 7, 9, 11–14, 16, 28, 47, 54, 63, 65, 71, 73, 75–76, 78–79, 83, 98, 103–4, 110, 113–14, 121, 125, 129, 133, 135, 142–44, 149–50, 162–63, 169, 195, 205–8, 210, 217, 224, 228, 231, 234, 237, 240, 246, 249–50, 258–59, 261–62, 264
    orthodoxy 13, 37, 104, 114, 130, 133, 142, 149, 194, 227, 259, 262–63

pagan 8–10, 27–28, 44, 53, 123–25, 170, 178, 187, 231–32, 234, 254
    p/Paganism 9–10, 245

pain 13, 30, 32, 68, 75, 129, 144, 149–50, 154, 156–57, 238, 240–44 *see: affliction, suffering*
p/Pantheism 22, 39, 41, 48, 56, 92, 139, 162, 177–79
    Pantheist 92
    pantheistic 41, 93, 162, 179–80
    panentheism 139, 259
parable 42, 51, 53, 63, 68, 94, 116, 188, 235–36
paradox 57, 89, 112, 142, 156, 165, 168–70, 186, 190, 235–36, 239, 250
    Paradoxical 89 *see: analogy, dialectic*
parousia 249–50
particular/ity 11, 13, 20, 32, 41, 48, 59, 67, 79–81, 90, 96, 103–4, 114, 117, 136, 142, 155, 159, 170, 172, 180–81, 183–84, 190, 195–96, 202, 204, 208, 217–18, 241, 248, 253, 259–60, 262
passion, the 35, 201, 214, 219, 229, 237–38, 242
patristic 7, 13, 15, 69, 75, 86–87, 103–7, 110, 112–16, 119, 121, 122, 124–26, 129, 131, 133, 136, 142–43, 189, 162, 177, 197, 200–201, 204, 208, 211, 216, 241, 233, 242, 145
Pelagian 255
    Pelagianism 247, 255–56
perception 2, 6, 16, 41, 52, 56–57, 61, 65, 73, 116, 121, 123, 128, 162, 164, 184–85, 196, 222, 231–33, 236, 238, 250
person 2–6, 13, 15, 19, 27, 30–31, 42, 47, 52, 61, 63, 65, 69–70, 73, 76–78, 83, 90–91, 96, 98, 117, 124, 126, 134, 138, 149, 157, 159, 162, 169–72, 177, 184, 187, 192–94, 196, 203, 208, 212, 214, 216, 218, 220, 224, 227–28, 230–31, 233, 235, 241, 244, 246–47, 252, 258–59, 263
    personality 58, 63, 65–66, 170, 174, 179–80
    persons 10, 32, 77, 89, 156, 170–71, 252, 258, 259
p/Philosophy 6–7, 9–10, 27, 34–35, 47, 73, 86, 88–89, 91, 97, 107, 123–26, 130, 134, 137, 142, 149, 151, 180, 183, 192–93, 199, 207, 235, 254, 264 *see: reason*
    philosopher(s) 5–8, 11, 41, 65, 70–71, 78, 87, 90, 103–4, 113, 119, 123–26, 128, 131, 137, 145, 151, 162, 165, 180, 184, 196, 200, 203–4, 207–8, 225, 240–42, 245, 254, 257–58
    philosophical 5, 26, 31, 35–36, 39, 41–42, 44, 47–48, 69, 71, 76, 97, 126, 134, 149, 151, 154–55, 156–57, 159, 162, 175, 178, 182, 199, 206–7, 209, 229, 241, 244–45, 261
    philosophically 35, 124, 126, 159, 181

philosophies 8, 28, 40, 48, 115, 124, 136, 150, 200
pilgrim 20, 39
    pilgrimage 20–21, 32, 46, 48, 55, 70–71, 87, 191, 212
Platonism 7, 116, 124, 128, 151, 170, 217
    form(s), the 2, 3, 5, 7, 9, 15–16, 21, 27, 30, 35, 47, 52, 54, 67, 71, 74–75, 81, 84, 86–87, 93, 95, 106–7, 114, 119–120, 142, 158, 179–180, 183, 185–186, 190–194, 196, 200, 204, 207–208, 218, 221, 229, 232–34, 240–41, 244, 246, 249, 255–57, 261–62, 264
    intelligible 7, 119, 128, 200
    Neo-Platonism 7
    perceivable 7, 70, 86, 119, 128, 184
    Platonic 7, 14, 36, 80, 116, 128, 131, 138, 142, 144, 202, 208
    Platonic Realism 7
    Platonists 7, 116
pneumatological 144, 213, 228, 232
polytheism 76
postmodern 96, 126, 262
    postmodernism 6, 103, 114–15
praeparatio evangelica 13, 119, 122–23, 162
prayer 25, 27–28, 36, 92–93, 151, 173, 192–93, 209, 215, 219, 221, 227, 237–38, 242, 251–52
prefigurement 164, 186–87, 264
Presbyterian 3, 23, 63, 104, 110, 122, 152
prevenient 94, 210, 245, 255, 256, 260
    prevenience 94, 210 *see: grace*
pride 42, 82, 95–96, 131, 144, 158, 167, 192, 211
prophet 81, 85, 130, 164, 234, 259
proposition(s) 74, 112, 250
Protestant 7, 11, 26, 48, 78–80, 84, 108–10, 112–13, 117, 122, 126–27, 158, 199–200, 239, 241, 82
    Protestantism 65, 75–76, 84, 91, 103–4, 117
    Protestants 12, 109, 117, 122
purgatory 4–5, 121, 193
puritanical 23

rationalism 10, 48 *see: reason*
    rationality 124, 222
realism 41, 48, 65, 73, 184
reality 7, 12, 14–16, 27–28, 32–33, 41–42, 47, 52–53, 56, 78, 84, 88, 137, 140–45, 162–63, 165–66, 173, 177–78, 180, 184–86, 188, 190–95, 201, 203–5, 219–20, 222, 224–25, 228, 231–32, 239–40, 245, 249–50, 252, 254, 258

Index of Subjects

reason 3, 4, 7, 15, 20, 27, 65, 72, 84, 97–98, 106–7, 124, 127, 151, 156, 171, 177, 181, 184, 190, 196, 201, 203, 206–7, 214, 227, 242, 244, 246–50, 252, 254, 262, 264 *see: rationalism, revelation*
rebirth 61, 104, 187, 224
reconciliation 25, 172–73, 233, 235
redeemer 2, 159
    redeeming 216, 237
redemption 2, 15, 20, 43, 83, 86, 174, 183, 187–89, 190, 218, 231, 237
reductio ad absurdum 13, 149
Reformation 78, 103–4, 110, 112, 114, 127, 129, 168, 204, 227
    Reformed 7, 12, 63, 73–75, 79, 84, 86, 91, 104, 110, 113, 122, 127, 158, 217
    Reformers 122
religion 2–5, 8–10, 21, 23, 26–30, 35–36, 47–48, 54, 66–68, 75–76, 83–85, 87, 89, 91–93, 96, 103–5, 109, 114–15, 119, 122–23, 126–28, 140, 152, 154, 156–57, 161, 163, 170, 177–84, 187, 191–93, 195–96, 207, 215, 230, 233, 234–35, 238–40, 244–45, 253, 257, 263
    religions 8–9, 27–28, 44, 47–48, 63, 67, 86, 108, 112, 115, 123–24, 137, 155, 162, 164, 170, 178–79, 187, 195, 205, 208, 212–13, 219, 228, 230–31, 235, 245, 255, 261
    religiosity 13, 149, 195, 227
    religious 1–3, 5, 9–10, 12, 14, 16, 19–26, 28, 32–33, 36, 41, 47, 57–58, 61, 63, 65–66, 67–68, 70–71, 73, 75–76, 78, 81–84, 87, 91–92, 97–98, 103, 108, 115, 119, 120–22, 125–26, 133–34, 137, 144–45, 150, 152–53, 155–57, 159, 164–65, 167, 170, 177, 179, 180–82, 184, 191–96, 202–203, 205, 212, 219, 222–23, 225, 233–34, 239, 243–246, 248–49, 253–54, 260
    Religious Experience 65–67, 69, 70–71
Renaissance 114, 253
repentance 16, 61, 63, 157, 162, 165, 211–12, 214–15, 229, 237, 239, 241
resurrection 2, 7–9, 12, 15, 19–20, 24, 40, 42–44, 59, 61, 63, 76, 78, 105, 112, 137, 140, 143, 157, 164–65, 167, 172, 179, 183, 185, 187, 190, 194, 198, 205, 207–8, 211, 215–18, 220, 222–24, 228, 237, 245, 250
    resurrected 8, 30, 37, 46, 50, 58, 61, 67, 72, 124, 127, 187, 223, 229, 231, 238, 240, 250
    risen 15, 33, 39 40, 42, 47, 59, 66, 68, 115, 138, 253

Retraktation 20, 65, 73, 79, 80, 87, 91–92, 97 *see: Wendung*
revelation 1, 2, 4–8, 10, 12–13, 15, 19, 37, 39, 45–47, 57, 61–62, 65, 73–76, 83, 86, 89, 90–93, 97, 104, 106, 119–20, 124–25, 131, 134, 144, 149–51, 155–57, 159, 162–67, 170–71, 177–83, 187–88, 191–92, 194–96, 199–201, 203–7, 216–17, 227, 234, 244–47, 249, 252, 258–59, 261, 263–64 *see: rationalism, reason*
    realization 2, 6, 32, 36, 39–40, 44, 46, 57, 65, 73, 76, 81–83, 86–87, 88, 90–91, 165, 193, 245, 257
    revealed 2, 5, 7, 12, 15, 19, 25, 29, 36–37, 47, 55–57, 67, 78, 83, 90, 97–98, 106–108, 119, 156, 167, 179–80, 192–94, 200–202, 205, 216, 219, 248, 259
    self-revelation 1, 4–5, 7, 12, 15, 61, 83, 89, 97, 263
righteous 62, 156–57, 162, 164, 180, 201, 215, 219, 232, 235, 248
Roman Catholic 3–4, 15, 43, 71, 78, 96, 104, 106, 109–10, 116–17, 121–22, 126–28, 131, 145, 183, 210, 219, 263
Romantic 10, 12, 22, 27, 34, 41, 98, 262
    Romanticism 10, 32, 175, 199, 208, 262
    Romantics 10

sacrament(s) 4, 44, 51, 56–57, 74, 121, 165
    sacramental 5, 46, 56–57, 121
    sacramentally 57
sacrifice 14, 44, 94, 113, 124, 157–58, 193, 205, 211–12, 214, 218–24, 227, 230, 232–33, 237–38, 253–54
    sacrificial 194, 205, 218, 222–24, 231
saga 27, 32 *see: myth*
salvation 1–2, 5, 6, 12–7, 19–20, 30, 42–43, 70, 73–74, 94, 96, 104, 112, 115–16, 139, 158, 164–65, 168–69, 171–72, 187, 189, 192, 201, 205, 210–12, 216–17, 228–29, 231–32, 237, 245–46, 248, 255–57, 225
    saved 2, 43, 73, 95, 121, 127, 165, 169, 172, 189, 215, 218, 256
sanctification 15, 143–44, 173, 210–11, 235
Schleiermachian 84, 86
science 56, 114, 140, 163, 184, 192, 252
    scientific 10, 67, 81, 184–85, 188, 248, 252
    scientism 151, 207
    scientist(s) 8, 20, 87, 104, 177, 248–49, 257
Scripture 2, 9, 11–13, 40, 65, 67, 73–74, 78–79, 103, 105–7, 109–10, 112–13, 116–17, 120–22, 129, 131, 142, 151, 167, 194, 200–203, 206, 216–17, 246–50, 255, 264 *see: Bible*

scriptural 71, 200, 202
second coming 8, 105, 131, 249–50, 251
secular 30, 83, 86, 115, 129, 136, 144, 191, 219, 243 *see: liberal*
    secularism 73, 83–84
Sehnsucht 19, 23, 29, 30–31, 33–36, 48, 54, 56–57, 166, 199–202, 228 *see: joy*
shadowlands 15, 52, 54, 58, 123
sin 4, 8, 14–15, 22, 30, 40, 45, 47–48, 50, 55, 65, 67, 69–70, 72–74, 78, 85–87, 94–96, 98, 101, 119, 121, 127, 136–37, 140, 157–58, 162–63, 164–65, 167, 169, 172, 177, 188, 190–91, 194, 198, 205, 210, 213–15, 217–24, 228–29, 230–31, 233, 240–41, 253–55 *see: fall, original sin*
    sinfulness 70, 136, 219
    sinned 40
    sinners 40, 95, 127, 229, 261
skeptic 58, 81
    skepticism 74, 81, 98, 114, 124, 136, 213, 244–46, 251–53
    skeptics 11, 79, 250–51
Socialism 81, 86, 129
    socialist(s) 81
soteriology 169, 210, 212 *see: salvation*
sovereignty 43, 86, 89–91, 97
spiritual 21–24, 27, 31, 33, 41, 44, 55, 58, 62–63, 66, 108, 136, 138, 152, 156–57, 172, 190–92, 219, 223, 22–28
    spirituality 26–27, 126, 165, 239, 255
status 13, 26, 61, 78, 83, 91, 94, 133–35, 140, 142, 145, 153, 164, 169, 188, 194, 234–35
steady state theory 248–49, 257
story 8, 28, 31, 44, 53, 55, 63, 76, 114–15, 135, 163, 182, 184–85, 187, 215, 224, 228, 236, 251, 254, 256–57
subject 15, 17, 20, 61, 68, 89, 95, 98–99, 123, 128, 134–45, 173, 181, 203, 217, 231, 238, 244, 245, 250 *see: object*
suffering 25, 71, 129, 138, 144, 149–50, 154–55, 157–58, 163, 188, 214, 217, 227, 230–31, 233, 235–38, 240–44, 247, 252, 257 *see: affliction, pain*
summa 149, 164, 205, 207, 210, 216, 262
supernatural 9, 27, 51, 59, 86, 120, 139, 151, 155, 177, 186, 198, 241, 252
symbolic 15–16, 138, 200–201
systematic 3, 5–6, 31, 82–83, 123, 125, 130, 168, 191–92, 206, 215–16, 263–64 *see: theology, doctrine*
    systematician 5

Temple religion 2

t/Theism 10, 19, 37–39, 41–43, 47–49, 75, 80, 139, 144, 193, 209, 227, 244 *see: atheism*
    theist 20, 42–43, 46, 49
    theistic 10, 19, 120, 155, 198
theodicy 13, 149, 154–55, 241
theology 3–9, 13, 16, 20–21, 52–54, 57, 63, 65–67, 72–76, 78, 79, 80–82, 84, 86–87, 92, 97–99, 103–5, 107, 110, 112–15, 121–22, 124–26, 129–30, 133–34, 137, 139, 142, 144, 149–51, 154–56, 169–71, 182–83, 194–95, 199, 206, 209, 215, 220–21, 227, 229, 246, 248, 253, 257–61, 263–64 *see: doctrine*
    theologian(s) 3–8, 11–14, 20, 37, 39–40, 65–66, 69, 72–74, 78–79, 83, 85–86, 90–91, 96, 98, 104, 112–14, 119, 121, 123–26, 128, 129–31, 133–38, 140–41, 144–45, 149, 154, 164, 165, 168–69, 179, 183, 189, 194, 197–98, 203–5, 208, 211, 215–18, 232, 240, 250, 258–59, 262
    theological 5, 6, 8–9, 11, 13–14, 50, 52, 57, 74, 80–84, 87, 90, 97–98, 104, 112–13, 119–21, 125–27, 129–30, 133–35, 137, 139, 140, 142, 144, 151, 154–55, 167, 169, 171, 182, 193, 196, 206–7, 246–47, 249, 252–54, 260
traditional 3–5, 8–9, 12, 26, 47, 58, 63, 65, 73, 75, 78–79, 83, 92, 96, 105, 113, 120–21, 133, 138, 152, 162, 195, 210, 241, 246, 251, 257–58 *see: orthodox*
transcendent 7, 15, 67, 86, 98, 128, 139, 181, 195, 235
    transcendental 33, 229
transposition 14, 130, 150–51, 165, 175, 177, 181–83, 186, 196, 203, 209, 217, 246–47, 264 *see: Platonism*
    translates 227, 232–33
    translation 1, 24, 29, 107, 204, 232
    transposed 165, 180–82, 200, 212, 246, 203
transubstantiation 117, 239
Trinity 2, 15, 32, 37, 46, 76–77, 83, 117, 156–57, 169–72, 174, 179–80, 184, 187, 192–193, 196, 203–4, 208, 212, 215–16, 218, 228, 230, 245–46, 258–59
    economic Trinity 171, 215, 228, 245
    immanent Trinity 32, 156, 171, 181, 212, 228
    triune 32, 65, 73, 98, 145, 171, 258–59
    t/Trinitarian 2, 5, 20, 76–77, 89, 156, 168–70, 173, 180, 212, 258–59
truth 8, 15, 19, 24, 27–28, 34, 40, 46–47, 52, 61–62, 67, 69, 74–75, 78–79, 89–91, 93, 105, 108, 112, 115–17, 119–20, 126, 128, 130–31, 138, 144–45, 153, 156, 162, 165,

179, 181, 187, 195–96, 200, 203, 207–8, 216, 218–19, 222, 228–29, 231, 233, 246, 249, 253–54, 257, 260

ubique et ab omnibus 105
understanding 1–7, 10, 13–15, 27–28, 42, 51–54, 57, 62–63, 68, 71, 76, 81, 83–84, 86–87, 89–90, 96, 98, 103, 108, 112, 114, 120–22, 124, 131, 133, 135, 140, 144–45, 149, 151, 155–59, 163, 167–69, 170, 172, 177–82, 185–87, 191–93, 195–97, 200, 203–8, 210–12, 217–19, 227, 234–35, 240–41, 243, 245–46, 250, 252–55, 261, 264 *see: knowledge*

universal 3, 11, 15, 49, 67, 94, 103, 109, 117, 124, 126, 128, 138, 155, 169, 178, 180, 182–83, 189, 195–96, 208, 212, 215, 240, 261 *see: imagination*
universalism 117, 125, 183, 189

vicariousness 186–88, 190
visible 52, 90, 109, 121–22, 240

Wendung 65, 73, 79–80, 87, 91–93, 97 *see: Retraktation*
zeitgeist 12, 76, 79, 83, 254

Index of C. S. Lewis's Works
An index of Lewis's works cited or quoted

Allegory of Love, The 170–71, 195, 260
"Avant-Propos a l'édition Française" 128 see: *Le Problème de la Souffrance*

Beyond Personality: The Christian Idea of God 167, 180–81, 188, 192–93, 195, 233–35, 242, 250–51
Broadcast Talks: Reprinted with some alterations from two series of Broadcast Talks "Right and Wrong: A Clue to the Meaning of the Universe" and "What Christians Believe" given in 1941 and 1942 33, 169–71, 179–81, 184, 186, 189, 194–95, 199, 211, 219, 226–28, 230, 233–37, 250–51, 267, 274, 283

Christian Behaviour 180–81, 186, 195, 233–34
"Christian Hope—Its Meaning for Today" 229, 268
Chronicles of Narnia, The 34–35, 43, 73, 158, 162, 171, 174, 202, 225–26, 229, 242, 247, 276
  Horse and His Boy, The 229
  Last Battle, The 229, 244
  Lion, the Witch and the Wardrobe, The 209, 222
  Magician's Nephew, The 162, 229
  Prince Caspian: the Return to Narnia 229, 242
  Silver Chair, The 225, 229, 243

Voyage of the Dawn Treader, The 229, 242–43[/2nd level]
Collected Letters Vol. I 63–64, 195, 238
Collected Letters Vol. II 92, 126, 136–37, 142, 195
Collected Letters Vol. III 28, 114, 125, 128, 133, 195, 229, 232, 253, 256
"Cross-Examination" 118, 140, 142, 147, 279

"De Descriptione Temporum" 30, 229, 273–75

"Early Prose Joy" 69
"Efficacy of Prayer, The" 229, 271, 272
English Literature in the Sixteenth Century 224, 229, 276

"God in the Dock" 40
"Grand Miracle, The" 33, 197–98
Great Divorce, The 72–73, 80, 116, 170–71, 195, 197, 202, 211, 213, 216–19, 226, 242, 244, 245, 248, 251, 260, 268, 281
Grief Observed, A 118, 164, 229, 247, 260–62

"Heaven, Earth and Outer Space" 115, 229 see: "Cross Examinations"

"I was Decided Upon" 115, 229 see: "Cross Examinations"

285

"Is Theism Important?" 30, 229, 247, 264
"Is Theology Poetry" 135
"It All Began with a Picture" 229, 277

Le Problème de la Souffrance 128 see: "Avant-Propos a l'édition Française"
Letter to A. J. Lewis (father), Mar. 28, 1921   195
Letter to Arthur Greeves, Aug. 4, 1917   195
Letter to Arthur Greeves, Dec. 6, 1931   137, 195
Letter to Arthur Greeves, Feb. 28, 1916   195
Letter to Arthur Greeves, Jan. 30, 1944   195
Letter to Arthur Greeves, Oct. 1, 1931   195
Letter to Arthur Greeves, Oct. 12, 1916   195
Letter to Arthur Greeves, Oct. 18, 1931   64, 195, 238
Letter to Arthur Greeves, Sept. 22, 1931   63, 195
Letter to Clyde S. Kilby, Feb. 10, 1957   253, 256
Letter to Clyde S. Kilby, May 7, 1959   229
Letter to Corbin Scott Carnell, Oct. 13, 1958   133, 229, 232
Letter to Dom Bede Griffiths, Apr. 4, 1934   126, 195
Letter to Dom Bede Griffiths, May 28, 1952   229
Letter to Emily McLay, Aug. 8, 1953   229
Letter to Genia Goelz, June 20, 1952   229
Letter to Genia Goelz, Mar. 18, 1952   229
Letter to H. Lyman Stebbins, May 8, 1945   136, 195
Letter to Janet Wise, Oct. 5, 1955   229
Letter to Lee Turner, July 19, 1958   229
Letter to Mr Allcock, Mar. 24, 1955   229
Letter to Mrs Emily McLay, Aug. 3, 1953   114
Letter to Mrs Green, Jun. 18, 1962   229
Letter to Mrs Hook, Dec. 29, 1958   229
Letter to Mrs Johnson, Nov. 8, 1952   229
Letter to Mrs Mary Neylan, Mar. 26, 1940   195
Letter to Owen Barfield, Aug 1939   195
Letter to Sr. Penelope CSMV, May 15, 1941   142, 195
Letter to *The Church Times*, Feb. 8, 1952   28, 125, 128
Letter to the editor of *The Spectator*, Dec. 11, 1942   195
Letter to Vera Gebbert, Oct. 16, 1960   229
Letter to W. H. Lewis (brother), Apr. 28, 1940   92, 195
Letters to Malcolm: Chiefly on Prayer 112, 171, 229, 247, 257–58, 262, 271

Mere Christianity 23–24, 33–34, 123, 125–27, 129–30, 132–33, 135, 145, 147, 149, 150, 158, 169–70, 173, 179, 188, 224–25, 227–37, 242, 244, 273

Miracles (1st and 2nd eds.) 113, 156, 158–59, 170–71, 195, 197–98, 201–3, 205, 211, 219, 226, 229, 231, 244, 247–48, 266, 271
"Modern Theology and Biblical Criticism" 99, 150, 174, 229, 247, 266
"Must Our Image of God Go?" 229, 278

"New Learning and New Ignorance" 224, 229 see: *English Literature in the Sixteenth Century*

Out of the Silent Planet 170–71, 175, 195, 252, 273

Perelandra 170, 183, 195, 248, 252
Pilgrim's Regress, The 39, 49, 51, 59, 61, 67–9, 112, 118, 142, 170, 175, 273, 283
"Poison of Subjectivism, The" 151
Problem of Pain, The 33, 128, 149, 157–58, 164, 169–71, 173, 175, 178, 195, 235, 257, 261–63, 283
"Psalms, The" 229, 257

Reflections on the Psalms 34, 170–71, 198, 229, 247, 257–58
"Rejoinder to Dr Pittenger" 155, 158–62, 229, 247, 252, 279

Screwtape Letters, The 80, 170–71, 195, 197, 202, 211–13, 216–17, 219, 226, 244, 251
"Screwtape Proposes a Toast" 229
"Sometimes Fairy Stories may say best what's to be said" 276
Surprised by Joy: The Shape of my Early Life 39, 42–44, 46–47, 51, 55, 59, 62, 64, 66–67, 69–70, 72, 79, 108, 111, 114–15, 118, 141, 143, 229, 247–48, 249–50, 271, 273

That Hideous Strength 170, 195
They Asked for a Paper 150
Till We Have Faces 34, 170, 229, 247, 252, 255–56
"Transposition" (1st and 2nd eds.) 150, 170–71, 195, 197, 201–2, 223, 229, 266

"We Have No 'Right to Happiness'" 229, 280
"Weight of Glory, The" 170–71, 195, 197, 219, 222
"What Are We to Make of Jesus Christ?" 229, 247, 267–68
"World's Last Night, The" 151, 268–69, 277

Sectional Contents

Foreword | xiii

Introduction. C. S. Lewis—Revelation, Conversion, and Apologetics | 1
1. Who or What is the Christ | 1
2. Why C. S. Lewis | 3
3. Aims and Objectives | 4
4. Explanations, Qualifications | 6
    i. Revelation and Reason | 6
    ii. Patristic | 7
    iii. Platonism | 7
    iv. Apologist/Apologetics | 8
    v. Creation, Fall, Incarnation, Resurrection, Second Coming, and the Four LastThings | 8
    vi. Liberal/liberal, Modernism | 9
    vii. Pagan | 9
    viii. Romantic | 10
5. "... and the Collected Works of C. S. Lewis" | 11
6. Lewis on the Christ: God and Redeemer | 12
    i. Part One, The Personal God of Salvation—Conversion and Acceptance | 12
    ii. Part Two, C. S. Lewis—Theologian and "Mere" Christian | 13
    iii. Part Three, C. S. Lewis—Apologist, Broadcaster, and Public Figure | 13
7. Lewis's Christ | 14

PART ONE THE PERSONAL GOD OF SALVATION—
CONVERSION AND ACCEPTANCE

Chapter 1 Conversion: God is God | 19

1. Introduction | 19
2. C. S. Lewis's Pilgrimage: Childhood | 20
    i. Lewis's Background | 20
    ii. Childhood Religion | 21
    iii. Moments of Grace | 22
    iv. Death | 24
3. C. S. Lewis's Pilgrimage: Youth | 25
    i. Schooling, Anglo-Catholicism, and Northernness | 25

    ii. Atheism | 27
    iii. *Sehnsucht* | 29
  4. C. S. Lewis's Pilgrimage: Conversion | 31
    i. "Huge Waves of Wagnerian Music" | 31
    ii. "The Fox had been Dislodged from the Hegelian Wood" | 34
    iii. "A Young Atheist Cannot Guard his Faith too Carefully" | 36

Chapter 2 Acceptance: God is God, in Christ | 39

  1. Encounters | 39
  2. A Protracted Conversion | 41
    i. Popular Realism and Pantheism | 41
    ii. Idealism and Theism | 41
  3. Lewis, Dyson, Tolkien . . . and Realization | 43
    i. Debate | 43
    ii. Awareness and Comprehension | 44
  4. Encounters . . . and the Church | 45
    i. The Bus Journey | 45
    ii. The Capitulating Don | 45
    iii. The Critical Conversation | 46
    iv. The Motorcycle Journey | 47
  5. The Progress and Regress of the Pilgrim | 47

Chapter 3 Helen Joy Davidman: Intellect and Imagination | 51

  1. A Baptized Imagination | 51
  2. Helen Joy Davidman | 54
    i. Cultural Judaism: New York | 54
    ii. Cultural Judaism: Childhood | 55
  3. Christ Haunted Me | 56
    i. "The Sacrament at the Heart of all Beauty" | 56
    ii. Poetry and Imagination | 58
    iii. Communism and Intellect | 59
  4. And God Came In | 60
  5. The Hound of Heaven | 62

Chapter 4 C. S. Lewis and Karl Barth I: Religious Experience— Revelation and Modernity | 65

  1. A Converted Intellect? | 66
    i. Intellectual Sins and Religious Experience | 66
    ii. The Measure of Religious Experience | 67
    iii. The Human Filtering of Religious Experience | 68
  2. A Shared Encounter? | 69
    i. Augustine and Religious Experience | 69
    ii. Simone Weil and Edith Stein and Religious Experience | 70
  3. C. S. Lewis and Karl Barth | 72
  4. Karl Barth | 73

- i. The Castigation of Liberalism | 73
  - ii. Trinitarian Considerations | 76
    - Nineteenth-Century Liberal Neo-Protestantism | 76
    - A De-Christianized Jesus | 78
  - iii. Barth: *Wendung* and *Retraktation* | 79

Chapter 5 C. S. Lewis and Karl Barth II: A Doctrinal Realization—God is God, in Christ | 83

1. God is God | 83
2. Lewis and Barth: A Doctrinal Realization— God is God, in Christ | 87
   - i. The Lord as "I Am." | 88
   - ii. The Paradoxical Difficulties of Defining the Complement in God is God | 89
   - iii. *fides quaerens intellectum* | 90
   - iv. The Problem of Religious Professionals | 91
   - v. The Problem of Religion | 91
3. Lewis and Barth: Acceptance | 93
   - i. Prevenience | 93
   - ii. "I did not choose Christ: He chose me" | 94
   - iii. "I was decided upon" | 95
4. Barth and Lewis: Similarities and Dissimilarities | 96

PART TWO C. S. LEWIS—THEOLOGIAN AND "MERE" CHRISTIAN

Chapter 6 C. S. Lewis the Classical Philosopher Theologian I: Witness and Method—"Mere" Christianity | 103

1. C. S. Lewis: Commission | 103
2. C. S. Lewis: "Mere Christianity" | 105
   - i. "What has been held Always, Everywhere, by Everybody" | 105
   - ii. "I am a Christian, a Mere Christian" | 106
3. Content Method in C. S. Lewis's Theology | 110
   - i. An Appeal | 110
   - ii. A Patristic Appeal | 112
   - iii. History, Modernism and Postmodernism | 114
   - iv. A Unifying Universal Principle | 116

Chapter 7 C. S. Lewis the Classical Philosopher Theologian II: *praeparatio evangelica*—A Catholic-Evangelical | 119

1. Introduction: Lewis's Adversary—Religious Atheism | 120
2. C. S. Lewis: A Catholic Evangelical? | 121
   - i. Theologian and Missionary | 121
   - ii. "*praeparatio evangelica*" | 122
3. C. S. Lewis: A Classical Philosopher Theologian | 123
4. "The One Who Saves Us from Our Sins?" | 126
   - i. Lewisianity? | 126
   - ii. The Confusion of Men and the Providence of God | 128

5. "Missionary to the Priests of One's Own Church" | 129
   i. A Prophetic Outsider? | 129
   ii. Lewis: *"in mirabilibus supra me"* | 130

Chapter 8 C. S. Lewis the Classical Philosopher Theologian III: Orthodoxy and Heresy—The Pittenger-Lewis Debate | 133

1. Introduction | 133
2. The Pittenger-Lewis Debate | 135
   i. Orthodoxy and Heresy | 135
   ii. W. Norman Pittenger | 137
   iii. Lewis's Reply | 137
3. Pittenger's Christology: "is," or "of the value of"? | 139
   i. An Ontological Distinction | 140
   ii. The λογος ἄσαρκος–λογος ἔνσαρκος | 141
   iii. Lewis the Logician | 142
4. Pittenger-Lewis: Conclusion | 143

PART THREE C. S. LEWIS—APOLOGIST, BROADCASTER, AND PUBLIC FIGURE

Chapter 9 Apologist and Defender of the Faith I: Revelation and Christology, 1931–44—The Early Works | 149

1. Introduction | 149
   The Early Works: 1931–44 | 150
   The Middle Works: 1941–47 | 151
   The Later Works: 1948–63 | 151
2. Revelation and Christology: The Early Period, 1931–44—The Key Theological and Philosophical Works | 151
   i. Lewis the Broadcaster | 152
   ii. A Professional Network and Context | 153
3. Theodicy and Pain: God's Justification | 154
   i. Strengths and Weaknesses | 155
   ii. Suffering and the Christ Event | 156
   iii. The Person and the Office | 157
4. *The Broadcast Talks*: A Summa? | 159
   i. The First and Second Series—"Right and Wrong" and "What Christians Believe" | 159
      Absolute Goodness | 159
      The Need for Forgiveness | 162
      A Dualistic Heresy | 162
      The Rightful King | 163
      Freedom and Happiness | 163
      The Christ of Salvation History | 164
      The Perfect Death | 165
   ii. The Third Series—"Christian Behaviour" | 166
      A New Morality | 166

The Great Sin | 167
Grace Initiates—Works Respond | 168
iii. The Fourth Series—"Beyond Personality" | 168
A Trinitarian Paradox | 168
The Universal Christ | 169
A Temporal Paradox: the Universal and Particular | 170
"The Son of God became a man to enable men to become sons of God" | 171
Carriers of Christ | 173

Chapter 10 Apologist and Defender of the Faith II: Revelation and Christology, 1941–47—The Middle Works | 177

1. Introduction | 177
2. The Revelatory "I Am," and "The Grand Miracle" | 178
    i. Revelation over and against Religion | 178
    ii. *infinitum capax finiti*: The Contradiction of our Religious Expectations | 180
    iii. Transposition and Analogy | 181
    iv. Those that make religion their "god," will not have "God" for their religion | 182
    v. The Incarnate God | 183
    vi. Fitness, Contingency, and Improbability | 184
    vii. Three Paradigms: "Descent/Re-ascent," "Christological Prefigurement," and "Selectiveness and Vicariousness" | 186
        "Descent/Re-Ascent" | 187
        "Christological Prefigurement" | 187
        "Selectiveness and Vicariousness" | 187
    viii. Rebellion and Death | 188
3. Doctrine . . . by Analogy | 191
    i. Screwtape's Correspondence . . . and *The Great Divorce* | 191
    ii. Christian Atheism? | 194
    iii. The Denial of the Particular | 196
4. Revelation and Christology, 1941–47: The Key Theological and Philosophical Essays | 199
    i. The Inconsolable Secret | 199
    ii. Revelation and Transposition | 203

Chapter 11 Apologist and Defender of the Faith III: Revelation and Christology, 1948–63— The Later Works: Mere Christology | 205

1. Revelation and Christology, 1948–63: The Key Theological and Philosophical Works | 206
2. Anscombe-Lewis | 207
3. An Orthodox Christ: Mere Christianity | 207
    i. Mere Christology? | 207
        The Historical Jesus? | 208
        Salvation and Sanctification | 210
    ii. The Death of Jesus of Nazareth | 211
        The Cross | 211
        The Death | 213

The Debt | 214
  iii. Jesus the Jew | 215
4. The Blood of the Lamb | 217
  i. Death, and New Life—A Means to an End? | 217
  ii. A Hebrew Concept | 219
  iii. An Haematological Perspective? | 221
    "The Blood of our Lord Jesus Christ, which was shed for thee..." | 221
    An Haematological Sacrifice | 222

Chapter 12 Apologist and Defender of the Faith IV: Revelation and Christology, 1948–63—The Later Works: Christlikeness | 227

1. Christlikeness | 228
  i. The Lord and Haunter of Creation | 228
  ii. The *imago Christi* | 230
2. Translating Christ | 232
  i. *Till We Have Faces* | 232
    anima naturaliter Christiana | 233
    The Paradox of Christlikeness | 235
  ii. "We are Christians not Stoics" | 237
    The Cry of Prayer | 237
    "There is Danger in the very Concept of Religion" | 238
    Comfort and Consolation | 240
3. Revelation and Christology, 1948–63: The Key Theological and Philosophical Essays | 244
  i. *fides*—Faith and Religion | 244
  ii. Eschatology and Pelagianism: A Lewisian Perspective | 247
    Identity | 247
    Judgment | 247
    A Theological Perspective | 251
    History: Teleology and Meaning | 253
    Pelagianism and Prevenient Grace | 255
  iii. Analogy and Apologetics | 256
    Story, Analogy, and Pictures | 256
    Apologetics and Witness | 257
4. Towards Death | 259

Conclusion. Apologist and Defender of the Faith | 261

Select Bibliography | 265

  Letters and Articles by C. S. Lewis | 265
  Books by C. S. Lewis | 266
  Other Books and Articles | 267

Indexes | 273

www.ingramcontent.com/pod-product-compliance
Lightning Source LLC
Chambersburg PA
CBHW060508300426
44112CB00017B/2591